D1567775

Fiction Across Borders

SHAMEEM BLACK

Fiction Across Borders

Imagining the Lives of Others in Late Twentieth-Century Novels

COLUMBIA UNIVERSITY PRESS   NEW YORK

Columbia University Press

Publishers Since 1893

New York   Chichester, West Sussex

Copyright © 2010 Columbia University Press

Library of Congress Cataloging-in-Publication Data

Black, Shameem, 1976–

Fiction across borders : imagining the lives of others in late twentieth-century
novels / Shameem Black.

p. cm.

Includes bibliographical references and index.

ISBN 978-0-231-14978-5 (cloth : alk. paper)—ISBN 978-0-231-52061-4 (e-book)

1. American fiction—Minority authors—History and criticism.   2. American
fiction—20th century—History and criticism.   3. Commonwealth fiction
(English)—History and criticism.   4. Other (Philosophy) in literature.
5. Difference (Philosophy) in literature.   6. Ethics in literature.
I. Title.

PS153.M56B62   2009

810.9′920693—dc22

2009017743

Columbia University Press books are printed on permanent and durable acid-free paper.

This book is printed on paper with recycled content.

Printed in the United States of America

c   10 9 8 7 6 5 4 3 2 1

References to Internet Web sites (URLs) were accurate at the time of writing. Neither the
author nor Columbia University Press is responsible for URLs that may have expired or
changed since the manuscript was prepared.

For my parents, Sena and Earl Black

CONTENTS

ACKNOWLEDGMENTS

I would like to thank the many individuals who have helped this book come to light. At Stanford University, where this project originally took root, I benefited in numerous ways from the warm and lively environment of graduate students and faculty members in the English department and beyond. Since I first began to work on these questions, Arnold Rampersad gave me more unfailing support, professional advice, and intellectual guidance than I can ever hope to repay. As my ideas developed, David Palumbo-Liu offered the benefit of his considerable expertise and generously shared his work on globalization with me. Shirley Brice Heath read my work in more time zones than I can count, and her discipline, acumen, and enthusiasm continually revived my love for writing and research.

During my time at Yale University, I was equally fortunate. I am extremely grateful to Tanya Agathocleous, who regularly read working sections of this project and helped me think through many of its governing ideas. This book is very much in debt to her insight and generosity. As readers of my work, Terry Castle, Geetanjali Singh Chanda, Wai Chee Dimock, Gloria Fisk, Paul Fry, Langdon Hammer, Amy Hungerford,

Patricia Parker, Linda Peterson, Claude Rawson, Kate Stanton, Jeremy Tucker, and Ruth Yeazell gave me invaluable critique and encouragement. Conversations with David Bromwich, Dan Ho, Sharmila Sen, and Karin Gosselink provided fruitful leads and stimulating questions. Suzanne Keen kindly shared her extensive knowledge of the psychological literature on social cognition. Amitav Ghosh graciously answered my questions about multilingualism in his writing. In the late stages of this project, I was fortunate to find a wonderful editor in Philip Leventhal at Columbia University Press, whose advice has made this book a stronger one.

Institutional support and encouragement were also invaluable. The practical assistance of Mellon, English department, and Whiting fellowships made this project much easier to begin at Stanford, and the intellectual and material support of the English department; the Ethnicity, Race, and Migration program; the Twentieth-Century Colloquium, and the Whitney Humanities Center at Yale allowed it to develop in a collegial environment. The manuscript was completed during a Morse Junior Faculty Fellowship, which provided a vital period of sustained writing and reflection. I am grateful to the libraries of Yale, Harvard, Georgetown, and Stanford, which offered important resources for my research. The wonderful undergraduates in my Fiction Without Borders seminars provided thoughtful comments and fresh questions on the problem of imagining social difference. Early and evolving versions of the ideas in this book found constructive and helpful audiences at American University, Bowdoin College, Claremont McKenna College, Fudan University, Harvard University, Stanford University, the University of California at Berkeley, the University of Denver, the University of Texas at Austin, the University of Toronto, Yale University, the American Comparative Literature Association, the International Association of Word and Image Studies, the New England Association for Asian Studies, and the Northeast Modern Language Association. The questions and insights I received on all these occasions have made a great difference. I would also like to express my appreciation for the thoughtful comments of the anonymous manuscript reviewers for Columbia University Press. Small portions of chapter 1 first appeared in an essay on Amitav Ghosh's *The Shadow Lines*; the final, definitive version of that essay was published as "Cosmopolitanism at Home: Amitav Ghosh's *The Shadow Lines*," *The Journal of Commonwealth Literature* 41, no. 3 (September 2006): 45–65, © Sage Publications. I am grateful to Sage Publications and to *The Journal of Commonwealth Literature* for the ability to reprint a portion of that essay in this book. An early version of chapter 2 appeared as "Fertile Cosmofeminism: Ruth L. Ozeki and Transnational Reproduction," *Meridians: feminism, race, transnationalism* 5, no. 1 (2004): 226–256, © Indiana University Press. I thank Indiana University Press and *Meridians* for permission to reprint this material in revised and elaborated form. I also thank Amitav Ghosh for permission to publish material from my interview with him. At Columbia University Press, I am grateful to Avni Majithia for her work and to Robert Fellman for his invariably helpful copy editing. This book was published with the assistance of the Frederick W. Hilles Publication Fund of Yale University, for which I offer warm thanks.

To acknowledge my broader debts, I should note that many individuals made crucial contributions in indirect but invaluable ways. In New Haven, I count myself lucky for all the lunches at Berkeley, coffees at Book Trader, and drinks at Scoozi with my many wonderful colleagues. During the years when I worked on this book in Cambridge, I deeply appreciated the friendship of political scientists who often asked just the right questions about literature. In much earlier points in my life, extraordinary scholars and mentors such as Jonathan Spence and Beth Charlebois made me want to pursue a life shaped by literature. From conversations about American Buddhism, Indian fiction, and South African literature to generous hospitality on research trips, my continually expanding family has provided me with love and assistance on three continents. And inventing stories for my growing nieces and nephews never fails to remind me afresh of why fiction really matters.

My parents, to whom this work is dedicated, have fostered my love of literature throughout my entire life. During the writing of this book, they offered pointed questions and steadying confidence in equal measure. My father, with whom I spent many blissful childhood hours browsing in bookstores, taught by example of the rewards of thinking and writing. From my mother, whose life has spanned four countries, I learned to appreciate the importance of crossing borders in all its pleasures and difficulties. This book bears my family's imprint on each page.

Finally, without the help of Andy Kennedy, writing this book would have been a deeply lonely task. As he read my writing with a compassionate but critical eye, he always helped me discover what I really meant to say. His love continually sustains me in all parts of my life.

Fiction Across Borders

Toward an Ethics of Border-Crossing Fiction

At the turn of the new millennium, might it be possible to imagine another without doing violence to one's object of description? Considering this question is the central task of this book. While envisioning alterity is fundamental to the making of literature, the difficulties of this task arise in particularly vivid and urgent form in fiction produced in the late twentieth and early twenty-first centuries. The stakes of this endeavor are perhaps best exemplified by J. M. Coetzee's novel *Disgrace* (1999), which dramatizes the agonizing necessity of the search to imagine the other. David Lurie, the protagonist of the novel, is a white South African literary scholar who finds himself equally out of place in the changing world of academia and in the shifting landscape of South Africa after apartheid. After David's daughter Lucy is raped, David finds himself repeatedly denied access to the details of what she was forced to endure. His exclusion provokes an anguished meditation on the problem of knowing others: "Do they think he does not know what rape is? Do they think he has not suffered with his daughter? What more could he have witnessed than he is capable of imagining? Or do they think that, where rape is concerned, no man can be where the woman is?

Whatever the answer, he is outraged, outraged at being treated like an outsider."[1] Is there a way for David to understand the experience of his daughter without inflicting new violence upon her? To imagine Lucy's rape, to "be where the woman is," provides a crucial ethical challenge that goes well beyond the specific trauma evoked in the novel. As David tries to sympathize with Lucy's suffering, Coetzee invites us to consider the problem of conceptualizing experiences that seem well beyond one's social location. David's predicament illuminates a central crisis of representation that haunts the academic study of literature, and it also bespeaks a wider concern with the ethics of encounter in a violently divided world. As the brutal landscape of *Disgrace* reveals, imagining the perspectives of others—or failing to do so—carries real consequences.

In the pages that follow, I explore how an emerging wave of fiction published in English between 1980 and 2005 speaks to this challenge. In tackling the question of envisioning alterity, this body of literature strives to offer new approaches to representing social difference. By "social difference," I mean the many distinctions by which otherness is created as a category with significant social implications.[2] These forms of difference can be perceived as political, cultural, economic, linguistic, or even biological.[3] Throughout this book, "social difference" includes differences of nationality, ethnicity, religion, gender, language, class, species, or other recognizable categories; at the same time, it also encompasses the many divisions in experience that separate, for example, the healthy from the suffering or the literate from the illiterate. These constructions of difference are often overlapping, irregular, and unevenly intense; one particular vision might be animated in a particular place and time while muted in another. Although, in the right circumstance, virtually any experiential distinction can be used to create the perception of otherness, my book is particularly concerned with dramatic visions of alterity that invoke troubling (though never stable nor singular) hierarchies of power. I concentrate on moments when subjects seek to represent forms of social difference that have been associated with oppression, marginality, or ideologies of inferiority, as when David Lurie yearns to sympathize with his daughter's experience of rape.

Representations of this sort have long been considered a problem. Postcolonial, feminist, and ethnic-minority forms of literary criticism produced in the late twentieth century tend to describe such endeavors as hegemonic exercises that commit new forms of representational violence, even (and often especially) when the subject hopes to valorize or redeem its object of description. In such theories of representation, attempts to write across borders informed by histories of oppression appear as complex fantasies that reveal much more about the subject than about the object of imagination.[4] These practices of reading underwrite a vast and varied body of cultural study, producing a critical metanarrative that exposes the hidden workings of hegemonic power in the act of what Satya Mohanty calls "discursive domination."[5] The very desire to know another is frequently marked as a suspect and contaminated longing, one that leads to new forms of self-deceit in the guise of seeking the truthful and real.[6] While such theories were once radical and necessary challenges to hegemonic forms of representation, their influence is now so widespread as to constitute a new set of critical givens.

To provide an alternative to these pervasive metanarratives, this book will propose a new interpretative lens that will help us identify an ethics of representing social difference. As articulated in the recent revival of ethical criticism, ethics connotes not behavioral codes, dogma, or a singular idea of the good but instead illuminates how literary works grapple with problems that pervade a world of competing values.[7] Throughout this book, I use "ethics" to signal the workings of an ethos of responsibility to one's object of inquiry, a responsibility opposed to hegemonic domination and representational violence.[8] I define ethics in such contrastive and negative terms because I understand it as an open field of possible emancipatory alternatives whose contours are continually being imagined. But, in stressing the language of attentiveness, I also explicitly acknowledge its immersion in questions of value.[9] To describe the scope of such responsibility to alterity, I borrow Donna Haraway's concept of "significant otherness." Haraway uses this phrase both descriptively, to indicate many kinds of possible alterity, and normatively, to envision encounters that "are accountable both to their disparate inherited histories and to their barely possible but absolutely necessary joint futures."[10] The interpretative lens I will offer brings into focus the specific utopian ideal evident in Haraway's description.

I explore this ethics of representation in an emergent body of what I call "border-crossing fiction." Such fiction is defined by two criteria: first, it foregrounds a dramatic dissonance between the subject and object of representation; second, it seeks to surmount these productions of social difference. Border-crossing fiction therefore embraces the challenge of representation with an intensity that surpasses the general concern with alterity that preoccupies fiction at large. As a small fraction of published literature, the fiction considered in this book envisions a special kind of meditation on the concerns of crossing borders. Works that struggle to surmount the problem of speaking across social difference should not be conflated with writings on themes of border-crossing more generally, which presuppose no particular engagement with the ethics of representation. Just as one might argue that not all work written by or about women constitutes feminist literature, not all writing on themes of border-crossing challenges its readers to consider the ethical stakes of imagining alterity. The novels included here all call attention to the problem of writing across borders and suggest responses that can be defended as alternatives to hegemonic or identitarian effects.

I argue that these works accomplish these tasks by calling attention to their own representational dilemmas, inviting their readers to question assumptions about identity and imaginative projection that underlie calcified forms of discursive domination. Although at some moments this book will evaluate how effectively these works of fiction actually represent forms of otherness, it will primarily seek to explain how they present the *process* of imagining social difference. As a result, while some of these novels do not always perform the emancipatory imaginative practices valorized in their pages, they nonetheless help their readers understand new ways to challenge hegemonic or identitarian positions.

The goal of this book, thus, is twofold. First, although border-crossing novels themselves suggest that the political and philosophical problems they raise will never be fully resolved, my account seeks to explore how very different kinds of fiction choose to wrestle with the terms of this problem. As the novels considered here strive to develop nuanced responses to different kinds of alterity, they offer the makings of a literature that expresses openness toward social difference and challenges debilitating political hierarchies. Second, my account seeks to provide an interpretative lens that helps us see a productive ethics of representational border crossing defined by its resistance to established patterns of hegemonic violence. This lens helps us challenge the dominant optic of scholarly inquiry, which currently emphasizes what

Eve Kosofsky Sedgwick calls the "tracing-and-exposure project." "Subversive and demystifying parody, suspicious archaeologies of the present, the detection of hidden patterns of violence and their exposure: as I have been arguing," Sedgwick claims, "these infinitely doable and teachable protocols of unveiling have become the common currency of cultural and historicist studies."[11] My account offers a theoretical and methodological alternative to such tracing-and-exposure projects by defending the specific strengths of the novels I explore. To enable this new critical metanarrative of possibilities for border crossing, my account will propose a set of shared principles that inform this search for an ethics of representation. This book, therefore, seeks to elaborate on alternatives to discursive domination in fiction and to offer a new scholarly metanarrative that makes this ethics visible.

While markers of alterity are never permanently fixed nor evenly weighted, one of the central findings of this book is that certain literary subgenres and philosophical stances often effectively correlate with different degrees of perceived difficulty in crossing social borders. Focusing in depth on novels that exemplify a spectrum of possible narrative choices, my account moves from the most moderate of circumstances, where social divides are seen as weak, to the most extreme situations, where such divides seem almost insurmountable. Sentimental and comic energies emerge in concert with relatively modest social differences, while sacrificial and antihumanist impulses more effectively address situations where such differences appear robust. Rather than dismissing sentimentality as mere agitprop or extolling it as an undervalued genre, my account specifies the conditions under which the sentimental makes sense as a productive ethical response. Similarly, I suggest that antihumanist approaches may prove useful in extreme situations without advocating them as appropriate to all instances of imaginative border crossing. We need certain choices for the ordinary, and we need others for the extraordinary.

In describing the different social situations with which these works grapple, I refer to moments when social differences *seem* weak or *appear* strong. This phrasing seeks to acknowledge that situations, by themselves, cannot simply be assigned ethical levels of difficulty. While clearly no one would want to discount the importance of measurable discrepancies in material power, how those discrepancies are constructed also matters a great deal. Ruth L. Ozeki and J. M. Coetzee, for instance, who reflect opposite ends of the spectrum, both prominently figure the rape of women and the suffering of animals as central challenges for border-crossing fiction. In Ozeki's polemical and sentimental work, these problems are amenable to liberal humanism and transnational feminism; Coetzee's haunting minimalism critiques the limits of these ideologies in favor of a more circumspect and elusive antihumanism. These antithetical responses both work, I suggest, because the first stresses the crucial similarities that underlie distinctions on the surface, while the second exposes the gaping fault lines within a small and proximate community. By staging these events within very different kinds of social relationships (one within a history of consensual bonds mediated through first-world television, the other within a history of violently inscribed sexual and racial ideologies), Ozeki and Coetzee are able to offer two radically distinct responses that both provide effective engagements with significant otherness. Their narrative choices, though diametrically opposed, both enable an ethics of representing alterity.

Produced on the stage of late twentieth- and early twenty-first-century globalization, the novels I consider emerge in an age characterized by a fundamental paradox in the role of social borders. On the one hand, circuits transporting bodies, goods, and ideas have never linked so many in so short a period of time. The pressures of late capitalism, the proliferation of mass media, and the forces of migration have created new conditions of visibility that make distant parts of the world suddenly seem much more entwined. Arjun Appadurai describes this world as one of "global cultural flows," defined by shifting landscapes of persons, technologies, capital, media images, and ideas. These landscapes represent "deeply perspectival constructs, inflected by the historical, linguistic, and political situatedness of different sorts of actors: nation-states, multinationals, diasporic communities, as well as subnational groupings and movements (whether religious, political, or economic), and even intimate face-to-face groups, such as villages, neighborhoods, and families."[12] But even as these flows pervade many walks of life, the markedly uneven effects of globalization have also provoked renewed interest in the value of social barriers. Evoked schematically but vividly in Benjamin Barber's image of "jihad vs. McWorld," powerful voices at the turn of the millennium have protested against dehumanizing effects of globalization and advocated new forms of local, tribal, or communitarian identity.[13] From resurging ethnic violence to fundamentalist religious movements to antiglobalization coalitions, this historical period encompasses many moments of profound resistance to the possibility and desirability of surmounting social difference. Writing across borders at the turn of the millennium is arguably both easier and harder than it has ever been.

As part of this historical period's obsession with breaking and solidifying social borders, the novels considered in this book are deeply informed by many of the faces of globalization. In particular, they register and reveal the impact of travel and migration on new contact zones of encounter. Influenced by competing genres of mass media, they draw attention to technologies such as television, which make distant (and sometimes nearby) others increasingly visible across the globe. They explore how cultural practices, religious beliefs, and aesthetic forms migrate beyond the social groups with which they are conventionally identified. And they call attention to the changing power of English as a global language. As they chart these social manifestations of globalization, these works of fiction seek alternatives to the neoimperial tendencies of global capital, the depredations of military violence, and the resurgent assertions of fundamentalist xenophobia. Although they address such concerns in specifically literary ways, these works betray a larger anxiety about the ethics of representation in an era of globalization.

Such global flows not only inform these novels but also call them into historical relation. For all their intimate affinities with specific geographies and literary traditions in different parts of the world, the novels I include share a formative historical moment. Though these novelists come from the United States, India, and South Africa, their works of fiction were all written in an era of heightened awareness about the possible pitfalls of writing across borders. Unlike literature from earlier periods, these works of fiction cannot plausibly claim ignorance of exoticism, stereotyping, idealization, sexism, or other forms of discursive domination that late twentieth-century anti-imperialism, feminism, and identity politics made visible. In contrast to many of its antecedents, fiction at the turn of the millennium frequently expresses diminished confidence that an individual can easily put himself or herself in the place of another.[14] Because inhabiting a world unlike one's own requires crossing barriers shaped by sharp inequities of material and social power, many of these novels wrestle with the need to validate their own thematic and formal embrace of the lives and languages of others. This shared location, in the wake of identity politics and post-colonial critiques of power, explains why I explore works of prose fiction published between 1980 and 2005. These social critiques provide a context, I contend, in which it becomes historically appropriate to read works of fiction for an ethics of imagining others. In light of the widespread pressure placed on literature to defend its representations of social difference, these novels struggle to avoid charges of invasive imagination.[15] They therefore illuminate how literary representations might be transfigured by the chastening critiques of postcolonial, ethno-centric, and feminist discourses. Furthermore, these novels emerge in an era characterized by rapid systems of publication and translation that, while markedly uneven in practice, nonetheless enable particular works of fiction to reach audiences in many parts of the world. An awareness of such theoretically available, if not always practically possible, circulation, I suggest, places further demands on writers to consider how their acts of imaginative projection might be viewed by the very others whom they seek to represent. While not all novelists in the period respond to these pressures or do so effectively, the culture wars of the late twentieth century have helped create new kinds of possibility for representational practice. As part of the intensifying global flows of ideas at the turn of the millennium, these influential meditations on the power of representation help create the conditions for this emerging literature.

Although any form of writing can attempt to figure significant oth-erness, the literary genre perhaps most prominently identified with rep-resenting social difference is prose fiction—in particular, the novel.[16] Because fiction conventionally calls attention to the texture of experi-ential life through emplotted action, the novel almost always partici-pates in one form or another of social border crossing. This participa-tion can become powerful and prickly, as Edward Said notes when he begins his argument in *Culture and Imperialism* (1993): "the power to narrate, or to block other narratives from forming and emerging, is very important to culture and imperialism."[17] Such a fraught contest is similarly central to ideologies of race, sex, class, and language, where competing accounts of human possibility play themselves out in the worlds of the novel. Precisely because prose fiction occupies a privi-leged role within influential critiques of border crossing, this book aims to suggest how this special intimacy might be rethought in the era of globalization.

If the novel brings a burdensome history to the problem of representational ethics, it also lays claim to certain rhetorical advantages. As a literary form associated with greater levels of commercial consumption and circulation than, for example, poetry, novels often project an air of accessibility that enhances their ability to shape readers' perceptions about social life. Given its capacity for multivocality, the genre of fiction is also well suited to the task of considering diverse and even conflicting perspectives simultaneously. The traditional commitment of the genre to many voices and many styles, as evoked in Mikhail Bakhtin's theories of polyphony and heteroglossia, allows competing points of view within the space of a single novel or story that can encourage active perspective taking across social borders. While novels have been blamed for fostering images of cultural constraint, they have also been credited with helping shape expanded views of human potential.[18] As late twentieth- and early twenty-first-century novels draw strength from the belief that they can foster ethically resonant identifications with others, they work to revitalize this legacy of expansive engagement for the turn of the millennium. Although poetry, performance, nonfiction narrative, and other forms of representation can and do aspire to such an ethics of border crossing, they bring significantly different formal strategies to bear on this endeavor, and thus they deserve a separate investigation that is beyond the scope of this book.[19]

As it appears in fiction at the turn of the millennium, the impulse toward an ethics of literary border crossing is a fundamentally decentralized one that spans diverse novelistic terrain. The writers I consider are not part of a self-defined movement or a critically coherent school (such as the kind associated with, for example, futurism, the Black Arts movement, or language poetry). Some of these writers, for instance, might be highly critical of, or unfamiliar with, the other authors with whom they are compared. Their works vary in aesthetic sophistication and cultural capital, they address different kinds of social barriers, they challenge different specters of representational violence, and they choose diverse formal ways to consider the risks and benefits of border crossing. Despite these differences, however, all of the novels considered here share two common attributes. First, in varied ways, they are fundamentally *about* the ethical problem of representing social difference.

Through metafictional moments, plot designs, or authorial statements, these writings struggle actively with the challenge of significant otherness. Second, these novels all offer narrative choices that work to elude complete recuperation into Orientalist, primitivist, sexist, classist, or other modes of representational constraint. No matter how different their stylistic strategies or thematic focus, these works favor, reflect on, and offer valuable contributions to the ethics of surmounting social difference.

The specific authors I assemble—Ruth Ozeki, Charles Johnson, Gish Jen, Jeffrey Eugenides, Rupa Bajwa, Amitav Ghosh, and J. M. Coetzee—aim to provide a balance between singularity and exemplarity. Seen individually, each of these writers offers an especially vivid and instructive encounter with the question of what it means to challenge invasive imagination. Focusing on one or two writers in each chapter, this book provides detailed explorations of representational possibilities that speak to specific intellectual predicaments and confront varied forms of discursive domination. At the same time, bringing these particular novelists together shows how the problem of imagining social difference pervades a broad range of late twentieth- and early twenty-first-century fiction. These novels envision very different worlds across three continents, exploring geographies as startlingly diverse as American television in Japan, American slavery read through Buddhism, suburban New York in an age of immigration, topographies of intersexuality, sari shops in Amritsar, the Indian diaspora in Southeast Asia, and post-apartheid South Africa. The novelists who offer us these visions vary in their national, ethnic, religious, and philosophical affiliations. They differ in their stylistic attractions to novelistic subgenres, revealing the particular contributions of entertainment-education fiction, comic writing, historical epic, and dramatic prose. They vary in how they articulate acts of border crossing and diverge in the scope and caliber of their responses. While the novels considered here by no means reflect the *only* possible productive forms of writing across borders, they allow this book to develop a flexible account of border-crossing fiction that remains open to many kinds of social, stylistic, and conceptual variation. Read together, these novels offer the beginnings of a map that delineates key contours in the struggle for emancipatory imaginative practices.

This constellation of novelists emphasizes writers who work within postcolonial, feminist, and ethnic-minority literary traditions. By privileging the responses found in minority or minoritized works of fiction, I hope to show that the yearning for new perceptions of significant otherness is not simply a veiled way of legitimating white or Western representations of other parts of the world. But I also turn to these writers to show how these minority or minoritized literary traditions are themselves afflicted by the ethical problems of writing about others: they are not always writing back to a dominant tradition but often envisioning social differences that require attention to their own social privileges. Since these works often begin with a heightened awareness of the dangers of "imperial eyes," they offer many of the most innovative and impassioned responses to the problems of representing others. Charles Johnson, for instance, explicitly asks if it is possible "to write well the lived experience of the racial Other," and Amitav Ghosh reveals his own ambivalence about representing languages he does not speak: "You flinch to represent a character thinking in Burmese in English. But one has to take that risk because something is better than nothing."[20] The critical consciousness of these writers, I suggest, helps them think through many of the ethical impasses of representational border crossing.

To align these writers through their shared participation in a specific intellectual preoccupation, as I do here, is to suggest that three of the most accepted ways to organize literary scholarship—shared nationality, shared ethnicity, and shared gender—can limit our ability to apprehend the intellectual contours of the late twentieth and early twenty-first centuries.[21] I do not contest the continuing salience of nation-states, minority identities, or gendered experiences of the world, particularly as such social formations underwrite legal and material forms of belonging. Indeed, each of my chapters seeks to explore how particular novels identify relevant forms of significant otherness through intimate dialogues with specific constructions of the social. The story I hope to tell, in short, is not a story of homogenization that renders nations, ethnicities, or genders obsolete. However, I do wish to argue that fiction in English at the turn of the millennium participates in a wider planetary conversation. Such a planetary conversation is uneven and certainly not comprehensive, but it exceeds the boundaries of national, ethnic, or gendered dialogue. The comparative reading practice I employ allows this conversation to come into focus, revealing new and surprising relationships between works that, on the surface, may seem to have nothing in common.[22] If my comparative methodology is thus vital to my argument, it is also integral in another sense: a book about representations of boundary crossing should be willing to cross a few boundaries itself.

The novels I consider invent a wide range of responses to confront the specter of invasive imagination. Since each writer situates his or her work in a different geographical, historical, and literary location, each faces different barriers to the problem of writing about others. While J. M. Coetzee confronts the burdens of apartheid and violence in South Africa, Amitav Ghosh points to the global spread of English and the problem of representing linguistic alterity. With Derek Attridge, I assume that "otherness is always *perspectival* and that it is always produced. In other words, there is no transcendent other . . . there is only an other that presents itself to a specific subject in a particular place and time; otherness is always otherness to someone."[23] Similarly, with Tzvetan Todorov, I begin from the premise that "others are also I's" (*CA*, 3). The terms of sameness and difference are never stable ones; they transform from novel to novel (and often within novels as well). Social identities themselves are always internally diverse, requiring ethical strategies to navigate within as well as across them.

The novels in the first half of this book, where social borders appear more moderate, tend to be accessible middlebrow works that favor sentimental and comic sensibilities. In referring to works as middlebrow, I suggest that they encourage and circulate in a mode of reading that falls between a highbrow emphasis on aesthetic sophistication and a lowbrow emphasis on unmediated pleasure. Writers such as Ruth Ozeki or Jeffrey Eugenides often garner more popular than scholarly acclaim, and even writers who attract more critical attention, such as Charles Johnson, still produce novels that are often easily consumed within middlebrow paradigms of reading. In the more ambitious and complex works of Amitav Ghosh and J. M. Coetzee, discussed in the second half of this book, crossing social borders appears as a significantly more vexed ethical undertaking. As these novels assign themselves increasingly challenging tasks, refusing the comforts of easy resolutions, their literary optics project increasingly tragic and dissatisfied sensibilities.

Why should we spend time thinking about fictions that many might see as enjoyable reads but not consider serious novels? Why not simply concentrate on writers such as Ghosh and Coetzee, where the pleasures and rewards of formal analysis are arguably greater? To ignore the popular or the middlebrow, I suggest, would be to miss an important avenue through which new representational ethics can infiltrate the public sphere. As scholars of constraining ideologies have so powerfully revealed, debilitating assumptions of social difference emerged not only through elite productions of scholarship and literature but also through such popular or subliterary forms as travelogues, detective stories, children's fiction, and comic books. While my choice of novels remains within the frame of adult fiction, this selection nonetheless reflects the principle that even works of questionable aesthetic sophistication may make significant contributions to social discourses on representational practices. This book hopes to show how even (and sometimes especially) formulaic subgenres can offer important meditations on ethical concerns. Including both popular novels and serious literature allows for a multidimensional portrait of border-crossing fiction, one that directs our attention both to readily reproducible forms of prose and to truly rare species of writing.

Considering fiction in this light may help envision a set of responses that can be described as ethical but not unduly prescriptive, committed to a certain set of values without requiring a rigid commitment to particular forms of fiction. This literary terrain is living and dynamic, capable of changing in inventive and surprising directions. As the following chapters of this book unfold, they tell the story of how the narrative choices of border-crossing fiction adapt to confront the changing circumstances of a world where ideas, images, material goods, and social practices circulate with increasing rapidity. Identifying multiple and overlapping experiments with theme and form, these chapters consider the challenges posed by nation, ethnicity, religion, gender, class, language, and other forms of significant otherness that elude recuperation into such established categories. As these chapters move from ordinary to extraordinary situations, they invite us to apprehend different histories of representational violence that bedevil specific borders. These chapters consider challenges to dehumanizing optics of global capital, Orientalist and ethnic stereotypes, rigid theories of gender, imperialist uses of English, and literary scripts of sexual privilege and racial bestiality. As these readings seek to cover a wide territory, they reveal the possibilities and the limitations of an ethics of imagining others.

In chapter 1, "Crowded Self and Crowded Style," I set forth my theoretical account of an ethics of border crossing. I begin by asking why imagining others has been considered such a problem, identifying influential critical metanarratives in postcolonial, feminist, and ethnic-minority theories that have presented representations of alterity as forms of discursive domination. To propose an alternative metanarrative, I argue that developing an ethics of border crossing requires thinking about its underlying principles of identity and imaginative projection. Working through philosophical and psychological accounts of representation, I propose three central concepts that help create practices that elude hegemonic or identitarian effects. These practices of representation enable what I call "crowded selves" and "crowded styles," or images of subjectivity and literary form that work against familiar forms of invasive imagination in their encounters with difference. Through their engagements with alterity, these selves and styles model acts of perspective taking, undergo active self-reflection, and work to diminish their own privileges. Thinking in terms of crowded selves and crowded styles, I suggest, provides a new set of portable reading practices to make visible the ethical contributions of border-crossing fiction.

My subsequent chapters use these concepts of crowded selves and crowded styles to identify a spectrum of approaches to alterity in very different works of fiction. Chapter 2, "Everyday Sentiment," begins with the most limited experiment in the ethics of imagining social difference. In the work of the Japanese American writer Ruth Ozeki, the transpacific circuits between America and Japan enable a mediated form of community, figured through the image of transnational television, in which no one seems radically different from one another. Within this representation of minimal alterity, Ozeki's novel turns to the codes of sentimental fiction and feminist politics to encourage her characters and readers to sympathize and act with others across national borders. These practices work to contest the dehumanizing discursive domination that the novel associates with global capital. As a popular novel with a strong didactic impulse, exemplifying what I call entertainment-education fiction, *My Year of Meats* (1998) reveals the usefulness of its everyday sentiment in furthering the growth of moderately crowded selves. This vision, compatible with the strategies of transnational feminist activism and the practices of television advertising, remains squarely within the comforts of liberal humanism. Ozeki's vision of engaging significant otherness, I contend, is not appropriate for situations of grave discrepancies in access to power. However, I suggest that the novel does help us understand the specific condition of limited alterity in which sentimental bonding allows for the emergence of moderately crowded selves.

If Ozeki's sentimental identifications succeed because the novel deploys them in a representational world of plausibly moderate otherness, chapter 3, "Ethnic Reversals," moves to the work of writers who begin to complicate such visions of limited alterity. The African American writer Charles Johnson and the Chinese American novelist Gish Jen craft worlds in which social difference is marked by deceptive and unstable inequalities: social borders seem rigid to some but invisible to others. In this context, their novels combat the histories of representational violence found in Orientalist and ethnic stereotyping. Focusing in particular on mismatching perceptions about the importance of ethnic and religious difference, Johnson and Jen rely on comic reversals to enable effective representations of significant otherness. When a multiracial American slave learns Chinese, or when a Chinese American girl becomes Jewish, the comedy of these linguistic and religious conversions asks us to question why these performances seem funny in the first place. In calling attention to the very stereotypes that make these crossings seem so incongruous, Johnson and Jen's novels inhabit these forms of discursive domination in order to transform them into productive antihegemonic and anti-identitarian signifiers. This disorienting doubleness, a flamboyant performance of comic reversal that continually makes its own theatricality visible, enables the formation of crowded selves and styles. While comedy has often been used as a disciplinary strategy to promote hegemonic images of superiority or to disparage the ineffectiveness of border crossing, I argue that the kind of comic style Johnson and Jen offer—one characterized by absurdity, anachronism, parody, and mockery—uses the playful dissonance of laughter to create effective forms of imaginative border crossing.

In both chapters 2 and 3, significant resistance to border crossing is relatively restricted. The success of Ozeki's novel relies upon a form of manufactured consent: her characters seek representation in the eyes of others, and this eagerness to be imagined is part of what makes the novel's sentimental identifications seem appropriate and useful. Johnson and Jen, for their part, destabilize the matter of consent by making fun of the claims to mastery and coherence that often provoke such resistance. But what about novels that deal more directly with objections to imaginative border crossing? To extend this project into more difficult territory, chapter 4, "Middle Grounds," turns to two novels that begin to confront this problem. Whereas chapters 2 and 3 concentrate on national, ethnic, and religious differences, chapter 4 takes gendered borders as the focus of its investigation. In the work of the Greek American writer Jeffrey Eugenides and the Indian novelist Rupa Bajwa, tragicomic narrative choices produce crowded selves and styles that flourish in the contested middle ground between privilege and abjection. While their novels are strikingly different—the first offers a sprawling epic tale of a Greek American hermaphrodite; the second crafts an intimate story of an Amritsar shop clerk—I argue that they offer surprisingly similar visions about how to approach resistant significant otherness. The most effective place for imagining social difference, these novels imply, lies in a middle ground between competing forms of knowing. For Eugenides, this middle ground is figured textually, as a compromise between the rigidities of essentialist certainty and postmodern skepticism in its portrait of gender differences. For Bajwa, this middle ground is figured materially, in the lower-middle-class position of a male protagonist who comes to sympathize with women from higher and lower social classes. Whereas Ozeki, Johnson, and Jen ultimately retain important elements of comfort for their crowded selves and styles, Eugenides and Bajwa's novels seek to balance privilege against marginality in their efforts to surmount social differences of gender.

Yet sometimes this middle ground is not always enough. Chapter 5, "Challenging Language," explores two works of fiction that exhibit even greater sensitivity to the pressures of alterity. In the work of the Indian novelist Amitav Ghosh, increasingly radical textual sacrifices prove vital to acts of imaginative border crossing. Ghosh focuses attention on the particular problem of representing linguistic difference, asking how a novel written in English might ethically reflect the nuances of translingual, multilingual, and even antilingual experience in South Asia and Southeast Asia. Given the history of English as an imperial and neoimperial language, Ghosh's fiction invites us to consider that English may need to renounce elements of its own aesthetic privilege before it can accommodate these different forms of expression. This renunciation takes an unusual form in his historical epic, *The Glass Palace* (2000), which turns a seemingly conventional historical-realist style into a surprising form of linguistic border crossing. Rejecting obvious markers of linguistic difference, such as dialect, Ghosh's work flattens the sonic dimension of English to create a tone that different readers are meant to hear differently. The logic of the novel implies that the less aurally determinative the language on the page, the more capable of producing heterogeneous reading experiences it becomes. The radicalism of this approach deepens in *The Hungry Tide* (2004), which produces expansive crowded selves and styles to embrace the significant linguistic otherness of hyperverbal translation and nonhuman communication.

Perhaps more than any other writer at the turn of the millennium, the South African–born novelist J. M. Coetzee takes the practice of imagining social difference to its utmost limit. Coetzee confronts a postapartheid world deeply scarred by enduring inequalities of oppression and violence, and many of his characters strenuously resist being imagined by others. With Coetzee, we reach the outermost extremes of border-crossing fiction: he speaks from a place where an ethics of imagining social difference is both virtually impossible and yet always demanded. Chapter 6, "Sacrificing the Self," examines how Coetzee's response to this predicament results in the most uncomfortably crowded selves and styles of all. Addressing the problem of imagining across gender, race, and species, Coetzee suggests that engaging significant otherness is possible only from the place of the rights losing, not from the place of the rights bearing. As his fictions suggest the inadequacy of traditional liberal rights, they imply that challenging the representational violence of sexual privilege and racist dehumanization requires a radical identification with figures who have never been considered the bearers of rights, namely nonhuman species. Coetzee's tragic vision of imagining the lives of others posits a self so dangerously crowded that it must renounce even the privilege of being human, and his crowded style similarly embraces threatening forms of racialized discourse to transfigure their meaning. As Coetzee pushes representational capacity to its fullest extent, his fictions suggest how the ethics of such an endeavor threatens to annihilate itself in the end.

The unfolding of this book thus maps the changing contours of representational ethics as novelists seek to confront different kinds and intensities of alterity. In responding to these inquiries, these chapters ultimately act as inverted mirrors of each other. Ozeki and Coetzee both locate concerns with imaginative projection in the specter of violence against women and in the treatment of other species, but they provide almost antithetical stylistic and philosophical responses. Johnson and Ghosh both seek to draw upon a vocabulary beyond English, but the former dramatically advertises the inclusion of such linguistic material, and the latter flattens, displaces, and virtually erases it within his novel. These paradoxical presentations of subjectivity and style, I suggest, best illuminate how the ethical strategies of border-crossing fiction can never be confined within a predetermined shape. Through such a diversity of responses, I hope to show how many distinct novelistic subgenres and philosophical positions can prompt narrative choices that surmount the barriers of hegemonic or identitarian practices. Under what conditions might it make sense to turn to the sentimental, the comic, or the tragic? When might it make most sense to amplify social difference through literary form, and when might it seem effective to evict such markers of difference from the language of a novel? When and how do the comforts of liberal individualism appear adequate, and when and how do the sacrifices of a more radical antihumanism seem called for? These are the kinds of questions the following chapters seek to answer. Taken together, these readings enable a new critical metanarrative that contests familiar accounts of invasive imagination.

1

Crowded Self and Crowded Style

Why do we so often act as if it is easier, or better, to represent one's own world than to imagine the world of another? Why do we assume that we can necessarily tell the two apart? "Everywhere was now a part of everywhere else," Salman Rushdie writes in *Shalimar the Clown* (2005). "Russia, America, London, Kashmir. Our lives, our stories, flowed into one another's, were no longer our own, individual, discrete. This unsettled people."[1] The unsettlement evoked in Rushdie's novel pervades a wide range of twentieth-century scholarly metanarratives about representing social difference. Telling stories that are not considered one's own, particularly when the teller approaches these stories from a position of privilege, is often described as a form of invasive imagination. Representing alterity is frequently understood as an act of discursive domination that replicates, in literary form, the violent operations of political, economic, and social inequality.

This approach has proven itself to be a powerful and necessary one. Yet is such uneasiness the only viable way to think about novelistic acts of border crossing? Might it not be possible to attribute positive ethical significance to telling stories about others? Proposing such an alternative optic is the purpose of this chapter. I begin by considering debates about representing alterity, asking why imagining others has been considered such a problem in the late twentieth century. I acknowledge where skeptics are right to question the act of representation, and I reject some commonly held assumptions about literary authority that predominate in popular understandings of fiction. But I also seek to challenge the pervasive metanarrative that describes the representation of otherness as a form inherently contaminated by discursive domination. Tracing the source of this skeptical metanarrative in late twentieth-century postcolonial, ethnic, and feminist studies, I suggest that these literary and cultural theories encourage two central ways of thinking about representing alterity from positions of relative privilege. The first influential strain of thought reads representations of others as displaced representations of the self, and the second important thread locates alternatives to invasive imagination in spaces of silence beyond representation itself. Neither of these underlying critical stances, I suggest, has fully offered a clear and coherent path toward an ethics of representing social difference, particularly when ideologies of inferiority are at stake.

To offer such a path, I suggest the need to reconsider underlying ideas about social and stylistic identity. By thinking through modern philosophical and psychological accounts of representation, I propose a set of principles that helps novels represent social difference without falling into familiar forms of discursive domination. Socially shaped selfhood and language, critical self-reflection, and diminishment of privilege emerge as the cornerstones of this ethics of representing others. These principles allow works of fiction to produce emancipatory practices that I call "crowded selves" and "crowded styles." These keywords help identify productive novelistic engagements with what I call (following Donna Haraway) significant otherness. Turning finally to a compact series of three readings, I suggest how specific works of fiction dramatize important aspects of crowded selves and crowded styles. Through these readings, I seek to show how such narrative choices may help resolve controversies about the ethics of representing others. Even in a world marked by radical inequality, oppression, and violence, not all imaginative acts are doomed to be invasive.

Why Is Imagining Others a Problem?

Since prose fiction cannot help but speak for and about others, the problem of social difference plagues virtually all fictional representations. If we insist that writers ought to represent only what they personally experience, every book devolves into solipsistic autobiography written ideally for its author's own consumption. This constricting conclusion suggests that the risks of imagining beyond one's experience can rarely be divided from the making of fiction. Even works that strongly reject the socially mimetic capacity of language force their readers to confront the unsettling presence of alterity, expanding conventional ideas about what social differences are and what it means to imagine them. In terms of both production and consumption, fiction continually spurs questions about one's capacity to inhabit the perspectives of others.

In what I call border-crossing fiction, or writing with a dramatic dissonance between the subject and object of representation, anxieties about the intimacy between representational power and social privilege loom particularly large. How can novels dramatize the representation of figures and forms with sensitivity to the distortions of inequality, especially when the social location of the perceiver seems distant from the world he or she imagines? In light of such kinds of questions, fiction of this sort is legitimately considered an enterprise fraught with a special kind of ethical difficulty. From a distance, border crossing often appears uncontroversial, but close up, it frequently inflames vexed debates about authority and domination.

As commonly conceived, such fiction often provokes a battle between those who claim uncomplicated freedom of artistic expression and those who defend exclusive rights to the representation of one's own experience (however broadly or narrowly construed). These two stances can best be understood through what the discourse theorist Amy Shuman calls narratives of "allegory" and of "entitlement." Allegorical positions mark "the use of stories to represent not just individual, but collective, experience," and so they are told by many different kinds of tellers. Entitlement positions, in contrast, reflect "the rights accorded firsthand experience: individuals have firsthand knowledge that grants them a privileged position as knowers and a legitimate stake in the interpretation of their own experiences."[2]

While these positions make sense under specific circumstances, I suggest that both of them reveal their limitations when held over time. Uncritical celebrations of authorial freedom of expression often articulate the allegorical principle as a veiled form of dominance, as the American novelist John Updike does in a comic mock interview with one of his fictional creations. Updike's character, a Jewish figure named Henry Bech, demands to know Updike's credentials for inventing Bech's life.

> **Q [Bech].**   And this Jewishness you give me. What do you know about being Jewish? *Très peu*, I venture to estimate. As much as you learned listening to the *Jack Benny* program back in Shillington, Pennsylvania. Ask Cynthia Ozick. Ask Leon Wieseltier. Ask Orlando Cohen.
> **A [Updike].**   Cohen is my invention. . . .
> **Q.**   You're no more Jewish than Henry Adams, and not near as funny about it.
> **A.**   It is my American right to give it a try, even in today's strident climate of defensive diversity.[3]

As Bech mixes real people with Updike's own characters as sources of authority on Jewish identity, Updike pokes fun at Bech's demand for an authentic authorial voice. Though Updike goes on in the interview to defend his characterizations more precisely, shaping specific analogies between writers and Jews, his use of "my American right to give it a try" seeks to protect authorial expression against any restrictions on his scope of inquiry.[4] As this rhetoric suggests, Updike's claim to universal imaginative access reflects a particularly national sense of might and prowess, confirming his critics' suspicions that border-crossing fictions conceal a neoimperial sensibility in the making.

This defense of unlimited authorial right sometimes appears not in bristling indignation, as in Updike's case, but in omission or dismissal. In the approach of late twentieth- and early twenty-first-century writing manuals, many readers and writers simply take expansive authorial power for granted. Because the genre of the literary guidebook indexes the changing concerns that beset generations of aspiring authors, we might expect such writing guides to address the public debates about representation that emerged in the wake of anticolonial activism and identity politics. However, in a survey of twenty-three manuals and advice books published between 1982 and 2004 (approximately the period covered in this book), only five acknowledged the potential controversies of writing across social borders.[5] Even fewer qualifications appear in journalistic discourse, which abounds with the uninhibited retelling of personal narratives.[6] This silence might be taken as evidence of the allegorical position, in which any writer is invited to represent any kind of story.

Yet this silence can also be seen to support the entitlement position, for one of the most commonly repeated dictums in the modern creative-writing guidebook is the principle "write what you know." If aspiring novelists are not strongly encouraged to contemplate the ethics of representing others, they *are* frequently encouraged to write about events and relationships that they have personally experienced or witnessed firsthand. "Start with your childhood," the bestselling writer Anne Lamott urges her creative-writing students.[7] "Your writing comes out of a relationship with your life and its texture," suggests Natalie Goldberg.[8] While these injunctions are not necessarily cast in the spirit of experiential essentialism, they do reinforce the popular assumption that good writing is more likely to emerge from memories and experiences in which the teller claims a strong firsthand stake. Indeed, when writing manuals do discourage aspiring writers from writing about radically different social experiences, they often do so not from ethical concerns about representational violence or discursive domination but because such writing is less likely to be *aesthetically* successful.

If institutions of modern Anglophone authorship thus tend to circumvent the ethical questions of writing across borders by (paradoxically) encouraging the operation of both allegorical and entitlement positions, theories of literary representation in the late twentieth century have created a powerful critical metanarrative that relies on sophisticated versions of the entitlement critique to question the possibility and value of imaginative border crossing. In many accounts of such writing, a novel's attempt to represent social difference is read as a disguised version of the aspirations or anxieties of the novel's own social location. This idea has gained greatest prominence through the influence of Edward Said's landmark *Orientalism* (1978), which exposes imperialist assumptions behind Western representations of the "Orient."[9]

In Said's terms, these representations damage those whom they claim to depict, at best imprisoning so-called Orientals in the narrow worlds of exoticism and at worst validating regimes of imperial control. Theories of related discourses, such as Western primitivism, have extended Said's core insight to suggest similar effects in Euro-American representations of African and South American cultures. As Marianna Torgovnick argues in her study of primitivism, "The West seems to need the primitive as a precondition and a supplement to its sense of self: it always creates heightened versions of the primitive as nightmare or pleasant dream."[10] The skeleton of such claims relies on what I call the mirror argument: representations of others, in specular fashion, ultimately offer only displaced versions of the subject's own social condition. While not all investigations of these discourses consider them to be exercises in domination,[11] this critical metanarrative encourages us to understand the troubling political implications of representing alterity. Put most bluntly in Abdul JanMohamed's speculation, "every desire is at base a desire to impose oneself upon another."[12] This infectious logic has generated a crisis in representational ethics that continues to haunt literature at the turn of the millennium.

The skepticism and occasional determinism that characterizes theories of Orientalism and primitivism has also surfaced in the growth of feminist, postcolonial, and ethnic-minority literature, where writers from marginalized social positions have sometimes implied exclusive powers of community self-representation. Especially prevalent during the wave of feminism, ethnic activism, and anticolonial struggles of the 1960s and 1970s, frustration with the legacy of repression emboldened many writers to claim the right to retell their collective histories. Feminist theorists vigorously contested the reliability of male images of women, echoing Jane Austen's insights in *Persuasion* (1818): "I do not think I ever opened a book in my life which had not something to say upon woman's inconstancy," Austen's Captain Harville argues. "Songs and proverbs, all talk of woman's fickleness. But perhaps you will say, these were all written by men."[13] Much as feminist activists pointed out the problem of judging women by male evidence, postcolonial and ethnic-minority theorists fought against the legacy of demeaning and constraining representations produced through imperial and racist articulations. As the vibrant explosion of minority and postcolonial writing offered innovative, powerful, and vital alternatives to white or Western representations, these writings were often publicly framed within the language of authenticity and essentialism. The Asian American editors of *The Big Aiiieeeee!* (1991), for instance, energetically sought to divide "real" from "fake" representations of Asian American culture.[14] Geary Hobson, critiquing white appropriations of Native American shamans, declared that "I doubt very seriously if there is anything in [white writers'] own cultural environments that really affords them such power, or even the access to such power, to say nothing of the spuriousness of their ancestors being shamans." Instead, Hobson defended "the great need which Indian people have of being the ones to speak for themselves, of being the ones to define themselves and their cultures."[15] Similarly, Rana Kabbani's account of European representations of the Middle East argued that "my sincere hope is that Orientalism—in both its new and its old forms—will eventually become extinct, as more of us describe ourselves from our own experience."[16] Such entitlement claims frequently encourage the assumption that community self-representations offer the most, and sometimes the only, valid forms of literary work, even as they grapple with anxieties that self-representations can also replicate modes of hegemonic domination.[17]

The legacy of this emphasis on self-representation appears in many common critical practices at the end of the twentieth century. It is evident in an exculpatory gesture of address, in which speakers scrupulously qualify their insights with reference to their nationality, gender, race, class, or sexuality.[18] More radically, concern with the structural possibilities (or impossibilities) of speech characterizes postcolonial debates about the politics of language choice. Prominent writers, most famously Ngugi wa Thiong'o, have argued that languages such as English, disseminated through colonialism and neoimperialism, cannot adequately convey the richness of lived and literary experience under postcolonial conditions. Drawing strength from Marxist theories of the relationship between material power and cultural expression, critics of border crossing have contended that the unequal conditions of literary production, circulation, and reception can limit the liberatory potential of a work written in English.[19] Suspicious of ethical claims to representing alterity, these challenges seek to expose how larger systems of inequality perpetuate new forms of discursive domination.

To run the risk of oversimplification, I suggest that the metanarrative that forms the basis of such criticism implies that those from relatively dominant positions of power experience difficulty effectively representing those whose place in the world appears more marginal. Kabbani articulates this logic of the mirror argument in the most expansive and transhistorical of terms: "Descriptions of distant lands peopled by fantastic beings have universally abounded, as one dominant group became able to forge images of the 'alien' by imposing its own self-perpetuating categories and deviations from the norm."[20] David Richards describes this pattern as the "euphemisation of power," in which practices of reading identify "misrepresentations through which power is legitimated, transfigured, and misrecognized."[21] Seen in this light, such representations ventriloquize the desires, anxieties, and hierarchies of authors who wish (wittingly or not) to maintain or acquire established forms of privilege. As such, the mirror argument establishes the possibility or impossibility of conceptualizing alterity along predictable axes of power.

This correlation between dominance and discourse persists even in accounts that trouble Said's reliance on monolithic binaries between strong and weak groups. Since power can be diffused and exercised in many different ways, theorists revising Said have described the heterogeneity of Orientalist discourse, and they have shown how subjects can never be simply reduced to those who possess power and those who lack it. Lisa Lowe, for example, argues convincingly that "when we maintain a static dualism of identity and difference, and uphold the logic of the dualism as the means of explaining how a discourse expresses domination and subordination, we fail to account for the differences inherent in each term."[22] Yet Lowe's revisions of Orientalism nonetheless continue to reflect the reading practices that the mirror argument would predict. In her interpretation of Lady Mary Wortley Montagu's sketches of Turkish court women, for instance, Montagu pushes against masculinist perceptions from a protofeminist stance but replicates Orientalist evocations in her European optic. As a result, Montagu's writing reveals "an orientalism generated by differently gender-determined and class-determined positions" (32). While Montagu's Orientalism is not monolithic, the terms of her identification—Montagu identifies with those who are, like her, women and aristocrats—remain exactly along the lines that the mirror argument in its many variants would lead us to expect.

Because this predictive logic suggests that displaced representations reflect the workings of social privilege, modern inquiries into border-crossing fiction tend to be more optimistic about postcolonial or minority artists who reshape dominant cultural exports. Though often taken as symbol of an increasingly complex interpretation of hybrid identity, these accounts continue to remain remarkably compatible with the assumptions of difference criticism. Following the structure of Hegel's master-slave relationship, in which the slave necessarily perceives more than the master, these arguments remain indebted to the theories of power and knowledge that sustain different versions of the mirror argument.[23] Katrin Sieg's nuanced study of ethnic drag in German theater, for instance, highlights the political complexity of drag as a genre but concludes by finding white impersonations of Native Americans repressive and Native American impersonations of ethnic others liberating. As Sieg puts it, "cultural transactions are framed by, and reproduce, unequal power relations."[24] While these investigations recognize the creative powers of the marginalized and afford what Paula Moya calls "epistemic privilege" to the oppressed, they often leave unexplored the question of whether comparatively privileged social forms can avoid domesticating or demonizing whatever enters their gaze.[25] Even Richards, who works to show that the "euphemisation of power . . . is not the whole truth," focuses his attention primarily on alternatives that are provided by colonized or postcolonial subjects.[26] These readings thus remain indebted to the mirror argument, which they refine and qualify but do not fundamentally elude. To read a representation as reproducing relations of power, even when these relations do not operate in isolation, is to remain within the conceptual thrust of Said's original claim.

Gayatri Chakravorty Spivak's essay "Can the Subaltern Speak?" (1988) takes this metanarrative further by refusing to offer any comfortable or reliable path out of representational violence. "We should also welcome all the information retrieval in these silenced areas that is taking place in anthropology, political science, history, and sociology," Spivak argues. "Yet the assumption and construction of a consciousness of subject sustains such work and will, in the long run, cohere with the work of imperialist subject-constitution, mingling epistemic violence with the advancement of learning and civilization. And the subaltern woman will be as mute as ever."[27] While some have challenged her conclusions, arguing (in a manner that recalls the entitlement position) for more nuanced attention to the discourse of communities outside the reach of Western institutions, Spivak's essay contends that such recuperation ironically works to reinscribe the very narrative of domination it was intended to contest.[28] As an epistemological effect of the material conditions of imperialism and inequality, Spivak's logic suggests, the problem of subaltern speech cannot necessarily be remedied by deepened qualities of attention or heightened claims to voice.

Contesting the mirror argument has thus frequently come at the expense of the possibility of representation itself. This sacrifice of representational ethics emerges in the work of Homi Bhabha, who defends poststructuralist theory from the patterns of Saidian critique by shifting focus from what he calls "cultural diversity," or "culture as an object of empirical knowledge," to "cultural difference," or "the process of the *enunciation* of culture as 'knowledge*able*.' "[29] By thus redirecting attention from an epistemological object to a condition of possibility, Bhabha hopes to show that any act of speaking about others will be troubled by the instabilities that poststructuralist theories consider constitutive of language. No speech act will simply reflect the privilege of its speaker; it will always be challenged from within, undercut by the traces and hauntings of the otherness it seeks to contain. Bhabha thus offers up an utopian Third Space that allows for the redescription of cultural symbols, but, as the condition for enunciation rather than any specific portrait, this Third Space is "unrepresentable in itself."[30] Theorists who draw upon Bhabha to explore the ethics of representing social difference, therefore, are likely to emphasize absence over presence, pointing us toward what eludes or defies representational practice.[31] While reading practices that emerge from this account can challenge the Manicheanism often attributed to Said, their emphasis on what cannot be represented makes them difficult to assimilate to a vision of nonviolent imaginative relationships between self and other.[32] Despite their crucial contributions to practices of reading, these responses have not aimed to offer a clear path toward a robust ethics of representing social difference.

These critical metanarratives—one emphasizing relentless mirroring, the other directing attention beyond representation—both suggest that imaginative practices cannot easily contest the inequitable power relations from which they emerge. Even if we accept that power is not something possessed or lacked but is the invisible condition for social relationships,[33] this description is not incompatible with remaining attuned to the inequalities that continue to haunt relationships between specific selves and specific others. Testifying to the salience of these inequalities, the influence of these paradigms of difference has continued to exert residual authority in shaping late twentieth- and twenty-first-century intellectual discourse. Indeed, the genius of the mirror argument lies in its supreme portability and its capacity for virtually limitless migration. Extended well beyond Said's original study of colonialism in the Middle East to many different parts of the world in many different periods of time, it even enables an understanding of the precarious border between culture and nature. Donna Haraway, for example, speaks of "simian orientalism" that describes how "western primatology has been about the construction of the self from the raw material of the other."[34] As the mirror argument has proliferated into many fields of inquiry, the shadowy presence of its critical double, identitarian logic, also continues to undergird many practices of both professional and lay reading. Such an expectation is palpable in a frequent autobiographical elision of author and subject. For example, ethnic-minority writers receive much more attention when they write about their own ethnicity than about another ethnic group.[35] It enables the very production of the problematic category of "ethnic" author: theoretically everyone should possess ethnicity, but "ethnic" is frequently simply a code for "nonwhite." J. M. Coetzee, for example, is never described as an "ethnic" writer, even though he was born into an ethnic minority in South Africa. It emerges in readings that ultimately conclude, as Kathleen Lundeen does, that "in literature, as in life, there are shared borders of identity that we are compelled to recognize but cannot cross."[36] Most broadly, this influence can be found in the more general hermeneutics of suspicion—what Eve Kosofsky Sedgwick calls "paranoid reading"—that predominates within literary criticism.[37]

While many literary scholars might accept that, in theory, one can sensitively envision social difference from positions of relative privilege, they rarely provide specific examples of such work or elaborate upon how it might succeed.[38] Said explicitly admitted that his view of literature was deeply concerned with conflict and therefore ill suited to address the "sanity and calm reflectiveness" that non-Orientalist writing might offer.[39] More open to these possibilities, Torgovnick qualifies her powerful critiques of the pitfalls of Western primitivism by noting glimpses of alternative modes of enunciation that suggest the possibility of escape from the epistemological effects of imperialism. But these glimpses offer only fragmentary and elusive sightings that remain, in Torgovnick's words, "variously turned aside or undeveloped."[40] In effect, these readings leave undisturbed a metanarrative of discursive domination as the most powerful interpretative lens.[41] This lacuna, not simply in these visions but in the broader preoccupations of the 1990s, suggests that fundamental problems of border crossing have yet to be fully resolved in literary discourse. Only in recent years have modern theorists begun to work through some of the impasses of earlier moments, asking, as B. Venkat Mani does, "is there any redeemable factor left in speaking for/about/as the Other?"[42] Though many have articulated the ambivalences and ambiguities that complicate these representations, they have often seemed skeptical of attempts to identify the positive ethical value in representing alterity.

This residual suspicion of border-crossing fiction appears in more strident form within popular print culture. In 2006, the Australian cultural critic Germaine Greer publicly attacked the Bangladeshi British writer Monica Ali for the portrait of London immigrant communities that appears in Ali's novel *Brick Lane* (2003). Greer claimed that since Ali is only half Bangladeshi and spent most of her childhood in Britain, she lacked the proper credentials to write about the Sylheti immigrants who populate London's Brick Lane. Basing her claims on a few biographical details, Greer sought to undermine Ali's legitimacy as a writer of fiction without ever substantially referring to the language of Ali's novel. Ali's crime toward her characters, Greer's article argues, is simply that "she has dared to create them."[43] While Greer claimed the authority of critiquing Orientalism, her argument debased the power of this tradition by turning it into an excuse for racial essentialism. In taking it upon herself to police the authenticity of a multiethnic and multinational writer, Greer revealed the sinister logic that an extreme and distorted form of the mirror argument allows. While critiques based on this metanarrative allow us to explain troubling portraits of social difference, they are sometimes taken to imply that fiction can rarely, if ever, speak legitimately outside what is considered its own world. (As we see in the case of Monica Ali, "what is considered" one's world is often a source of debate in its own right.) If every attempt to write beyond the experiential scope of the author forms only a displaced mirror of the author's own predicament, the resulting view of the world yields only a portrait of imaginative imprisonment. This portrait, as I will suggest, is not actually consonant with the way individuals experience their lives.

In the end, while no representation will ever be above criticism or untouched by the workings of inequality, I suggest that it is crucial to consider why some representations may be less prone toward representational violence than others. As Ihab Hassan argues, the predilection for difference over similarity that characterizes many forms of critique "can discourage mutual obligation, cripple empathy, defeat transcultural judgments, leaving only raw power to resolve human conflicts." Following Hassan, the interpretative lens I will propose asks, *"How and when, pragmatically, do we honor differences, ignore them, negotiate them?"* [44] In explicitly seeking forms of viable imaginative border crossing, this book attempts to make visible the implicit value judgments that pervade influential ideas about writing across borders. While readings based upon metanarratives of discursive domination do not always identify themselves in terms of such judgment, they suggest that such writings present others in ways that modern readers would hope to resist. Their readings contend that texts commit particular errors of perception, and they argue that these errors usually work to the detriment of the people and places represented. Such approaches rely on a covert claim to knowledge, for only in reference to an implied ideal can their critiques of representational failure make sense. Through the invisible assumptions of such criticism, readers are constantly encouraged to make value judgments about the status of literary works.

This book thus seeks to restate this hidden preoccupation with representational insufficiency as a positive set of questions. In turning to the language of ethics rather than to the language of politics, I should be clear that I am not advocating a cloistered, apolitical, or privatistic approach to the reading of fiction. However, I understand the language of ethics as offering a more open form of engagement with significant otherness than politics, with its commitment to the generalizable, may always be able to offer. To talk about politics is often to reveal how literary forms reproduce political hierarchies and inequalities; to talk about ethics, I suggest, allows us to identify forms of fiction that may exceed such reproduction. The language of ethics thus offers a way to discuss value that is not limited to what Satya Mohanty defines as political criticism, namely "the common desire to expose the social interests at work in the reading and writing of literature." [45] Seen from one angle, my approach could fit within this definition comfortably: after all, I seek to understand the social interests that emerge through the production of border-crossing fiction. But I also suspect that Mohanty means to stress the word "expose," and in this sense he gestures toward the kind of exposure plot that characterizes dominant assumptions of critical reading. An interpretative lens that magnifies the language of ethics, I suggest, is one that seeks to move beyond this plot of exposure.

Rethinking the ethos of invasive imagination, the novels considered in this book produce relationships between self and other that allow for productive dialogue across perceived social borders. These novels attempt to engage significant otherness without inevitably trapping their objects of representation within the prisons of their own fantasies and fears. My work thus builds upon the arguments of Tzvetan Todorov, one of the most optimistic theorists of representing otherness in the late twentieth century. Chastising many of his fellow scholars for overly mystifying the capacity to imagine others, Todorov argues that "my culture is not a negligible quantity, but neither is it all. . . . Affirming the existence of incommunicability among cultures . . . presupposes adherence to a racialist, apartheid-like set of beliefs, postulating as it does insurmountable discontinuity within the human species." [46] Todorov's *The Conquest of America: The Question of the Other* (1982) turns to the example of Spanish conquest in the Americas to evaluate what it terms "the problematics of the exterior and remote other" (*CA*, 3). "We want *equality* without its compelling us to accept identity; but also *difference* without its degenerating into superiority/inferiority," Todorov argues (249; italics in the original). His assessment of Spanish colonial encounters with Indians reflects a considered, though highly circumscribed, optimism about how this ideal might be realized. [47] "To experience difference in equality is easier said than done," Todorov writes. "Yet several figures of my exemplary history came close to it, in various ways. On the axiological level, a Las Casas managed in his old age to love and esteem the Indians as a function not of his own ideal, but of theirs: this is a nonunifying love" (249). Such "nonunifying" love emerges from dialogic practices of "speaking to" rather than simply "speaking of " (even the choice of the word "love" affirms the importance of direct engagement). This dialogic commitment will be important to many of the works of fiction I explore. Imagining others as Todorov suggests will not lead to positivist knowledge of them, but in contrast to neoimperial, racialized, or sexist perceptions, it may offer a better foundation for a representational practice commensurate with the demands of a globalizing world.

Given my emphasis on social-border crossing, it might be objected that such an exploration of social constructions of difference siphons attention from the reality of material exploitation.[48] While economic inequality presents a crucial set of problems, to dismiss the importance of social difference may allow us to forget that, in many parts of the world at the turn of the twenty-first century, people kill and die for such ideas of identity. Amitav Ghosh, writing of his experience as an Indian Hindu anthropologist in an Egyptian Muslim village, notes his own rising panic when the villagers ask him if he is circumcised. Even though their questions mean him no real harm, Ghosh is immediately overwhelmed with memories of communalist riots among Hindus, Sikhs, and Muslims in India that led to "men dismembered for the state of their foreskins."[49] While not all writers considered here explore symbolism (here figured through the religious molding of the body) in such harrowing circumstances, this specter may help us appreciate the urgency of the social distinctions they highlight. As the ethics of border crossing in these novels can be a fragile and rare phenomenon, even the most modest of its victories may offer important symbolic alternatives to the inscription of social difference through repression and violence.

Furthermore, the symbolic structure of literary works has often been called to account for its effect on the material world. If as scholars we accept, loosely following Foucault, that fiction can do real damage through its representations, we should logically ask if fiction also possesses the latent power to propose new forms of expression. If readers know enough to be able to critique literary representations, it should be possible to be able to identify moments that provide productive alternatives. One novel alone, of course, cannot erase pervasive epistemic violence. Only the relationship between widespread forms of representation and systems of education, economics, and governance enables literature to speak with audible force. For a new generation of novels to exert measurable social power, there will need to be more of them, and they will need to be reinforced by cultural, political, and economic elements currently missing from much of twenty-first-century life. The compassionate empathy supposedly fostered by literature, in Suzanne Keen's convincing demonstration, is often overestimated by supporters of the novel when it comes to measurable social behavior on behalf of others. [50] While psychological studies of reading do provide some evidence of an impact on its audience, the power of books to change minds and actions is far from certain. [51] In a broader social context, as Elaine Scarry rightly argues, legal and constitutional documents must solidify the insights found in the imaginary worlds of fiction. [52] But these works still need to be written, read, and studied for the insights they provide into how such transformation might evolve. [53] With Arjun Appadurai, I take imaginative work as (among many other things) social work. [54] Although new theories and practices of representing others are unlikely to inspire readers to change lives or systems in dramatic ways, they may well exert more subtle influences that, combined with other forces, might alter the character of the public sphere.

Whether or not these works inspire new forms of civic behavior, their innovations in representational ethics are also worth defending in their own right as contributions to the history of ideas. Scholars have extensively elaborated on the ways in which representations consolidate particularly privileged identities through troubling manipulations of others, but they have not given equal attention to how representations might do otherwise. Although such emancipatory moments are frequently fleeting, partial, or full of painful sacrifices, the narrative choices described in this book reveal how fiction at the turn of the millennium yearns to abandon dystopic styles of representation. As readers, we are only beginning to trace the contours of such emergent literature.

Crowded Self and Crowded Style

How might we begin to identify the underlying ideas and practices that could enable a new metanarrative of imaginative border crossing? In the pages that follow, I will propose two keywords—*crowded self* and *crowded style*—that figure such alternatives. In order to set forth these concepts, my account first works through the specific theories of identity and imaginative projection that underwrite such an ethics. Going beyond the logic of the dominant metanarrative requires adopting different understandings of how self and other can relate under conditions of social difference. With reference to modern philosophical and psychological accounts of representation, I propose three characteristics that, taken together, shape the ethical family resemblances of the novels considered in this study. While these conceptual values are not new in themselves, I suggest that their intermeshing helps specify how innovative alternatives to the mirror argument and the unrepresentability argument might emerge. My account will then explore how prose fictions work through these concepts as they envision encounters with significant otherness.

The first idea that informs an ethics of border-crossing fiction is a recognition of selfhood and language as socially shaped. As many novels and antiessentialist theories insist, self-knowledge is a frail and often unreliable construct. Although theories of liberal and autonomous subjectivity might claim self-knowledge as fundamentally reliable, more modern understandings of selfhood stress its fluidity and provisionality, so that no single perspective on the self—including the self's own view—will ever offer a fully complete account. As psychologists argue, present selves often dramatically fail to predict accurately the needs and wants of their future incarnations.[55]

More specifically, the closer we look, the more the boundaries between selfhood and otherness begin to blur. Although individuals often assume that they speak authoritatively about their own social location and tentatively about experiences they have not had, this distinction is actually a difficult one to maintain with perfect coherence. Indeed, the complicated relationship between personal experience and acquired knowledge enables the very construction of identity in the first place. I draw here upon Satya Mohanty's theorization of experience, which he argues is never simply a sufficient and self-evident category: "'Personal experience' is socially and 'theoretically' constructed. . . . Our access to our remotest personal feelings is dependent upon social narratives, paradigms, and even ideologies."[56] Many of the acts that constitute personal experience are thus acquisitions of exterior knowledge, so that a sense of one's identity as (for example) "Indian" might stem not only from the lived practices of everyday life but also from the kind of Indian history one has studied or from the kind of Indian literature one has read. An individual immersed in a secular-nationalist history of India might understand being Indian very differently from an individual steeped in ideologies of Hindutva. Such practices provide narratives that make sense of inchoate individual experiences, offering important interpretative windows that frame how individuals identify and understand their own social locations. Indeed, as Benedict Anderson has famously argued in the case of nationality, group identities are constructed precisely by linking together individuals who do *not* share the lived practices of their daily lives.[57] Of course, not all aspects of identity formation are voluntary. Important kinds of unchosen experience (especially of oppression and discrimination) provide crucial and privileged forms of theoretical knowledge about the self. However, to assume that identity is only constructed externally (by the state, by what others perceive one to be) or negatively (by discriminatory or exclusionary practices) is to overlook a wide range of practices that make a social identity rich and significant.[58] Learning about others—through history, literature, mass media, or other avenues—constitutes an important part of one's own social identity. Many of the acts that help individuals shape themselves cannot always be distinguished from the acts that help them learn about different parts of the world or about different kinds of world experience.

Why should learning Indian history construct Indianness for someone we know in advance to be Indian but not for someone we know in advance to be a citizen of a different nation? It may be useful here to consider Walter Benn Michaels's critique of the paradoxical logic behind the pluralist conception of identity, which "requires in fact that the question of who we are continues to be understood as prior to questions about what we do."[59] This assumption explains why many border-crossing representations continue to be plagued with accusations of fraudulence, even though what individuals do to constitute their own identities often resembles what they do to comprehend those of others. Avoiding this residual essentialism, Michaels's analysis suggests, requires thinking much more radically about the similarity between how persons learn about what they consider their social identities and how they learn about the lives and traditions of others. "If history were learned, not remembered," Michaels parses this logic, "then no history could be more truly ours than any other. Indeed, no history, except the things that had actually happened to us, would be truly ours at all."[60] While one can use this point to contend that individuals have a less intimate relationship to "their" past than is commonly presumed, I suggest that it also allows individuals the possibility of claiming a *more* intimate imaginative relationship to the experiences of others.[61] This relationship is not equivalent to one's own experience, but it may not be as distant as formerly assumed.[62] Abandoning the expectation of equivalence between these forms of imaginative affiliation allows the African American protagonist of Samuel Delany's novella *Atlantis: Model 1924* (1995) to offer a manifesto of socially shaped selfhood that claims them both:

> I'm going to originate everywhere. . . . From now on, I come from all times before me—and all my origins will feed me. Some in Africa I get through my daddy. And my momma. And my step-daddy. Some in Europe I get through the library: Greece and Rome, China and India. . . . Every time I read a new book, every time I hear something new about history, every time I make a new friend, see a new color in the oil slicked over a puddle in the mud, a new origin joins me to make me what I am to be—what I'm always becoming.[63]

Subjectivities are forged in the libraries as well as on the streets, in the cacophony of written histories as well as in the crucible of embodied encounters.

If selfhood is shaped by experiences and practices that go well beyond what the logic of pluralism would identify as its social identity, literary discourse can also be understood as a negotiation between the innovations specific to a particular novel and the language as it is used by other speakers and writers. Even across linguistic divides, different languages continually influence the shape and circulation of other tongues. Amitav Ghosh articulates the effects of such multilingualism in an Indian context, arguing that, though each language is unique, "no body of literature anywhere develops within a closed room, and each of India's languages has resounded to the echoes of its surroundings—both immediate and distant."[64] The same might be said even of parts of the world, such as the United States or Britain, where fewer languages dominate public discourse. Writers from immigrant and postcolonial communities frequently reshape the tone and texture of English, interweaving new vocabularies and linguistic structures while transforming grammatical mistakes into sources of aesthetic power.[65] Strong divisions between indigenous and foreign languages, therefore, are often difficult ones to maintain.

At the broadest level, then, it becomes easier to recognize the impossibility of impermeable conceptual divides between the selves and styles considered one's own and the selves and styles considered another's. But what about the nature of the specific engagement between one point of view (psychological or formal) and another? Particular instances of imaginative projection veer toward two extremes that make us question the value of adopting the perspectives and discourses of others. The first extreme leaves an identity effectively unchanged; the second seeks to erase that identity's existing markings. An evocation of the first position appears in the variants of the mirror argument I have already discussed, in which attempts to represent the other offer displaced versions of the subject's own condition and lead to forms of discursive domination.[66] This predicament appears vividly in Charles Johnson's novel *Oxherding Tale* (1982), which exposes the pathological intimacy between domination and inescapable selfhood. Flo Hatfield, a slave owner who exerts mastery through sexual encounters, reveals the solipsistic violence behind the ostensibly other-oriented act of desire. Her slave Andrew comes to comprehend the true form of his enslavement in his virtual erasure from her point of view:

> She lay her chin on my chest, looking up, and I wondered if, really, there were two of us here, or—for each of us—only one. I asked her, "What do you feel when you touch me?"
>
> "Me." Now her lips were on my fingertips. "I feel my own pulse. My own sensations." She laughed. "I have a pulse everywhere."
>
> "That's all you feel?"
>
> "Yes."[67]

As the logical evocation of the mirror argument, such self-conservation offers a deeply problematic model for an ethics of representing others.

Yet the other end of the philosophical spectrum—an end that often circles back to its beginning—offers an equally unsatisfying vision of engagement with others. If individuals identify so closely with someone else that they repress or conceal their own pasts and perspectives, they are usually known through the language of impersonation or passing. Amy Hungerford illuminates this problem in her work on falsified Holocaust memoirs, suggesting that taking over someone else's identity and "memorizing memory" offer an unsatisfying ethical vision of imaginative projection in both subjectivity and style.[68] At the clearest level, the specter of Holocaust impersonation dramatizes the ethical stakes of border crossing: to claim Holocaust survival is to make particular moral and political demands on the public sphere in ways that are consequential, not trivial. At the same time, such impersonation is not only a matter of subjectivity but also of literary form. Once a Holocaust trauma acquires generic conventions of representation, Hungerford shows, it becomes copyable, so that the relationship between the experience of trauma and the production of memoir is no longer a necessary one. The writer's own location thus vanishes into the conventions of particular narrative pathways.

If impersonation raises one specific set of concerns about the visibility of selfhood, the discourse of passing provokes another form of anxiety. While impersonation marks the claim to a set of experiences, passing marks the claim to a certain definition of social identity. As I use it here, passing means cultivating the perception of a social identity by suppressing information about the self that would contradict the governing definition of that social identity.[69] Though passing of the racial or gendered variety is usually available only to a limited number of people whose physical presence in the world allows for a variety of public perceptions, the idea of passing exerts an influence on discourses of social identity that goes well beyond the small number of actual passers. Passing, I argue, offers at best a troubling model for border crossing because it depends on the practice of conscious concealment or repression (if a person considers herself white because she has never learned of any black ancestors, she is not usually described as a passer).[70] Passing not only denies aspects of the self but, to its duped audience, also denies its very status as border crossing. Perhaps most crucially, passing provides a troubling model because it is often (though not necessarily) complicit with social hierarchies. Passers frequently gain benefits that would be denied if their ancestry, anatomy, or upbringing were fully known. Even in cases where an individual passes "down," adopting the identity of a group marked by ideologies of inferiority, this act is frequently reabsorbed within a frame of interpretation that reaffirms existing social hierarchies. For example, the experiences of John Howard Griffin, a white American liberal who passed as black in an ethnojournalistic experiment in understanding racism, often served to displace those of black Americans in public discourse. Even within his own writing, Griffin's method relies on a division between a white observant consciousness and a black experiential body that continues to practice discursive domination.[71] Sara Ahmed, contemplating such cases, is led to describe passing as a phenomenon that "involves an apparatus of knowledge that masters the stranger by taking its place."[72] In a case like Griffin's, the visible erasure of white identity ironically doubles back into a mode of self-conservation, revealing the secret sharing between these ethically unsatisfying modes of imagining alterity.

The practice I seek to identify, therefore, neither upholds the self-conservation of hegemonic mirroring nor enacts the self-erasure of impersonation and passing.[73] Instead, the border-crossing fiction I defend presents the most useful form of imaginative projection as an *expansion* of selfhood and style. In such an expansion, significant otherness counts simultaneously as part of what is considered one's own and as a legitimate part of what is considered another's. A model for such a balance can be found in modern psychological accounts of sympathy, which seek to explain how selves engage with the lives of others unlike them. The psychologist Lauren Wispé reconciles subjectivity with sympathy by saying that "all experiences are subjective; they are all 'my' experiences; but some of 'my' experiences include the experiences of others. Although some of my experiences include what is happening to me, some of my experiences also include what is happening to you."[74] As narratives of globalization emphasize the increasingly intricate connections between distant parts of the world, documenting "what is happening to you" includes not only the near and immediate but also the far and remote.[75] In Charles Johnson's short story "Dr. King's Refrigerator" (2003), for instance, a young Dr. King suddenly appreciates the force of such newly visible links. "When we get up in the morning," he says to his wife, "we go into the bathroom where we reach for a sponge provided for us by a Pacific Islander. We reach for soap created by a Frenchman. The towel is provided by a Turk. Before we leave for our jobs, we are beholden to more than half the world."[76]

This expanded sense of selfhood resonates with the account of identity offered by Derek Parfit, who argues that "a person is not like a Cartesian Ego, a being whose existence must be all-or-nothing."[77] Instead of a coherent selfhood tied together by its narrational links between earlier and later experiences (a conventional way of understanding personal identity), Parfit instead puts forward the claim that "persons are not separately existing entities. The existence of a person, during any period, just consists in the existence of his brain and body, and the thinking of his thoughts, and the doing of his deeds, and the occurrence of many other physical and mental events" (RP, 275). In short, for Parfit, "a person is like a nation" (RP, 275). Crucially, this impersonal conception of selfhood enables an ethics that diminishes the role of self-interest and encourages an intensified concern for the experiences of others. Parfit writes:

> When I believed my existence was [a conventional Cartesian account of personal identity], I seemed imprisoned in myself. My life seemed like a glass tunnel, though which I was moving faster every year, at the end of which there was darkness. When I changed my view, the walls of my glass tunnel disappeared. I now live in the open air. There is still a difference between my life and the lives of other people. But the difference is less. Other people are closer. I am less concerned about the rest of my own life, and more concerned about the lives of others.
>
> (RP, 281)

When Parfit contemplates his own death, for instance, he claims comfort in rejecting the idea that identity is all or nothing, present or absent. Redescribing his death through his counterintuitive view of personhood, he anticipates that while there will be no future experiences that relate in a specific way to his present experiences, there will be other future experiences (how other people remember him, how he influences their thoughts, and so on) that do relate to his present experiences. For Parfit, *whose* experiences these are is much less important than *what* these experiences are, so that personhood becomes a diffused and portable phenomenon. "My conclusions again," he writes, "give less importance both to the unity of each life and to the boundaries between lives" (*RP*, 446). His account allows the speculation that just as one's own personhood extends far beyond the conventional borders of the self, the self is also composed of the similarly diffused personhood of others. Parfit's account can also be applied to literary style, which might be characterized by analogous forms of interpenetration. Although any discourse included in a novel by definition then belongs to the social location of that novel, this description need not prevent us from recognizing how some such discourses may also belong to literary cultures from other parts of the world. Amitav Ghosh, for instance, writes in English but borrows linguistic structures from Bengali, arguably participating simultaneously in two literary traditions. While heightened consciousness about such links does not guarantee radical sympathy or prosocial behavior,[78] a Parfitian theory of subjective and stylistic identity offers a necessary step beyond the views of identity that inform the mirror argument.

If the first general characteristic of an ethics of representing social difference thus rests on this balance, in which selfhood and style are understood to be neither unchangeable nor eradicable, the second characteristic takes this point one step further: it suggests that the act of imagining others requires actively reimagining one's own social location. This twinned endeavor builds upon Richard Rorty's claim that "coming to see other human beings as 'one of us' rather than as 'them' is a matter of detailed description of what unfamiliar people are like and of redescription of what we ourselves are like."[79] While self-knowledge is partial, and thus it is impossible to assert an impenetrable divide between authoritative knowledge of the self and inadequate knowledge of others, the challenge of conceptualizing others benefits from subjective or stylistic self-awareness.[80] Indeed, this awareness often means acknowledging how one has been shaped by the experiences of others. Without such visible efforts, border-crossing fictions can easily replicate the unconscious mirroring of desire and anxiety that marks hegemonic representation.[81] Ross Posnock makes such a point in his study of American literary culture, where he suggests that "the scandal of white plagiarism resides not in violation of black ownership but in the refusal to acknowledge indebtedness."[82] This pairing of inward and outward effort seeks to surmount what Beatrice Hanssen, alluding to Julia Kristeva, calls "a romanticized melancholia that remains in the thralls of an internalized or incorporated alterity, where one complacently revels in the awareness that one always already is a 'stranger to oneself.' "[83] Thinking about oneself thus helps prevent one from *only* thinking about oneself.

Without this interplay between imagining other worlds and scrutinizing one's own, border-crossing fiction quails before the virulence of its critics. When concern for the lives of others is perceived as an unselfconscious paternalism, it loses its credentials to forge imaginative solidarity. "Sometimes strangers don't like being loved," Maxine Hong Kingston reminds us as she depicts the perils of extending consideration in *The Fifth Book of Peace* (2003).[84] In more astringent fashion, V. S. Naipaul suggests the limits of naively altruistic border crossing in his novel *Guerillas* (1975). Featuring a white couple who hopes to abet a Caribbean revolution, it traces the disintegration of both the couple and the political process to the point where "everybody wants to fight his own little war, everybody is a guerilla."[85] Although the novel is hardly sympathetic to any of its characters, who illustrate different kinds of charlatanism, it most vividly punishes its white female protagonist, who yearns to be a revolutionary hero. A literary descendent of Jane Eyre's liberal conscience, Naipaul's Jane is portrayed as a self-deluded and ineffective subject who provides an available body for revolutionaries to rape, maim, and kill. Though Naipaul's portrait of Jane is scarred by the misogyny of much of his writing (her male partner receives far more respect from the story), *Guerillas*' savage indictment of border-crossing aspirations makes a powerful point. Part of Jane's problem lies in her naïve desire to inhabit a new world without seriously reconsidering the contours of her own. This principle suggests why the most extreme experiments in imagining social difference, in which the subject's social location is omitted entirely, are often seen as untrustworthy guides for thinking about the worlds they represent. In their quest to inhabit very different social spaces, these novels frequently either offer no space to reevaluate the meaning of their social worlds or present these portraits of difference only as allegories for their local conditions. Effectively, they replicate the problems of self-conservation and self-erasure I have described. Surmounting this problem requires reconsidering one's own location.

Complementing socially shaped identity and active self-reflection, the third characteristic of productive border crossing requires self and style to abandon aspects of privilege and to embrace a capacity to be vulnerable. I will expand below on just how works of fiction can diminish their own privilege, but for now I want to emphasize the broader theoretical importance of undermining the sense of mastery that writing about others is often said to afford. Because critiques of hegemonic writing expose the troubling effects of hierarchical vision, as we see in Mary Louise Pratt's description of the "monarch-of-all-I-survey,"[86] any robust form of imagining social difference will need to attend critically to its own position of authority. Although the language of vulnerability has become a staple of popular psychology, where it often works to forward a veiled self-absorption or a covert form of manipulation, I use it here in the more critical sense of attentiveness toward asymmetries in privilege and of efforts to level such inequality, even at great cost to the imagining subject.

In stressing the importance of vulnerability, my account draws upon the Levinasian tradition of conceptualizing ethical obligation, which encourages a turn away from the rights of the self to the needs of others. For Emmanuel Levinas, otherness is prior to being; the other punctures the self's claim to a world where everything is assimilable to the consciousness of the self. This rupture entails responsibility, so that existence and obligation are very difficult to distinguish in Levinas's conception. To be, in a way, is to experience unending responsibility to the humans who mark this fundamental alterity. Sara Ahmed, working through the problem of encountering strangers, offers a useful interpretation of this Levinasian stance when she argues that ethical encounters require individuals to engage with the particular demands of others while also recognizing that their responsibility to those others is fundamentally unlimited. Encountering another world, therefore, acknowledges a moment of failure as a paradoxical part of its ethical success. "One gets close enough to others to be touched by that which cannot be simply got across," she contends.[87] Admitting one's inability to inhabit the perspectives of others sometimes enables the very breakthrough that allows for the encounter with significant otherness once considered impossible. The vulnerability modeled in the texture and tone of subjectivity and style can provoke such a transformative touch.

If the invocation of vulnerability can sometimes suggest an emphasis on rigorous sacrifice or austere diminishment, as it often does in Levinas's writings, it need not always be expressed in such extreme form. Vulnerability can also emerge through a kind of play, such as that described in the work of the feminist philosopher María Lugones, who advocates playfulness as the best antidote to the arrogant perception that can be associated with border-crossing fiction. "The playful attitude involves openness to surprise, openness to being a fool, openness to self-construction or reconstruction and to construction or reconstruction of the 'worlds' we inhabit playfully," Lugones writes.[88] This imaginative practice requires generous dialogue between self and other, which counterpoints concern for others with a willingness to reconsider the limitations of the self. Renunciations of privilege, therefore, can range in intensity from the sacrifice of one's life to the "openness to being a fool."

Ironically, the importance of such vulnerability reflects a paradox in the relationship between literature and imaginative projection. Although novels may emphasize the ethical importance of fragility and uncertainty, particularly for privileged subjects, they actually provide their readers with safe spaces in which to inhabit the perspectives of others. As Suzanne Keen hypothesizes through her experiments with reader responses, "fiction deactivates readers' suspicions and opens the way to easier empathy."[89] Through their very fictiveness, novels can offer their audience a form of protection often conspicuously denied their characters or their language. In Ian McEwan's *Saturday* (2005), for instance, readers can offer nuanced responses to the life of a hostage taker because these readers, unlike the novel's main characters, are not actually being held hostage. But, as we will see, novels can also work to push against this generic contract. From encouraging readers to take risky ethical and political actions to making identification with compromised characters feel distinctly uncomfortable, novels can invite degrees of vulnerability in their audience—although, of course, nothing approaching the sacrifices these authors inflict on the worlds they invent.

In allowing fiction to provide representations of social difference that we might take seriously rather than dismiss as fatally flawed, these three characteristics of representational ethics resonate with certain principles of postpositivist realism. I gravitate here toward Paula Moya's account of this philosophy of identity, which contends that a postpositivist form of reliable representation does not require a transcendent knowing subject. "Because I have given up on the dream of transcendence," Moya writes, "I understand objective knowledge as an ongoing process involving the careful analysis of the different kinds of subjective or theoretical bias through which humans apprehend the world. . . . I justify my commitments with reference to a normative conception of the human good—one that I am willing to interrogate, and if necessary, revise."[90] In offering a description of representation that accounts for the role of mediating values and lends itself to future alteration, this theory navigates between the philosophical extremes of essentialist certainty and postmodern skepticism. In similar fashion, the representations of significant otherness that I defend are neither primarily static nor primarily fluid. Instead, these conceptions occupy a middle space that acknowledges elements of what Pheng Cheah calls "given culture" while still insisting that both self and other can change.[91] The viability of border-crossing fiction thus appears in its susceptibility to the modifications that come with dialogue.

Although Moya's work is primarily concerned with defending the epistemic privilege of (minority) personal experience, and in this sense could be considered antithetical to my approach, our projects are actually mutually implicated.[92] As her title *Learning from Experience* (2002) suggests, Moya wants to claim that it is possible to "learn from" the experiences of others.[93] What I explore, in its fictional form, might be considered the descriptions and effects of such learning. Understood in terms of fiction, the literature I consider is not invested in producing a positivist view of another (should such a view even be considered possible). Rather, these novels work toward representations that seek to avoid reinscribing socially repressive hierarchies of value: their practices are fundamentally *relational*, not solely descriptive. Such an ethical, as opposed to positivist, view of another visualizes that other as having the capacity to engage and alter the self. Representations that acknowledge their own indebtedness to others, that express self-consciousness about their own limitations, and that exhibit fragility in the face of alterity may stand the best chance of eventually surmounting those limits and weaknesses.

How might the ideas discussed above take shape within fiction? When border-crossing fictions choose to dramatize expanded, self-aware, and vulnerable perspective taking through their representations of character, they frequently envision what I call a *crowded self*. In this metaphor for subjectivity, the borders of the self jostle against the edges of others, and this mediating position allows for the contours of each to become more porous and flexible. Characters attempt to see the world as another does without wholly letting go of their own original vision, because this perspective-taking exercise may alter that initial point of view. Developing a crowded self is not the same as looking for one's "lost half"; it is not an exercise in literary narcissism, in which perspective taking is only valued as means to heightened self-knowledge or self-completion.[94] Instead, this expansive concept of selfhood helps visualize a subject that is always already multiple, flexible, and open to future metamorphosis. As the adjective "crowded" pulls us in the direction of the expanding and unknown multitude, the noun "self" asserts the importance of a specific individuality. This tension between the centrifugal and the centripetal seeks to capture the central balancing act of border-crossing fiction, as representations strive to offer more than displacements and impersonations. Although many theories of subject formation suggest that a self consolidates its own identity by expelling unwanted others or defining itself against them, the crowded self expands to include diverse, sometimes contradictory, and occasionally even threatening points of view.

Novels can visualize the making of crowded selves in many different ways. Some works emphasize the changing relationship of two characters across specific social divides (Ozeki, Bajwa, Coetzee). Other works of fiction prioritize figures who attempt to adopt the vocabulary and practices of another way of life (Johnson, Jen, Bajwa). Still others dramatize characters who offer explicit philosophical disquisitions on the problem of conceptualizing lives unlike their own (Eugenides, Ghosh, Coetzee). As these overlaps should suggest, these approaches are not mutually exclusive, and many authors portray different kinds of crowded selves to great effect. Despite these distinctions in how subjectivity is dramatized, however, all of these portraits share an underlying family resemblance that I describe through the language of crowding.

Why turn to this language for a governing keyword? To invoke the crowd, after all, is to conjure up a vexed history of literary representations. In their most frightening form, crowds often signify the dangers of the irrational mob from which the exceptional individual seeks escape, while in more utopian moments, they frequently illuminate the pleasures and possibilities of collective social action.[95] Whether considered emblems of tribal culture or visions of modernity itself, crowds have inspired both anxiety and aspiration in those who seek to portray their power. Yet within this divided and often troubled representational history, the image of crowding offers several concepts that prove extremely useful for a theory of engaging significant otherness. Elias Canetti provides such productive associations in his classic *Crowds and Power* (1960), where he argues that crowds tend to work against the divisive force of social stratification. In the most extreme form, Canetti contends, there comes a moment when "all who belong to the crowd get rid of their differences and feel equal."[96] While the crowded self I envision does not require the dissolution of personal identity, it does draw strength from this emphasis on surmounting social distinctions and seeking equality. Jeffrey Schnapp and Matthew Tiews reinforce this presupposition when they suggest the continuing importance of border crossing in their cultural history of crowds: "Heterogeneous and unstable, they arise as the result of the promiscuous intermingling and physical massing of social classes, age groups, races, nationalities, and genders."[97] The space of the crowd in modern life, then, is a space that invites its members to confront affinity and alterity in the same moment. Such a confrontation characterizes the metaphor of the crowded self.

This trajectory toward an egalitarian sense of community requires members of crowds to move *through* their own sense of difference. As the space where, in Canetti's formulation, a fear of being touched suddenly becomes a desire to press together, crowds compel their members to recognize the palpable presence of strangers.[98] Because individuals often perceive anew the extension of their bodies in the company of the crowd, this practice invites them to reassess the literal and figurative place they occupy in the world even as they begin to share symbolic space with others. This reevaluation arguably continues even as physical crowds grow less common in the increasingly mediated and virtual world of the turn of the millennium. Indeed, as Schnapp and Tiews imply, this mediation may even work to make new modes of otherness visible to viewers in first-world spaces, when "the face of contemporary multitudes has increasingly become a foreign face associated with conflicts in Asia, the Middle East, and Africa relayed into first world living rooms and bedrooms via electronic media."[99] As figures for confrontations with social difference, such crowds often feel unpleasant, especially at first, as they threaten to unsettle the comforting protections of individual space. The formation of a crowded self is similarly founded in a disturbing intrusion, sometimes slight and sometimes severe, as the lives of others thrust themselves into view.

The rhetoric of crowding helps illustrate the difference between potentially transformative crossings and conventional conceptions of liberal multicultural tolerance. As opposed to a crowd, a multicultural public sphere insists on norms of behavior that, despite egalitarian rhetoric, frequently instantiate one particular group's social practices as the template for sanctioned public interaction. As multiculturalism preserves precisely the decorum in the public sphere that crowds often sacrifice, it threatens to drain full complexity from those encounters with others. Gesturing toward the limits of such decorum, Abdul Jan-Mohamed and David Lloyd contend that "pluralism tolerates the existence of salsa, it even enjoys Mexican restaurants, but it bans Spanish as a medium of instruction in American schools."[100] In short, conventional multiculturalist accounts celebrate consensual and market-oriented pleasures but do little to challenge formative institutions or fundamental structures of power. This rhetoric of liberal tolerance—even when it claims the contrary—often cannot make room for real alterity within its logic. This point best reflects my difference from Martha Nussbaum, who has written with passion and elegance on the possibility and usefulness of imagining others through drama, poetry, and fiction. While her arguments sometimes assert the *theoretical* value of the unknown and the mysterious, as in *Cultivating Humanity* (1997), following her arguments to their conclusion leaves very little room *in practice* for nonliberal ideas inside her governing Kantian framework.[101] The crowd, as a place where the irrational is traditionally more welcome, can better accommodate competing and even incommensurate points of view. Without overstraining the metaphor (for it is, in the end, a figure of speech), I suggest that the crowded self draws upon these transformative qualities to offer an alternative to multicultural toleration.

Although it might be argued that the impact of such crowding depends on what has often been considered a specifically Western notion of personal privacy, writers from densely populated nations outside the West have also played with its potential as a mode of engaging significant otherness. Indeed, one might argue that coping with the claims of multitudes in public space brings non-Western writers to the forefront of engagements with social difference. It may not be a coincidence, then, that perhaps the most literal exemplar of a crowded self in late twentieth-century literature appears in an Indian novel. In Salman Rushdie's epic *Midnight's Children* (1980), the narrator Saleem Sinai suddenly finds himself a vessel for the thoughts and feelings of other Indians.[102] Exemplifying Parfit's view of personhood, in which a person is like a collectivity,[103] Saleem records with wonder how "the inner monologues of all the so-called teeming millions, of masses and classes alike, jostled for space within my head."[104] While Saleem's crowded self is a specifically national construction, an "All-India Radio" (*MC*, 198) that mimics national political forms, it dramatizes the promises and possibilities of expanded selfhood across many different kinds of social barriers. These voices break into multiple layers of Saleem's consciousness, felt both as a cacophony of different languages and as an "insistent pulsing" (*MC*, 200) in the prelingual levels of his mind. As Saleem works to make sense of his new mental porousness, he struggles to adjudicate between the claims of the self and the claims of the voices in his head. His narration clearly exposes the dangers of a crowded self, showing how Saleem quickly manipulates the minds of those around him in an attempt to avoid being lost in the crowd. "If I had not believed myself in control of the flooding multitudes, their massed identities would have annihilated mine," Saleem argues, seeking to rationalize his exploitation of unsuspecting characters whose behavior he telepathically directs (*MC*, 207). Yet, in critiquing both the idea of controlling the flooding multitudes (a vision of unchanged selfhood) and the threat of annihilation beneath a mass of identities (a vision of erased selfhood), the novel gestures toward an utopian space of expanded selfhood between these two extremes. At his best, Saleem figures the productive and transfigurative jostling between his own identity and his identification with others as the magically crowded space in his mind.

Even as the metaphor of the crowded self stresses the importance of expansion, it nonetheless suggests that the capacity for inclusive engagement may be limited. As I show in the chapters that follow, writers frequently disagree on how crowded this space can ultimately become. Writers working from within traditions of liberalism stake out comfortable territory for an individual selfhood; novelists drawn to more radical positions suggest that conceptualizing social difference requires surrendering more room to the needs and perspectives of others. Struggling with the choices that characterize Saleem's predicament, some authors favor a crowded self that tends more toward self-preservation; others advocate a crowded self that veers precariously close to self-annihilation. Some articulate the action of crowding as a relatively peaceful form of collaboration; others present it as a competitive space of constant quarrels and vexed negotiations. In all cases, however, these writers suggest that the creation of such expanded subjectivity is an ethical act of imagination. Refusing to allow others entry can be as troubling as misrepresenting them.

The question of expanded, self-conscious, and antihierarchical perspective taking that enables the crowded self is not only a matter of subjectivity but also a matter of literary form. If subject matter, and especially characterization, offer a novel one place in which to embed the values of representational ethics, literary style offers another space where novels can perform their ethos. Content and form, of course, are not binary opposites or even separable in practice, but I distinguish them analytically here to illuminate how engagements with significant otherness are not limited to images of selves seeking deepened identifications with the world around them. For some writers, the struggle toward an ethics of border crossing is most evident in *how* they write: their works invite us to meditate on how the process of conceptualizing social difference affects and is affected by the texture, tone, and patterning of their language. I refer to such fictions as displaying *crowded style*.

Just as there is no single way to construct a crowded self, there is no single way to display a crowded style.[105] Some novels meld a range of literary forms and voices from different cultural traditions (Ozeki, Johnson, Eugenides, Ghosh). Others deploy parody, irony, flattening, or other distancing devices to force a wedge between their own rhetoric and ossified literary conventions of discursive domination (Johnson, Jen, Eugenides, Ghosh, Coetzee). Yet others turn to structural patternings and imagistic echoes to suggest underlying connections that belie surface divides (Ozeki, Jen, Coetzee). Crowded styles can reflect many different aesthetic stances, which change to suit the intellectual and political terrain they engage. Rebecca Walkowitz, for instance, shows how particular stylistic postures of "naturalness, triviality, evasion, mix-ups, treason, and vertigo" can "generate specific projects of democratic individualism, on the one hand, and of antifascism or anti-imperialism, on the other."[106] Although Walkowitz's interests are organized around challenges to nationality and not always explicitly or exclusively identified with the ethics of representing alterity, many of the stances she describes could be considered contributions to the conceptual problem of engaging significant otherness. What makes literary forms "crowded," in the metaphorical sense at stake here, is their ability to embody an openness toward difference and a sensitivity toward the specter of hegemonic representation and ideological constraint.

The literary techniques offered as examples above, of course, are not new developments in fiction. It is important, then, to ask what differentiates crowded styles from the use of such techniques in writing from earlier periods. Forms, I suggest, do not embody ethical meanings irrespective of their literary content, historical period, and intellectual context. They signify differently across time and place, accruing ethical significance in organic relation to many changing factors. As an example of the importance of intellectual context, modernist writing is often characterized by an abiding interest in the aesthetic bricolage and formal mixing of styles that appear in many late twentieth-century border-crossing fictions. But this modernist stylistic catholicity is often read as a testament to the metanarrative of Orientalism and primitivism. It tends to reflect, in Jed Esty's diagnosis, "modernism's general capacity to rise above, while incorporating, the local materials of any given cultural tradition."[107] The phenomenon I observe in fiction at the turn of the millennium looks distinctly different, responsive as it is to an intensifying set of historical concerns that have troubled the idea of "rising above." Walkowitz's work, which spans both early and late twentieth-century writing, also reveals such important distinctions in historical context. Although her work shows how early twentieth-century modernist writers disturb common assumptions about essential cultural or national attributes, it also suggests that these works are shaped by pressures and constraints that differ from the field of possibility experienced by late twentieth-century writers. For example, Walkowitz is careful to note that Joseph Conrad's attempts to disturb essentialist views of nationality are uneven and that they are best figured as a critique rather than as a positive replacement for problematic views of identity. In contrast, Walkowitz finds it more appropriate to read Salman Rushdie and Kazuo Ishiguro's deployments of stereotypes as more fully productive—a distinction, I suggest, that may have much to do with the different context of Rushdie and Ishiguro's emergence in the multicultural Britain of the 1980s.[108] Though it is certainly conceivable that one could identify crowded styles in different periods, these particular historical moments of enunciation afford varying significance to formal techniques.

It is also important to ask what differentiates crowded styles from similar stylistic choices that appear in writings we might not view as particularly emancipatory in effect. While form cannot be simply collapsed into its content and context, it is in dialogue with its content and context that a narrative technique serves as a crowded style. Amitav Ghosh, for example, embeds a metafictional passage in his novel *The Glass Palace* (2000) on the problem of evoking multilingual speech within a single written language. Given this clue that the novel actively struggles with the problem of representing linguistic alterity, it makes sense to read Ghosh's own choice of style as a response to this concern. Moving outside a particular novel to consider its specific conditions of intellectual production also affects the significance of its style. On the surface, read simply as a formal artifact, Ghosh's historical-realist rhetoric might not seem radically different from the historical realism of many other writers; indeed, many scholars have found Ghosh's prose to be the least compelling and original aspect of *The Glass Palace*. But by looking at his work in light of particular language debates on the use of English that have shaped South Asian writing, we can appreciate the significance of his choices and feel the weight of his stylistic embraces and textual refusals. In this historical and intellectual location, Ghosh's language of narration gains visibility as a crowded style.

One exemplary vision of crowded style emerges in the work of the African American writer Charles Johnson, who frequently draws upon

Asian spiritual discourses in his representations of African American lives. In Johnson's novel *Oxherding Tale*, many of the characters represent both recognizable images from the genre of the American slave narrative and allegorical figures from Asian spiritual discourses. Combining the insights and associations of multiple religious and literary traditions, these images contest the constraints of Orientalist representation. The slave master can be read as the icon of samsara, the coffin maker as the Daoist sage, the slave catcher as the arm of Shiva, and the fugitive slave narrator as the classic seeker from numerous Asian spiritual traditions. Sliding in and out of different rhetorical conventions, these hybrid figures engage both Western and Asian canons of representation. In casting these characters to resonate with images and icons across borders, Johnson unsettles the principles of difference that promote hegemonic or identitarian effects. As a crucial element of this unsettling, *Oxherding Tale* emphasizes the importance of mistakes over authoritative knowledge in performing its translation. For example, although it inscribes what look like handwritten Chinese characters within the English text, most of those characters are not recognizable units of Chinese written language. This playfulness works against the performance of mastery that has often been associated with hegemonic border-crossing impulses.

Crowded selves and crowded styles emerge in many different guises. Some writers emphasize one over another; more commonly, works of fiction interweave the two strategies in varying proportions, and the creation of a crowded style is often intimately linked to the formation of a crowded self. The mixing of the two underpins Charles Johnson's definition of intersubjectivity, which provides one model for such border-crossing fiction. Intersubjectivity occurs when one observer describes a subjective interpretation to another onlooker and, in doing so, makes the representation mutually intelligible. "So at one point," Johnson asserts, "what is entirely subjective becomes intersubjective. . . . Somebody else on the other side of the room coming from another part of the world, or world experience, will through language, as Heidegger says, allow this object to be disclosed for somebody else."[109] This emphasis on continual redisclosure foregrounds communicative values, suggesting how new linguistic descriptions can allow for expanded engagement with what is being described and perhaps with the describer as well.

As ways of marking productive forms of border crossing, the concepts of crowded self and crowded style are indebted to the influential discourse of hybridity emblematized by such theorists and novelists as Homi Bhabha and Salman Rushdie. As more and more scholars reveal how hybridity emerges in numerous forms, the idea of pure and self-contained social worlds seems increasingly fallacious. But precisely because hybridity now appears as the standard rather than the exception at the turn of the millennium, it appears in guises liberating and radical as well as confining and exploitative. Michael Hardt and Antonio Negri argue that hybridity alone is revolutionary only when pitted against a stable essence, such as the idea of the imperialist nation. Since many major late twentieth- and early twenty-first-century forces no longer claim such stable essences as their domain, hybrid practices serve multiple masters, ranging from grassroots alliances to corporate strategies.[110] In Rushdie's *The Moor's Last Sigh* (1995), hybridity energizes fundamentalist and violent repression as much as it emboldens expansive and syncretic forms of community. Hybridity by itself is not always enough to push against the force of imperialist or nativist thought. In contrast, crowded selves and styles exemplify hybrid moments that both challenge ideas of stable essence and suggest possible alternatives to the conflicts and impasses that often afflict encounters with alterity.

My approach also seeks to provide an alternative to hidden identitarian assumptions that infiltrate discourses of hybridity commonly perceived as antiessentialist. Ironically, accounts that celebrate the transgression of social borders often unwittingly restrict imaginative authority to personal experience in much the same manner as theories of difference criticism. Salman Rushdie, for example, is treated as a central figure with the right to write about South Asian, British, and American hybrid geographies because he himself is historically shaped by those worlds: he was raised in India and Pakistan and has been professionally based in England and the United States. It is less clear that his readers would accept his authority to write about, hypothetically, Vietnamese refugees in Hong Kong or Turkish communities in Germany; indeed, Rushdie is sometimes criticized for his depictions of African British communities. In other words, the category of hybrid literature was created to reflect and address the experiences of people whose historical lives no longer fit existing social categories. A wealth of studies about hybridity focus on multinational or multiethnic novelists who write about their particular form of cultural mixture. This situation creates an odd nativism of the hybrid, for, as in conventional identitarian accounts, personal experience and ancestral affiliation shape the range of subjects about which an author is taken seriously. While this book tries to account for writers with an intimate historical relationship to the worlds they portray, it also investigates authors who are not affiliated in easily visible ways with the ideas and images that populate their writings. For this reason, I look not at Charles Johnson's interest in African histories and practices, which weave their way into a substantial part of his work, but instead at his commitment to Asian spiritual discourses. Johnson's fiction explores the way in which practices not previously thought to be organically connected can be placed in dialogue with each other, and thus his creations not only reflect historical hybridity but also produce new forms of engagement with significant otherness.

With these values and concepts in mind, I will turn to three exemplary works of fiction to suggest how the underlying principles I have discussed become visible as crowded selves and crowded styles. Although critiques of border-crossing fiction often imply that writers speak with greater authority about what is considered to be "theirs," many works of fiction destabilize the very ground of such presumed authority. This idea pervades the work of Anita Desai, a writer who not only writes about India (where she is from) and the United States (where she has been professionally based) but also about parts of the world with which she is not closely identified. *Diamond Dust* (2000), a collection that showcases Desai's position as a border-crossing writer, meditates on this question through its representations of character and its formal structure. In a fabulist short story called "The Man Who Saw Himself Drown," readers encounter a protagonist who finds himself simultaneously inside and outside his own life. As the title suggests, the protagonist of the story begins to perceive himself as if he were a separate person. Looking at the body of a drowned man, the bewildered narrator reports that "every detail, in every detail, he was myself: I was looking at myself—after having spent half an hour, or an hour, underwater, sodden with river and mud—but it was I, in every detail."[111] Since "The Man Who Saw Himself Drown" begins in the third person and only moves to first-person narration when the character spies himself from the outside, the protagonist literally usurps the space that the reader occupies at the beginning of the work. In doing so, the "I" of the short story creates his own crowded self. As he reads his life from an outsider's perspective, the story suggests that looking at one's own life may not be fundamentally different from looking at the lives of others.

The prose style of the story reflects these continuities as well. Like the protagonist, who emphasizes the sameness of "every detail" between his past and present selves, the only technical aspect that stylistically differentiates this story from the realist fictions in Desai's collection is the fabulist plot. Except for its premise, "The Man Who Saw Himself Drown" resembles other narratives in *Diamond Dust* in its pacing, tone, and texture. As the story emerges in the very heart of the collection, its placement asserts a literal and metaphorical centrality to the problem of self-knowledge. Taken as a whole, the crowded style of *Diamond Dust* suggests that the projects of knowing the self and knowing another are mutually constitutive endeavors. Imagining others may be easier than many theories suggest, and conceptualizing the self harder.

As border-crossing novels struggle to surmount social difference, I have suggested that they pair this sense of permeable identity with self-critical reflection. One vivid example of this endeavor appears in Amitav Ghosh's novel *The Shadow Lines* (1988), which elaborates on its approach to significant otherness. *The Shadow Lines* refers to this project as "imagination with precision,"[112] and as Ghosh's novel implies in many different ways, the freedom to imagine others is enhanced by the guiding precepts of self-conscious observation. The novel thus offers an ethical vision grounded in intense scrutiny of the boundaries between its world and the worlds of others. Such an ethically nuanced form of storytelling explicitly contrasts the confining narrative choices of Orientalist rhetoric. On vacation in India, the narrator's aunt (tellingly nicknamed Queen Victoria) refers to a gripping story about a cobra and a thala-goya she encountered in Sri Lanka. Echoing strains of Rudyard Kipling's Rikki-Tikki-Tavi, the story exploits the drama of exotic danger to entice the narrator under its spell. However, after the family party, the narrator's cousin Tridib gently takes the narrator aside to suggest that the significance of the tale lies not in flamboyant Sri Lankan cobras but in the minute architectural details of the aunt's house in Colombo. Tridib's tutelage provides a concrete model of imaginative practice that begins with the scrutiny of one's supposedly familiar world:

When we had almost reached the ground floor, [Tridib] said: Did you notice that [the] house had a sloping roof?

I shook my head: the detail had escaped me . . . he put his hands on my shoulders, turned me around and asked me whether I could imagine what it would be like to live under a sloping roof—no place to fly kites, nowhere to hide when one wanted to sulk, nowhere to shout across to one's friends.

. . . in a while I began to imagine the sloping roofs of Colombo for myself: the pattern they made if one wheeled in the sky above them, how sharply they rose if one looked at them from below, the mossiness of their tiles when one saw them close up, from a first floor window, and soon I felt that I too could see how much more interesting they were than the snake and the lizard, in the very ordinariness of their difference.

And still, I knew that the sights Tridib saw in his imagination were infinitely more detailed, more precise than anything I would ever see.[113]

This vision of the precise imagination, which explores the hidden rather than the obvious, encourages the narrator to begin his invention of distant places with an exploration of his own world. Attending to the sloping roofs of Colombo reveals anew the significance of the narrator's familiar flat roofs of Calcutta, shedding new light on the architecture that shapes the play, the escapes, and the friendships of his daily life. From this moment of awakened self-perception, the narrator's imagination roves outward to envision a foreign world in which roofs slope at unexpected angles. His mind's eye explores the roofs from three different spatial perspectives—above, below, and close up—to prevent any single view of the roofs from gaining dominance, and the novel scrupulously documents how each of these views springs from a specific place: "if one wheeled in the sky above them," "if one looked at them from below," "from a first floor window." This passage dramatizes the miniature formation of the crowded self, which begins with its own world and then generously reaches out to other possible experiences. Although some theories imply that forging an identity is fundamentally a process of othering, the novel suggests that self-reflection does not always require a calcified opponent to consolidate its own identity. Novels like *The Shadow Lines* attempt to move past the critique of liberal self-importance masquerading as altruism by linking visions of alterity to an evolving sense of expanding selfhood. This interrogative interplay within the precise imagination forms a central aspect of the emerging representational ethics I defend.

The importance of vulnerability further underwrites this approach to social difference. Sometimes this vulnerability is radical, as is Tridib's in *The Shadow Lines* when he enters a rioting mob in a quixotic quest to save the lives of other people. The sacrifice of his life, the climax of the novel, articulates one extreme of ethical action. However, *The Shadow Lines* suggests that not all sacrifices need be so final to further these ends. In particular, it suggests specifically textual ways in which the abandonment of one privilege in particular—the privilege to be at the center of a story—can enable an ethics of border crossing. In this context, Elaine Scarry's theories of perception in literature can illuminate how Ghosh's narrator reverses the Orientalist gesture in which the imagined other primarily bolsters an enfeebled or anxious sense of self. Scarry argues that novels often convince us of the vivid and solid character of imaginary objects through a form of imaginative contrast, in which particular elements gain solidity when compared with gauzier visual images. Invoking Proust's scenes of shadow puppets skimming over comparatively dense walls, Scarry claims that "a film passes over and hence coaxes into solidity the walls behind it."[114] This technique helps explain how Ghosh's narrator persuades his readers of the vivid reality of the roofs of Colombo. In the passage quoted above, the narrator becomes the translucent substance against which the sheer angles and the mossy tiles gain imaginative weight. The multiple perspectives of his vision require us to imagine a viewer who is sometimes grounded (literally, when he beholds the roofs from below) but also disembodied and weightless (when he wheels in the sky above). The narrator both gives us the specificity of plural and precisely identified angles of vision and offers himself up as the comparatively thin specter against which the roofs come into being. Rather than using the sloping roofs of Colombo as a prop for the narrator's own selfhood, *The Shadow Lines* suggests how the very shadowiness of the narrator's persona can allow concern for the vivacity of other worlds. Although scholars tend to associate omniscient narrative voices with the godlike view from nowhere that often characterizes such narration in nineteenth-century fiction, the narrator's crowded self presents omniscience as a deliberately flimsy production whose strength lies not in absolute control but precisely in this refusal of traditional narrative authority. This sacrifice of the novel's storyteller, who lacks even his own name, is one example of the ethical possibility of textual vulnerability.

As a final example, a specific literary controversy from the late twentieth century reveals how thinking in terms of crowded selves and crowded styles might help address public concerns about border-crossing fiction. In an essay called "The Problem of Speaking for Others" (1991), the philosopher Linda Alcoff contends that although the self is socially shaped and thus always in some sense spoken for, speech acts need to be evaluated in light of their political effect. Her argument begins and ends with the story of Anne Cameron, a white Canadian writer whose novels include first-person narratives of Native Canadian women. "At the 1988 International Feminist Book Fair in Montreal," Alcoff writes, "a group of Native Canadian writers decided to ask Cameron to, in their words, 'move over' on the grounds that her writings are disempowering for Native authors. She agree[d]."[115] Alcoff's essay encourages her readers to support these choices, because if Cameron's works do constrain Native Canadian women, "they are counterproductive to Cameron's own stated intentions, and she should indeed 'move over'" to let Native Canadians tell their own stories.[116]

However, to look more closely at the Cameron case is also to question some of the assumptions that sustain these requests to "move over." In the writings of Lee Maracle, the Native Canadian writer who asked Cameron to stop writing about Native Canadians, Cameron's work is not described as rhetorically racist or socially exploitative. To the contrary, Maracle reveals that, to her surprise and discomfort, Cameron's feisty approach provided a model for her own literary development.[117] Why, then, is Cameron's work considered so debilitating for Native readers? Maracle suggests quite clearly that the problem lies in the suffocating structures of power that govern white and Native Canadian writing. "When I'm on the bookshelf and she's on the bookshelf, I know what the citizenship of this country is going to buy," Maracle writes.[118] Her argument denies the efficacy of individual action, so that not even Cameron's financial and rhetorical efforts to promote Native writing earn her the right to work within a Native storytelling lineage.

In making this case for why Cameron should "move over," Maracle fights the wrong battle. If the problem lies in the prejudice of a readership, then working to combat that prejudice makes more practical sense than encouraging self-censorship among writers. More important, Maracle implicitly accepts the idea that writing about Native Canadians occupies a constant market share in which she and Cameron can coexist only as competitors for the telling of Native Canadian stories. Maracle thus forgets that literal and symbolic markets can grow, and the central task shared by both Maracle and Cameron is to broaden and deepen the share that Native Canadians possess in their country's self-image and in the world at large. Although in situations of genuinely limited space and time, border-crossing fictions should not be allowed to usurp the place of work from marginalized communities, such works can potentially collaborate rather than compete with self-representations to extend the reach of their shared project. Although the political problem of speaking for others stems from historical injustice and unequal social privilege, border-crossing fiction need not always remain a passive casualty of such inequities in power. Maracle herself admits that the call to "move over" provides a temporary rather than an enduring answer to the problem of imagining others. "It is not itself a solution," she writes.[119] Silence may satisfy specific political concerns, but it neglects the ethical imperative to consider other people's lives as worthy of sustained investigation, and it denies the ways in which group identities shape each other. Although writing about alterity has often been described as dangerous, *not* writing about the lives of others may be equally troubling.

Far from offering a naïve form of border crossing, Anne Cameron addresses the complexity of literary authority as an integral part of the stories she seeks to tell. Her narrative choices suggest that the project of imagining others requires her to reconceptualize her own authorial position. In a collection of Native myths called *Dzelarhons: Myths of the Northwest Coast* (1986), Cameron prefaces her stories with a foreword that purports to explain the origins of the tales. The narrator of her foreword is a young girl, implicitly from a white family, whose mother singlehandedly supports her children by working long hours at a local hospital for Native Canadian children. During the day, the narrator is cared for by a surrogate mother named Klopinum, who shares with her charge a wealth of Native fables about Raven, Snipe, Eagle, and the Creator. When the narrator suggests that Klopinum write down her stories to share with the world, Klopinum shakes her head. "Who listens to me? Who listens to us? Who listens? Anyway, I can't read and I can't write, and I never went to school and writers go to university."[120] When the narrator suggests that she tell the stories to someone who can write, Klopinum pats the narrator's hand. "'You think so? Tell you what,' she said, 'I'll give them stories to you. You want it done, you do it'" (DZ, 20). As a gift of language passed down to the narrator, this passage suggests that Cameron recognizes the need for a clear authorizing strategy to legitimate her work.

What makes this exchange plausible as a portrait of emerging crowded style, rather than simply as a transparently self-serving fiction, is the role of the narrator's own mother. As an adult, the narrator encounters a fisherman who was cared for as a child in the Native hospital by the narrator's mother. Inviting the narrator back to his house, he shares an old photograph of her mother attending his childhood birthday party. "She was like my own mom when I didn't have one," he tells her (DZ, 13). When the narrator tells her mother of the chance encounter, "out came her photo album and there was Sonny with my mom again" (DZ, 13). If Klopinum serves as the narrator's surrogate mother who passes down stories beyond the social bonds of tribe, the narrator's mother simultaneously spreads maternal affection far beyond the limits of her own immediate family. These crossing affiliations between the Native and white communities suggest that for the narrator to accept Klopinum's gift of language, she must relinquish the exclusivity of her own mother's love. The self-authorizing strategy of the foreword, therefore, asks the developing crowded self of the narrator to pay its own price in return. Robust representational ethics thus requires a legitimating sacrifice. By acknowledging the problem of literary authority in her foreword, Cameron's work takes shape as a crowded style by performing one form of such legitimating sacrifice: it gives up the commonly held allegorical position (discussed earlier) that any writer can, unproblematically, write about any subject, and it works to envision more equal conditions of exchange. This textual trade gains material weight through Cameron's financial commitments, since she has used profits from her writing to promote Native authorship. In her foreword to Dzelarhons, Cameron offers self-authorizing strategies that seek to differentiate her work from exploitative appropriations of Native imaginative resources. Her writings suggest how narrative choices might stage new forms of representational ethics rather than inevitably reproducing political and material inequalities.

To cross borders productively, works of fiction encourage both vivid affective responses to the lives of others and nuanced learning about their predicaments. Representational ethics cannot simply reflect a dutiful response to an abstract moral principle; it requires the energy of active sympathy and imaginative commitment. As Bruce Robbins puts it in the specific context of the transnational, "internationalism demands feeling as well as knowing, or feeling combined in some proportion with knowing, if it is going to rouse any support." He concludes that questions about justice and rights "require an education in global or internationalist feeling."[121] Yet these powerful emotions also need to be placed within a wider history that allows us to question why individuals suffer or succeed in the particular ways that they do. Identifying invisible structural problems matters as much as acknowledging the palpable pain of the person before us. The relationship between education and feeling, therefore, is twofold: feelings need to be educated, or linked to larger knowledge, and then (in Robbins's terms) individuals need to be educated in such feeling. In insisting on both emotion and knowledge, such self-aware engagement seeks to counteract the expansive and uninhibited universalism that pervades many defenses of unmediated encounters. Although I would argue that social borders may all be crossed, doing so may require far more work than universalist accounts often imply.

The search for an ethics of imaginative border crossing thus contributes to the process of rethinking the promise of universalism after the chastening critiques of postcolonial, poststructuralist, feminist, and ethnic-minority studies. When Seyla Benhabib calls for a philosophical understanding of post-Enlightenment universalism, she argues that it "would be interactive not legislative, cognizant of gender difference not gender blind, contextually sensitive and not situation indifferent."[122] When novels convey the hope that readers might experiment with previously unconsidered perspectives, they help visualize a specific and delimited potential of universalism: the promise that individuals need not remain hopelessly trapped within particular hegemonic or identitarian constructions. It may be possible to retain some of the attractions of universalism without what many have identified as its insensitivity to the way power shapes social borders and the way local identities contribute to ethical flourishing.

Within such fiction, can angry and implacable novels perform this kind of ethical work? Theorists such as Doris Sommer have argued that the value of many literary works lies in their resistance to the border-crossing energies of reading, so that minority writings challenge the assumptions of mainstream readers by denying them access into the full world of the novel, play, or poem. "By marking off an impassable distance between reader and text, and thereby raising questions of access or welcome, resistant authors intend to produce constraints that more reading will not overcome," Sommer claims.[123] Arguing that mutual understanding is a fantasy that masks asymmetries in power, Sommer valorizes the ethical value of a minority text in its difficulty, unavailability, and resistance. Clearly, anger and silence offer important contributions, because they assert that imagining significant otherness is not always easy. As these performances of unavailability illuminate inequalities in social and material power, they assert that those constructed as "others" need not be grateful for the interest shown in their lives. They also remind their readers that sympathetic connection should not be used to justify or obscure unjust structural systems. Anger and silence thus offer a bracing counterpoint to ideals of identification and engagement, and they help ensure that such practices do not devolve into a masked form of superiority. Imagining subjects must frequently reconceptualize their own positions when they apprehend the anger or silence of another: in J. M. Coetzee's *Disgrace* (1999) for instance, Lucy does not want to allow her father easy access to her experience of rape. David's fatherly love and his liberal concern pale in the face of her experience, and her desire to elude representation forces David to acknowledge the source of his exclusion in his male heterosexual privilege. In this respect, there is certainly a place for unavailability within the ethics of border crossing.

Nonetheless, while angry fictions can spur a larger transformation, they can also calcify into an excuse to avoid creative responses to the problems they vividly present. Since anger requires a stable object to maintain its own energies, it is ill suited to further a breakdown of social difference. *Disgrace*, for example, does not allow David to simply accept Lucy's obdurate silence and move on with his life. He cannot abandon the imperative to imagine her perspective, even though she does not want to be imagined. Instead, *Disgrace* suggests that working through rather than passively accepting anger and silence can ultimately enable new kinds of imaginative projection. In the moments of greatest loss, the ongoing sacrifices of the imagining subject lead to a fragile encounter between father and daughter that models the difficulty, but also the possibility, of imaginative reconstruction. Novels must confront and move through the difficulties of rage and resistance if they wish to generate reconstructive hope.

Although rage, silence, and resistance can address momentary and vital political concerns, they ultimately prolong the problem they ostensibly oppose. In pushing against what Lee Maracle calls the temporary resolution of silence, crowded selves and crowded styles seek to operate in a new scale of time. While the image of border crossing is a spatial one, I suggest that we can also consider it as an attempt to reconcile different scales of temporality: Anne Cameron's works, for example, attempt to remain sensitive to the then-present problem of identity politics in 1980s Canada, but they also struggle to envision responses for a future time when the solutions of silence will no longer seem adequate or even desirable.

Focusing on a spectrum of late twentieth- and early twenty-first-century fiction in English, this book explores how this emerging group of authors seeks to contest repressive modes of representation. Through their diverse and contextually specific responses, these novels ask readers to move beyond a fascination with otherness as a cipher for displaced selfhood or as a figure beyond representation. Their strategies range from everyday practices, such as political activism, to extreme commitments, such as spiritual abjection. Although some writers point to the value of pleasure while others assert the need for sacrifice, all of the novelists in this study share a vivid commitment to the production of crowded selves and crowded styles. Their narrative choices invite their readers to share in forms of border crossing that can question, rather than inevitably reinscribe, the inequalities and injustices of a globalizing world.

As I ask how novels might stage new ways of imagining the lives of others, I offer a new critical metanarrative that allows this ethics of representation to become fully visible. For the past thirty years, the study of literature has profited from a skeptical optic that focuses on the trickiness of words and their impact on the ideas that inform experiential lives. Though the power of such a critique remains strong, I believe that our current moment calls for criticism to do more than chart representational failings and imaginative inadequacies. In the spirit of Paul Gilroy's sociology, which defends the "conviviality" of living together in local and planetary multicultures, this book attempts to consider ideas about literary imaginative projection *through*, rather than against, the importance of social difference.[124] In confronting some of the many challenges of globalization, these works of fiction struggle toward a new representational ethics for the twenty-first century.

2

Everyday Sentiment

Jane Takagi-Little, the central conscience of Ruth L. Ozeki's *My Year of Meats* (1998), hopes to tell the truth about people unlike her. As a documentary filmmaker, Jane believes in correcting the cultural misperceptions that marred her youth as a Japanese American in Minnesota, even as she comes to realize that the objects of her camera's gaze will never be singular nor stable. Both earnestly naïve and knowingly postmodern about the possibility of adequately representing social difference, Ozeki's novel meditates on the difficulties of conceptualizing the lives of others in an era of globalizing media. While Jane recognizes that no claim to imaginative border crossing can ever be conclusive, she struggles to make the small daily choices that enable flexible and capacious engagements with significant otherness. Her questions, therefore, speak to late twentieth-century concerns about envisioning others across an increasingly mediated planet. Jane's search, so ordinary in its nature, addresses Bruce Robbins's call for ways of border crossing that make sense not in extreme circumstances but in embedded first-world daily life. "We need an internationalist ethic of the everyday, one that will not tell us solely what to die or kill for but also how action at a distance can be part of how we live," Robbins argues.[1] Foregrounding the search for an ethics of conceptualizing alterity through late twentieth-century global media, Ozeki's popular novel speaks to the pervasive need for such everyday action at a distance.

Although *My Year of Meats* represents a wealth of figures from different nations, ethnicities, social classes, and sexualities in the Pacific Rim circuits between Japan and America, the novel presents these social divides as only mild obstacles to the pursuit of imagining significant otherness. When Ozeki's novel asks how subjects might best perceive others at a distance, it offers solutions that correspondingly remain conceptually conservative. With its reformist rather than radical sensibility, *My Year of Meats* insists that individuals can challenge the representational violence it associates with a dehumanizing optic of global capital by reappropriating existing circuits of late capitalist simulacra. The novel might be said to exemplify Rey Chow's suggestion that "the morally impassioned rebuke of images always goes hand in hand with the massive production and circulation of more images—be those images about classes, races, nations, or persons of different sexual orientations."[2] The novel rewrites the premade familiarity of transnational media circuits into an alternative feminist network where women sympathize with others unlike them, reimagine their own possibilities, develop alliances across nation and ethnicity, and generate grassroots political action. In visualizing such possibilities, the novel asks its readers to break down the depersonalizing circuits of global trade in images, as its characters learn to do.

This everyday representational ethics emerges through the novel's subgeneric affiliation with entertainment education, a form of storytelling explicitly designed to educate its audience about political or cultural issues through melodramatic narratives. Though usually associated with television programming in developing countries, this genre perhaps most accurately describes the fast-paced and didactic structure of *My Year of Meats*. A central feature of this form is its reliance on sentimental perceptions to generate forms of affective bonding with its objects of representation. This chapter investigates the possibilities of representational ethics grounded in such sentimentality to reveal the productive, albeit limited, contributions that entertainment education might make to representations of social difference.

Throughout the pages that follow, I suggest that sentiment is most useful for border-crossing fiction under two conditions: (1) when only moderately strong imbalances in access to power separate the subject and object of sympathy, and (2) when sympathizers take action to alleviate the suffering of others. If asymmetries in power seem intense, as in a context of imperialism, then sentiment is likely to be perceived as a deeply inadequate response to the problem at hand. Since sentimentality frequently presupposes a consensual alliance between its subject and object, it will not work well with figures who resist being represented. It will also seem ineffective, if not unethical, if it appears to usurp the ameliorative energies of practical and political action. The strength of sentimental sympathy thus works best across relatively weak social borders with objects who actively desire representation in the minds of others. If asymmetries in power are considered relatively mild, sentiment can help increase the visibility of suffering subjects and inspire action to alleviate the source of the problem. Ozeki's work, I suggest, presents sentimental experiences of border crossing under precisely these conditions.

I begin by examining how Ozeki's narrative choices mitigate alterity by producing a world of hypervisible but paradoxically weak social differences between Japanese and American subjects. In this context of limited otherness, I explore how Ozeki's figures develop moderately crowded selves through sentimental perceptions that encourage both self-reflection and vulnerability. These perceptions challenge the discursive domination associated with the instrumentalist optic of global capital. I then turn to examine how the novel embeds these sentimental conceptions of significant otherness within a political framework that bespeaks the theoretical breakthroughs of 1990s transnational feminist advocacy. Ozeki's novel, I suggest, can be read as part of a larger debate in late twentieth-century transnational feminist movements over how to establish productive alliances between women in many parts of the world without homogenizing those experiences or assuming their incommensurability: in short, without doing violence to their objects of description. Feminist advocacy networks most successfully navigated this problem of representation by inventing the concept of "violence against women," a phrase that draws upon sentimental practice to articulate commonalities in the oppression of women while allowing particular forms of oppression to remain distinct. *My Year of Meats*, I argue, draws upon and extends this optic to create a crowded style that encourages simultaneous attention both to specific individual suffering and to larger structural forces that cause this pain. Finally, I conclude by exploring how the novel seeks to transform imaginative engagements with significant otherness into demands for political rights through the power of global advertising. Relying on the pleasures of liberal selfhood, Ozeki's vision of productive border crossing emerges through practices of commercial self-fashioning, transnational alliances, and grassroots activism. Because most of the subjects in the novel already consider themselves part of a global first-world community, Ozeki's world offers little resistance to border crossing, and her narrative choices provide moderate and reformist means of imagining others. Her crowded selves and styles, on the whole, provide comfortable spaces that remain compatible with ideals of liberal humanism.

This representational ethics, however, is not without its difficulties. Despite its best intentions, the attraction of *My Year of Meats* to postmodern sentiment sometimes leads it back toward conventional forms of imaginative constraint. Thwarting its own aspirations, the novel frequently offers excessively contrived and uncritical visions of specific cultural groups and social practices. Indeed, Ozeki's novel reflects specifically liberal stereotypes at work (multiracial vegetarian lesbians, heartwarming African American families, luminous disabled children) that testify to the limits of its own approach. *My Year of Meats* can persuasively be read as a novel that uncritically exports Western liberal feminism to other parts of the world, that presents American immigration as the triumphal answer to most problems, and that remains overly naïve about the insidious effects of global capital and global media.

However, the conceptual acts found in the novel offer an important counternarrative that elucidates one contribution to imagining social difference. Although Ozeki's narrative choices do not always avoid rhetorical constraints, her work searches productively for an alternative to the corporate-sponsored images that suffuse the circuits of global capital she describes. *My Year of Meats* thus reveals how questions of representational ethics can emerge in works with admittedly modest aesthetic ambitions. In showing how women come to feel for each other at a distance, the novel models an imaginative process of limited, but nonetheless useful, writing across borders. Although this contribution lacks the pleasures of formal literary complexity that characterize the more sophisticated novels considered in later parts of this book, popular works such as *My Year of Meats* matter because of their investment in larger social phenomena—in this case, discourses of global media, transnational feminism, and advertising—that wrestle with everyday problems of representational ethics.

Elusive Borders: Ruth Ozeki's My Year of Meats

Since *My Year of Meats* is a novel about a television series, it may come as no surprise that Ruth Ozeki began her career in the arts as a filmmaker. After designing sets for horror movies and working in Japanese television production, Ozeki created autobiographical documentaries, such as *Halving the Bones* (1995), which meditate on the cultural crossings of her Japanese American family. *My Year of Meats*, her first novel, abandons the lyrical melancholy of *Halving the Bones* but continues its concern with the social significance of everyday life in an increasingly migratory world. Her second novel, *All Over Creation* (2003), furthers this interest in the intimacy between the personal and the political. A critique of genetic engineering and industrial food production, *All Over Creation* champions a mode of local and seasonal agriculture while simultaneously contesting the potentially xenophobic overtones of such an emphasis on indigenous production. As Ozeki's work explores the implications of basic acts, such as eating or reproducing, in a world of global circuits, it invites its audience to question how these practices testify to implicit ideas about the significance of social difference.

Borders are already falling in the first pages of *My Year of Meats*. "Eventually we're all going to be brown, sort of," Jane declares as she meditates on her role as a multiethnic individual.[3] As the children of white American fathers and Japanese mothers, both Ozeki and Jane represent multiracial subjects who navigate the hybrid cultural terrains of both sides of their families. While ancestry offers no guarantees of affinity or alienation, both Ozeki and Jane express relatively high levels of comfort in traversing both American and Japanese representational spaces. While Jane speaks eloquently of not quite fitting into either American or Japanese worlds, that degree of separation emerges in *My Year of Meats* as a strength rather than an inhibition. Comfortable in her multiethnic body, refreshingly free of oppressive anxieties about ethnic belonging, and exuberant in her comic energy, Jane explores the dissonances of cultural travel through the style of comic satire even when her subject matter commands tragic seriousness.

When assertions of rigid cultural borders surface in the world of *My Year of Meats*, they provoke the destabilizing response of subversive laughter. When Jane receives a fax from her Japanese employer's wife that alludes to her husband's proclivity for wife beating, Jane's Japanese co-worker Kenji responds unsympathetically to this vulnerable outreach from his fellow national. He suggests that Jane ignore the fax:

> "I'm warning you, Takagi. Leave it alone. You're not Japanese. You're just going to make it worse for everyone."
>
> Ma used to do this to me and Dad all the time, cop this attitude of *you are a crude, uncivilized foreigner and cannot possibly understand our delicate and unique Japanese sensibility*, and there is absolutely no point in arguing. They've been practicing this one for over a millennium.
>
> (*YM*, 228, italics in the original)

How does Jane treat this claim to impenetrable cultural secrecy? She turns it into a source of satire. Rather than arguing rationally with Kenji about the possibilities of cultural translation, Jane responds with comic subversion. Offering him a souvenir from her latest shooting location in the Midwest, she hands him a t-shirt emblazoned with the logo "Sidewinders"—a reference to bulls whose surgically altered penises prevent them from impregnating cows. "It's a baseball team," Jane tells him with a straight face (*YM*, 228). As Kenji unwittingly admires his new shirt, the gift subverts his claim to cultural authority. In spontaneously contriving the impenetrability of American culture, Jane asserts its *likeness* with Kenji's idea of what it means to be Japanese. The novel thus turns an assertion of difference (the untranslatability of Japanese sensibility) into a comic production of cultural similarity. At the same time, Jane's cruel humor suggests that there is nothing inherently mysterious about American, or implicitly Japanese, culture. Kenji does not get the joke because, unlike the readers of the novel, he has not read an article on sidewinders printed a few pages earlier in *My Year of Meats*. Ozeki and Jane's narrative choices imply that cultural barriers reflect deliberately staged denials of information rather than the mysterious operations of unique cultural sensibility.

The formal construction of *My Year of Meats* further confirms the novel's commitment to breaking down the mystique of cultural separation. In choosing to tell the story from the perspectives of two narrators, one Japanese American (Jane) and one Japanese (Akiko), Ozeki's style minimizes the social barriers that exist between American and Japanese national identities. While the two narrators are unknown to each other until midway through the novel, they are both familiar to their readers, and so neither character marks a space of radical otherness. Although the narratives are asymmetric, with Jane's voice in the first person and Akiko's in the third, the novel's method of alternating between the two voices immediately lessens the degree of alterity that the novel encourages its readers to experience. Such a narrative choice is a conventional one, of course, but it nonetheless helps to construct Ozeki's liberal portrait of a world with markedly commensurable social differences.

Jane, the impoverished filmmaker, takes a job producing Japanese television documentaries for an American meat lobby called BEEF-EX. "BEEF-EX was the sole sponsor of our program," Jane tells us, "and its mandate was clear: 'to foster among Japanese housewives a proper understanding of the wholesomeness of U.S. meats'" (*YM*, 10). Part cooking show, part lifestyle documentary, and all advertisement for the red meat BEEF-EX hopes to export to Japan, the series *My American Wife!* features regionally diverse American Wives as they prepare hearty, meat-filled meals for their families.[4] While this ideological export of normative and conservative femininity might be disturbing enough, Jane's research for the series soon links this representational violence to an even more insidious set of problems in the capitalist production of American beef. The more Jane learns about the meat industry and its relationship to women, the more she discovers metaphoric and literal connections between women and cattle in U.S. culture. After Jane encounters the illegal use of the hormone DES as a growth stimulant in the meat industry, she discovers that the same hormone was once prescribed to pregnant women, including her mother. When Jane traces her own infertility to fetal exposure to DES, she realizes that her private sadness forms part of a larger problem of international public health.[5] Because BEEF-EX seeks to export this hormone-contaminated meat to the newly opened markets of Japan, Jane comes to realize the insidious financial imperative that her documentaries serve, and she begins to film covert footage for a private documentary that exposes risks to public health in the meat supply. She does so with the help of numerous American Wives, whom she enlists as allies in the political fight against the global spread of DES.

If Jane's narrative charts the vicissitudes of transnational production, the second thread of the novel explores the effects of transnational consumption. Akiko, the unhappy, bulimic Japanese wife of the advertising executive who invented *My American Wife!*, regularly watches Jane's documentaries and prepares the recipes filmed on the show. As Jane begins to feature families who diverge from a normative ideal of a white, middle-class, and healthy household, Akiko finds herself energized by these new visions of black, lesbian, and adoptive families. Consumption of global media turns Akiko into a liberal feminist subject, and she eventually leaves her abusive husband to begin a new life in the United States with Jane and the American Wives. This second feminist alliance, which counterpoints Jane's documentary network, creates a feedback loop between consumers and producers of transnational imagery.

Although Jane and Akiko do not know each other in the first half of the novel, Ozeki's narrative choices place them within a shared imagined community. As avid readers of Sei Shōnagon, the Heian court writer whose famous *Pillow Book* inspires Jane's documentary impulse, both Jane and Akiko treat this medieval text as a touchstone for their own experiences. Their shared reference point in Shōnagon allows Jane to produce and Akiko to decode the feminist messages inscribed within *My American Wife!*, creating an alternative viewing community through the circuits of transnational media. Watching the inaugural episode of the series, Akiko thinks of a line from one of Shōnagon's lists: "A rather unattractive woman who looks after a large brood of children. That was a perfect description of Flowers, the Coca-Cola lady, and she was a housewife from Iowa in the United States of America" (YM, 40). As Akiko interprets these early episodes with reference to *The Pillow Book*, her assessment of the television show aligns her with Jane's optic rather than with the official marketing messages of the program. Much as Akiko surreptitiously reads *The Pillow Book* at night to escape her overbearing husband John, Jane too reaches mentally for Shōnagon when that same John burdens her with inappropriate sexual confidences on a trip to America. "I started counting categories," Jane tells us with distaste as she tries to banish John's presence from her mind. "Hateful / Unsuitable / Depressing / Annoying / Presumptuous / Things That Give a Hot Feeling / Things That Give a Pathetic Impression. . . . When I'd put enough distance between us, it occurred to me that I was probably the only person in the history of the world who has ever recalled Shōnagon in a strip joint in Texas" (*YM*, 44). In distancing themselves from the same man through the same set of Japanese writings in similarly incongruous spaces, Akiko and Jane unwittingly bring themselves closer to each other in the novel.

As Jane and Akiko emerge as distinct voices in the novel, Ozeki's stylistic juxtapositions encourage her readers to appreciate the intricate affinities between them. One of Jane's sections ends with her admission of guilt about her role as a documentarian: "I felt bad about Suzie Flowers—like I'd stolen something from her that could never be replaced" (*YM*, 37). The next sentence of the novel, told from Akiko's point of view, inherits Jane's rhetoric of robbery. "Sometimes Akiko felt like a thief, sneaking through the desolate corners of her own life, stealing back moments and pieces of herself" (*YM*, 37). The metaphor of theft opens a translational space that Jane and Akiko inhabit together, so that the juxtaposed sentences crowd their experiences together within a shared figure of speech. This rhetorical communion does not merge their experiences into an indistinguishable or homogenous state; instead, it draws attention to the specificity of their self-conceptions as very different metaphorical thieves. In balancing the uniqueness of each character while asserting their commonalities, this narrative choice minimizes the difference between the two figures in the novel.

Through multiethnic identity, comic subversion, shared literary touchstones, and mutual metaphors, *My Year of Meats* fosters a crowded style that presents its world as a community of individuals already connected through the cracks in moderate social borders. In large and small ways, these narrative choices remind us that myths of cultural autonomy require tremendous effort to repress the many fragments of evidence that contradict their claims. Although this imagined world is filled with violence, exploitation, and misunderstanding, it fundamentally asks its readers to perceive social borders as crossable rather than as signs of radical alterity. In a fiction where figures share more with others than they may know, Ozeki explores how these unspoken connections might flower into robust engagements with significant otherness.

Sentimental Crowded Selves

In order to encourage sympathetic imagination across borders, the novel suggests the need for figures like Jane and Akiko to link the project of imagining others to a reassessment of their own social location. For both American and Japanese characters, sentimental concern for others eventually leads to self-examination, so that the self serves as both subject and object of its own sentimental gaze. This form of crowded self emerges for both Akiko and Jane as a form of commercial self-fashioning. By altering their habits of production and consumption within a global economy of dehumanizing images, they change themselves in the face of the other. Reformist rather than radical, this sentimental realignment articulates the self within, rather than against, the circuits of global media and transnational capital.

As discourse, sentimentality is often characterized by a perceived reliance on uncritical emotional responses. When individuals experience sentimental sympathy with others, they do so not because they have deduced from philosophical principles that they should care about others' suffering but because they feel viscerally for bodies in pain. But although sentimental sympathy often presents itself in the mask of the immediate and instinctive, it is always culturally coded and socially shaped. As it reflects assumptions about whose suffering is worthy of concern, it plays a powerful role in shaping the visibility of particular kinds of people. Such visibility can help develop new conceptions of obligation and responsibility; as Lynn Hunt suggests, the Western legal concept of human rights may owe much to the mode of tearful compassion exemplified by the novel.[6] Moreover, sentiment is not without its own philosophical underpinnings. I draw here upon Joanne Dobson's definition, which describes literary sentimentalism as "an emotional and philosophical ethos that celebrates human connection, both personal and communal, and acknowledges the shared devastation of affectional loss."[7] Implying a form of selfhood that recognizes its own lack of autonomy, sentimentality bespeaks a subjectivity that is fundamentally ecological, bound up in its relationships to other beings. This impulse toward bonding enables Martha Nussbaum's contention that emotions, such as compassion, can embody the "judgment that others (even distant others) are an important part of one's own scheme of goals and projects, important as ends in their own right."[8] As a conduit for such assumptions, sentiment may prove effective in establishing robust affective bonds between subjects at a distance.

Such power enables incipient crowded selves to emerge in the novel. Akiko, for instance, enters as a thin and passive self who gains a new vivacity through her sentimental identification with the television images on *My American Wife!* Touched by the American families represented on screen, Akiko begins to regard her own alienated life with renewed affection, and these spectacles on American television propel her toward new forms of self-knowledge that play themselves out through the market. When she is thrilled by the sounds of zydeco music on an episode of *My American Wife!* set in Louisiana, Akiko, with a visceral feeling of liberation, travels through Tokyo to buy the song. "She'd written down the names of Bobby Joe and also Rockin' Dopsie at the bottom of the paper where she copied the week's recipe. The next day she took the bullet train to town and found the CDs at Tower Records in Shibuya" (*YM*, 78). Akiko's burgeoning move toward liberal feminist bonding occurs through an act of material consumption. Not only buying American music but buying it from the recognizably American music chain Tower Records, Akiko develops her new sense of self by embedding her life further into the workings of global capitalism. For many readers, Akiko's instinctive response reveals the failures in this particular portrait of Western liberal feminism. At the moment when Akiko feels to herself most like an individual in solidarity with others, she is actually best described as a cog in the wheel of transnational trade.[9] In this light, Akiko's immediate affinity for zydeco signals an inauthentic masquerade, a sign of simple consumerism rather than of cultural exchange or serious self-reflection.

But why should the fact that Akiko spends money invalidate her growing impulse to expand her range of cultural engagement? Presumably the Louisiana audience for Bobby Joe's songs also pays for albums or concert tickets, and in this novel, the fantasy of an authentic identity built outside capitalism is just that: a fantasy.[10] In Ozeki's writings, the circuits of global capital are value neutral. They can be used to transmit harmful products, such as hormone-contaminated beef or repressive images of women, but they can also be used to spread cultural objects of value, offering Akiko new emotions and new desires. "She'd never seen heat rising before, or met a woman like the one in the song, who carried a straight razor. Akiko didn't know what a straight razor was, but suddenly she wished she could have one too" (*YM*, 79). The song embodies a powerful marketing tool, in the sense that it inspires Akiko with desires she did not know she had for products she does not fully comprehend. Yet the tone of the novel, if not the content, suggests that Akiko's response may be less of a simple capitalist colonization of consumerist desire and more of an emergence of a crowded self. As her emotional response to the music changes her emotional response to herself, it expands her capacity for sympathy toward her own condition. Breaking a barrier through consumption does not mean that the breaking is inauthentic; instead, it implies that the barrier was relatively weak in the first place.

This impulse toward expanded social engagement intensifies Akiko's yearning for sentimental connection with those she has seen on television. Emboldened by her new music purchase, Akiko finds herself brave enough to send a fax to Jane that confesses her newly discovered sexual desires and her husband's domestic abuse. The power of sentimental representation in the novel reaches its apex in this startling document, where Akiko reveals her yearning to bond with Americans and insists upon making herself visible to them.

> *Dear Miss Takagi-Little,*
>
> *You do not know me because I am only the wife of Ueno of BEEF-EX so I regret to bothering you at all. But I feel compelled to writing for the reason of your program of the Lesbian's couple with two childrens was very emotional for me. So thank you firstly for change my life. Because of this program, I feel I can trust you so that I can be so bold.*
>
> *. . .*
>
> *But I am most wanting to say that I listen to the black lady say she never want man in her life, and all of a sudden I agree! I am so surprising*

that I cry! . . . I feel such sadness for my lying life. So now I wish to ask
you where can I go to live my happy life like her? Please tell me this.
Sincerely yours,
Akiko Ueno

. . .

p.s. please do not tell my husband I write this to you because he will
anger and maybe hit me as he is sometimes wont to do.

(YM, 213–214, 215, italics in the original)

This missive, recording Akiko's engagement with the significant otherness she experiences on screen, draws upon the power of sentimental
identification to foster a crowded self of layered perspectives.[11] In stepping out of her receptive role as the consumer of media images and demanding direct personal communication, Akiko performs a form of
intimate bonding that draws upon the images of global television but
also rejects the one-way dissemination of such media from America to
Japan.[12]

In giving us Akiko's response to "the program of the Lesbian's couple," Ozeki reveals how late twentieth-century transnational media inherit the historical potential of sentiment to shape communities across
national borders. Speaking of eighteenth- and nineteenth-century British, French, and American fiction, Margaret Cohen argues that "the sentimental subgenre was a *transnational* literary form during the century
of sentimentality's prestige, and sentimental novels were the most translated of all literary fiction."[13] Although audiences in diverse social spaces
interpreted these images differently, the codes of sentimental fiction op-
erated on a larger scale than the national or the regional, much as Akiko
responds to Jane's documentary vision from her home in Japan.[14] As Cohen contends, these codes historically enabled "sentimental communities" that bonded with each other through the experience of witnessing
figures in pain.[15] Within such imagined literary worlds, sentimental fiction also modeled expanded communities for its avid readership. "Sympathy continues to work to establish bonds that *specifically transgress and
replace those of kinship and nation*," April Alliston claims.[16] When Akiko
finds herself moved by Jane's sentimental shots of American families, we
can appreciate how the traditional power of such female-centered representation infiltrates the new mass media of the late twentieth century.

The sentimental power of this moment is not only evident in Akiko's response to television imagery but also in Ozeki's representation of this response. Akiko's English, imperfect but expressive, enhances the impression of vulnerability. The childlike diction, coupled with the distinctly adult content, offers what Evelyn Nien-Ming Ch'ien calls "weird English," or the transformation of non-native grammatical mistakes into forms of literary power. "The use of weird English is a calculated effect," Ch'ien argues. "For polycultural writers, weird English is not simply the temporary adoption of a spelling disorder, but a conscious appropriation of hybridity."[17] Despite—or, I suggest, because of—its seeming transparency and grammatical errors, the fax represents one of the most concise moments of layered imaginative border crossing in the novel. As Akiko suddenly inhabits the perspectives of others through a sentimental encounter (*"I am so surprising that I cry!"*), her substitution of "surprising" for "surprised" offers a much better description of the actual cognitive process that creates her crowded self.[18] What reflects aesthetic control for Ozeki (Ch'ien's "weird English") represents an out-of-control experience of expansion for Akiko as she slips between different forms of identity and expression. In the moment of engaging with the significant otherness she sees on television, Akiko "surprises" herself, and as she turns her sentimental gaze on her own life, she quickly moves to take action on her own behalf. Her emerging crowded self thus pulls her both outward and inward simultaneously, breaking down divides not only between subjects of different nationalities but also between individuals on different ends of media production and consumption.

For her own part, Jane also finds herself propelled into a sentimental form of border crossing when she receives this astonishing fax. After reading the document, Jane tells us:

> Maybe it was because my shows were broadcast in Japan, on the other side of the globe, but up until now I'd never really imagined my audience before. She was an abstract concept: at most, a stereotypical housewife, limited in experience but eager to learn, to be inspired by my programs and my American wives; at the very least, a demographic statistic, a percentage point I'd hungered after, to rub in a pesky executive's face . . . suddenly here was the audience, embodied in Akiko, with a name and a vulnerable identity.
>
> (*YM*, 231)

The vividness of Akiko's physical suffering stimulates in Jane a sentimental response that causes her to rethink the character of her Japanese audience. As Jane abandons her quantitative approach, the novel
offers us Jane's conceptual transformation as a basis for dialogue among
women from different social locations. Her moment of self-reflection
enables an incipient crowded self that looks at the world from multiple
perspectives that engage and alter each other. If we accept David
Palumbo-Liu's contention in his reading of the novel that so-called rational choices (such as Jane's desire for heightened viewer ratings) cannot guarantee the ethical treatment of others,[19] the power of sentimentality becomes vital to an ethics of representing social difference. The
sentimental impulse that seizes Jane ("suddenly here was Akiko, with a
name and a vulnerable identity") fosters a larger evaluation of her own
role as a maker of modern images. "Maybe my shows weren't much as
documentaries, but I had believed in them," Jane confesses. "And
Akiko's fax brought my audience, and my responsibility, into sharp
focus. It was clear to me that I couldn't continue to celebrate beef. I had
to tell some truths about meats, even if it meant getting fired" (*YM*, 232).
If Akiko mimics what she perceives as Jane's power as she (Akiko) re-
makes herself, Jane mimics what she perceives as Akiko's vulnerability.
Both figures reimagine themselves as producers and consumers of
global products, subverting transnational circuits to serve new feminist
emotions of attachment.

Ozeki's strong reliance on such feeling may seem troubling, because
there are many reasons to distrust the aesthetic or political efficacy of
sentiment in modern literature.[20] Within twentieth-century discourse,
sentimentality frequently suggests the low levels of cultural capital that
accrue to social insincerity, political complacency, or aesthetic manipulation.[21] These low levels of cultural capital reflect sentimentality's history as an emotion associated primarily with femininity and effemi-
nacy.[22] Since sentimentality implies not simply sympathy with pain but
also *pleasurable* sympathy with pain, it affiliates itself with such phenomena as masochism, exoticism, and self-absorbed pleasure in the
wonder of difference.[23] If this pleasure leads observers to ignore their
own possible complicity with the pain of others, it fuels skepticism
about the ethical utility of such emotion. Because sentimentality allows
individuals to feel good as they commiserate with other people's hard-
ship, it often masks the underlying structures of power that precipitate

individual moments of suffering. Sympathy personalizes structural inequities, allowing sympathizers to indulge in feelings of superiority or relief while ignoring their own investment in unjust social systems. For many writers from postcolonial or minoritized situations, pity on the part of the powerful reflects and reinforces yet another psychological hierarchy that helps perpetuate discursive domination. The desire to sympathize with others, in such cases, represents the luxury of an elite, thus reinforcing the social divide that it ostensibly surmounts. Richard Rorty identifies one source of anxiety about this practice when he notes that relying on sentimental education means appealing to discretionary good will rather than legislating ethical demands. We fear sentimentality, Rorty argues, because we fear that "if we hand our hopes for moral progress over to sentiment, we are in effect handing them over to *condescension*."[24] If we perceive a significant gap in power between subject and object, sentimental compassion is likely to be resented and dismissed as an exercise in guilt-assuaging complacency.

Because Ozeki offers us a world in which her main characters do not confront high levels of alterity, experience intransigent obstacles in their search for power, or resist being represented, I suggest that sentiment offers a viable tool for her portrait of crossing social borders. While *My Year of Meats* is not exclusively sentimental literature (Jane Smiley, in a blurb printed on the cover of the paperback edition, calls it "a comical-satirical-farcical-epical-tragical-romantical novel"), it uses the historic power of sympathy to catalyze new conceptions of those far away. "While we might cringe at the clichés and the 'nationalist' sentimentality found in Ozeki's novel," Palumbo-Liu argues, "I believe we ignore the sentimental at our own risk—rather than simple knowledge or 'rationality' it might be the most powerful tool in persuasive storytelling, and progressives should reclaim that as a tool. To be effective, we need to think more closely about our inherited forms for sadness."[25] I suggest that part of the power Palumbo-Liu describes lies in the ability of sentiment not only to make others vivid but also to make the self more vivid to its own perception. This practice is not only "nationalist," in Palumbo-Liu's terms, but also (as we see with Jane and Akiko) capable of generating transnational engagements that reappropriate circuits of global media. This interplay between imagining others and reimagining the self enables everyday action at a distance across social borders.

With its blend of sentimental narrative codes and didactic activist energy, the novel allows us to consider the implications of Sara Ahmed's theory of the cultural politics of emotion. According to Ahmed's argument,

> Emotions are what move us, and how we are moved involves interpretations of sensations and feelings not only in the sense that we interpret what we feel, but also in that what we feel might be dependent on past interpretations that are not necessarily made by us, but that come before us. Focusing on emotions as mediated rather than immediate reminds us that knowledge cannot be separated from the bodily world of feeling and sensation; knowledge is bound up with what makes us sweat, shudder, tremble, all those feelings that are crucially felt on the bodily surface, the skin surface where we touch and are touched by the world.[26]

Dramatizing emotional responses to transnational media such as the television program and the fax, Ozeki's novel calls our attention both to the literal mediation of such feelings and to the more extensive philosophical mediation that Ahmed foregrounds. Through sentimental perception, *My Year of Meats* works out a role for the interior and exterior body within its search for engagement with significant otherness.

Feminism Across Borders

But are such sentimental crowded selves enough? Meditating on the transnational imagery of pain, Susan Sontag forcefully argues that sympathizing with others cannot stand alone as an ethical response to evidence of suffering. She writes: "Compassion is an unstable emotion. It needs to be translated into action, or it withers. The question is what to do with the feelings that have been aroused, the knowledge that has been communicated. If one feels that there is nothing 'we' can do—but who is that 'we'?—and nothing 'they' can do either—and who are 'they'?—then one starts to get bored, cynical, apathetic."[27] The force of sentiment, or the shock the viewer experiences when confronted with evidence of pain, must propel concrete action to offer a robust form of imaginative projection. Such a transformation of compassionate energy marks a central aspiration of Ozeki's representational ethics.

As the novel locates this question through its portrait of an emerging transnational feminist community, it partakes in an expansive twentieth-century history of gender-based internationalism. Is the process of imagining others as part of a larger community easier because that community is primarily composed of women? In the early twentieth century, many thinkers did in fact suggest that shared gender enabled women to comprehend each other's ambitions and anxieties across social divides. Virginia Woolf famously declared in her antiwar polemic *Three Guineas* (1938) that "in fact, as a woman, I have no country. As a woman I want no country. As a woman my country is the whole world."[28] Woolf implied that the exclusion of women from the spaces of nation making, such as the university, the army, and the government, could be turned into a radical advantage for global politics. Echoes of her words resounded into the 1980s, when the American activist Robin Morgan began her encyclopedic attempt to unify all feminist movements into one shared global endeavor. The fruit of Morgan's efforts, *Sisterhood Is Global: The International Women's Movement Anthology* (1984), revitalized the rhetoric of sorority that had long permeated the discourse of twentieth-century Western women's internationalism,[29] and it resonated with the renewed emotional fervor of women's movements in the 1960s and 1970s. Arguing for a universal understanding of feminism, *Sisterhood Is Global* asserts that "women seem, cross-culturally, to be deeply opposed to nationalism—at least as practiced in patriarchal society."[30] Anything less than an international vision of women's solidarity reflects a patriarchal subversion of feminist political strength through divisive appeals to class, ethnicity, religion, and nation.[31] Morgan's anthology documents the hope, in the retrospective words of the journal *Public Culture*, that "feminism was to be a global touchstone for all humankind."[32]

This hope, however, did not come to pass. Though Morgan understood feminism to oppose nationalist ideology, many women's movements (especially in the postcolonial world) articulated strong philosophical and practical links to campaigns for national liberation. Morgan's idealistic global sisterhood was soon attacked as a new form of American imperialism, in which particular middle-class, liberal feminist ideals first developed in the United States were then thrust upon women around the globe.[33] Morgan's ideas endured further challenge from within the United States, where women of different races, religions, sexual orientations, and social classes sought to define their own struggles on their own terms. As Chandra Talpade Mohanty forcefully reminded feminist thinkers, "Beyond sisterhood there are still racism, colonialism, and imperialism!"[34] Many feminist activists called upon their colleagues to remember how women oppress other women, complementing the celebratory ideal of sorority with an awareness of racial and economic hierarchies.[35] Responding to these new challenges, feminist theorists began to dismantle the rhetoric of global sisterhood.[36] As more and more women asserted different ways of interpreting feminism or forged their own rhetoric of social change, shared gender began to seem inadequate when compared to the power of local identities and local histories.

Thus the ethical task for transnational feminism was to maintain the power of capacious alliances without blurring the critical differences among women's goals and beliefs.[37] While some scholars have advocated feminist projects of only modest ambition, Sara Ahmed offers an important critique of this position when she argues that failing to account for the experiences of different women poses a challenge as serious as usurping their voices in the name of a supposedly universal feminism. Too restrained an approach, in Ahmed's words, "functions as a kind of solipsism that confirms the privilege that it seeks to refuse (I can only speak about myself, or I can only speak about the impossibility of my speaking)."[38] Such self-centered effects are precisely what an ethics of border-crossing representational practices seeks to counter. This search for a new understanding of solidarity and alliance energizes the threads of third-wave feminism of which *My Year of Meats* forms a part.[39]

The novel attempts to address this problem of engaging significant otherness through narrative choices that resonate with the conceptual breakthroughs of late twentieth-century feminist politics. In particular, the novel adopts many of the rhetorical practices that made the concept of violence against women the centerpiece of transnational feminist advocacy in the mid-1990s. *My Year of Meats* is not only a novel about the experiences of women; it is also a novel that relies upon the political strategies of transnational feminist activism to develop important aspects of its crowded style. Though, to the best of my knowledge, the book was not consciously constructed in relation to organized political activity, the novel effectively works to shape a theoretical framework for a transnational feminist community. Like the advocacy networks that search for viable ways to unite women politically, the novel seeks to avoid both the silence of cultural relativism and the arrogance of cultural imperialism.

In a study of first-wave transnational advocacy networks, the political scientists Margaret Keck and Kathryn Sikkink tell a story of transnational feminist activism that anticipates the narrative choices of *My Year of Meats*. By the mid-1970s, Keck and Sikkink note, Western feminists sought to cast women's issues internationally through the rhetoric of discrimination and equality. Rooted in struggles for suffrage and rights in the workplace, this form of feminism found itself severely challenged at the 1975 International Women's Year Conference in Mexico City. For many women from the global South, discrimination and equality described pressing problems for women in industrialized nations but ignored serious difficulties faced by women in the developing world.[40] This fissure left a vacuum in the project of global feminism, reminding women of the historical, economic, and cultural biases that afflicted attempts to set an international feminist agenda.

What succeeded where discrimination, equality, and other feminist causes failed, however, was the idea of violence against women. In the mid-1970s, the phrase "violence against women" was neither a unified nor a unifying category. Initially, campaigns concerning violence against women were isolated local movements that focused on specific problems such as wife battery, military brutality, rape, dowry deaths, prostitution, or female genital cutting. "The category 'violence against women' had to be constructed and popularized before people could think of these practices as the 'same' in some basic way," Keck and Sikkink argue. "This one caught on because in some way it 'made sense' and it captured the imagination" (*AB*, 171–172). This shift reveals the success of a transnational feminist network that managed to unify women's activism (*AB*, 165–167).[41] The United Nations promulgated its Declaration on the Elimination of Violence Against Women in 1993 and subsequently established a trust fund to support efforts against gender-based violence worldwide. By 1995, just before *My Year of Meats* was published, violence against women had triumphed as the heart of transnational women's movements. This historical surge in conceptual prominence depended largely on the transformative powers of political rhetoric. Since that time, global attention to violence against women has continued to rise in prominence throughout the 1990s and into the twenty-first century.

Keck and Sikkink argue that violence against women succeeded in mobilizing transnational advocacy networks because it focused attention on issues of bodily pain that translate easily around the world. "We argue that issues involving bodily harm to vulnerable individuals or issues about legal equality of opportunity are most likely to result in successful transnational networks" (AB, 192). The concept of violence against women successfully exploited this basic concern for physical well-being among less powerful members of society, and it worked in large part because it elicited a sentimental response. While physical pain has been convincingly read as a sign of untranslatable experience (as in Elaine Scarry's influential theory of the body in pain),[42] descriptions of suffering often paradoxically also prove to be uniquely portable across social borders. Sad and sentimental stories have proven to be effective political unifiers.

Resonating with this larger pattern, violence against women constitutes the central structuring device that links Jane's discoveries of public-health abuses to the private sufferings of women in the novel. These cases center on the specter of female fertility, in which practices designed to enhance or regulate the reproductive capacities of women ultimately damage those bodies in physical and psychological ways.[43] As Jane discovers more and more women and girls who suffer at the site of their fertility, the novel invites us to apprehend the similarities between public and private abuse. My Year of Meats relies upon the parallelism of the documentary series and its episodic format to invite comparison among the stories of violence that emerge in the off-screen lives of each American Wife. After a Wal-Mart truck crashes into Christina Bukowsky and leaves her comatose and infertile, her languishing condition mirrors the economic downturn of her town when the Wal-Mart diverts business from local stores. Rosie Dunn, a five-year-old growing up on a feedlot in Texas, develops breasts and menstruates as a result of her exposure to DES-treated cattle. Akiko's husband, desperately seeking to control his increasingly elusive wife, resorts to emotional abuse, physical attacks, and outright rape to assert his ownership of her reproductive capacities. Because of her fetal exposure to DES, Jane struggles through the sadness of miscarriage in her quest to bear a child. As these microstories provide an alternative series to the official storylines of *My American Wife!*, the parallel format of the documentary series identifies recurring causes of violence, such as patriarchal privilege, capitalist expansion, dehumanizing forms of labor, and normative images of femininity, while attending to the diverse ways that women experience and respond to such literal and representational violence.

As the novel adopts strategies that work in the political world, *My Year of Meats* emphasizes the strand of feminist thought that stresses the vivacity of health and suffering rather than the abstract articulation of human rights. Although the rhetoric of violence against women gained a measure of international force through its association with human rights, which allowed many activists in the 1990s to argue that women's rights should be recognized as human rights,[44] this rhetoric was not embraced as an unqualified blessing. Even activists who support flexible definitions of human rights have admitted that its privileging of international law, its identification with Western jurisprudence and theory, its emphasis on male political rights, and its individualism have sometimes made it tactically inappropriate or philosophically troubling for feminist advocacy networks.[45] To offer an alternative ground for political critique, one thread of transnational activism has begun to cast violence against women as a concern of public health.[46] *My Year of Meats* operates within this political framework, which allows the novel to criticize individual, medical, and corporate practices across national borders without relying on legal definitions of essential human rights. Doctors who prescribe DES to pregnant women or farmers who lace cattle feed with hormones signal betrayals of public health that affect the lives and the bodily integrity of women. In a late twentieth-century American context where concerns about food safety, environmental toxins, and health care have bordered on a national middle-class obsession, Ozeki's strategy speaks to the pressing practical concerns of this readership. Through images like Jane's new conception of Akiko, the power of feeling for a body in pain proves more persuasive than a philosophical description of entitlement and obligation.

Despite the efficacy of this expansive concept of violence against women, this unifying device has not always been welcome in many late twentieth-century conversations about transnational politics. The transnational campaign against violence against women has often been accused of allowing its dramatic narrative—the kind of viscerally moving drama that powers such scenes as Akiko's rape—to forestall alternative possibilities for feminist critique. After a groundbreaking international conference for human rights in Vienna, where the theme of violence gained center stage as a successful form of transnational advocacy, some intellectuals lamented that the success of first-person female narratives about violence sensationalized human rights and usurped the rightful place of poverty and development. Writing for *The Nation*, Laura Flanders (quoted in Bruce Robbins's study of human-rights culture) contended that "the experience of violence provides a powerful common ground. It's also sexy; sexier than labor rights, illiteracy, or poverty. . . . What bleeds, as the familiar press maxim has it, leads." Robbins also looks with suspicion on "sad and sentimental" stories that animate human-rights discourse, citing their "inconclusiveness." "The apparent universality of suffering," he argues, "and the apparent universality of the sentiments in the face of suffering are no less open to possible abuse than any other universality."[47] Violence against women, thus, may have served to muffle dissent and detract attention from problems that lack strong sentimental appeal.

Many theorists of violence lend credence to this problem by continuing to define violence in relatively narrow terms. Believing that to include all material forms of injury is to rob gender violence of precise explanatory power, these theorists focus on forms of violence with short and direct causal connections, where the desire to harm can be plausibly proven.[48] One common definition of violence, "an act carried out with the intention or perceived intention of physically hurting another person,"[49] clearly encompasses domestic and state-sponsored brutality but excludes impersonal actors whose capacity to inflict harm exceeds demonstrable intention. Transnational corporations that sell dangerous products, regulatory agencies that fail to enforce public safety, or media productions that manipulate public images elude the grasp of this definition of violence. Even analysts who focus specifically on violence against women as a matter of public health sometimes fail to articulate the ways that transnational trade, poverty, and development endanger women's physical well-being.[50] Even as feminists successfully challenged the artificial divide between state-sponsored and domestic injury, their emphasis on physical abuse has been perceived as a distraction from problems of global capital. Amrita Basu thus concludes in her discussion of transnational feminist organizing that global campaigns "are more effective in challenging physical violence than structural violence against women."[51]

What sets *My Year of Meats* apart in its portrait of violence against women? As the novel organizes the micronarratives of women into a transnational story about diverse forms of harm, it uses the power of sympathy to expand the political imagination of its readers. Against narrow understandings of violence, *My Year of Meats* seeks to stretch its readers' imagination to appreciate structural as well as personal sources of harm. Mediating between the one and the many, it uses the vivacity associated with the individual body to direct attention to less easily imaginable abstractions. In the novel, the repressive optics of medical establishments, transnational corporations, and global media form one of the most powerful sources of violence against the bodies of women. As Jane sees more and more of her American wives and families damaged by the failures of public health, she presents us with a form of representation that combines the short causal chains of domestic abuse with the longer, more subtle effects of violence through medicine, food consumption, unhealthy work environments, and poverty. As feeling at a distance allows readers to grasp structural problems, the power of sentimental sympathy works to enlarge their own crowded selves and to further more penetrating critiques of domination, whether discursive or physical.

One of the most vivid sources of violence in the novel is the specter of global capital, which directly and indirectly reinforces representations and practices that lead to serious harm. To be sure, the novel is not hostile to entrepreneurial activity, or even to commodification and consumption per se, and its irreverent enjoyment of these pleasures prevents its critique from devolving into an overly predictable indictment of modern consumer culture. However, the novel emphasizes how the search for profit leads to abuses of public health that most keenly affect poor communities, which are also often ethnic-minority communities as well. When an African American man grows breasts from consuming inexpensive cuts of chicken that contain high hormone residues, the novel invokes the specter of feminization to suggest the literally emasculating effect of such corporate practices on the body politic and to assert the heightened vulnerability of the poor to environmental toxins. Internationally, as well, the collusion between American agribusiness and Japanese television reveals how the violence of public-health abuses increasingly targets nonwhite communities. Jane's "Documentary Interlude," which exposes how the hormone DES enabled the mass production of meat, makes clear the financial imperatives that her documentaries serve:

> In 1989, Europe banned the import of U.S. meat because of the use of hormones in production. BEEF-EX started looking for a new market.
>
> In 1990, as a result of pressure by the U.S. government, the New Beef Agreement was signed with Japan, relaxing import quotas and increasing the American share of Japan's red-meat market.
>
> In 1991, we started production on *My American Wife!*
>
> (*YM*, 126–127)

When Jane's work turns out to advertise meat grown with the same hormone that damaged her own reproductive abilities, the novel allies the imaginatively vivid image of her body to the political and financial decisions that serve the spread of capital markets. Indeed, the search for new markets to conquer is described in the book through the language of sexual conquest. "A liberal meat supply," Akiko's husband quotes to her, "has always been associated with a happy and virile people and invariably has been the main food available to settlers of new and undeveloped territory" (*YM*, 20). Violence against women is not simply a metaphor for the violence of capitalist conquest but a literal consequence of its structural investment in virility. This ability to direct attention in complementary ways, I suggest, enables a central aspect of the novel's crowded style. In making her argument so clearly throughout the novel, through explicit devices such as the "Documentary Interlude," Ozeki seeks to expand a reader's ability to imagine the structural scope of violence against women.[52]

As the novel indicts male behavior, patriarchal attitudes, transnational capital, and structural inequality as contributing factors to all its represented forms of violence, *My Year of Meats* is also careful to explore how women themselves contribute to the dissemination of transnational harm. This issue emerges most clearly in the realm of the media, where Jane tries to confront her own role as a maker of commercial images she does not wholly support. Even more provocatively, Akiko embodies the contradictions of becoming both producer and consumer of media violence against women. Before her marriage, Akiko works happily as a copywriter for Japanese manga comics, where she relishes the gory captions she invents for public consumption. Though the novel presents this moment as one of the more liberated periods of Akiko's life, her work enhances a genre in which the victims of its spectacular horror are most commonly women. "In the pages of the comics read by male students and workers on rush hour trains," writes Vera Mackie, "women are subjected to violence, rape, and mutilation."[53] Though in no way is Akiko held responsible for her husband's abuse, Akiko (like Jane) finds that her work enters a feedback loop in which her power to produce imaginaries of violence is undermined by her physical suffering at the hands of those who consume such fantasies. Jane's work as a filmmaker enacts Akiko's role on a transnational stage, enabling the novel to articulate how women themselves contribute to media violence against other women. In showing us their complicity with the suffering of others, *My Year of Meats* complements its portraits of feminist sympathies with what Susan Sontag calls "a reflection on how our privileges are located on the same map as their suffering."[54] While Sontag argues that we should replace the false intimacy of sympathy with the austere solemnity of such recognition, Ozeki's novel attempts to retain both the power of emotional identification and the haunting critique of transnationally intertwined fates.

As Ozeki shows how sentiment can enable transnational feminist alliances and expand activist imagination, she asserts the importance of educated feelings. It is not enough for Jane to simply feel sorry for girls whose bodies are deformed by DES exposure; she actively works to educate herself and her audience about the reasons DES remains vital to American agribusiness. This oscillation between education and feeling models an everyday act of representational ethics for the readership of the novel that works against the fetishization of individualized pain. Individual suffering matters in and of itself, not simply as a symptom of a larger problem, but respect for that individual suffering also demands that we confront the subterranean workings of structural ills. The crowded style of *My Year of Meats* not only helps to balance between viewing others as similar and as different but also oscillates between the detailed, focused scale of the individual and the larger, systematic scale of the problem. Sentimental representation can, in the right time and place, enable that reconciliation.

Advertising Action

How might sentiment not only enable nuanced conceptions of others but also encourage activism in the readership of the novel? To address this concern, *My Year of Meats* asks its readers to rethink the power of firm narrative conclusions. The novel contends that happy endings, often dismissed as unsophisticated and regressive, can ironically work to foster political energy across borders. A meditation on the importance of narrative closure emerges early in the novel, when Jane shoots the first episode of *My American Wife!* "Well, Fred," Jane explains to the husband in the family being filmed, "In TV, sometimes you have to shoot the endings first" (*YM*, 3). Fortunately for her episode, Jane captures a kiss between Fred and Suzie Flowers long before their marriage dissolves acrimoniously on camera. After Fred admits to an affair on screen and abandons his wife, Jane's director surreptitiously edits the video tape to follow Fred's angry revelation with a moment of artificial forgiveness. The early kiss appears in the show, framed by "a cartoon heart" that resembles, in Jane's opinion, "a TV ad for phone sex," so that the audience need never appreciate the shambles of the Flowers' off-camera lives (*YM*, 29). As an aesthetic and ethical moment in documentary, the "ending" of the Suzie Flowers episode represents one of the lowest imaginative moments in *My Year of Meats*. Mortified by the deception and poor taste of the episode, Jane regrets having precipitated the breakup and refuses Suzie's repeated demands for a copy of the show. However, when Suzie finally does acquire a videotape, her response confounds Jane's fearful expectations. Unoffended by the optimistic editing, Suzie passes the tape on to Fred, who arrives penitently on her doorstep with a peace offering of flowers. Watching the false happy ending of the show inspires the couple to mimic its possibilities for reconciliation.

The episode of Suzie Flowers directs us toward a serious question that the novel raises about narrative closure and practical action. Before Suzie sees the taped version of the show, she exists in the narrative stasis of repeated action (namely, constant calls to Jane). Watching the representation of closure on the tape breaks the stasis, allowing both Suzie and Fred the emotional breakthrough they need to move forward with their relationship. Paradoxically, the artifice of the sentimental happy ending allows renewed action in the world off-camera, turning the ending (as Jane hints earlier) into a space of beginning. Though the happy endings of the novel are less deceptive (and more artful) than the garish scenes that satisfy Suzie and Fred, the novel as a whole still invites its readers to behave as Suzie and Fred do. In particular, it urges its readers to move from thinking about others to acting in concert with them.

In its ending, *My Year of Meats* neatly concludes its narrative threads in emotionally satisfying ways that reward the good and punish the bad. (As a telling emblem of what this internationalist novel considers punishment, Akiko's rapist husband John is demoted and sent to the Japanese provinces to produce local advertisements for hot-springs resorts.) As a result, the conclusion of the novel may appear excessively contrived to a readership sympathetic to the critiques of the novel but skeptical of such a successful outcome. While the comic tone of *My Year of Meats* rarely adopts the heavily humorless style of early twentieth-century social realism, the dominant impulse of the novel reflects an interpretation of social-realist aesthetics in its desire to portray a world capable of change and reform. As Ozeki defends herself against charges of an unearned ending in an interview included with the Penguin paperback edition of the novel, "You cannot make a better world unless you can imagine it so, and the first step toward change depends on the imagination's ability to perform this radical act of faith."[55]

Though Jane declares that "I don't think I can change my future simply by writing a happy ending" (*YM*, 361), this ambivalence sinks beneath the weight of the novel's celebratory closure. In defending the choice to make the closing note of the novel an optimistic one, Ozeki contests the conventional criticism that satisfying endings subvert progressive change by substituting the pleasures of vicarious action for the more difficult comforts of historical reform. Happy endings are often thought to be escapist opiates, robbing the reader of the desire to connect the world of the novel to the world of lived experience. Ozeki, however, makes an interesting argument for an inverted relationship between the pleasures of narrative closure and the desire for historical change. "I wrote a happy ending, although, like Jane, I am suspicious of the efficacy of doing so," Ozeki asserts in the interview accompanying the novel. "But happy endings satisfy the emotions, and I wanted to provide the type of satisfying narrative closure in the hope that it would free the intellect to continue its trajectory beyond the story line, pondering the issues the book raises."[56] The governing assumption behind her explanation assumes that the emotional paralysis and ambiguity of ambivalent narrative endings directly translate into intellectual and political stasis. Complex and open endings, she implies, mire the reader within the social space of the novel and prohibit the translation of affect into action.[57] As Ozeki argues that novels need to evict the reader from the imagined world of literature, this interpretation of narrative closure complements her claim that novels need to perform the social work of imagining viable futures. To encourage that trajectory, *My Year of Meats* concludes with references that direct the reader to nonfiction accounts of American meat industries and DES action networks.

The narrative choices that impel the celebratory ending of *My Year of Meats* thus ask to be read as a marketing device for social action, in which the imperatives of selling the novel and selling its activism merge into a seamless whole. As with Jane, whose multicultural shows actually enhance television ratings and sales of meat, Ozeki seems to argue that the novel can spread ethical ideals while it provides a particular audience the happy endings it enjoys. The merger of these two goals reflects the very points of contradiction produced within the flows of transnational capital.[58] Although the book is a powerful critique of the depredations of the global market, it also contends that the success of the novel in an era of globalization depends in part on how works of fiction learn to exploit the techniques of visual media marketing for their own ends. Like *My American Wife!*, the novel instills desire for its ideological product and relies on emotionally satisfying closure in order to encourage its readers to learn from the book. Just as the audience of the television show should feel inspired to purchase the meat and prepare the recipes filmed on camera, the audience of *My Year of Meats* is also expected to act upon its narrative consumption, enacting what Nina Cornyetz calls the novel's "performative rather than strictly literary function."[59] Ozeki's work suggests that, ironically, the model best known for its ability to produce new emotions of yearning, aspiration, and action—commercial advertising—may enable one such link between the sentimental emotions generated within the novel and the political energy encouraged in its readers.

According to Ozeki, this model may even be working. After a translation of the novel was published in Israel, she received a call from an Israeli civil-rights lawyer. "He wanted to tell me about a case he was working on, representing a group of DES daughters in a class-action lawsuit against the pharmaceutical company who had distributed the drug," Ozeki recorded on her blog. "He told me that after *My Year of Meats* was published in Israel, the story of DES poisoning was covered by the media, which resulted in an additional 80 or so women calling his office and joining the plaintiffs in the suit. So indirectly it seems my book had helped his case."[60] The image of the class action, in which plaintiffs fight both for themselves and for others, offers a particularly appropriate transformation of sentimental sympathy into active liberal demands on the public sphere.

In choosing to develop engagements with significant otherness through sentiment and sentimental narrative codes, *My Year of Meats* effectively wrestles with the crucial problem of feeling at a distance. The project of imagining across borders, as Jane finds when she reads Akiko's revelatory fax, requires us to refigure the "we" and "they" that Sontag hints at in her essay on compassion. As the novel asserts solidarity among its women through their shared (and diverse) forms of suffering, it reminds us that robust and enduring sympathy requires an acknowledgement of one's own vulnerability. Precisely because the women in the book feel threatened by similar transnational practices, they are able to avoid the indifference that Sontag associates with complacency, and they learn to act in concert against transnational sources of harm. Just as Jane is inspired to rethink her own role as a producer of global media, the novel asks its readers to reevaluate their own actions and alliances in an increasingly interconnected world. Through the projection of emotion onto injured bodies, the novel suggests, in Sara Ahmed's terms, "how feminism involves an emotional response to 'the world,' where the form of that response involves a reorientation of one's bodily relation to social norms."[61]

Rethinking the way one's own daily habits of production or consumption affect others far away, adopting political strategies of feminist representation, and turning postmodern compassion into concrete ethical action all emerge as cornerstones of Ozeki's representational ethics. These practices are all compatible with a comfortable, middle-class life in a developed nation, even though they need not be limited to such a social position. Ozeki's vision provides ample space for the needs and desires of the imagining subject, asserting that one can experience pleasure while still making worthwhile ethical gestures. Although these solutions are philosophically moderate because they do not require severe sacrifices on the part of the crowded self, these visions nonetheless require the energy of ongoing effort. For Ozeki, conceptualizing others is only the first step in the process of ethical representation; one must also translate such perspectives into political activism.

Despite the evident dangers of sentimentality, an ethics of imagining across borders need not always abandon the power of its passionate presence. In particular, affect can be particularly compelling in helping make heterogeneous communities more than empty abstractions. A "we," in one sense, is not just a community defined by legal documents or principled ideas about social obligations but is also a community that feels viscerally for its members. Many theorists have argued that large-scale communities are bound to fail because their members will not, in the end, feel deeply for each other.[62] Even with an abundance of good will, these critics argue, members of an overly capacious social order will not share the emotional commitments that bring imagined communities to life. But if sentiment is vital to the health and liveliness of smaller communities, then it stands to reason that sentiment may have a crucial role to play in helping shape enduring relationships across social borders. Sentimental emotions help us feel at a distance, and indeed, as Rorty has argued, the creation of actually existing transnational communities (like human-rights cultures) owes its existence to the power of "sad and sentimental stories."[63] *My Year of Meats* testifies to one such vision at work.

Given the novel's contributions to the ethics of representation, it is ironic that many moments in the novel fall short of its own ideals. Readers have found many of Ozeki's portraits of multicultural America and Japan artificial, sometimes embarrassingly so, and in these moments of failure we can best apprehend the limits of sentiment-based representation. Sentimental sympathy and good will cannot enable all forms of imaginative border crossing. Yet while many of Ozeki's characterizations remain within the confines of prepackaged vision, her novel still offers important insights into one process of imaginative projection. Though the novel does not always live up to its own best impulses, it suggests how we might strive toward an ethics of conceptualizing others in an increasingly mediated world.

Although—or because—*My Year of Meats* is not a radical novel, it offers us a compelling portrait of what Bruce Robbins calls "ordinary" global culture.[64] Jane is the rare companion who reveals both a social conscience and a sense of humor; no sterile puritanism diminishes her relish for the pleasures of life. Her comic sensibility allows her to decry the corrosive effects of global capital while cheerfully admitting the fun of shopping at Wal-Mart, and ironically, this satirical doubling of perspective makes her ethical conscience more durable and appealing. The comic sentimentality of *My Year of Meats* thus seeks to provide a sustainable ethics of engaging significant otherness for everyday first-world life. This vision is neither radical in its demands nor adequate to extreme circumstances, but it may be livable, replicable, and workable for many who are entangled as producers and consumers in a global economy.

3

Ethnic Reversals

In an essay on Harriet Beecher Stowe's *Uncle Tom's Cabin* (1852), the African American novelist Charles Johnson ponders the ethics of representing racial difference. Like many modern readers, Johnson understands *Uncle Tom's Cabin* as a testament to the history of representational violence and discursive domination. Describing its figuration of black Americans as "ineluctably racist" and "truly beyond salvage," Johnson suggests that the novel reveals more about the cultural fantasies of Stowe and her world than about the complexities and contradictions of life under slavery.[1] In trying to present black characters as worthy of white Americans' moral concern, Stowe imprisons African Americans in a debilitating form of racial discourse that continues to haunt black writers like Johnson.

Yet despite Stowe's failure to craft a novel that black Americans can celebrate, Johnson argues that *Uncle Tom's Cabin* still raises vital questions about the possibility of imagining social difference. "One hundred and fifty years after its publication, *Uncle Tom's Cabin* can still serve us, though not in the way that Stowe and her admirers intended," he declares. "It invites us to discuss whether a white author can successfully portray a black person *in his own terms*, instead of through the distorting, fun-house mirror of white, Eurocentric ideas about people of color" (*TW*, 103). Though Stowe fails to offer such representation, her aspiration invokes the ideal of conceptualizing others beyond the metanarrative of the mirror argument. Although self-representations, as Johnson argues, may provide richer and fuller portraits of a people, abandoning the responsibility to imagine the lives of others ensures that border-crossing fictions remain locked in the "fun-house mirror" of distorted and demeaning thought. "Stowe's book challenges us today to ask whether it is possible ever to write well the lived experience of the racial Other," Johnson concludes (*TW*, 104).

This chapter turns Johnson's question back on himself, asking how he and writers like him seek to represent social discourses and practices not conventionally considered their own. What alternatives might such novelists offer to contest racially distorted perceptions? In the pages that follow, I investigate how two ethnic American writers approach this task of imaginative border crossing. Working under slightly more challenging conditions than those depicted in Ruth Ozeki's fiction, these novelists offer an expanded range of narrative choices that focus in particular on the role of ethnic and religious discourses. Charles Johnson, along with the Chinese American novelist Gish Jen, both embrace this endeavor by turning to comic performances of border crossing. While Ozeki's work hints at how comedy might mitigate perceptions of alterity, Johnson and Jen elaborate more fully on the possible contributions of the comic to an ethics of representation.

Johnson and Jen represent important voices in a trend that presents multiethnic and multiracial identity as a source of comic integration rather than as a tragic narrative of cultural alienation. In this respect, they share an ethos with many novelists in other parts of the English-speaking world. This comic turn is especially pronounced in British fiction, where such writers as the novelist and screenwriter Meera Syal trace the comic possibilities of working-class life for Asian British communities. Such flamboyant parodic energy characterizes the fiction of Zadie Smith, whose *White Teeth* (2000), *The Autograph Man* (2002), and *On Beauty* (2005) all relish the absurdities of life within multiracial families on both sides of the Atlantic. In similar fashion, Hari Kunzru's novel *Transmission* (2004) turns to the subversively comic powers of a global South Asian diasporic network visualized through the workings of mass media. Even more clearly than these authors, however, Johnson and Jen not only seek representational border crossing through comedy but also make an account of that search an integral part of the stories they tell.

The form of representational violence that most haunts the work of Johnson and Jen is that of the stereotype, an emblem of imaginative constraint that is most likely to produce concern about the ethics of representation in both popular and critical discourse. Stereotypes mark anxieties about the limits and borders of group belonging, figuring not simply simplified portraits of complex phenomena but also questions about the power to control through representation. In Homi Bhabha's terms, racial stereotypes offer "a form of knowledge and identification that vacillates between what is always 'in place,' already known, and something that must be anxiously repeated . . . as if the essential duplicity of the Asiatic or the bestial sexual license of the African that needs no proof, can never really, in discourse, be proved."[2] In this sense, as a quality both assumed in advance *and* constantly in need of being performed, the stereotype can be seen as the microcosm of what Walter Benn Michaels describes as the pluralist conception of culture itself. In Michaels's assessment of pluralist logic, although concepts of cultural identity claim to escape racial essentialism, "the assertion of cultural identity depends upon an identity that cannot be cultural—we are not Jews because we do Jewish things, we do Jewish things because we are Jews."[3] Jewishness, or any other ethnic identity, is thus both already known *and* in need of constant proof. The comedy of Johnson and Jen, I argue, inhabits stereotypical discourses in order to invert their hegemonic and identitarian effects. Their playful reversals of the stereotype can be read as a comic exploitation of the paradoxical logic of pluralism, through which a new representational ethics may come into view.

In alluding to such reversals, I should be clear that neither Johnson nor Jen replace discursive domination with visions of ennobled otherness. Instead, they work toward a form of representation that resembles a process that Rey Chow describes in her analysis of cross-ethnic stereotyping. Chow understands stereotypes as generative and creative as well as repressive and troubling, arguing that their use can some-times provide a "way of impersonating those [one] mocks—for the sake of annihilating them from within with that healthiest of anarchistic explosives, laughter."[4] In order to reverse constraining expectations about social borders, after all, those expectations must be acknowledged in the first place. In this sense, it should not be surprising that writers and actors for ethnic television comedies, such as Meera Syal and Sanjeev Bhaskar in Britain, have claimed that stereotypes provide "indispensable tools" for the beginnings of ethnic comic representation.[5] As Johnson's and Jen's novels move to the edge of such constraining discourse in order to finally question the logic of those constraints, they produce crowded selves and styles in a dizzying game of representing social difference.

In stressing the role of the comic, these novels ironically deploy a form of writing with a history of perpetuating social distinctions. In order to laugh at someone else, individuals often need to feel safely distant from the object of their laughter, and such distance easily creates a hierarchy to distinguish the mockers from the mocked. Comedy thus can both reflect and reinforce unequal social relations, constraining its targets within restrictive ideas about proper social borders. Laughter from below can also serve to enforce social distance, venting suppressed anger against unjust social systems or performing inscrutability in the face of dominant cultures' desire for knowledge.[6] Scathing laughter can rebuff too easy an intimacy, telling subjects they have more work to do before they can fully engage with the lives of others.[7] Explicitly and implicitly, comic modes often raise ethical difficulties in the practice of representing social difference.

In contrast to forms of humor that work to discipline subjects into existing social categories, the narrative choices of Johnson and Jen instead valorize comic incongruity through ethnic discourses and religious practices that collide in surprising ways.[8] Pointing to the gap between what we see and what we assume, this form of humor challenges assumptions about the proper relationship between one's own life and the lives of others. Throughout this chapter, humor, laughter, and comedy serve as rough synonyms to describe textual effects that appear comic or absurd against the cultural expectations implied by the narrative.[9] Because laughter emerges through such historically specific assumptions about particular social barriers, this humor invites readers to question the ideas that make its effect legible in the first place. As comic incongruity provokes laughter through the juxtaposition of difference, it can ironically work to unsettle the social barriers it describes.

Such practices of representation emerge through the vicissitudes of comically incongruous dramas of border crossing, in which Johnson's and Jen's characters weave the rhetoric of other social groups into their own everyday lives. Whereas Ozeki figures the cognitive state of characters, like Jane, who suddenly begin to represent others differently to themselves, Johnson and Jen focus attention less on explicit acts of perspective taking and more on performative border crossing, the adoption of ethnic and religious practices from a different way of life. Their protagonists, and their literary styles, experiment with the possibilities of encounter that arise from inhabiting a different social identity. When a multiracial American slave learns Chinese or a Chinese American girl decides to become Jewish, the comedy of these ethnic performances asks us to question why these cultural discourses are considered incompatible enough to provoke a comic response. In the United States of the late twentieth century, such acts of performative border crossing are often marked as surprising objects of comment. Because we commonly expect cultural crossings to reflect ascents in power, in which subjects adopt the practices of those with greater cultural capital, crossings among ethnic minorities or peoples of color challenge such hierarchical ascent and the values it assumes. "In the inequitable reality of the United States," Amy Ling argues, "two types of cultural cross-dressing occur: one we might call 'lateral'—from minority to minority; the other vertical—from minority to majority."[10] Lateral movements, in an American context, thwart conventional expectations about the incentives for adopting new social practices, and thus they create the conditions for a destabilizing laughter that can engage significant otherness.

Through the destabilizing power of such topsy-turviness, Johnson's and Jen's narrative choices exploit the dissonance of mismatching perceptions. I begin my exploration of this dissonance by locating Johnson's work within traditions of romantic Orientalism. When Johnson writes of Zen slave narratives in *Oxherding Tale* (1982), he generates rhetoric akin to stereotypical Orientalist discourse in order to overturn that form of discursive domination. His prose invokes self-mockery, comic absurdity, historical improbability, asymmetric framing, and productive misreading to enable his burgeoning crowded style. Elaborating on this comic logic, I suggest that Jen's work calls our attention to hyperracialized perceptions of ethnic stereotypes in order to trouble the stable line between the familiar and the foreign. Situating Jen within American debates on political correctness, I explore how her approach to representation complicates the underlying assumptions of identity politics. Even more clearly than Johnson, Jen's *Mona in the Promised Land* (1996) contends that a sustainable crowded self requires the ongoing experience of comic reversals. As Jen suggests that there is no ideal or correct life beyond mockery, she implies that a robust subjectivity must accept the sympathetic satire of others. Although many novels include moments of comic anarchy only to restore social order in the end, Jen's fiction maintains the openness of the unexpected in performative border crossing. Exposing the perceptual processes that make social identities rigid to some but porous to others, these novels contest invasive imagination by unsettling underlying ideas about the meaning and stability of social difference.

These novels further challenge discursive domination through their attention to imaginative engagements between ethnic minorities or peoples of color. Although adopting the social signifiers of others has often been read as the privilege of hegemonic identities such as whiteness, the novels of Johnson and Jen help articulate the importance of border crossing for nondominant groups. These works strive for the vision that the theorist R. Radhakrishnan describes as "rooted in the politics of representation and yet daring enough to visualize a postrepresentational space where one group will have earned the right to speak for the other in a spirit of equal reciprocity."[11] Both writers turn to the power of surprising reversals to enable this energetic formation of crowded selves and styles. In their refusal to support the essentialism that, in its most destructive form, gives rise to what the Kenyan politician Koigi wa Wamwere calls "negative ethnicity,"[12] their novels work to articulate robust views of ethnic belonging that also embrace ethnic transformation. These fictions testify to Paul Gilroy's claim that "the powerful and pleasurable fantasy of transgressing that impassable boundary [of race] has started to circulate through the core of popular culture."[13]

Reversing Orientalism: Charles Johnson's Oxherding Tale

Born into an African American family in the Midwest, Charles Johnson first began his artistic career as a cartoonist, then trained as a philosopher, and finally became a writer of fiction in the 1970s. Throughout much of his diverse literary career, Johnson has been an extremely vocal opponent of identitarianism and enthusiastically accepts a place in the history of what Ross Posnock calls the *"antirace race man."*[14] "For Johnson," Posnock contends, "there is no striving to enter the kingdom of culture, one is already in residence."[15] Indeed, as passages quoted in earlier chapters attest, Johnson is fond of proclaiming his allegiance to an expansive view of artistic inheritance and even of embedding didactic declarations on the inseparability of self and other within his fiction. A young Dr. King, for instance, opens his refrigerator to behold the universe in one of Johnson's short stories: "He saw in each succulent fruit, each slice of bread, and each grain of rice a fragile, inescapable network of mutuality in which all earthly creatures were codependent, integrated, and tied in a single garment of destiny."[16] Although Johnson's affinity for this kind of writing, and his disinclination to identify his work in terms of racial exclusion or cultural opposition, made him an anomaly in the decades when cultural nationalism and identity politics dominated American public debate, it has afforded him increasing prominence in the late 1990s and early 2000s. Indeed, the first decade of the new millennium has witnessed the publication of four scholarly volumes dedicated solely to his work.[17] This revival of interest in Johnson's novels, which has inspired the republication of some of his early stories as well as a wealth of literary studies, suggests the prescience and ongoing relevance of much of his claim to border-crossing fiction. Indeed, his novel *Oxherding Tale*, published in 1982, provides the earliest example of the representational ethics considered in this book.

While Johnson's interest in diverse cultural practices ranges widely across the world, among the most important ideas in his work have been Asian spiritual theories, which he seized upon to illuminate the vicissitudes of African American history. First introduced to yoga by his mother, Johnson trained as a martial artist in his teens and found himself drawn to the Buddhist theories that sustained the principles of the martial arts he practiced.[18] One of his unpublished collections of cartoons, a book on Zen called *It's Lonely at the Top*, both sympathizes with and satirizes the American countercultural quest for spiritual enlightenment.[19] When Johnson turned from cartoons to fiction, he began by writing a naturalistic novel about a young black man's experience in a martial-arts training hall. Although Johnson never published that book, his desire to theorize African American experiences through performative border crossing of Asian discourses pervades his oeuvre.

Johnson's abiding interest in Asian discourses takes him into contested cultural territory. Throughout the twentieth century, specific historical conditions have rendered black-Asian border crossings in the United States particularly vexed. Because Asian communities have often been marked as model minorities in American racial discourse to position them in opposition to African Americans, this hierarchical discourse (sometimes reinforced by Asian immigrants themselves) splinters a shared sense of minority identity and reinforces a perceived gap between the social capital of different ethnicities.[20] Registered in such films as Mira Nair's *Mississippi Masala* (1991), the tension between these communities marks a potentially explosive social engagement. In forging an alliance between black and Asian discourses, Johnson is already caught up in a project with recuperative implications.

From the screenplays and short stories "The Green Belt," "China," and "Kwoon" to the novel *Oxherding Tale*, much of Johnson's early writing insists upon reading black American history as a thoroughly syncretic set of narratives. Fusing the journey from slavery to freedom with Buddhist quests for enlightenment, Hindu searches for dharma, and Daoist hunts for "the way," Johnson claims for black Americans a metaphysical as well as a material quest for liberation. In his epic adventure *Middle Passage* (1990), this pull toward eclectic Asian metaphysics emerges through the book's portrait of the semi-Buddhist Allmuseri tribe and its critique of American Orientalism. His novel *Dreamer* (1998) archives the late twentieth-century history of Afro-Asian encounters, where a fictionalized Martin Luther King Jr. and his double Chaym Smith both turn to Asian spiritual practices to shape their responses to American racial conflict. As an essayist for the American Buddhist magazine *Tricycle*, Johnson frequently explores how Buddhist teachings illuminate black Americans' struggles for political and civil rights. "Were it not for the Buddhadharma, I'm convinced that, as a black American and an artist, I would not have been able to successfully negotiate my last half century of life in this country," Johnson declares.[21] His understanding of racial and national history relies upon a commitment to these ethnic and religious resources.

In offering us Zen slave narratives, black Buddhist monks, African American martial artists, and mulatto mokshas, Johnson's fiction attempts to answer the haunting question he poses in his introduction to *Oxherding Tale*: "what might these eastern traditions, which inspired Gandhi, poet Gary Snyder, and even led Richard Wright to compose hundreds of hiaku [*sic*], have to *say* to black Americans?"[22] If scholars of African American literature have often read spirituality in black literature as a guide to indigenous African or African American practices, Johnson confounds the presumed connection between spirituality and ancestry.[23] In engaging the significant otherness of Asian religious texts, his work seeks to create new readings of black experiences that transfigure the contours of both black and Asian signifiers in the process.

This dedication to Asian spiritual discourse is heavily indebted to the mediating genre of the Western spiritual narrative. Just as Johnson read hundreds of slave narratives before embarking on *Oxherding Tale*, so too did he immerse himself in exegeses of Buddhism, Hinduism, and Daoism before weaving them into his fiction. As he writes,

> I studied over and over the "Ten Oxherding Pictures" of twelfth-century Zen artist Kakuan Shien, the stunningly spiritual art of Nicholas Roerich, western writers who'd imaginatively "journeyed to the east"—Somerset Maugham in *The Razor's Edge*, Herman Hesse in *Siddhartha*, James Hilton in *Lost Horizon*, Jean Toomer in "Blue Meridian," Thomas Mann in *The Transposed Heads*—and devoured everything in print on zen by D. T. Suzuki, Eugen Herrigel, Christmas Humphreys, Alan Watts, and a library of esoteric books by authors from India, China, and Japan.
>
> (*OT*, xi)

While Johnson's capacious catalogue encompasses both Western and Asian sources, the asymmetry of his list, which names mostly European and American writers and leaves many Asian authors unidentified, suggests the primacy of Euro-American spiritual narratives for his own work. Although many readers of *Oxherding Tale* (and of Johnson's other novels) have shown how his fiction dramatizes Asian ideas through detailed source studies, they have done so primarily on Johnson's own terms.[24] This chapter seeks instead to go beyond Johnson's own claims, considering how Johnson's work fares when read in light of the specter of discursive domination. Rather than taking its liberatory potential as self-evident, I inquire into the representational practices that might affiliate the novel with familiar modes of Orientalist constraint. By exploring Johnson's proximity to Orientalist gestures, I hope to illuminate a larger point about the usefulness of his comic practices for an ethics of representing social differences.

The genre of the "journey to the east," which locates spiritual quests within the imagined worlds of Asia, is now most commonly read as a genre deeply embroiled in stereotypes of romantic Orientalism. For the most part, the spiritual narratives that Johnson read envision Asian pastoral spaces as both displacements of and escapes from European modernity (thus remaining within familiar paradigms of self-conservation and self-erasure). Thomas Mann and Herman Hesse's German novels, which offer philosophical parables set in premodern Indian landscapes, resonate with Friedrich Schlegel's nineteenth-century identification of Germany with ancient Aryan India.[25] Drawing upon related discursive traditions, the commercially successful books of James Hilton and Somerset Maugham link Western dominance of the interwar period to images of Asian passivity. Hilton, who invented the spectacular world of Shangri-la, imagines this retreat as an idealized Eurocentric regime that depends on the original violence of colonialism. In Shangri-la, the barely visible labor of Tibetan Buddhist peasants sustains an aristocratic spiritual hideaway of unnaturally long-lived Europeans. Maugham's book, which presents a spiritual experience in India as the unseen but essential core of the novel, invites its readers to consider mysticism as one among many American consumerist choices that make Western life more bearable. In their different ways, all of these authors lend themselves easily to Orientalist fantasies that privilege the construction of Western selfhood and culture. As one of the major axes along which Orientalist ideas cohered in Europe and America, Asian religious traditions have often proven irresistible to Westerners seeking escapes from industrial modernity and consumer culture. In turning to Asian spiritual discourse to avoid constraints on African American representation, has Johnson simply entered a parallel prison of Orientalist rhetoric? Because Johnson's novels favor spiritual over material discourse, one might be tempted to understand Johnson much as Johnson perceives Stowe: as a well-meaning attempt to think beyond one's social borders, but one that finally reaffirms confining representations of otherworldly and exclusively religious "Orientals."

However, the question of Johnson's Orientalism is complicated by the problem of ethnic differentials in power. Edward Said's argument relies on the premise that one important "feature of Oriental-European relations was that Europe was always in a position of strength, not to say domination . . . the essential relationship, on political, cultural, and even religious grounds was seen—in the West, which is what concerns us here—to be one between a strong and a weak partner."[26] Given their ambivalent relationship to the politics of Western modernity, do black writers necessarily replicate the dynamics of "a strong and a weak partner" that Orientalism implies? Spiritual narratives within black American writing suggest the possibility of another story. Like Jean Toomer, who captured Johnson's imagination, a small but vital tradition of black American writers has imagined Afro-Asian interconnections as a blow against the limitations of life under racist regimes. W. E. B. Du Bois's *Dark Princess* (1928), a love story that places African American and Indian political struggles within a global movement of the colored races, documents an important aspect of Du Bois's internationalism and global antiracism.[27] Similarly, Langston Hughes's socialist travelogue *I Wonder as I Wander* (1956) attempts to find strength for black Americans in the Soviet Union's treatment of its eastern ethnic minorities. Martin Luther King Jr. owes a debt to Gandhi's spiritualized anticolonial resistance, and his sympathy with the Vietnamese Buddhist peace activist Thich Nhat Hanh further supports King's global concerns. During the 1960s and 1970s, black nationalists also sought common cause with Asian resistance movements as they theorized the mystical identity of "the Asiatic black man."[28] Reflecting increasingly idealist, spiritual, and philosophical perspectives on cultural syncretism, Jean Toomer's mystical poetry, Richard Wright's late proliferation of haikus, bell hooks's discussions of her Buddhism, Lucille

Clifton's Zen-inspired poems, and Pearl Cleage's portraits of tai chi practitioners all seek to expand the contours of black aesthetic practice as they ask how different conceptions of Asian spirituality speak to the contradictions of race. Including himself within this numerically minor but intellectually important tradition, Johnson inherits a vision of spiritual discourse as one path to worldly solidarity and sustenance among peoples of color.[29]

Yet this tradition offers only the possibility, not the guarantee, of a new ethics of representation. Although racial identity complicates the differentials in power that underlie Said's claim, it provides no guarantee that black authors will actively challenge the rhetorical and philosophical assumptions of European Orientalism. Although their political ambitions diverge, works such as *Dark Princess* and black nationalist tracts often indulge in the tropes of romantic Orientalism that also pervade Eurocentric writings. Their representations bolster ideas of "the mysterious East," turning it into a blank slate upon which they inscribe their own cultural fantasies of rising black power.

To explore how Johnson both inhabits and subverts this discourse of romantic Orientalism, I turn to *Oxherding Tale*, the "platform book" that introduces the governing questions that inform much of Johnson's work. Prescient in its experimental form, this novel prefigures many of the questions that have preoccupied more and more novelists at the turn of the millennium. As a neo–slave narrative that traces the journey of its multiracial narrator from slavery to freedom, *Oxherding Tale* fuses this historical movement with a metaphysical journey from many forms of slavery to many forms of freedom. The novel unfolds not only through the Christian rhetoric of bondage and salvation but also through Buddhist, Hindu, and Daoist tales of liberation from the prisons of desire. Referring to a Zen Buddhist cycle of paintings that depicts a man in search of his ox, the title of *Oxherding Tale* invokes a classic parable of the quest for selfhood.[30] The seeker hunts for his ox in myriad places, finds the ox, lives with it, and then, in the end, realizes that self and ox are one. With the plot line of the novel loosely based upon this parable (and upon others, including Herman Hesse's 1922 novel *Siddhartha*), Johnson relies upon these questions about the meaning of selfhood, desire, suffering, and liberation to illuminate the specific predicaments of enslaved and enslaving individuals.

Like most of Johnson's work, *Oxherding Tale* does not attempt to tell us any documentary truth about Asian history. Nor, despite the proliferation of allusions to Asian art and philosophy in his writings, do many Asian characters appear in the novel. The challenge of representing Asian individuals thus poses a philosophical and technical problem that Johnson has yet to address substantially in any of his works.[31] Although one response to the problems of Orientalism could provide a renewed appraisal of social realism, Johnson's work eschews any claim to novelistic ethnography. Instead, its significance lies in its attempt to develop innovative ways of inhabiting Asian discourses in order to implode the textual markers of Orientalist discursive violence.

While, in theory, Johnson could achieve such a crowded style through a rhetorical engagement with any spiritual philosophy not conventionally associated with African American history, the actual content of the spiritual discourses he espouses bolsters his novel's claim to an ethics of border crossing. When his Buddhist-inspired characters claim the illusory quality of personal selfhood and encourage fluid interpenetration between one life and another, they dramatize why Derek Parfit claims that Buddhist ideas resonate with his own philosophy of expanded personhood.[32] Though I will not be discussing the Buddhist ideas dramatized within Johnson's characters, as many others offer such an account, I suggest that we can understand the formal strategies I will explore in light of the novel's commitment to a view of identity that resonates with the underlying principles of the crowded self.

To work toward such a representational ethics in *Oxherding Tale*, Johnson begins with the wonderfully surprising and historically improbable education of his narrator, a multiracial slave named Andrew. While Andrew's black and white heritage places him within the rich tradition of American interracial literature, and indeed the novel ponders the implications of miscegenation and passing, Andrew's education moves him beyond the central racial dynamic of American life through an invocation of Asian history and culture.[33] Although it is not impossible to believe that an enslaved individual could learn Chinese under the aegis of his nineteenth-century master, the unlikeliness of such an education provides an unsettlingly comic anachronism that deepens through the self-mocking force of parody. Laughter reverses our expectations about both slaves and Asian discourses in the self-parodying moment of Andrew's education, which includes thorough immersion in nineteenth-century American Orientalist scholarship. Under the instruction of his obsessive tutor Ezekiel, Andrew finds himself lost in a dizzyingly comic cycle of metaphysical speculation:

> [Ezekiel] taught me the 165 Considerations, Four Noble Truths, the Eight-Fold Path, the 3,000 Good Manners, and 80,000 Graceful Conducts; but I must confess that reading Chinese thought was a little like eating Chinese food: the more one read Lao tzu and Chaung tzu [*sic*], or ate subgum chop suey, the emptier one's head and stomach felt hours later. Too, I could never remember if it was ▽ before ┴ except after 合, or 灸 before 呆 except after 曾, and always got the meanings confused.

(OT, 13)

Because Western representations of Asian spirituality are often characterized by excessively sententious language that bespeaks a yearning for transcendence, Johnson's comedic excess punctures pompous spiritual rhetoric and knocks it from its pedestal of mystical remove. The self-mockery of the passage differentiates Andrew from the countercultural fascination with Asian ideas in the 1960s and 1970s (a period in time, as Ashraf Rushdy has convincingly argued, that *Oxherding Tale* opposes).[34] Because Andrew has a sense of humor, he figures a parodic alternative to the stereotype of the student whose glazed reverence for Asian religions signals a fleeting encounter with philosophical insights rather than a significant commitment to public and private change.

The educational program outlined above proffers a systematic vision of social behavior that the novel renders extremely ironic. Ezekiel's chosen texts place great value on social order (Considerations, Good Manners, Graceful Conducts), and with 83,165 precepts to learn, these tracts suggest to Andrew an impossible standard of social behavior. Ezekiel himself is spectacularly unable to achieve the standards implied in these texts. With "a splendid future as an Orientalist ordained for him, provided he isn't hanged, say, for high treason, or heresy," the tutor metonymically yokes Orientalist expertise to derangement, violence, and social disorder (*OT*, 9). Nothing in Ezekiel's canon of considerations and conducts saves him from the psychological demons that dog his steps. In exposing the emptiness of Ezekiel's philosophy of teaching, Andrew's voice paves the way for a new framework to mediate between the ideas in Asian scriptures and the lived reality of his own life on American racial frontiers.

Having established some self-mocking distance between himself and conventions of Orientalist scholarship, Andrew relies on the comedy of cultural anachronism to explore the fissures through which an engagement with significant otherness might emerge. His description of his education mocks the idea of rule-based knowledge, contesting the idea that other cultural discourses can be memorized and contained in adequate fashion. Having just critiqued the influx of rules from Asian scriptures, Andrew proceeds to apply an English rule of his own to equally ludicrous effect: "I could never remember if it was ▽ before ⊥ except after 👓." In trying to apply the English spelling rule of "i before e except after c" to Chinese calligraphy, Andrew illustrates one of the problems of using Western theory to interpret non-Western texts. As Dipesh Chakrabarty argues, a culturally inflected hierarchy separates what counts as legitimate theory from what is available as content. Modern scholars, no matter what geographic region they study, are asked to place their insights within the genealogy of European concepts, but non-Western theories are not afforded similar centrality. As Chakrabarty notes, "few if any Indian social scientists or social scientists of India would argue seriously with, say, the thirteenth-century logician Gangesa. . . . And yet past European thinkers and their categories are never quite dead for us in the same way."[35] In facetiously applying English rules to Chinese grammar, Johnson satirizes the tendency to rely upon Western concepts to shape an understanding of non-Western ideas. Displaced to the level of a child's spelling mnemonic, Andrew's jaunty confession hints that the syntax of his crowded style requires a reevaluation of its own conceptual grammar. In staging this moment as parodic, Johnson dramatizes the ability of a theory to question its own usefulness and its own limitations. Without suggesting that only Chinese linguistics can explain different forms of Chinese, the cultural anachronism points to a need for self-consciousness in border-crossing fiction.

This passage mocks the ideal of authentic knowledge, for Andrew's command of Chinese is unusual in more ways than one. Handwritten into the Plume paperback edition of the book, most of the characters that Andrew claims to know do not appear in a Chinese dictionary, nor are they recognizable to native readers of Chinese.[36] They resemble commonly used existing characters, but they displace or omit particular strokes. As the risk of imposing my own false analogy, we might think of them as the equivalent of English words with misformed letters.[37] What Andrew is being taught is thus itself an invention, with meanings perceptibly and literally transfigured in translation.[38] The handwritten characters look like they are written by someone not trained from childhood to write in Chinese, thus visually and obviously performing a form of writing that dramatizes its own status as border crossing. This passage encourages the reader to be skeptical of claims to knowledge, which may be much more illusory than the trappings of their mastery, and to embrace the inevitable losses and gains of cultural translation. Including these transfigured characters creates an effect that Rebecca Walkowitz has theorized as the "mix-up," in which "ordinary social and semantic mistakes . . . can create opportunities for effective, if sometimes impermanent agency."[39] This productive instability, however, is only visible to those readers familiar enough with Chinese characters to understand how different Andrew's are. This condition of visibility, I suggest, works less to affirm the supposedly correct knowledge of such a reader than it does to both celebrate and trouble the act of bilingual reading. As the novel calls attention to the changing character of language, the reader must "know" some Chinese in order to have that knowledge exploded.[40] This sort of paradoxical oscillation, I suggest, constitutes a central feature of Johnson's approach to imaginative border crossing.

Though parody allows this crowded style to include Asian signifiers under the guise of critiquing their inclusion, the parodic also encounters its limits as a mode of sustained narrative ethics. Unlike many works of postmodern writing, *Oxherding Tale* refuses to remain within the tonal registers of an ironic negativity. In offering us many voices, some of them mocking and some of them reverent, Johnson's crowded style destabilizes the monopoly that any one tone might maintain. This polyphony thus enables an active field of interpretations that make no claim on singular truths. Johnson offers a comedy of absurdity, filled with surprising reversals and asymmetries, to escape the constraints of totalizing systems.

Such energetic polyphony appears in one guise as asymmetric framing. One of Johnson's selected Asian narratives, the tale of Trishanku, begins in the world of high rhetoric and ends with the power of vernacular speech. Walking by the river one night, Ezekiel relates to Andrew a Hindu parable on the meaning of samsara. The passage begins with Andrew's decidedly Romantic sense of the natural world, which juxtaposes the lushly specific description of landscape with Andrew's abstract spiritual musings: "Oddly like a sacrament, the sand was penciled with patterns by porridgy waters that came crashing in, carrying catfish to shore" (*OT*, 31). Andrew's thoughts on freedom weave in and out of this rich sense of the natural world, where the penciled sand provides the visible text of his spiritual desires. The point of departure for the tale of Trishanku thus gestures toward an Emersonian transparent unity of nature.

Though Romantic idealism has been associated with one form of Orientalist discursive domination, Johnson works against such constraint through the asymmetric framing of the story. As Ezekiel tells the tale of his Trishanku, the novel moves farther and farther away from Ezekiel's mediating voice. Ultimately, we forget that anyone is telling this tale at all. As both Ezekiel and Andrew disappear from the pages, the story moves into its own level of textual time and space. In the narrative's final moment, when Trishanku attains enlightenment, the novel returns not to Ezekiel and Andrew in the pastoral moonlight but to Andrew and his father George at Flo Hatfield's slave plantation. Trishanku's tale thus marks a seminal moment of material transition between Andrew's education in the hands of Ezekiel and his future tutelage in Flo Hatfield's school of desire. As a moment of transfer, the tale translates multiple movements across different registers of space and time. In effect, we are given three stories crowded into one: the scene of Ezekiel's philosophical musings on the shore, the tale of Trishanku itself, and Andrew's parting from his father at Flo Hatfield's plantation, Leviathan. Trishanku's story thus forms the luminous center of a narrative polyphony that no single frame tale dominates or contains. We cannot tell whether Trishanku's story is Andrew's memory or his dream, and this uncertainty enables the novel to engage the significant otherness of an Asian parable without fixing it into any single site of Western fantasy.

Reversing expectations about the affinity between the parable and Emersonian Romantic discourse, the asymmetric frame tales also produce a crowded style as Johnson encodes Asian discourse into a black vernacular. Complementing the high rhetoric of the passage's beginning, the ending suddenly thrusts us into the world of an earthier voice.

> there was Brahma in a sea, a miracle, of light. He was a little impatient now, tapping his foot. "Trishanku," asked the Most High, "where is my pillow?"
> "Wake hup, Hawk." George elbowed me. "We heah, son."
>
> (OT, 34)

While it is not surprising that the story melds well with the elevated discourse of Romantic prose, its ethical viability draws strength from its reverberation with the rural inflections of George's speech. Although George's wake-up call fits in the plot as a literal summons to the sleeping Andrew, it serves more powerfully as a vernacular restatement of Brahma's question to Trishanku. At the end of the novel, when Andrew experiences his own epiphany, he beholds the face of George much as Trishanku here perceives the floodlit Brahma. Although George is never presented as an enlightened character himself (he is constrained by his racial essentialism and manic paranoia), he provides the key to Andrew's own enlightenment. His call to "wake hup," therefore, prefigures the awakening that Andrew's final vision of his father inspires. This merging of Asian discourse into George's black vernacular challenges the discourse of alterity that Orientalist poetics requires, yielding instead a stylistic topsy-turviness.

The polyphony of Johnson's prose, which inscribes Asian discourse among high and low registers of narrative and in and out of Asian spaces, reemerges when *Oxherding Tale* retells the Daoist parable of the uncarved block. As a classic set piece of Daoist literature, the uncarved block ostensibly visualizes the direct, unmediated simplicity of the self toward which Daoist philosophy encourages one to return. Andrew encounters such a block in the hands of Reb, the Allmuseri coffin maker whose detachment from the pains and desires of the world ultimately enables Andrew's own liberation. Left alone in Reb's workshop,

Andrew discovers among the many carvings an image of himself. "The replica was finished, but only the first side bore my likeness," Andrew tells us (OT, 77). The second side of the block reveals a face caught in the throes of desire and anguish, the third side depicts an aging town father, and the fourth side remains smooth and uncarved. "The back, I supposed as I drifted off mercifully to sleep, was where one mounted this odd figurine" (OT, 77). If the carving suggests a visual allegory for Andrew's past and future progress through the worlds of desire, domesticity, and enlightenment, it also offers a powerful metaphor for the many faces of Johnson's novel.

Johnson turns to productive misreading to unmoor the significance of rhetorical figures like the uncarved block. Much as the block's representation of Andrew includes both the familiar ("only the first side bore my likeness") and the unrecognizable (the sufferer, the social pillar, and the blank slate), Johnson's representation of Asian spiritual discourses mingles together the recognizable symbol of the uncarved block with Andrew's new (mis)interpretation of what the blank side is for. Since standard explanations of the uncarved block in Western discourse often stress its importance as the natural simplicity of the undesiring self, Andrew's guess that the uncarved side represents "where one mounted this odd figurine" seems to mistake the meaning of the block's blank slate. But in supposing the uncarved side to be the block's interface with the wall, Andrew turns the classic emblem of Daoist philosophy into the side that melds most seamlessly with the architecture of Andrew's local world. The uncarved side becomes a part of Andrew's hypothetical home, binding the block to domestic structures. What seems to be a mistake, then, actually expands how the uncarved block can be interpreted in different local spaces. The last line of Andrew's description perfectly captures the textual oscillation between received interpretations of Asian spiritual discourse and Andrew's considerably different vision of the uncarved block's role. Inscribing Asian figures in a way that unsettles their significance and sets their meanings in motion, Johnson contests the Orientalist logic of confining misreading with new and emancipatory misreadings of his own.

Throughout *Oxherding Tale*, the novel's insistence on polyphonic form disturbs singular conceptions of realism. As Johnson has argued, different forms imply different assumptions about the way the world works, and in choosing to mingle and fracture tones and genres in his novel, his crowded style encodes and disrupts all forms' claim to singular truths. Through this multivocality, Johnson disturbs the concept of a unitary and fixed Asian discourse to be appropriated. Offering us the eclectic and broken vision of collage rather than the systematic and totalizing vision of Orientalist scholarship, *Oxherding Tale* gives us hints of a border-crossing dialogue in constant motion. Johnson's parodic mockery, comedy of the absurd, historical and cultural anachronism, asymmetrical framing, and productive misreading all work to reverse conventional expectations about the social barriers between black and Asian ethnic and religious practices. The workings of his crowded style emerge through these experiments, which inhabit old forms of discursive domination to explode their significance.

Performance Past Correction: Gish Jen's **Mona in the Promised Land**

Like Charles Johnson, the Chinese American writer Gish Jen trains her literary eye on the performative border crossings of American ethnic minorities. Whereas Johnson's work draws our attention to the significance of literary discourse, preferring to conceptualize Asian texts and cultural practices rather than people, Jen takes a more embodied approach to the question of representing social difference. Raised in suburban New York, Jen initially trained in business school but left the world of finance to pursue her career as a writer of fiction. Her novels and short stories trace the emotional and sociological contours of Chinese immigration to the United States, illuminating a multicultural terrain that frequently takes her protagonists by surprise. Jen's novels *Typical American* (1991) and *Mona in the Promised Land* (1996), as well as some of her early short stories, chart the vicissitudes of the Chang family as its members migrate from Shanghai to the suburbs of New York. Building a life together, the Changs watch in bewilderment as their daughters make unexpected accommodations to different visions of American identity. Jen's collection of short stories, *Who's Irish?* (1999), meditates on the multiplicities of transnational experience between the

United States and China, and her novel *The Love Wife* (2004) explores the makings of a multiracial American family.

Jen's body of work poses these insistent questions about migration through an invigorating commitment to comic strategies. Although her fiction addresses serious and sometimes even tragic subjects, Jen's distinctive prose style finds something to laugh at within even the most troubled circumstances of modern life. In continually returning to a comic mode, Jen suggests that humor comprises a necessary aspect of her border-crossing fiction. As she invites us to laugh at and with her characters as they develop their distinctive crowded selves, she uses comedy not to satirically undermine their performances of alterity but to satirically endorse them.

This use of satire represents a significant departure from many traditional conceptions of mockery. Despite the anarchic irrepressibility associated with humor, many forms of comedy work to discipline their audience into a particular vision of the world. Such an impulse emerges most clearly in satire, which presupposes a better world through its critique of an existing one. As Northrop Frye defines it in his *Anatomy of Criticism* (1957), satire reflects "a combination of fantasy and morality."[41] If satirical laughter exposes a wrong to be corrected, satires of performative border crossing frequently work to reify the social borders challenged by transgressive acts. Depending on who is performing what, these performances can be denigrated as racial passing or social climbing, mocked as exotic and inauthentic, or condemned as exploitative and disrespectful. When satires mock an impulse toward cultural fusion as a form of self-indulgence, they imply that aspirations to conceptualize otherness offer yet another sign of Orientalist or primitivist narcissism: a masquerade of difference that only reflects the privileges of the embodied self. Such satire often seeks to expose the hollowness of border-crossing pretensions and put transgressive individuals back in what is considered their proper social place. Comedy that works in this way implicitly presumes a world of correct behavior, enacting Frye's "combination of fantasy and morality." Humor, in such Hobbesian terms, bespeaks a veiled assertion of superiority.[42] Although satire has thus been affiliated with the disciplinary power of the comic, Jen's writing insists that satire and sympathy can coexist within a single optic. The crowded style of her novel emerges through the destabilizing force of laughter, evocative of the paradoxical location conjured by R. Radhakrishnan when he speaks of a simultaneous "politics of representation" and "postrepresentational space." Sympathetic satires of border crossing call our attention to the specter of social divides, invite us to question them, and ultimately reverse their authority.

Turning comedy into a tool for border crossing rather than a form of cultural derision, Jen describes her literary approach in the context of the late twentieth-century rhetoric of political correctness. "Is this book un-p.c.? Yes," Jen said in an interview with the *Chicago Sun-Times* in 1996. "Is it anti-p.c.? Not exactly. The truth of the matter is, I think in some quarters [political correctness has] gone too far, but in some quarters it hasn't gone far enough."[43] "Political correctness," a keyword of American debates on the politics of representation, emerged initially in the 1980s on American college campuses and gained national media recognition in the early 1990s. In January 1991, *New York Magazine* published an article inquiring "Are you politically correct?" which catalyzed broad national conversations on representing social difference. How should individuals outside mainstream norms be represented in public discourse? What forms of speech constitute discursive domination? The energy and anxiety that crystallized over the heated term "political correctness" represented a fraught entry into the central question of imagining social difference. Proponents of political correctness have argued that cultural representations carry real ethical weight in the world, and thus part of campaigns for greater social justice should require attention to the way language can constrain or demean those whom it represents.

However, public debates about political correctness frequently abandoned broader ethical questions in favor of heated debates over discrete uses of language. While "politically correct" rhetoric replaced derogatory or hierarchical language with more seemingly neutral or inclusive terms, it often encouraged the use of sterile and euphemistic rhetoric in public discourse. As such, political correctness gestured toward an aim that many writers supported in theory—fuller and more complicated representations that acknowledged the complexity of power in social life—but promoted methods that were aesthetically unappealing and simplistic in practice. Leftist skeptics of political correctness, such as Sarah Dunant, wondered "what price racial and sexual equality if it can only be achieved by the imposition of another set of rules, in some cases amounting to what many see as direct censorship of speech or behavior? You don't achieve freedom by being frightened of what you can and can't say."[44] In extreme form, such rhetoric devolved into a new literary constraint that discouraged writers from tackling difficult and complex subjects for fear of giving offense to different social groups. While such writers as Jen share the larger goal of ethical representation, they reject the quick solutions and artistic tentativeness associated (fairly or unfairly) with the term "political correctness."

Being "un-p.c." but not "anti-p.c." uses humor as a tool to break social hierarchies rather than to bolster them. Although the term "political correctness" implies that there is, in fact, such a stable entity as a "correct" stance that could emerge in the absence of offensive language,[45] Jen's comic portrayals of ethnic and religious border crossing suggest that there is no such thing as a "politically correct" life beyond critique. The ethical robustness of border crossing emerges through a willingness to let others mock what will never be correct, what will never be above laughter. While traditional satire in Northrop Frye's terms illuminates a social problem in order to call for implicit correction, Jen's humor does not expose wrongs to be remedied. Jen thus inherits Bakhtin's egalitarian tradition of "festive laughter," which is "directed at all and everyone," including "those who laugh."[46] The teasing laughter that attends such performances, modeled by the novel's own tone of sympathetic satire, provides an alternative to racist derision without abandoning the energies of comic reversal. Mocking and being mocked constitute the condition of everyday border crossing.

This narrative choice succeeds, I suggest, because many of the borders in Jen's novel are not as rigid as they initially seem. Like Johnson, Jen continually plays with the idea that what we consider strong divides are much less durable than they first appear. Throughout her fiction, characters who seem different on the surface turn out to share much in common, often much more than characters of the same ethnicity or religion. Like many writers, Jen suggests that the strongest fissures frequently develop *within*, not across, social categories of identity. A relationship between a parent and a child, therefore, is far more fraught with alterity than a relationship across ethnic borders. Jen's comedy suggests that as individuals develop their crowded selves by reaching out to others, they can ultimately establish closer ties with the significant otherness of those nearby.

Located in the fictional New York suburb of Scarshill, *Mona in the Promised Land* charts the tensions of multiethnic modernity. Set during the rise of American identity politics in the late 1960s and written in the midst of the American culture wars in the early 1990s, the novel explores the struggle to develop new ethnic modes of belonging in the intersections among different minority communities. Like the actual town of Scarsdale, New York, where Jen grew up, the Scarshill of the novel is an affluent suburban community with a large Jewish population and an excellent public-school system. When the Chang family decides to move there for their daughters' education, the novel tells us on the first page that they are migrating in more ways than one: "they, the Changs, are The New Jews."[47] The Changs' younger daughter Mona soon finds her niche within the suburban Jewish community, and when her best friend Barbara Gugelstein decides to rediscover her Jewish roots, Mona follows along: "before you can say matzoh ball, Mona too is turning Jewish" (*M*, 32).

Unlike Charles Johnson, whose work emerges in the context of political tension between black and Asian communities, Jen explores the collision of communities that lack such history of antagonism in mainstream American discourse. Asian American and Jewish communities are both likely to be described in the late twentieth century as model minorities, and Asian American writers at the turn of the millennium are sometimes cast as the true heirs of such midcentury Jewish American writers as Henry Roth or Bernard Malamud.[48] Lacking the perceived level of racially inflected separation that often mars black-Asian relations in the United States, the affinity between Chinese and Jewish communities occurs in a much more comfortable historical space. Yet that comfort does not prevent Chinese-Jewish border crossings from seeming comic, and thus the very impulse to laugh hints at expectations of difference that lie below the surface of these seemingly compatible ethnic identities. To create alliances under these conditions, therefore, immediately challenges the expectations manufactured by mainstream American discourse.

The comedy of the novel arises through its playful manipulation of the pluralist paradox of culture, in which (in the phrase of Michaels quoted earlier) "we are not Jews because we do Jewish things, we do Jewish things because we are Jewish." Mona first exemplifies the absurd potential latent in this position. Before her friends' ethnic revival of Judaism, Mona makes a place for herself in middle school as an exotic curiosity who invents a comical "Chinese" identity to impress her classmates. On a whim, she tells her friend Barbara that she knows karate; Barbara is duly impressed, having witnessed a karate demonstration on television the night before. "That's when Mona recalls that she too saw it on TV last night, in fact at Barbara's house. She rushes on to tell Barbara she knows how to get pregnant with tea" (*M*, 5). Mona's wonderfully inventive set of fabulations, based on her very small foundation of cultural capital (her Chinese is limited to the Shanghai dialect for "stop acting crazy," "soy sauce," and "rice gruel"), remind us that Mona's "Chineseness" can never be understood as an uncomplicated inheritance or an unproblematically authentic identity. Mona believes she needs to do Chinese things because she is Chinese, undaunted by the fact that she has little idea of what such Chinese things might be.

Ironically, when Mona turns to Judaism, she finds herself unwittingly engaging with a deeper idea of what it means to be Chinese in America.

> [The members of the Jewish youth groups] talk about what it means to be Jewish, which so far as they've been able to tell mostly seems to be about remembering that you are. . . . Mona tries to imagine what it would be like to forget she's Chinese, which is easy and hard. It is easy because by her lonesome she in fact often does. Out in the world of other people, though, Mona has people like Miss Feeble [a teacher who asks her naïve questions about her ethnicity] to keep the subject shiny. So here's the question: Does the fact that Mona remembers all too well who she is make her more Jewish than, say, Barbara Gugelstein?
>
> (*M*, 32)

Jen anchors the comedy of this passage around the contradiction between what is meant by self and other. Is it the content of remembrance or the act of remembering that makes one Jewish? As the passage implies that supposedly given identities like Judaism need continual work to remain alive, it reveals the fissures within the idea of the self as a known and familiar construct. While the Jewish youths seek to recapture a lost sense of community, Mona finds a paradigm that rewrites her experience of everyday soft racism into a constructive form of spiritual belonging. The familiar turns out to be foreign, while the foreign is after all familiar.

Here, the logic of Jen's approach to identity becomes something more like "we do Jewish things because we are Chinese." Mona's youthful Rabbi Horowitz reminds Mona that truly turning Jewish is not an escape from being Chinese but instead a deepening of it. "*The more Jewish you become, the more Chinese you'll be*," she remembers him saying (*M*, 190, italics in the original). Mona wonders "why it is that now that she's Jewish, she feels like more of a Chinese than ever" (*M*, 66). The novel suggests that this process is not simply a version of the mirror argument, in which an ostensible performance of border crossing collapses into a projection of displaced selfhood. Mona is "doing Jewish things," often with more facility than her Jewish friends, and the novel invites us to hold together both the inherited and the performative aspects of identity in a way that is both pluralist (in the sense that the novel does not invite us to think of being Chinese as better or worse than being Jewish) but also twists the pluralist logic (we do Jewish things because we are Chinese). In Jen's literary world, both forms of identity exist simultaneously in a crowded self; in some sense, Mona is not Chinese until she becomes Jewish.

This vision resonates with Jen's own description of her own location as an author. Although Jen claims that the events in the novel are not autobiographical in a literal sense, she credits her development as a writer with her own affinities with Judaism. "There's a way in which the book is more true than the truth. The culture to which I assimilated was predominantly Jewish, and there are many parts of me that I feel to be fundamental to who I am that come from that culture," Jen says. "For instance, the writer part. . . . Since I assimilated into this culture that greatly esteemed voice, and writing, and fiction in particular, I became a writer."[49] Much as Jen does not describe a contradiction between what is her own and what belongs to a supposedly different culture, Jen's portrait of Mona offers a vision of a crowded self in which self and other blur distinctions between them. The crowding of ethnic and religious identities expands the borders of Mona's identity, allowing both Chinese and Jewish identities to flourish at once.

This ongoing practice of imagining others while reimagining the self occurs even more dramatically through Mona's relationship with her friend Sherman, a Japanese exchange student who spends a year in her town. As eighth graders, Mona and Sherman are first thrown together in school because they fit into the 1960s category of "Oriental," even though their actual cultural backgrounds are very different. Called upon to establish this connection, Mona tries out her only words of Chinese on her new classmate: " '*Ji-nu*,' she says. '*Shee-veh*' " (*M*, 10). Sherman, not surprisingly, does not comprehend the Shanghai dialect for soy sauce and rice gruel, and as it turns out, he understands relatively little English as well. Despite the bankruptcy of their shared identity as "Oriental," however, Mona is elated by the idea of being with someone who is supposedly like her. As she takes it upon herself to teach Sherman English and American cultural conventions, their relationship begins to fill the gaps between their histories as Chinese and Japanese in their new shared environment of America. If Mona's Jewish friends are presumed to be unlike her but turn out to be not altogether different, Sherman embodies the opposite relationship between perception and reality. To generate connections with Sherman, Mona must break down not only the language barrier between them but also the intense historical animosities between Chinese and Japanese subjects. Her mother, scarred by the violence of Japanese brutality during World War II, evicts Sherman from the house after he draws a Japanese flag on a napkin. Talking to Sherman makes Mona feel that she pursues a natural connection with someone like her, while in reality she arduously creates a relationship with someone very different.

In high school, when she mans a temple hotline, Mona begins to receive phone calls from a person who identifies himself as Sherman. The phone calls continue over several years, and the novel keeps us, like Mona, in suspense over the real identity of the caller. Is it truly Sherman, now living in Hawaii and traveling across America, or is it Mona's classmate Andy Kaplan playing an elongated practical joke? Just when we think that surely the caller is Andy, Mona is approached by a Japanese student who identifies himself as Sherman. It is with real surprise, then, that we discover that the original caller is in fact Andy, who ultimately passes on the phone identity of "Sherman" to Seth, Mona's Jewish ex-boyfriend. Being "Sherman" allows Seth to speak with Mona after the end of their relationship, and it raises again the apparent and deceptive discrepancy between the familiar and the foreign. In transforming "Sherman" into Seth, the novel plays with these social borders that continually turn presupposed others into familiar figures. If turning Jewish makes Mona more Chinese, trying to be "Oriental" with "Sherman" ironically reaffirms Mona's ties with another Jewish person. As the novel shows how difference can never be easily mapped onto social borders like ethnicity, it plays a dizzyingly comic game in which outsiders turn into insiders who then metamorphose into outsiders. Since the line between self and other is never stable, reconceptualizing the self is not just the necessary ethical counterpart to imagining the other: it actually becomes the same activity.

What kinds of narrative choices allow Jen to navigate this world of shifting borders between self and other? *Mona in the Promised Land* mingles together the tactics of Jen's characters with Jen's own representational choices, showing how both author and characters struggle to conceptualize others across moving, illusory, and unexpected social borders. These crossings confuse given and chosen cultural practices, asserting a space for the pleasures of cultural fantasy while also insisting on an openness to the unexpected topsy-turviness of imagining alterity.

The novel articulates its view of an ethics of border crossing through the linked metaphors of "switching" and "flipping." Mona first encounters the question of conceptualizing a different cultural identity through Sherman, who asks the thirteen-year-old Mona to marry him on his last day in America. "*How can I be Japanese?*" Mona asks him. "*Like you become American. Switch,*" Sherman tells her (*M*, 19, italics in the original). Mona has tried to persuade Sherman that changing one's cultural identity is merely a matter of "switching," of making a conscious decision to become someone new. But Sherman has different ideas about how change occurs. Without warning, "he flipped her. Two swift moves, and she went sprawling through the late afternoon, a flailing confusion of soft human parts such as had no idea where the ground was" (*M*, 21). As Sherman temporarily shatters Mona's confidence, the language of the passage literally breaks up

Mona's identity by momentarily transforming her into "a flailing confusion of soft human parts."

The novel suggests that performative border crossing is as indebted to the "flip" as it is to the "switch": its ethical impulse requires allowing others to disturb Mona's own comfortable sense of herself. Being flipped means exposing oneself to the gaze of another, making oneself vulnerable, and having the resilience to pick oneself up and carry on. These metaphors modify Werner Sollors's influential models of "descent" and "consent," in which "descent language emphasizes our position as heirs, our hereditary qualities, liabilities, and entitlements" and "consent language stresses our abilities as mature free agents to choose our spouses, our destinies, and our political systems."[50] While "switch" clearly resonates with "consent," "flip" suggests the importance of imposed culture beyond the language of hereditary "descent." Being flipped asserts a sense of surprise missing in the supposedly known worlds of descent and the supposedly desired worlds of consent. Jen's comedy relies precisely on this new combination of switch and flip to reverse conventional expectations about established ethnic identity.

Such comic flipping acquires new force through the telephone calls that proliferate in the novel, which allow characters to expand into crowded selves exclusively through language. When the Jewish boys Andy and Seth pretend to be Sherman, or when Mona impersonates her older sister Callie after running away from home, Jen's characters use the disembodied space of the telephone call to try out new possible identities. As the characters have only words with which to inhabit the lives of other people, their predicament mimics the condition of the novel itself. As Andy, Seth, and Mona all adopt the perspectives of others on the phone, the novel shows how these temporary moments of impersonation dramatize the metafictional project of border-crossing fiction. Unlike impersonations that seek to repress or submerge one's own experience within the life of another, these performances rely on the active interplay between actor and character. As we will see, these moments do not offer positivist conceptualizations of others—in fact, these representations are often heavily indebted to stereotype and cultural cliché. But the novel suggests that it is not in avoiding stereotype but in its parodic dismantling that emancipatory representation begins to emerge. When characters think they are switching but suddenly find themselves flipped, they explode the stereotypes—and implicitly the pluralist idea of culture—they often initially inhabit.

This process emerges most clearly when Seth explains to Mona why Andy Kaplan began, and then ceased, his impersonations of Sherman. "I think he liked the challenge of it. You know how his father is a Japan expert and everything," Seth speculates. Andy stopped, Seth says, because "he worried it was mean. Also it was getting too weird. It was weird how much he liked having an alter ego. And the secrecy. He said the secrecy had a life of its own" (M, 276). As Andy's invented phone persona takes on a significance beyond the original prank, Andy finds himself flipped by the increasing substance of his new verbal identity. Even though the content of his "Sherman" is a curious blend of Andy's erratic knowledge of Japan and the stereotype of an inscrutably poetic Japanese sensibility, this collage of confining representations paradoxically enables a significant intimacy between Mona and the voice on the phone. The novel thus flips the constraints of codified cultural representation into open and disorienting possibilities.

This crack within the stereotype enables the comic paradox of switching and flipping that propels the novel's signature reversals. Mona's mother Helen offers a vivid glimpse of this logic when her older daughter Callie expresses her contempt for a nice Chinese roommate at Harvard; Callie disdains a roommate who would surely spend all her time studying. "To which Helen managed to answer both 'Not everyone Chinese studies all the time, that's *stereotype*' and 'It would be good for you to study all the time with your roommate. Study together is nice'" (M, 37, italics in the original). Such a comic paradox defines many of the figures in the novel, who recognize the problems in particular cultural constructs even as they enthusiastically employ them. Seth too inhabits this contradiction in his role as "Sherman":

Seth says he's been reading about Japan, and culture, and Zen, even though Sherman as Seth understood him was more a guy than a monk. He says it's only American hippies who think that everyone in Japan is a Zen master. And maybe the real Sherman sleeps on a bed, who knows? Still, by way of getting into his part, Seth has been sleeping on a futon . . . it hasn't been easy trying to learn to cherish a certain exquisite melancholy. However, through all of this, he's begun to feel, actually, sort of Japanese. Or at least, that the Japanese manner corresponds to something in him.

(M, 278)

Like Helen, who defines an ideal Chineseness both against and through stereotype, Seth takes a similar approach to his conceptualization of Japanese identity. His clear pleasure in his new cultural exploration, coupled with his admission that "it hasn't been easy," asserts a place for aesthetic curiosity even as the humor of the passage punctures his pretensions.[51] The comedy of the scene models the making of a crowded self in Seth's embrace of exoticism and his simultaneous questioning of it.[52] Lest we think that Seth is simply barging into someone else's culture and making himself too much at home, Jen pairs this moment of revelation with a new change in behavior on Seth's part. When he stands on the threshold of Callie's college dorm room, where Mona is camping out, Mona notices a distinct difference in his approach. "Now he stands square in the doorway without laying claim to it. This is so unlike Seth that for a moment Mona cannot imagine what he is waiting for. What is he, shy? But no: He is simply waiting, patiently, for an invitation to enter" (M, 275). Seth as Sherman is actually becoming a different person; in stepping uninvited into the persona of a Japanese-turned-Hawaiian boy, he paradoxically becomes more circumspect about the act of inviting himself into the lives of others.

But of course Jen cannot let the joke end here. When Mona invites him to come inside, she invites him into Callie's space, not her own. No authentic place of cultural ownership remains, only Mona's provisional bedroom in the public living room of her sister's suite, where Seth and Mona crowd together in Callie's bed. Even Callie's space is itself a mimicry of Mona's room in Scarshill, thus continuing the dizzying question of what is really one's own. As two voices on the phone (Seth as Sherman, Mona as Callie) now delightfully embodied together in a single location, the novel suggests that their performances finally enable a literal and metaphoric reconciliation. By allowing themselves to see and be seen, or hear and be heard, through different eyes and ears, they find a new and ultimately durable union with each other. Their embrace of significant otherness models the "un-p.c." but not "anti-p.c." aesthetic of Jen's representational ethics. As they accept the laughter of others and learn to laugh at their own performances of border crossing, the novel creates new conditions of possibility for engaging social difference.

Yet we might well wonder what the real stakes of this love affair are: why should the playful escapades of two affluent American teenagers be taken as an emblem for a new ethics of border crossing? *Mona in the Promised Land* seems to wonder this as well, for the novel takes pains to incorporate the critique of a character who challenges the elitism that (perhaps necessarily, given her protagonist) characterizes Jen's central vision. Alfred, an African American cook who formerly worked for Mona's parents, looks askance at Mona's conversion to Judaism and challenges the idea of true ethnic choice. "'Jewish?' says Alfred, peering down. 'You expect me to believe that? Uh uh. Not until you grow your nose, baby.'" Alfred reminds her that some forms of performative border crossings may not be easy or even possible: "'And nobody is calling us Wasp, man, and nobody is forgetting we're a minority'" (*M*, 136, 137). As part of a subplot that focuses on the employment discrimination of Mona's parents, who initially prefer to promote Chinese employees over black ones, Alfred seems to figure the limitations rather than the flexibilities of ethnic and class identities. Yet even here, the novel suggests that the project of surmounting social difference is one that also matters to someone in Alfred's position. Given his sensitivity to the racial hierarchies that constrain such crossing, it becomes especially important that Alfred eventually builds a multiracial life of his own. In the end, Alfred ultimately marries Evie, a cousin of Mona's Jewish friend Barbara. While Alfred and Evie's early tumultuous courtship founders on the rocks of race and class, they eventually transform into "the love bugs, Mr. and Mrs. Community Organization. They've marched, they've cooked, they've given up denying that she married him to assuage her own guilt, or that he's a white-bitch-lover who shouldn't have needed her to get him through college" (*M*, 297). As Alfred and Evie surrender to the mocking gaze of each other, their community, and the novel itself, they burst forth as creative and generous crowded selves whose embrace of significant otherness thrives within the energy of laughter. The novel even contemplates placing them before the gaze of a larger audience: "Everyone's expecting the Knickerbocker clan to be made into a TV show" (*M*, 297). As they embrace these mocking critiques, Alfred and Evie assert themselves through comic reversals of their own inhabited stereotypes. As with Mona and Seth, Alfred and Evie make a sustainable life with each other only when they embrace the gaze of sympathetic mockery.

When Jen's characters reconcile with each other through these performative border crossings, their paths suggest one of the larger claims of Jen's novel: reaching out to others ultimately enables sympathy for those close by as well. As part of the novel's breakdown of difference, it shows that the further one moves to grapple with an unfamiliar world, the more sympathetic one might become to those close by. While *Mona in the Promised Land* offers a comedy to its readers, it also documents the great disappointment of Mona's life in her growing estrangement from her mother. Although Helen actively practices a life that blends together many different kinds of cultural identities, she resents Mona's growing commitment to Judaism and her challenge to Helen and Ralph's racial hierarchies. When Mona finally decides to run away from home, she finds herself sitting on a bench in Grand Central Station with no clear plans about where to go. Suddenly, she finds the foot of a homeless woman falling in her lap. "But so removed is Mona from her everyday ways that she finds a strange small comfort in this contact. And so she takes the lady in: oldish, the color of cherry bark, evidently asleep. Short matted hair. One might surmise her zip dress no longer zips, for she is wearing safety pins all down her front. . . . [Mona] clasps her hands on the lady's slim ankles, and holds on" (*M*, 255–256). Both offering the woman a secure place to rest and drawing comfort from her as well, Mona reaches out in a sympathetic gesture to a stranger. But the novel makes clear that in doing so, she is metaphorically reaching out to Helen. When Mona finally returns home, hopeful of a reconciliation with her mother, Helen appears at the top of the stairs in clothing that recalls the homeless woman in the train station. "Even though it is daytime, Helen is wearing her old quilted bathrobe, which features squarish diamond buttons. These look as if they were designed to light night games at Yankee Stadium. As three of them are missing, however, Helen is using safety pins in their stead. Mona shudders. Helen looks as though she has just woken up" (*M*, 294). Stitched together by the image of their safety pins, Jen's representations of the homeless woman and Helen entwine the familiar and the foreign. Holding the ankles of an unknown woman allows Mona to work toward a connection with her mother, showing how an ethical gesture toward a stranger transfigures what is considered one's own world. As these two scenes painfully reveal, the real alterity exists not between Mona and the stranger in Grand Central but between Mona and Helen. An ethics of border crossing may be most needed not only across what seem like clear social divides but also where they are least expected: in the world of what is ostensibly familiar.

In the end, as in the beginning, the comedy of the novel flips the boundaries between given and chosen, self and other, and familiar and foreign. The final ethical task of *Mona in the Promised Land* enacts a reconciliation between Helen and Mona, whose years of alienation reflect a divide more entrenched in the novel than any border between Chinese and Jewish ethnic practices. In order to reconnect mother and daughter, the novel implies that Mona and Helen must surrender themselves to the gaze of others. Living a sustainable life requires vulnerability in the eyes of a witness, and thus accepting being laughed at offers the best hope for robust performative identities. At the novel's very end, when Helen finally ends her long estrangement from Mona at Mona's wedding to Seth, their emotional homecoming transpires through the innocent gaze of Mona's young daughter Io. As Mona and Helen embrace in tears, as if they are the ones declaring their lifelong commitment before a crowd, Io looks up at her mother and grandmother "and like a fine little witness, claps" (*M*, 304). This ultimate moment of homecoming, an embrace of significant otherness between mother and daughter, becomes the final performance of border crossing in the novel.

Throughout their fiction, Charles Johnson and Gish Jen figure the possibility of an ethics of border crossing through such comic performance. Embracing the discourses of others, even in ways that may initially appear stereotypical or problematic, can enable real change across shifting ethnic and religious borders of culture. "The biggest, maybe the only advantage in being a stereotype is that you have the ability to continually surprise, to upturn audience expectation," argues Meera Syal.[53] As Johnson and Jen turn to a wide repertoire of comic strategies to unsettle the idea of fixed cultural practices, they envision ongoing ethical connections among ethnic minorities and peoples of color. These forms of outreach enhance the vitality of ethnic communities, so that, in the words of an epigraph to *Mona in the Promised Land*, "dispersion leads in turn to accumulation."

Johnson's and Jen's narrative choices, paired with the decisions of their characters, model images of possibility under conditions of moderately severe social borders. They both address worlds in which the divide between black and Asian communities, or Chinese and Jewish ones, can be considered either rigid or invisible, and they transform that instability of perception into the foundation of their comedy. As Johnson's novels work to reverse the rhetorical signatures of Orientalism, his fiction implies that this task does not require avoiding stereotypes or replacing them with sanitized positive imagery. Instead, both Johnson and Jen use comic techniques to unsettle the rhetorics of constraint and upend them from the inside. In this respect, they share an ethos with other writers at the turn of the millennium, for whom, in Rebecca Walkowitz's formulation, "correctness does not constitute an ethical model for antiracist or multicultural literature."[54] Conceptualizing others, in this context, requires coming to terms with the narratives that have governed their representation.

Sometimes this work strains at the edges of what the comic may be able to offer. Readers familiar with Johnson's work will note that I have not discussed *Oxherding Tale* as a comedy of *slavery*, an aspect of the novel that has deeply troubled many of Johnson's readers, and it remains an open question if the comic distancing of Johnson's crowded style can adequately deal with the specters of real violence represented in its pages. Jen, for her own part, compels us to ask if comedy really is the best way to represent the performance of border crossing. When Mona, expecting to see Sherman at last, encounters Seth on her threshold, the free indirect discourse of the passage turns her shock into an interrogation of the novel: "This is supposed to be some kind of comedy?" (*M*, 277). When Mona finally accepts that her life is part of a comedy, that Seth actually is her long-lost love reunited under improbable circumstances, she embraces the idea of being laughed at as the condition for a growing crowded self.

With no correct representation above laughter and absurdity, both Johnson and Jen suggest that the best ethical choice is to accept that laughter and learn to gently mock one's own desires to engage alterity. In that subversive yet sympathetic laughter, crowded selves and styles may flourish. The novels of Johnson and Jen identify ethical possibilities in the cultural pleasures of the ethnically crowded self and style, which envision new relationships between given and chosen cultural modes of identity. As the playfulness of their novels disturbs ethnic stereotypes and pluralist logics of cultural identity, Johnson and Jen show how imaginative border crossing replenishes rather than diminishes the energy of American ethnic communities. "Writing well the lived experience of the racial Other," or engaging with the practices of others, enables writing well the lived experience of the self.

4

Middle Grounds

How to imagine others who may not always wish to be imagined? In the works of Ozeki, Johnson, and Jen, resistance to the representation of social difference remains relatively limited. Ozeki figures a world where subjects willingly and often eagerly consent to be imagined; Johnson and Jen undermine the idea of consent by mocking the concepts of mastery and correctness that often inspire resistance to border crossing. In this chapter, I turn to two novels, one by the Greek American writer Jeffrey Eugenides and the other by the Indian novelist Rupa Bajwa, which extend the project of imagining alterity by beginning to account for the role of possible resistance. As the project of imagining across borders becomes more difficult to its practitioners, these novels turn to tragicomic forms of narration that flourish in formal, philosophical, and social middle grounds. Although their narrative choices complicate the relatively optimistic visions found in the fiction of Ozeki, Johnson, and Jen, they refrain from the radical sacrifices that will mark the work of Ghosh and Coetzee. As the novels of Eugenides and Bajwa confront intensified visions of alterity, they begin to lay a greater emphasis on the need for a critical consciousness of power and privilege. Although my earlier chapters suggest the need for relatively low levels of vulnerability, exemplified by Jen's metaphor of the flip, *Middle Grounds* identifies the increasing imperative for subjects to inhabit unprotected and ambiguous positions as they seek to surmount social borders. The crowded self, in other words, begins to give up more and more room to the needs of others.

Rather than emphasizing sentimental or comic forms of fiction, these novels investigate the middle grounds of the tragicomic novel and its philosophical and practical ambivalence toward the possibility of border crossing. This ambivalent approach to significant otherness characterizes such novels as Jamaica Kincaid's *Lucy* (1990), which offers an astringent critique of liberal paternalism and American feminism but nonetheless reveals a deep longing for love and intimacy across borders of race and gender. Caryl Phillips negotiates this tension in *Crossing the River* (1993) and *A Distant Shore* (2003), counterpointing transnational histories of violence and atrocity with accounts of growing personal intimacy between black and white outsiders from different ethnic and national cultures. Deeply comic and painful by turns, Arundhati Roy's *The God of Small Things* (1997) shows how a playful language of unity shared by a set of twins splinters apart through its encounter with the cruelties of caste violence in southern India. Looking back to the making of Black Britain in World War II and its aftermath, Andrea Levy's *Small Island* (2004) charts the construction of a crowded self through liberal gestures but ultimately testifies to the inadequacy of tolerant individualism in a world that forestalls an interracial social imaginary. In short, these novels place increasing weight on the constraints of inequitable histories and oppressive systems. As such novels struggle with the promises and pitfalls of liberal accounts of border crossing, they locate their ethics of representation in their philosophical and stylistic negotiation of this ambivalence.

Working within such terrain, Eugenides and Bajwa bring a new dimension to bear by anchoring their concern with significant otherness in the problem of crossing gender. I begin this chapter by asking in what ways we might understand borders of gender as analogous to the borders of national, ethnic, and religious practices that animate the work of Ozeki, Johnson, and Jen. I then turn to explore Jeffrey Eugenides' novel *Middlesex* (2002), which figures its middle grounds in the discursive space between constraining ideas of gender identity. *Middlesex*, a boisterous, Ovidian epic of the Greek diaspora, speaks from the first-person voice of a narrator who is "born twice: first as a baby girl . . . and then again, as a teenage boy."[1] Because the narrator shares the perspectives of both males and females but also finds himself alienated from them, his "middlesex" generates a crowded self that speaks from a position both authoritative and precarious. Even as Eugenides' representation of his narrator expands our vision of what it means to be an "I," it unsettles familiar constructions of resemblance and difference. Championing ambiguity in the gender of a narrative voice, the novel ultimately produces its crowded style through a textual middle ground between the representational violence associated with postmodern skepticism, on the one hand, and with essentialist certainty, on the other. My chapter then moves to address Rupa Bajwa's intimate novel of urban Indian life, *The Sari Shop* (2004), which despite its very different social terrain comes to offer a surprisingly similar portrait of ethical potential. Whereas Eugenides figures his middle ground by navigating competing theories of language and identity, Bajwa complements his project by exploring the meaning of middle grounds in social and material terms. As Bajwa charts the imaginative development of a sari shop assistant, the novel identifies the potential latent in the assistant's lower-middle-class position between excessive power and excessive vulnerability. While figures of authority or abjection commit new forms of representational violence, Bajwa's sari shop assistant uses his intermediate class position to develop a crowded self that expands to include the perspectives of the diverse women around him. The rhetorical choices of the novel mimic his capacity for engaging significant otherness, offering a crowded style that similarly navigates between privilege and sacrifice. Showing how gender boundaries are inscribed by competing theories of knowledge and by competing socioeconomic positions, both novels push against the forms of representational violence they associate with rigid perspectives on social identity. Their ethics of representing gender differences combat discursive domination by accepting both the pleasures and the perils of imagining across borders.

Speaking Across Gender

Since both Eugenides and Bajwa focus attention on the problem of crossing gender, they invite us to inquire how this project constitutes a form of border-crossing fiction. Can gender really be considered a social border comparable to nationality, ethnicity, or language? Although no one would wish to claim that gender works in exactly the same manner as other social markers, I suggest that the similarities among them may be as important to acknowledge as the differences. As Eugenides' inter-sex narrator Cal Stephanides would have us believe, life on the frontiers of sexual identity can mirror the experience of those in national or eth-nic borderlands. Layering a narrative of sexual transformation onto a plot of immigration, Eugenides' novel insists upon the parallels be-tween Cal's Greek grandparents fleeing from Turkey to America and Cal's migration from his girlhood into his adult masculinity.[2] Watching the work of a Turkish bread baker in Berlin, Cal muses on the similari-ties between the complications of ethnic, national, and gendered cross-ings: "An artist of bread baking. Stephanides, an American, grandchild of Greeks, admires this Turkish immigrant to Germany, this *Gastarbe-iter*, as he bakes bread on Hauptstrasse here in the year 2001. We're all made up of many parts, other halves. Not just me" (*M*, 440). Like these descriptions of other kinds of identity, gender provides a vocabulary for social divisions that can never be accepted as simply natural, even (or especially) when they claim such self-evident status. As an immigrant to the culture of masculinity, Cal, like the baker, finds himself both of and apart from his new world, where the distinctions between given and chosen identity become difficult to maintain.

As Cal's homology suggests, gendered identity frequently provides socially recognized ways of sorting individuals into groups and affects the amount and kind of power available to those individuals. Because of such tangible and intangible social effects, gender poses representa-tional challenges that parallel the roadblocks presented by other kinds of social borders. In twentieth-century feminist analyses of cultural imagery, the theoretical insights of feminist critiques often resonate with, and even replicate, the defining principles of Orientalist or primi-tivist perception. In the 1970s, many feminist critics argued that since men have frequently enjoyed more social power than women in many parts of the world, male representations frequently fail to offer trust-worthy guides for thinking about women. Although few scholars believe that such power exerts the same force or character in every place and time, many readers have looked warily upon androcentric representations that seem to legitimate unequal power relations among the sexes. Like imperialist novels about the colonized, male representations of women are thought to reveal more about the social anxieties and aspirations of the male writers themselves than about the female subjects on the page. Judith Fetterly, writing at the end of second-wave feminism, encapsulates the power of this view when she argues that literature "insists on its universality at the same time that it defines that universality in specifically male terms."[3] Such constraints not only mar representations on the page but also constitute the very conditions of possibility for reading. "To read the canon of what is currently considered classic American literature is perforce to identify as male," Fetterly contends (PL, 564). Such gendered cross-voicing provides a variant on what I have been calling the mirror argument, in which encounters with otherness conceal a form of veiled literary narcissism. Even adamant defenders of male representations of women such as Wendy Lesser fundamentally present this process as a self-oriented one. In valorizing "the search for one's lost half, and the perception and understanding of divisions within the self," Lesser identifies one ultimate goal of such art as a deepened purchase on the artist's own masculine identity.[4] This defense can be thought to confirm the suspicions of more skeptical feminist readers: male representations of women ultimately serve to benefit the subject rather than the objects of representation. Although these second-generation feminist concerns with reflection theory have been undermined by feminist and queer perspectives in the 1980s and 1990s, which contest the increasingly tenuous idea of a stable and unitary self that can be accurately reflected on the page, they have not yet been fully replaced by new models of representational ethics. Even as poststructuralist critics have exposed textual instabilities to recuperate works that might, on the surface, seem like exemplars of constraint, they tend to valorize a work's oppositional or negative tendencies over its possibilities for ethical perception of significant otherness. The epistemological and ethical challenge of gender, abstracted through this critique, remains affiliated with the challenge of the mirror argument.

At the turn of the new millennium, feminist theorists such as Sara Ahmed have begun to call for new ways of thinking about gender that do not simply confirm the theoretical impossibility or the ethical inadequacy of representing social difference. In the spirit of such inquiry, this chapter explores engagements with alterity that work toward cross-gendered representation. To confront the moderately severe social borders presented in their novels, Eugenides and Bajwa gesture toward the need to avoid extremes of certainty and control. Knowing too much or too little, or speaking from positions of too much or too little power, impede the act of conceptualizing the lives of others as visualized in their pages. As these middle grounds provide tragicomic alternatives to the mirror theories of aesthetic narcissism, they offer new possibilities for gendered crowded selves and styles.

Jeffrey Eugenides' Middlesex *Poetics*

A novelist of Greek American heritage, Jeffrey Eugenides came to fame in 1993 as the author of *The Virgin Suicides* and won the Pulitzer Prize for his second novel, *Middlesex*, in 2002. Raised in Detroit, where large parts of his novels are set, Eugenides embraces the tradition of Saul Bellow and Philip Roth as he probes the makings of an increasingly multicultural American landscape. Set in the rich and turbulent world of the Greek diaspora in Turkey and America, *Middlesex* tells the story of a girl who grows up to be a man. Known to us in childhood as Callie, then eventually as Cal, the narrative voice of Eugenides' novel asks us to think about gender as a metaphorically rich borderland that maps the diversity of human life. In choosing to represent a complicated and contested sexual identity not often found in realist fiction, Eugenides calls attention to the problem of authorial and individual gender crossing through the dramatic conceit of his writing.

As a structuring principle of the novel, Cal continually navigates the cognitive and ethical difficulties of envisioning, and being envisioned by, gendered lives unlike his own. Since few characters in *Middlesex* share his particular sexual identity, Cal constantly grapples with the barriers of social difference, yet Cal's particular sexual identity as both a girl and a man paradoxically proffers a source of shared experience and identification. The governing ethos of *Middlesex* insists that the bewilderments of hermaphrodism mirror the confusions of identity that multitudes confront in daily life. While Cal's story challenges conventions of representation in an unusual way, his convoluted map of sexual identity also shares much with changing ideas of gender in modern

American life.[5] "People hear that *Middlesex* is told by a hermaphrodite, and sometimes that repels them from reading it," Eugenides claims. "But I see it as a family story. I used a hermaphrodite not to tell the story of a freak or someone unlike the rest of us but as a correlative for sexual confusion and the confusion of identity that everyone goes through in adolescence."[6]

For Eugenides, the metaphor of Cal's hermaphrodism speaks directly to the metafictional predicament of the modern novelist. "With *Middlesex*, after a certain amount of trial and error, I came up with a narrative point of view that could do anything," Eugenides claims. "And I did want to use a hermaphrodite as the narrator. It seemed to me that a novelist has to have a hermaphroditic imagination, since you should be able to go into the heads of men and women if you want to write books."[7] This link between sexuality and authorship implicates Eugenides in the literary history of androgyny, popularized in English literature in the late nineteenth and early twentieth centuries. Perhaps the most celebrated moment of this cultural fascination with unified gender appears in Virginia Woolf's *A Room of One's Own* (1929), where she famously describes a man and a woman entering a taxi as a metaphor for artistic wholeness: "Perhaps to think, as I had been thinking these two days, of one sex as distinct from the other is an effort. It interferes with the unity of the mind. Now that effort had ceased and that unity had been restored by seeing two people come together and get into a taxi-cab."[8] Ending her indictment of gendered hierarchies with a vision of integration, Woolf yearns for a form of forward and progressive motion that dissolves the chasm between imaginative practice and social experience.

Eugenides inherits this optimism about the aesthetic benefits of crossing gender (and *Middlesex* builds upon the gender-switching legacy of Woolf's *Orlando* [1928]). But his work also revises the significance of multigendered imagination. Rather than emphasizing a harmonious "unity of mind," Eugenides asks us to recognize the active dissonance between different conceptions of what gendered identity entails. His choice of the rhetoric "hermaphrodite" emphasizes the contact zone between genders that "Hermes" and "Aphrodite" suggest. (Despite evident familiarity with the modern political identity of "intersex," Eugenides does not use such rhetoric when speaking of his work.) Although, in Ovid's *Metamorphoses*, Hermaphroditus's name precedes his transformation into a bisexual being, it comes to signify an appropriate mingling of anatomies and identities. In claiming the language of hermaphrodism, Eugenides chooses to maintain the image of border crossing (and Greek heritage) that the word connotes. Unlike earlier theories of androgynous imagination, which envision abstract syntheses of male and female, Eugenides' vision of hermaphrodism retains its sensitivity to the way power and desire shadow the complicated geographic terrain of gender. Cal not only offers the promise of access to many different kinds of experience but also provides cogent thoughts on the cultural assumptions and structural divisions that shape the changing maps of sexuality. The very process of Cal's crossing from female to male, which occurs during a trip across America, provides a metaphor for the long and active journey of border-crossing fiction. Unlike Virginia Woolf's *Orlando*, who wakes up one morning with an entirely new gender, Cal illuminates the vulnerability, pain, and sacrifice of gender crossing even as he demonstrates its possible liberation.

Because the portrait of Cal reflects an act of authorial gender crossing on Eugenides' part, Eugenides stresses the importance of Cal as an "I" rather than a "he" or a "she." To evade the constraints of representational violence and to allow more freedom to the subjects being imagined, *Middlesex* counterbalances its interest in gender as a force shaping identity with an insistence that the individual exceeds such definitions of sexual identity. Thus, only sentences after Cal tells us that he was born once as a girl and again as a man, he gives us this definition of who he considers himself to be:

> I'm a former field hockey goalie, long-standing member of the Save-the-Manatee Foundation, rare attendant at the Greek Orthodox liturgy, and, for most of my adult life, an employee of the U.S. State Department. Like Tiresias, I was first one thing and then the other. I've been ridiculed by classmates, guinea-pigged by doctors, palpated by specialists, and researched by the March of Dimes.
>
> (*M*, 3)

As Cal presents a self that appears crowded with heterogeneous experiences and perspectives, what clearer reminder could Eugenides provide that identity exceeds given social categories, even flexible ones? Kwame Anthony Appiah provides a similar catalogue when he encourages us to remember that we are "teachers, lawyers, autoworkers, and gardeners; fans of the Padres and the Bruins; amateurs of grunge rock and lovers of Wagner; movie buffs, MTV-holics, and mystery readers."[9] As these vivid lists expand the range of ways in which individuals might perceive affiliations with one another, both do so by moving from abstract categories (gender, nationality) to detailed social practices (hockey goalie, mystery reader). As Cal makes it clear that his "I" is larger than his gender, he reminds us that the expansiveness of the crowded self is something that the detailed world of the novel is particularly well suited to show us.

These nuances reinforce the novelist's truism that the most specific and unique descriptions of daily life speak most powerfully to diverse readers. As Eugenides' strategy affords characters like Cal the opportunity to speak outside the category of gender, it breaks down social differences by finding commonalities in details. The significance of these details is not located in the possibility of shared identification; surely Eugenides does not expect a significant proportion of his readership to actually be members of the Save-the-Manatee Foundation or even to know what it is. Instead, the rhetorical force of these descriptions asserts the particularity of identity. These markers cannot be fully subsumed within an abstract category; longstanding membership in the Save-the-Manatee Foundation does not simply collapse into an general signifier for liberal, environmentalist, and upper-middle-class status. It is precisely Cal's resolute irreducibility that makes him credible and sympathetic to his readership. While clearly a reader who grows up in a part of the world that plays field hockey will interpret Cal's self-definition differently from someone unfamiliar with the game, both readers should be able to appreciate the difference between these relatively thick descriptions and the clinical view of Cal as a stripped self, a medical curiosity "on page 578, standing naked beside a height chart with a black box covering my eyes" (M, 3). This contrast invites us to recognize the ways in which social difference does not stop at conventional categories; in Amy Hungerford's formulation, "particularity goes all the way down."[10]

This expansively confused and confusing particular self thus complicates the concept of what alterity might actually be. In terms of gender, is Cal both, neither, either, all? Since every character in the novel in some sense is like Cal and yet simultaneously unlike him as well, Cal disturbs and reaffirms gender norms at the same time.[11] Unlike other characters in the novel who dress in drag or celebrate the political possibilities of identifying as intersex, Cal ends the novel as a man whose life, on the surface, resembles other heterosexual men in his social circle. "Something you should understand: I'm not androgynous in the least," he reminds us (*M*, 41). At the same time, he claims, "I remain in essential ways Tessie's daughter. I'm still the one who remembers to call her every Sunday" (*M*, 520). Watching the streetwalkers in Germany, Cal tells us that "my feelings toward them were not a man's. I was aware of a good girl's reproachfulness and disdain, along with a perceptible, physical empathy" (*M*, 307). Embedded in conventional American social roles for both male and female, while at the same time not quite of them, Cal constantly performs his crowded self through an enabling paradox: the concept of "others unlike him" is neither stable nor fixed. This flexibility emerges in his relationship with Julie Kikuchi, a heterosexual woman whom Cal sporadically pursues in Germany. Julie worries that Cal is a closeted gay man and she his "last stop," claiming that closeted gay men seek out Asian women for their boyish figures (*M*, 184). When Cal finally divulges his history to her and they embark on a romantic relationship, Cal says, "I might be your last stop, too. . . . Did you ever think of that?" In reply, Julie tells him, "It crossed my mind" (*M*, 514). Julie's answer reminds us that all the novel's characters, not simply Cal, live in constant states of border crossing. Cal's experience suggests that fissures in the word "unlike" provide new possibilities for imagining across constructions of social difference, gendered and beyond.

The novel furthers this breakdown between similarity and difference through its formal narrative choices, which emphasize the importance of ambiguity in the gender of Cal's speech. Through the texture and tone of Cal's voice, the novel engages with larger theoretical debates on the relationship between aesthetics and gender. The problem of writing across gender is not only a question of cultural imagery but also a problem of style and rhetoric. In historical terms, narrative practices identified as female have been defined as techniques that appear commonly in women's writing but not frequently in men's, as well as forms of language that were culturally coded as feminine in the period when a particular work of literature was written.[12] Modern linguists such as Deborah Tannen argue that men and women use different rhetorical strategies of communication and thus metaphorically speak different languages.[13] In contrast to these historicist and linguistic arguments, which might be seen to convey a form of essentialism, post-structuralist theories have articulated masculine, feminine, or gender-based writing in theoretical rather than historical terms. In such readings, feminine writing is understood as language that reflects values associated with the theorists' understanding of the feminine: multivocal polyphony, open endings, visceral language, uncontainable rhetoric, and egalitarian impulses have all been considered such textual markers. Many of the examples given for these gendered effects have little to no relation to the socially experienced gender of the writer. Hélène Cixous's "The Laugh of the Medusa" (1975), for instance, famously hails James Joyce as a practitioner of *l'ecriture feminine* for his avant-garde narrative experiments in *Ulysses* (1922).[14] Yet, liberating as these readings can be, these patterns can also come to afford sophisticated stereotypes of gender that themselves call out for dismantling.

Middlesex challenges both of these aesthetic paradigms not by eschewing them but by transforming them into a crowded style of unique formal synthesis. Scholars of narrative discourse have argued that gender crossing in *Middlesex* transpires through the style of Cal's address, which draws upon differing markers of gender. Building upon her association between direct address and femininity in the novel, Robyn Warhol claims that "Cal periodically addresses his 'patient reader' directly, assuming a sympathy between narrator and narratee that operates to encourage the actual reader to identify with the figure of the narratee. In this respect, Cal performs as a feminine narrator at the same time that he is a male character."[15] Indeed, some of Cal's direct addresses seem designed to mimic famous signatures of nineteenth-century women writers. After Cal's tragicomic account of adolescent sex with a boy who fails to notice the unusual anatomy of his partner, Cal tells us, "Reader, believe this if you can: he hadn't noticed a thing" (*M*, 376). It is impossible to read this line without hearing an echo of Charlotte Bronte's famous "Reader, I married him" from the end of *Jane Eyre* (1847). Yet, even as Eugenides echoes Bronte's discourse, he also reverses and inverts its significance. Cal's line ends a chapter, whereas

Bronte's begins one; Cal's confession marks not the beginning of a marriage but his last sexual romance with a boy. In twisting as well as invoking the gendered conventions of direct address, Cal offers himself as a nineteenth-century female narrator while subverting the stable associations of such a position. This ambiguous linguistic ground serves as one vision of the novel's crowded style.

The novel does not present all middle grounds as equally emancipatory, suggesting that its balancing acts between essentialism and poststructuralism require attention to power and vulnerability. *Middlesex* illustrates the potential dangers of synthesizing essentialist and postmodern conceptions without such reflection through the spectacular failure of a medical practitioner, Dr. Luce. Given the vexed history of complicity between medical establishments and disciplinary ideas of the body, it should be no surprise that Luce dehumanizes Callie as he probes her anatomy and her inner life. Yet Luce is not simply a figure for repressive and paternalistic medicine; he also embodies specific ideas about literary discourse, representation, and identity. When Callie visits Luce, the doctor attempts to decipher her rhetoric much as literary critics might analyze characters in a novel. Scrutinizing Callie's manner of speech in psychological interviews, Luce listens for what he perceives as gendered clues: "Women prefer the anecdotal, men the deductive. It was impossible to be in Luce's line of work without falling back on such stereotypes. He knew their limitations. But they were clinically useful" (*M*, 417). While Luce's knowing use of stereotypes might be put to ethically productive purpose in a different context (as we saw in chapter 3), it serves as a form of discursive domination in a situation marked by large asymmetries in power: an authoritative adult doctor interrogating a vulnerable adolescent patient whose gender identity is unclear.

As Luce's parody of strategic essentialism links together the extremes of postmodern and essentialist ideas of gender, *Middlesex* suggests that rigid versions of either position lead to failures of sympathetic identification and thus to failures of representational ethics. Since Luce believes that the identifiable sex of rearing is more important than the ambiguous sex of anatomy, his perspective aligns him with social constructionists who argue that gender is fundamentally a social performance. As a scholar, Luce persuades his field that "gender was like a native tongue; it didn't exist before birth but was imprinted in the brain during childhood, never disappearing. Children learned to speak Male or Female the way they learn to speak English or French" (*M*, 411). Given the ambiguous form of narrative speech that characterizes Cal's voice in *Middlesex*, we might suspect that the novel distances itself from this point of view.

Despite this emphasis on gender as a social performance, Luce is also curiously dogmatic about his interpretations of gender. "Luce felt that parents weren't able to cope with an ambiguous gender assignment," Cal tells us. "You had to tell them if they had a boy or a girl" (*M*, 413). For Luce, language is literally a form of domination. Because Callie has been raised female, Luce defines her as such, even though medical tests reveal anatomical markers associated with men. This desire to specify a singular gender affiliates Luce with essentialism, even though he believes that this essence is found in social behavior rather than in the body. This particular combination emerges as a nefarious force in the novel, inspiring Luce to mislead Callie about her condition and the consequences of medical treatment to make her more like a girl. As Callie discovers when she stumbles across Luce's private medical reports, corrective surgery would effectively diminish her capacity for sexual pleasure and her ability to inhabit her body as a man. Luce's report judges what Callie would want in her future life, presuming that "the ability to marry and pass as a normal woman in society are also important goals" (*M*, 437). The sinister combination of postmodern performance and essentialist singularity, given authority through medical institutions, constitutes a repressive regulation of Callie as an embodied and aesthetic subject. Indeed, Luce's enthusiasm for intrusive surgery might be seen as an apt metaphor for invasive imagination.

Luce's failure speaks to the novel's larger critique of positivist methodology, showing how such methods mystify the very experiences they seek to explain. In his practice, Luce observes and measures Callie's body, asks her direct questions about her childhood experiences and sexual desires, and articulates a view of her life as best he can based on what he presumes to be medical facts. But his methodology also relies upon invasive psychological manipulation. After showing Callie a pornographic video, Luce asks her if she prefers the man or the woman. "'The pool boy? That's good. I dig the pizza girl myself. She's got a great bod. . . . She's got incredible tits,' he said. 'You like her tits? Do they turn you on?'" (*M*, 419). As Luce tries to communicate with Callie, he offers his own uninhibited preference in an attempt to make her feel comfortable discussing sexual desire. At the same time, he performs the stereotype of the male locker-room friend to see if Callie responds positively to this form of crude confessional, as he presumes a boy would do. Yet because this confessional is a calculated performance rather than a genuine moment of vulnerability, Callie lies to him out of confusion and discomfort. Concealing her desire for girls, Callie effectively performs a heterosexual feminine identity for Luce that corroborates his thesis that the sex of rearing matters more than the sex of the body.

Luce fails to understand that his form of measurement is hardly objective; his persona *produces* the Callie he then records. In writing and fictionalizing her autobiography for Luce, Callie tells us that "I also knew that I was writing for an audience—Dr. Luce—and that if I seemed normal enough, he might send me back home" (*M*, 418). In order to find a clearer view of Callie's inner life, Luce needs not positivist measurements but better sympathetic perception of Callie's desires. In short, his method lacks the self-awareness and vulnerability needed to acknowledge her resistance to his probing gaze. As he mingles postmodernist with essentialist beliefs in a way that represses the subject before him, the novel suggests that the certainties of his ideological commitments prevent him from perceiving the complexities of Callie's situation. Luce thus offers a parody and a perversion of *Middlesex*'s own narrative choices.

In contrast to Luce, who models a reductive combination of social construction and biological essentialism, *Middlesex* navigates a very different path between these two claims to knowledge.[16] As the novel suggests the importance of biological borders at the same time that it emphasizes the role of social performance, it embraces identity as a generous middle ground of multiplicity and even contradiction. As a girl who grows into a man, Cal chooses to match his social performance to his changing bodily impulses, rather than the other way around. In defending the importance of bodily voice and physical pleasure, the novel insists upon the salience of borders generated by anatomy. Cal cannot simply abandon signs of male maturation without serious psychological and physiological costs. Yet even at the moment when Callie transforms into Cal, we find that becoming a man requires more than an uncomplicated decision to heed the voice of the body. Embodiment offers an insufficient guarantee of gender or sexual identity, so Cal must perform his newfound masculinity in order to legitimate his claim to male anatomy. "To walk like a boy you let your shoulders sway, not your hips. And you kept your feet farther apart. All this I had learned in a day and a half on the road," the newly redefined Cal says of his engagement with the significant otherness he is making his own (*M*, 441). As Eugenides navigates between extreme versions of social constructionism and biological essence, the novel implies that the creation of crowded selves and crowded styles requires a middle ground between these two forms of representation.

Cal's flexible view of identity allows for resistance, hesitation, and uncertainty in its openness to the power of different kinds of gendered knowledge. Near the end of the novel, Eugenides offers an apt emblem of this accommodating form: on the verge of a sexual relationship, Cal and Julie leap together into a shared bed in a dark room. Generous toward Julie's reluctance and toward Cal's own resistance to being seen, the novel offers the cover of darkness to invite engagement with otherness without the glaring positivist light of the examining room. Linking the desires of the body with the performance of sexual identity, this moment gestures toward the ambiguous middle grounds inhabited by their crowded selves.

Such a middle space of accommodation further characterizes the formal style of Eugenides' novel. While *Middlesex* continually calls attention to its own making in classic postmodern fashion, it also refuses the strong social constructionism of postmodern philosophy in its willingness to entertain biological models for literature. Nodding to the genome that distinguishes Cal's gendered life, Eugenides shapes the form of the novel to echo the development of Western literature. "Since it's about genetics, I thought the book should be a novelistic genome; that is, it should contain some of the oldest traits of writing and storytelling," Eugenides says.[17] As a result of this decision, Cal's early narrative voice oscillates between a modern realist narrator (the forty-one year old cultural attaché at the U.S. embassy in Berlin) and an exultant Homeric bard. "Sing now, O Muse, of the recessive mutation on my fifth chromosome!" this voice boldly declaims (*M*, 4). Avoiding strong prior commitments to any particular literary style, *Middlesex* generously makes room for many forms of literary expression. Like the ambiguous gender of narration that characterizes Cal's voice, this middle voice displays a crowded style through its changing emphasis on social and biological models of writing.

As the novel debates whether gender is biologically or socially constituted, *Middlesex* rejects the hypothesis that gender is purely social but nonetheless asserts that biological borders can and must be imaginatively crossed. Indeed, Cal appears to *gain* the ability to inhabit the minds of women when he becomes a man: "Callie couldn't imagine the things [her mother] was seeing in her dreams back then. But I can," Cal tells us confidently (*M*, 422). The vision encouraged by the first-person narrative's crowded self lets Cal flourish in the wide borderland geography of gender rather than forcing him to abandon his male body or his feminine childhood.

Between Authority and Abjection: Rupa Bajwa's The Sari Shop

At first glance, the Indian novelist Rupa Bajwa presents us with a very different vision of what it means to cross borders of gender. While *Middlesex* is a vast and sprawling epic novel that plays with exaggerated modes of literary style, Bajwa's debut novel *The Sari Shop* (2004) provides an intimate and restrained account that mingles social satire with tragic drama in a much more muted manner. Whereas Eugenides' novel explores the makings of modern immigrant America, Bajwa's fiction dramatizes the vicissitudes of life in lower-middle-class urban India. A native of Amritsar, in which *The Sari Shop* is set, Bajwa eschews the grand transnational narratives that have often characterized South Asian writing in English at the turn of the millennium, and unlike Eugenides, whose work often bears the marks of immersion in cultural theory, Bajwa rejects attempts to affiliate her work with explicit theoretical paradigms. However, despite these differences, Bajwa resembles Eugenides in envisioning a compromise that both incorporates and challenges the ideals of liberal humanism. For Eugenides, this challenge occurs at the intersection of debates about knowledge and gender formation. Bajwa, instead, directs our attention to a different set of debates, which locate the problem of crossing gender within the complex matrix of social class. If Eugenides asserts ambiguous and accommodating claims to knowledge, Bajwa extends these claims into the middle grounds of social life between privilege and marginality.

As the novel offers an increasingly metafictional set of meditations on the ethics of engaging significant otherness, it invites us to inquire into the relationship between male and female projects of cross voicing. Because women writers have frequently been accorded lower levels of social capital than their male counterparts, female representations of male figures have more often been read as acts of empowerment rather than as modes of discursive domination. Although female authors have been chastised for replicating male fantasies or capitulating to plots that overdetermine the fates of women, their work has provoked markedly lower levels of anxiety about the theoretical problem of conceptualizing others. If critical concern about representation is greatest when the subject enjoys more social power than the object, it should be no surprise that women's writing provokes the most skepticism about female cross voicing when it transgresses borders of race, class, or sexual orientation.[18] Bajwa's novel intervenes in this debate by suggesting an alternative to the mirror argument of adequate imaginative perception that continues to inform cultural criticism.

This alternative emerges through the novel's commitment to a middle ground that is specifically class oriented. Ramchand, an assistant at an Amritsar sari shop, enters the novel as a member of the urban lower middle class. He thus inhabits a position of limited economic opportunities, one exacerbated by his lack of familial social structures to support him. Rita Felski contends in her analysis of the lower middle class that its amalgamation of "the traditional petite bourgeoisie of shop owners, small businesspeople, and farmers and the 'new' lower middle class of salaried employees such as clerical workers, technicians, and secretaries" often signifies a repressive cultural landscape of shame, joylessness, and conservatism.[19] Although Felski's analysis draws primarily on twentieth-century British class structures, her description resonates with the new economic order of twenty-first-century urban Amritsar as it appears in Bajwa's novel. Lacking both the elite's easy intimacy with high culture and the working class's unabashed bodily pleasures, the lower middle class, in Felski's terms, "does not generate an identity politics."[20]

More than simply being *from* the lower middle class, Ramchand provides a figure *for* it. As a passive character whose desires remain inchoate even to himself, he embodies the very absences that preclude the emergence of identity politics. "He wasn't articulate enough, that was the problem," Ramchand thinks to himself. "He knew it. Look at other people, look at how clearly they spoke. . . . And *his* own thoughts—they always fanned out, spiralled upwards and downwards unintelligibly, rolled themselves up into random curls, chased their own tails and came to nothing."[21] Ramchand's invisibility to himself mirrors the lacuna of his class identity, leaving him only with the one clear desire that marks lower-middle-class affiliation—the desire to escape. Yet if such a position has been culturally overdetermined as a space fit only to leave, *The Sari Shop* rewrites the indeterminacy of the lower middle class into a position of ethical possibility. Although the novel is careful to show that such a malleable space is also susceptible to the predations of national chauvinism and patriarchal privilege, Ramchand's trajectory reveals the possibility latent in such an invisible middle ground. Ramchand's increasing identification with women of different social classes simultaneously engages significant otherness and makes him more visible to himself. Read allegorically, the novel suggests that the act of identifying across borders of gender and class can revive a sense of ethical purpose for a lower-middle-class location in a post–identity politics era.

As a mediating voice between the privileged certainty of an upper-class woman and the abject anger of a woman living in poverty, Ramchand dramatizes how a crowded self might develop across varying fields of gendered power. When Ramchand develops increasingly vivid images of these two disparate women who compel his imagination, the novel suggests that his capacity to engage significant otherness reflects his middle position between excessive power and excessive vulnerability. This middle ground resonates with the social location that defines classical views of spectatorship, a position that exemplifies Ramchand's role as witness (he first appears in the novel watching a street scene unfold below his window). In her work on tragic emotions, Martha Nussbaum describes an Aristotelian understanding of the kind of spectatorship that plays out in Bajwa's novel:

> If you believe that you are so badly off that nothing further could happen to you to make things worse, you will not be likely to be capable of pity for others because you will be looking at their plight from the very bottom, from the point of view of one whose sufferings are complete. On the other hand, if you believe yourself self-sufficient *vis-à-vis eudaimonia*, secure in your posses-

sion of the good life, you will suppose that what happens to others cannot possibly happen to you.[22]

Bajwa's novel identifies this space of susceptibility as an important starting point for the practice of engaging significant otherness. Although not everyone in this middle ground will necessarily feel pity in the classical sense, I suggest that the novel identifies imaginative failures in the poles that Nussbaum describes. *The Sari Shop* thus reveals how the techniques of the novel draw upon the workings of tragedy, but it links this theatrical structure to the less elevated world of middle-class life that novels traditionally claim as their primary social territory. Connecting problems of sympathy to the conditions of consumption and class that form the fault lines of urban life, *The Sari Shop* thus offers a different approach to the tragicomic genre that complements the synthesis found in *Middlesex*.

As the main theater of the novel, the Sevak Sari House initially stands out for its lack of sympathetic engagement with the lives of others. The novel presents the shop as a cultural location where middle-class women *escape* domestic roles that ask them to place the concerns of others above their own desires, thus turning the setting into a fantasy of female assertion. This dominance of female power defines the architecture of the sari shop, which relegates men's clothing to the floor beneath the level that houses the rich collection of saris. "The suiting and shirting cut-pieces in the ground floor cowered under the sparkling, confident dazzle above" (*SS*, 6). Through its economic structure, the sari shop allows women to act as consumers not simply of clothing but also of social power. Although not all of the customers become tyrannical visitors, the organization of the shop encourages them to abandon sympathy for the shop assistants who serve them. Because the stock is shelved in spaces that only the shop assistants can access, the process of attending to a customer requires the labor-intensive act of continually unfolding and refolding saris for women to evaluate. The organizational format of the Sevak Sari House thus reflects the economic reality, common under postcolonial urban conditions, that labor is cheaper than the extra space needed to display the merchandise for customer access. When women abandon sympathy for shop assistants in the novel, they are not simply indulging in a personal inclination to revel in the power of condescension and contempt; they are actively encouraged to do so by the very structure of commercial activity. It is significant that although Sevak Sari House sells mostly clothes for women, all of the shop assistants are male. Part of the attraction of shopping, the novel suggests, lies in the opportunity for middle-class women to deny sympathy specifically to men (possibly in compensation for their vividly dramatized deference toward husbands and sons). Although many of these women prove perfectly capable of denying sympathy to other women as well, the assistant Ramchand's servile role in the shop underscores the reversals in gender power relations that shopping for saris affords.

Within such a theater of social power, the novel suggests that Ramchand's very passivity ironically enables him to move toward a more robust ethical form of imagining social difference. In the shop, expected to be attentive but invisible to the customers, Ramchand hones the observational skills that turn the sari shop into a space of ongoing drama. The shop trains his eye, teaching him not about distinctions in fabric but about gradations of human behavior. "Though women were otherwise strange, alien creatures to him, there was one part of them that he knew intimately—the way they chose saris" (SS, 63). Saris educate his imagination, providing the lens through which Ramchand develops an astonishing psychological acuity about people he considers "strange" and "alien." When young women come to the shop with relatives to buy saris for their wedding trousseau, Ramchand recognizes the "quiet nervous excitement" of the happy ones and the signs of more ambivalent brides: "Ramchand had also seen such girls look into the mirror with melancholic eyes, as if the *sari* was quite all right, it was the idea of this particular marriage that wasn't so happy. This happened rarely, but when it did, it would tug terribly at Ramchand's heart, though he would later tell himself that it must have been his imagination" (SS, 64, italics in original). The novel pauses over the irony of his last word, for Ramchand's "imagination" is of course presented as his strength, not his weakness.

As Ramchand is forced to look beyond the architectural familiarity of the sari shop, his capacity for sympathetic engagement gains the chance to develop more fully. When he delivers saris to the house of one of the city's wealthiest families, he enters a world of social opulence completely unlike his minimalist life in a spartan rented room. Overhearing the conversations of Rina Kapoor, the daughter of a rich industrialist, Ramchand first begins to conceptualize a world of hitherto unimaginable privilege and plenty. The escape from the sari shop invigorates his sense of self:

> The world was big, after all. He had just got into a rut—shop, room, shop, room, shop, room . . .
>
> Once you got out of that rut, it was easy to see that there were endless possibilities in the world. There were the hills where the Kapoors' servant boy had come from, there were mountain streams on those hills that were as clear as the boy's voice. There was the swimming pool that Tina frequented—maybe it was like the one in *Baazigar*, with blue tiles and a board to dive from, at the edge of which Shilpa Shetty had writhed during a song, wearing a backless blouse and a thin yellow chiffon sari. There was the college where Mrs. Sachdeva taught, there were the books that were written and read by many, there were cars and flowerpots and frosted glass trays with peacocks on them.
>
> (SS, 70, ellipses in the original)

This catalogue of possibilities, drawn from Ramchand's more extended meditations, affords a glimpse into his newly inspired optic on the world around him. His visions of significant otherness encompass a wide range of social classes, they reach out to the geographies of the natural world and the exclusive social spaces of privilege, and they blend the transparencies of film with the hidden worlds of written language. His growing crowded self views material objects not only for their role as status symbols but also for their ability to promise a defamiliarized aesthetic experience. Such a rare excursion inspires Ramchand to embark on an ambitious course of self-improvement. Entering Rina's world, for Ramchand, casts expanded imagination as an ascent in power that maps onto the trajectory of class mobility.

In coupling Ramchand's ventures into the lives of other people with this desire to change his own existence, the novel dramatizes the characteristic of representational ethics that links imagining others with a renewed conception of the self. After hearing the Kapoors communicate with each other in English, Ramchand decides that improving his English reading skills will afford him the expansive life he suddenly intuits. Learning to read English represents a significant step in shaping what he believes will be a fuller and more intentional life, and the novel suggests that Ramchand's imagination flourishes through this embrace of written language. At first, struggling through collections of dated letters in which young British women cheerfully propose motor tours in the English countryside, Ramchand invites the reader to lament the effort he expends engaging with a hopelessly outdated image of a colonial center. But, as Ramchand's English gradually improves, English does eventually transform into a language that opens up new opportunities. When Ramchand buys a child's scientific book from the bookseller, he delights in learning how the world works, and his pleasure in the text pushes at the limits of his everyday life. In taking up the study of English, Ramchand mirrors Rina's own intellectual aspirations, and his sympathy with her turns into a form of active imitation. Although this project follows predictable lines of social aspiration, the novel invests this mimicry with a new sense of ethical possibility.

If sympathy with Rina reflects an ascent in social class, Ramchand also finds himself called to sympathize with those more vulnerable than he. Over time, he enters the life of another shop assistant's wife, a troubled and angry woman named Kamla who endures terrible mistreatment and complicates her situation with self-destructive violence. Kamla's fate takes Ramchand into the underworld of the city, where women are beaten, raped, and treated as disposable objects. Abandoned by her family, abused by her husband, poorly served by medical establishments, and angry at the exploitative behavior of wealthy Amritsar employers, Kamla expresses her rage through her growing alcoholism and public displays of uncontrolled invective. This behavior enrages her husband and earns the disapproval of the other shop assistants, but Ramchand finds himself preoccupied by the plight of this angry, abused woman. Although entering Rina's world inspires Ramchand's confidence in the project of self-improvement, his capacity for sympathy also leads him downward toward self-annihilation.

In choosing to sympathize with her destructive misery, Ramchand begins to question the protective privileges of his own masculinity. After Kamla is brutally raped by the police as punishment for harassing a middle-class family, Ramchand finds himself overwhelmed by the testimony of her drunken, broken body. This encounter with significant otherness provides a space in which Ramchand surrenders the privileges of masculinity and makes himself vulnerable to the face of another: "The room was getting hotter and Ramchand was completely drenched in sweat. But he still sat there, knowing nothing but that he should not leave, that he was needed here. A dread was building up inside him. . . . It was like travelling into darkness and reaching the heart of it. Ramchand's mind went blank" (SS, 182). As Bajwa's language reaches back into the Conradian rhetoric of darkness, the novel implies that sympathy across borders of gender resembles the journey into strangeness that defines Conrad's novel. Whereas Ramchand's sympathy with Rina reflects his identification with her aspiration to better her life, identifying with Kamla offers no such optimistic connection between different parts of the crowded self. Instead, Kamla's situation reveals the need to recognize this abject and uncontrollable world of physical and emotional violence that eludes conventionally liberal conceptions of community. It demands that Ramchand, sitting with her in the "tomb-like atmosphere" (SS, 182), confront the specter of death, violation, and loss. The novel underscores an ethically charged moment in the instant of Kamla's gaze, in which Ramchand surrenders the privilege associated with a man viewing a woman's body.

> Her eyes were like dark, twin tunnels that led nowhere.
>
> Ramchand recoiled from her gaze.
>
> But he couldn't look away. Something in her face held him there on the spot, squatting silently. . . .
>
> Then her dead eyes blazed at him. She drew up her upper lip in a snarl, like an animal. Ramchand watched in horror. And suddenly she did erupt with an angry snarl. "*Help*? You want to *help* me?"
>
> (SS, 182–183, italics in original)

Bajwa's brief, punctuated paragraphs, designed in melodramatic fashion to heighten the emotional intensity of the encounter, emphasize the vulnerability inherent in meeting Kamla's eyes. The novel suggests that this moment of intense vulnerability offers an alternative to the gaze that simply mirrors the face of the onlooker. Even though no practical solution emerges from this vision of Ramchand's crowded self, the novel suggests the ethical value of his passive vulnerability through its materialist critique of Kamla's predicament. In submitting to the power of Kamla's stare, Ramchand implicitly puts himself in her position; he allows her to enact her rage upon him without defending himself from the misery of her anger. As Ramchand gradually realizes that Kamla is bleeding from the aftermath of rape, he begins to question his complicity in the structure that leads to her abjection. "Was it her blood that was wetting his hand. . . . He held up his hand before him" (*SS*, 184–185). As the scene literalizes the cliché of having blood on one's hands, this encounter suggests that Ramchand not only imagines himself in Kamla's position but that he also confronts his own metaphorical guilt in placing here there. This dual acknowledgement enables Ramchand to embrace his frailty as well as to admit the culpability of his male privilege, and his very fear bespeaks not voyeuristic horror at Kamla's condition but horror at his own place in a world marked by gendered violence. This sympathy that "leads nowhere" traps Ramchand in a world beyond remedy, where his only solution is to flee the scene of Kamla's misery. As his crowded self encompasses Kamla's anger, it becomes a far from comfortable space.

Whereas sympathy with Rina leads to a program of class mobility and self-improvement, sympathy with Kamla leads Ramchand down a path of frustration, failed communication, and inchoate anger: a journey into the "nowhere" of Kamla's life. Ramchand begins to mimic Kamla's capacity for anger and resistance that first tries to attack appropriate targets but then turns violently on the self. When Ramchand takes the bold move of confiding Kamla's plight to the college professor Mrs. Sachdeva, he finds himself rebuffed. "'I don't want to listen to all that vulgar rubbish again, that too in Hindi. Why are you bothering *me* about all this? It is no concern of mine,'" Mrs. Sachdeva says (*SS*, 214, italics in original). Although Mrs. Sachdeva actually is intimately linked to one source of the problem (her friends are the businessmen who laid off Kamla's husband without fairly paying back wages, thus throwing the couple into financial straits and sending them on their downward spiral), her rejection—couched in her class dismissal of Hindi as a nonelite language—eventually helps to turn Ramchand into another version of Kamla. After Kamla is brutally beaten and killed by the police, Ramchand finds himself filled with the inchoate combination of rage and impotence that distinguishes her as a character. Trapped in a nightmarish world of darkness and hallucinatory dreams, Ramchand returns to the sari shop to wreak violence on the men and the systems he has always unquestionably accepted as sources of authority. As in Kamla's case, Ramchand's protest fails to effect recognizable social change. Both of their protests are seen as madness, as inappropriate and inauspicious demonstrations of violence against seemingly innocent targets.

Through such actions, Ramchand's engagement with the significant otherness of gender comes to exceed the spectatorship that initially impels it. Adequate imaginative projection, in some sense, means that he momentarily shares the life of the women with whom he identifies. His sense of self provides a crowded space where different possible identities collide with one another, thus altering the contours of Ramchand's own subjectivity. In discovering shared emotional impulses with Rina and Kamla, and in mimicking their social behavior, Ramchand shows how crossing lines of gender asks him to negotiate many different forms of power. Although few readers will be surprised to witness Ramchand mimicking Rina's upper-class lifestyle, we *are* surprised to watch him reject this class ascent through sympathy with Kamla, and the force of the novel's critique of class- and gender-based exploitation emerges from this mimicry of abjection. Ramchand demonstrates that sympathy can be a dangerous practice, one that leads both to self-knowledge and to self-destruction. The novel suggests that it is Ramchand's willingness to make himself vulnerable, to expose his inner self to a wide range of threatening gazes, that makes his own return gaze an exemplar of imagining alterity.

If Ramchand seems to demonstrate the power of conceptualizing others across gender, he is in turn imagined by these women in a much less ethically productive way. The women of the novel possess either too much authority, or too little, to sympathize adequately with others in the terms that the novel puts forth. After Ramchand invites himself to Rina Kapoor's wedding, Rina suddenly seems to become aware of Ramchand's existence as a person rather than as one of the many nameless servants and vendors who populate her life. When she visits the sari shop alone a few days after her wedding, her visit is less to buy saris than to learn about Ramchand's life. However, Bajwa shows from the beginning that Rina's interest in Ramchand is very different from Ramchand's interest in Rina. Her gaze is one that asserts authority rather than openness to the unexpected: "She smiled without any reason, she looked as though she knew something about him, a secret about him, that he did not know himself" (SS, 134). Ramchand begins to suspect that he is an incomplete self when viewed through her eyes, and her penetrating questions unnerve him: "It was the first time that a woman was asking him such personal things, and that too such a magnificent woman, and it flustered him completely" (SS, 135). As Bajwa stresses the difference in class status between them, she reveals Rina's refusal to recognize Ramchand's desire not to be represented. The novel itself, in contrast, reports very little of their extended conversation, and thus *The Sari Shop* pairs its own reticence against Rina's invasive intrusion.

Rina wants to know Ramchand because she wants to put him in a novel, and her story—published midway through *The Sari Shop*—provides a counternarrative to the novel in which it resides. It soon becomes clear that *The Sari Shop* encourages us to think critically about Rina's literary endeavor: "The novel was the story of a shop assistant in a sari shop. The protagonist was called Sitaram. He was a funny guy, superstitious, clever and lovable. The other characters in the book were a sadhu who performed miracles, a mad dog and a middle-aged woman who was a kleptomaniac" (SS, 187). Although Bajwa writes that "it was a well-crafted book" (SS, 187), Rina's portrait of Sitaram seems almost unrecognizable as a portrait of Ramchand. The conventions of her story turn the mordant and inchoate Ramchand into the comic character of Sitaram, retaining only the awkwardness that characterizes both portraits. The specificity of Ramchand's lower-middle-class position, and its implication in larger patterns of exploitation and corruption, vanish into the classless world of dogs, sadhus, and middle-aged kleptomaniacs. Rina gives Sitaram a love interest in "a beautiful village girl" (SS, 187) whom he wins with the help of the old sadhu. These plot details seem only to intensify the irony of Rina's vision: Ramchand is far removed from any romance plot in his own life, content to worship his landlady from afar without any hope of fulfilling his desire. These discrepancies would not be troubling if the only similarity between the two characters were their occupations, but Rina seems to think that her portrait does reflect the real Ramchand. "She had even gone to see him, to speak to him, so that she could give a real identity to her sudden inspiration" (SS, 186–187). This emphasis on "a real identity" invites us to consider Rina's claims to imaginative projection.

The Sari Shop suggests that the problem with Rina's novel is not that it differs from the portrait of Ramchand; in other words, the problem is not one of positivist representation. Instead, it is a problem of inequitable power. As Bajwa's vision of urban anomie transforms into Rina's portrait of comic pastoralism, this particular turn to the comic reinforces the hierarchies that separate Rina and Ramchand in the first place. Rina is consistently amused by Ramchand: "how she had laughed with Tina about [Ramchand's desire to attend her wedding]" (SS, 186). Just as Rina shows "an amused smile" (SS, 129) when Ramchand arrives uninvited at her wedding or when she interviews him in the sari shop, her entire novel seems to train such a mocking gaze on the "slightly ridiculous but endearing" Sitaram (SS, 187). Although comedy, as we saw in chapter 3, can offer a powerful source for an ethics of border crossing, Rina's laughter does not exploit this potential opening. Neither Ramchand nor Sitaram are allowed to be anything to Rina but a source of laughter that reinforces her sense of social superiority.

If Ramchand's expanded crowded self opens him to women, even leading him to mimic their lives in a form of unwitting identification, Rina retreats to the reverse tactic of extreme self-protection. The love interest in her story bears some resemblance to herself, as the details of the novel show: the character is beautiful, with "almond-shaped, kohl-lined eyes" and "jasmine flowers in her hair" (SS, 187). This portrait recalls Rina herself on her wedding day, when she confronts Ramchand in a room with "a heady smell of jasmine flowers" (SS, 129). But this portrait is deeply indebted to type, and the classical details of "almond-shaped, kohl-lined eyes" describe literary conventions more than they evoke individual women. Rather than exposing herself to the gaze of her public, Rina fills up the space where a self could be with a literary convention limited to poetic typology. Whereas Ramchand takes risks in engaging with women unlike him, Rina remains aloof and untouchable, constantly writing at a safe distance from her subjects.

Although its stated commentary about Rina's novel is reserved and even sometimes positive, *The Sari Shop* uses the power of juxtaposition to offer its strongest critique of Rina's approach. In the scene directly following the publication of Rina's novel, Ramchand abandons his own interest in reading English books. This renunciation reflects his sinking awareness of the discrepancy between euphemism and action, for after

Kamla's rape by the police, he cannot read English passages like "*a policeman is a very useful and important public servant*" (SS, 187, italics in original) without shuddering at the distance between public rhetoric and private suffering. English, for Ramchand, ultimately reveals itself as a form of discursive domination that mystifies social relations of power. The alignment of these two scenes invites us to meditate on the discrepancy between Sitaram and Ramchand. Rina's harmless fantasies come to seem like sinister forms of representational violence as great as the difference between policemen as useful public servants and policemen as rapists and murderers. Her use of English, rather than promising the allure of self-improvement, comes to seem the repressive embodiment of elitism itself. When Rina and her novel appear again in *The Sari Shop*, they only emerge in the conversation of Mrs. Sachdeva, who praises Rina's initiative while denying any compassion to Ramchand's story of Kamla. Rina's novel thus comes to be associated with a trenchant form of intellectual hypocrisy, in which middle-class women hope to keep the world safely distant through comfortable cultural fantasies about the lives of others.

Rina's work thus poses metafictional questions about the larger possibilities of Bajwa's novel and, by extension, about the larger possibilities of its readers' critical investment in conceptualizing social difference. If the novel invites us to be suspicious of literature that defends its own safety, *The Sari Shop* relinquishes its own claims to immunity through Ramchand's rejection of English. If we, like Ramchand, stop reading, the novel sacrifices the conditions of its own existence. This challenge to the language of the novel is particularly important given the status of English as a language of neoimperial class privilege in South Asia (a problem discussed in more detail in the next chapter). As readers, we are asked to abandon the security of our own purchase on English and to acknowledge the power of Ramchand's lower-middle-class engagement with the language. Although Ramchand's English is imperfect and incomplete, testifying to his lack of opportunity for extensive formal education, he nonetheless remains sensitive to the violence that can masquerade in foreign tongues. Although the voice of *The Sari Shop* is written in the idiom of one comfortable with English, its narrative of Ramchand's linguistic engagement and abandonment helps constitute a middle position between exalting the social privileges of English and sacrificing the language altogether. This metafictional element of the novel thus works toward its own crowded style.

In keeping with the novel's tragicomic ambivalence toward liberal narratives of progress, Ramchand's ethical development coincides with the material failure of his perceptual shift. Ramchand ultimately abandons his quest to find a voice, either through English or through anger, and the novel returns him to the depressed, quiet stasis with which the novel began. Sympathy alone does not change the structural conditions of daily life; in the world of the novel, it cannot offer robust and enduring social change. But when we experience this ending with a sense of diminishment, we mourn the imaginative engagements with significant otherness that flower and unfold throughout the pages of the novel. In this moment of loss, the novel reinforces its commitment to the ethical value of crossing borders.

Although *Middlesex* and *The Sari Shop* offer very different points of entry into the problem of gendered cross voicing, they both explore how crowded selves and crowded styles can emerge from middle spaces. Cal literally dwells within such a position, since the "Middlesex" of the title refers not only to the "middle sex" of his gender but also to the street name of his childhood home. This middling space emerges rhetorically as an ambiguously gendered form of narration, and it attests to the novel's productive compromise between poststructuralist and essentialist claims to knowledge. Ramchand, figuring this balance in class terms, occupies a mediating location between the extremes of privilege and poverty that Rina and Kamla inhabit. Ramchand's relative success in sympathetic imagination suggests that imagining across borders requires a delicate balance between power and vulnerability: Rina seems to have too much power; Kamla seems to have too little. Both privilege and anger make it difficult for these characters to engage ethically with the inner lives of those around them, and thus it is fitting that Ramchand, the character poised in the precarious center between them, should be the one best able to inhabit their views of the world.

This middle ground between different forms of knowledge and different levels of social power best confronts a world in which subjects begin to resist being represented by others, a world in which the promises of liberal humanism are not always evident. Cal and Ramchand both find themselves exposed to destabilizing gazes—Cal beneath the scrutiny of medical specialists and curious voyeurs, Ramchand through the terrifying stares of Rina and Kamla—and these moments of literal and metaphorical nakedness contribute to the formation of their crowded selves. But neither of them are asked to remain indefinitely within these positions of vulnerability, and in fact both novels imply that an excess of abjection can inhibit the growth of representational ethics. Their vision offers a precarious balance between extremes of identification, neither aggrandizing nor erasing the self in their tragicomic encounters with significant otherness.

5

Challenging Language

As novels confront what seem to be increasingly opaque social barriers, their narrative choices begin to require more radical aesthetic and textual sacrifices. In this chapter, I explore two works by the Indian writer Amitav Ghosh that address the barriers imposed by different kinds of language. Shifting from the emphases on national, ethnic, religious, and gendered borders that have preoccupied this book to date, I now turn to investigate social differences marked by linguistic alterity. Given the status of English as a language linked to discursive domination through imperial and neoimperial practice, how can postcolonial narratives told in English effectively reflect the nuances of translingual, multilingual, and even antilingual experience? Under such circumstances, I suggest that English may need to relinquish elements of its own aesthetic privilege in order to engage the significant otherness of different forms of expression.

To confront the linguistic alterity of the twentieth century's South and Southeast Asian diasporas, Ghosh's fiction offers new crowded styles of narration that engage the multilingual worlds his characters inhabit. I begin by situating Ghosh's work within debates about English within South Asian writing. I then consider how these debates inform *The Glass Palace* (2000), a historical-realist account of nineteenth- and twentieth-century Burma, India, and Malaysia. Unlike the stylistic tradition of such writers as Raja Rao and Salman Rushdie, where English erupts with a distinctively South Asian sound, Ghosh flattens his rhetoric in *The Glass Palace* to render it legible across different social spaces. Because he refrains from representing different dialects as sonically distinct forms of English, Ghosh works against a tradition of discursive domination by refusing to place the many languages of his characters into constraining hierarchies of standard and nonstandard English. The flattened aesthetic, in which most characters sound somewhat alike, produces a crowded style by requiring readers to imagine linguistic difference for themselves. Although it may seem paradoxical to think of such a flattened, seemingly homogenous style as "crowded," Ghosh's approach actually invites a wealth of different readerly interpretations that expand the representational power of his prose. This approach is strikingly different from the incorporation of linguistic alterity found in Charles Johnson's work, where Johnson flamboyantly encodes not-quite-Chinese characters and Asian discourses under conditions of heightened visibility. Ghosh chooses the opposite approach, instead valorizing the visual optic of photography, which viewers can engage no matter what language they speak. In playing with the sonic and vocal registers of language, the crowded style of Ghosh's fiction ultimately fosters the development of crowded selves.

I argue that Ghosh mounts an even stronger response to the problem of representing linguistic difference in *The Hungry Tide* (2004), where he articulates questions of border crossing through encounters between Indian-American and Bengali subjects. Although characters in this novel yearn for an idealized nonverbal language that mimics the world of nature, they ultimately commit themselves to strategies of communication that combine the immediacy of nonverbal gestures with the unreliable but necessary power of translation. The novel dramatizes the growth of their crowded selves as they emerge through such mixed forms of communication. Taken together, *The Glass Palace* and *The Hungry Tide* invite us to meditate on how the material texture of language enables encounters with significant otherness. As Ghosh's work seeks an ethics of representing multilingual and antilingual alterity, his resulting crowded styles diminish the aesthetic privileges of

English. These renunciations, I argue, paradoxically expand the ethical capacity for English to resist hegemonic and identitarian effects.

In choosing to present strong social borders that require new practices of textuality, Ghosh's work partakes in a larger trend of late twentieth- and early twenty-first-century fiction that experiments with the relationship between linguistic form and social difference. Keri Hulme's novel of Maori and New Zealand life, *The Bone People* (1983), asserts the importance of many kinds of language—including silence and visual art—in its vision of a multiethnic family in the making. Through its challenges to realist narrative structure, Achmat Dangor's *Kafka's Curse* (1997) addresses the paradoxical slipperiness and resilience of ethnic identity in a South African Muslim community. Prominent works that accentuate regional dialect and subculture vernaculars, such as Irvine Welsh's *Trainspotting* (1993), James Kelman's *How Late It Was, How Late* (1994), and Gautam Malkani's *Londonstani* (2006), all seek to renegotiate what counts as English in public culture. Compared to such novels, Ghosh's stylistic approach on the surface may seem markedly modest. However, the apparent conventionality of his historical-realist discourse in fact enables a powerful response to the problem of social difference, one that resonates with the pervasive ethical themes of his fiction. Read in light of debates on English as a South Asian language, Ghosh's narrative choices create surprisingly effective forms of linguistic border crossing.

Abandoning Sound: Amitav Ghosh's The Glass Palace

One of the preeminent writers of the Indian diaspora, Ghosh has chronicled social-border crossing in histories, novels, reportage, and essays for over twenty years. As the child of a diplomatic family, Ghosh spent his childhood in what was then East Pakistan, Sri Lanka, Iran, and India. Throughout his professional career on four continents, including time spent in India, England, North Africa, and the United States, he has illuminated the underexplored worlds of the Indian Ocean and their relationship to the West. Associated with subaltern as well as elite forms of border crossing, Ghosh's writing excavates the lives of those outside the reach of conventional histories.[1] His first novel, *A Circle of Reason* (1986), tells the fabulist story of a weaver who flees his home in Bengal to start a new life in the Middle East and North Africa. A parody of extreme Western rationality, the novel explores the different kinds of reason that emerge in the shifting worlds of refugees and exiles. This legacy of contact between the Indian subcontinent and the Middle East resurfaces in Ghosh's memoir and history *In an Antique Land* (1992), which details his experience as an anthropologist in a village in Egypt. Subtitled "History in the Guise of a Traveler's Tale," the book weaves Ghosh's own meditations within the history of a medieval Indian slave in the service of an Egyptian trader. Returning once again to the histories of non-Western contacts, Ghosh's science-fiction thriller *The Calcutta Chromosome* (1995) traces an Egyptian computer programmer's attempt to understand an Indian form of underground scientific research. His best-known novel, *The Shadow Lines* (1988), focuses on the metaphorical mirrors between India and England and between different parts of the severed subcontinent, exploring how the legacies of colonialism and Partition bind their subjects even more closely through the language of ostensible division.

With *The Glass Palace*, Ghosh relinquishes the intense introspections of *The Shadow Lines* for the sweeping canvas of historical epic. Telling the story of the Indian diaspora in Burma and Southeast Asia, the novel returns to the theme of non-Western contact that much of Ghosh's oeuvre painstakingly interprets. As *The Glass Palace* illuminates the wealth of intra-Asian migrations during the nineteenth and twentieth centuries, it recounts an alternative history of globalization. Through its plethora of family narratives, the novel explores the exile of the royal Burmese family under British colonialism, the rise of the comprador Indian community in Burma, the Chinese development of Malaya, the growth of Indian independence movements, and the effect of World War II on South and Southeast Asia. Although these worlds are deeply touched by the reach of Western colonial powers, the novel draws attention to the complicated crossroads of Indian, Burmese, Chinese, and Malayan circuits. Believing that the West (and in particular, the Enlightenment) has no monopoly on the invention of modernity, Ghosh envisions how a new global era emerges through the powerful Chinese and Indian diasporas of the late nineteenth and twentieth centuries.[2] As *The Glass Palace* illuminates transnational maritime communities shaped by trade and travel, it chronicles the fall of the region from a porous world of open borders to a realm divided by the forces of nationalism after World War II.[3] The desire to explore new worlds without imperial eyes emerges in Ghosh's novel as an ironic challenge to the colonial legacy that enables these new migrations.

As part of its preoccupation with these contradictory and ambivalent conditions of globalization, *The Glass Palace* searches for the appropriate language in which to produce its border-crossing fiction. Striving toward an ethics of multilingual representation, the prose style of the novel attempts to recognize the burden placed on how narratives can be told. For many parts of its journey through the past, the novel shares as much with historical writing as it does with fiction. Signaling its concern with historical storytelling, the title of the novel alludes to the nineteenth-century Burmese classic of history and fiction *The Glass Palace Chronicles* (1829). Widely versed in historical scholarship, Ghosh turns the primary quarrels of the novel into struggles against obscured or inaccurate histories of subcontinental and Southeast Asia.[4] Long-standing friends with the Indian historians who developed the Subaltern Studies group, Ghosh shares their concerns (if not always their methods) for increasingly democratic forms of history.[5] Whether recovering the forgotten story of four hundred thousand Indians expelled from Burma or exposing the racist brutalities of Malaysian rubber plantations, *The Glass Palace* intervenes in historical debates about the role of race in liberal philosophy, the possibility of native resistance, and the coercive as well as persuasive forms of empire. As part of its concern with historiography, the novel reveals its anxiety about the languages in which such forgotten histories should be told.

This preoccupation with the ethics of historical language became a matter of public debate and scrutiny when Ghosh refused to accept the Eurasia regional Commonwealth Prize for *The Glass Palace* in 2001. Though he was pleased that the prize committee had liked the book, he wrote in his letter rejecting the prize, the historical principles behind the very idea of a Commonwealth Prize reflect the traces of colonial power that *The Glass Palace* attempts to resist. In part, Ghosh objected to the criteria of the Commonwealth Prize because only books written in English are considered for the award. "As a grouping of nations collected from the remains of the British Empire, the Commonwealth serves as an umbrella forum in global politics," he wrote to the prize administrators. "As a literary or cultural grouping, however, it seems to me that 'the Commonwealth' can only be a misnomer so long as it excludes the many languages that sustain the cultural and literary lives of these countries (it is surely inconceivable, for example, that athletes would have to be fluent in English in order to qualify for the Commonwealth Games)."[6] Privileging English memorializes the imprint of the British, suggesting that only their linguistic legacy enables legitimate international art.

Published on his Web site, Ghosh's gracious but firm refusal became a signature statement of principle for many authors and scholars on the troubled nexus of language, history, and globalization that shapes South Asian writing in English. Laments decrying the global dominance of English and the relative neglect of other languages pervade many conversations on the fate of subcontinental literatures, though rarely do these arguments alter the structures of publishing and reviewing that perpetuate such asymmetry. As Tabish Khair wrote in an open letter to his peers, "It is . . . rare that major writers actually question the paradigms that bestow 'global' visibility of [sic] certain individuals or literatures."[7] Although Ghosh is by no means the only author to bemoan the peripheral status of languages other than English, his willingness to forgo a major prize catalyzed renewed discussion about the role of English in South Asian literary history. In many respects, this question speaks to the heart of *The Glass Palace* and its attempt to forge an ethics of multilingual fiction.

In the 1960s, one of the central debates about South Asian writing in English focused on the legitimacy of English as a South Asian language. Meditations on the tensions of writing in English form a recognizable poetic complaint in many works of poetry and fiction from that era, charting how the burdens of history attend each choice of vocabulary and syntax.[8] Though writers in the 1980s and 1990s occasionally still found themselves attacked for using the tongue of former colonial rule, this debate no longer animates discussions of literature as it once did. Few critics at the turn of the millennium take writers to task simply for writing in English, and most writers and readers accept that English, like other dialects that migrated to the subcontinent, is now a legitimate South Asian language. Indeed, Indian English has been described by Bishnupriya Ghosh as "now the insider's tongue, a distended space of linguistic migration from the global to the local."[9]

Instead, late twentieth- and early twenty-first-century anxiety about subcontinental and diasporic English focuses less on the ghosts of a colonial past and more on the specters of a globalizing present.[10] Given its comparatively easy passage into the powerful world of Western publishing and distribution, literature in English threatens to obscure fiction written in what are often called South Asia's regional languages. Even the very rhetoric of "regional" provincializes such non-English writing from the start, implying that these languages are bound to territory in a way that English is not. Such a scenario occludes the diasporic possibilities of these different literary traditions, such as Tamil literature from and for Sri Lanka, Singapore, Malaysia, and Canada. It presumes, as Kwame Anthony Appiah has eloquently written, that the category of the local favors the center over the periphery. "It is not hard to be irritated by high-handed pronouncements from critics for whom detailed description of locale amounts to mere travelogue," Appiah points out, "unless, say, the locale is 'Wessex' and the author is Thomas Hardy."[11] Even if we abjure the rhetoric of "regional," however, English remains a language of the elite in South Asia that grasps the lion's share of literary publicity in the West. Ghosh has tried in his way to avoid a headlong embrace with the major Western institutions that manage global visibility, often choosing to publish his books first with the Indian publisher Ravi Dayal and only later to release them under Western imprints.

As part of this interrogation of the powerful circuits of global distribution, Ghosh's works meditate on how best to comprehend literature's role within the multilingual set of societies that his novels engage. "Of the languages that currently possess a significant body of modern writing, each has its own traditions, its own history, and its own canons," Ghosh wrote of subcontinental literature in an essay on the Indian short story. "These specificities are very real and demand absolute respect: differences are so important a part of Indian literature that it would be a travesty to subsume them under homogenizing generalities. But at the same time no body of literature anywhere develops within a closed room, and each of India's languages has resounded to the echoes of its surroundings—both immediate and distant."[12] In this description, Indian languages and literatures are best understood as crowded stylistic spaces that blur the lines between local and foreign.

Such a conception of crowded style crystallizes in the striking image that ends *The Glass Palace*. The great-grandson of the main protagonist Rajkumar reveals how once, as a child, he stumbled upon a scene that he could not fully understand: the aging Rajkumar and his onetime political adversary, Uma Dey, sleeping in bed together naked. Though they had lived together for many years, their relationship was understood as Uma's platonic gesture of charity toward a man bereft of his fortune with no place else to go. Hoping to alleviate their confusion and anxiety upon waking, the young narrator offers the bewildered couple a tumbler of their false teeth:

> It was only after [Rajkumar] had thrust his teeth into his mouth that he discovered that Uma's dentures were clamped within his. And then, as he was sitting there, staring in round-eyed befuddlement at the pink jaws that were protruding out of his own, an astonishing thing happened—Uma leant forward and fastened her mouth on her own teeth. Their mouths clung to each other and they shut their eyes.[13]

In this moment of new-found romance, Uma and Rajkumar's tangled false teeth conjure up the problem of interlocked speech. Once adversaries, now lovers, Uma and Rajkumar offer a poignant metaphor for the complicated relationships between different forms of linguistic alterity. Their artificial teeth point to the artifice that makes speech possible, reminding us that rhetoric is never simply a natural or self-sufficient form of communication. As Uma searches for her dentures, she cannot obtain them without also binding herself to Rajkumar and his own long history of speech. Offering a metaphor for Ghosh's theory of language development, the scene literally insists upon the impossibility of a "closed room" between different speakers. Not only are Uma and Rajkumar tangled together in the crowded space of their shared bed, but their room is also open to the young narrator, who wanders in and out to provide testimony of their interlocking mouths.

As the novel knots together such figures in a multilingual world, *The Glass Palace* teems with the energy of its many languages. Evoking the polyphonies of the subcontinent, Ghosh's characters speak Burmese, Hindustani, Tamil, Bengali, Japanese, and English, to name only the most prevalent languages. During the course of the novel, the narration documents the language choices of its speakers over seventy-five times (on average, once every six pages). In many cases, these allusions serve Ghosh's historical realism by persuading the reader that each conversation can plausibly take place. For example, in capturing a scene between a Westernized Bengali and a Malayan Tamil, *The Glass Palace* specifies that the dialogue ensues in the lingua franca of either Hindustani or English. As the book charts each shift in language, Ghosh reminds us of the struggles for power, social capital, and self-expression that attend each choice of tongue.[14]

"Multilingualism is a central problem in my work," Ghosh asserts. "I'm multilingual myself, speaking Hindi, Bengali, English, Arabic, French." His thoughts on the challenge of representing multiple languages draw upon a variety of literary traditions:

> The classical novel grows out of monolingual circumstances. Even Bakhtin's work is about different registers within the same language, not among them. The problem of multilingualism is also a problem for all Indian languages, not just English. In these patterns of heteroglossia, everyone speaks many languages at once. You can't represent that realistically. Magical realism is a response to this, though it's not my response. In classical Indian prosody, Sanskrit theater, you have certain characters speaking one kind of Sanskrit and certain characters speaking another. The trivial response to the problem is to represent it through words, interjections—I find this increasingly uninteresting. If you're creating a mishmash, well, maybe that is appropriate if you're trying to replicate the mishmash of Indian English, but it's not appropriate for representing a Hindi speaker, or a non-standard Bengali.[15]

As Ghosh rejects popular literary means of representing linguistic difference, such as the magical realism and mixed argot made famous by writers like Salman Rushdie, he hints at the need to consider multilingualism as a structural rather than a surface problem of significant otherness.

How might a novel develop an ethics of engaging such polyphony? The inclusion of foreign words and phrases in South Asian writing often touches on a sensitive nerve, namely the implied audience to whom the novel appears to speak. Postcolonial South Asian novels (and postcolonial novels in general) are often accused of pandering to the West, not only bypassing local institutions of publication and production but also abandoning any implied rhetorical address to a local readership. From this perspective, books that explain South Asian idioms or practices to an unfamiliar readership perform a service that many South Asians feel they never themselves received from Western fiction. As Rushdie's Saladin discovers painfully in *The Satanic Verses* (1988), "England was a peculiar-tasting smoked fish full of spikes and bones, and nobody would ever tell him how to eat it."[16] English novels, like Saladin's famous kipper, present many of their overseas readers with confusing cultural references that sometimes work to make these readers feel marginal, inadequate, and bereft of proper cultural capital. Given this history of social hierarchies constructed through language, to include foreign words or to translate them, to typeset them in italics or to present them in regular print, and to provide context or to assume comprehension all acquire heightened political stakes in shaping where the book stands in the politics of language. What should the novel assume as shared knowledge? Should it consciously attempt to teach implied readers who lack such cultural capital? To whom should it speak?

From the very beginning, the immense scope and linguistic excess of *The Glass Palace* work against the idea of secure cultural capital that Saladin's spiky kipper invokes. Although a novel set entirely in the world of upper-middle-class Bengal might well attract a bilingual readership who would feel patronized or excluded by excessive explanation of Bengali words, few readers are likely to have linguistic competence in all six or seven of the major languages that structure *The Glass Palace*. Virtually none of the characters, even the most polyglot, exhibit such linguistic mastery, and most of them find themselves linguistically alienated at some point in the novel. As the novel traces the characters' methods of navigating between comprehension and confusion, it exposes the shifting lines that constantly change what knowledge the novel can take for granted. As it suggests that alienation is as important an experience as mastery, the novel abjures the idea of an homogeneous implied readership.

Even as it acknowledges the significance of gaps and cracks in communication, the novel refuses to relinquish the project of creating a multilingual community of shared comprehension. "Some of the languages [in *The Glass Palace*], like Burmese, I don't even speak," Ghosh admits. "You flinch to represent a character thinking in Burmese in English. But one has to take that risk because something is better than nothing."[17]

To accomplish this goal, the novel treats all foreign languages equally through a consistent method of including non-English words that Ghosh developed in collaboration with his editor. When a foreign word first surfaces in the story, it appears in italics; subsequent uses are printed in typeface indistinguishable from the rest of the English prose. In most cases, the first appearance is glossed, explained, or made clear from the context; future appearances dispense with explanatory material. After the initial confrontation with non-English material, fragments of foreign languages merge smoothly into the visual and narrative registers of the story. This form of crowded style refrains from privileging any single foreign language and opens up English equally to all of their claims on expressive potential.

As the novel makes foreign words part of the expanded vocabulary of English, it engages with such significant otherness by also treating English as a foreign language. At selected moments in the novel, *The Glass Palace* italicizes English words in a manner that mimics the introduction of foreign phrases, and it asks its audience to rethink how these words resonate as they move around the world. For the most part, the English words so scrutinized are either negatively charged or ironically presented: *evil*, *scandal*, *slavery*, *mercenary*, *duty*, *country*, and *freedom* all appear as defamiliarized foreign words that demand new investigation. Against this litany of punitive moral judgment and empty promises, the novel positions the Pali term *karuna*, or compassion, as the most prominent non-English word with equivalent moral weight. In subjecting English words, and with them moral categories, to the same inquiry that other languages receive, the novel encourages its readers to learn English and its concepts anew as well. As English appears as a language both of and in translation, a crowded space of multilingual representation, it sacrifices the privilege of taking its own ethical vocabulary for granted.

Unlike many other postcolonial writers, Ghosh chooses to work in an English idiom that rarely compels his readers to hear the differences among the many languages it represents. This preference for a plain style characterizes much of his work, and scholars have tended to set Ghosh's eloquent but unadorned prose against the work of writers whose fictions manipulate the syntax, vocabulary, and tone of English to create distinctive vernacular sounds.[18] Although the theories of language that underlie vernaculars offer important contributions to new forms of representation in an era of globalization, as Bishnupriya Ghosh's work attests, *The Glass Palace* charts a different course.[19] Eschewing the Sanskritized communal voice of Raja Rao and the Bollywood pyrotechnics of Salman Rushdie, the narrative voice of *The Glass Palace* works within an alternate tradition of South Asian writing, exemplified by R. K. Narayan, which aims for a clear, public tone with no obvious markers to affiliate it with any particular part of the world. "*The Glass Palace* is such a big story that I decided early on it would be damaged by flamboyance," Ghosh claims.[20] Instead, as I have suggested earlier, the novel shares as much rhetorically with historical narrative as it does with conventions of fiction. As the title of the book implies, the tone of the novel mimics the seeming transparency of glass.

Just as the stately style of the novel approaches the restrained tone of historical storytelling, the voices of each character tend to mute the presence of linguistic difference. Although the novel mentions explicitly that Rajkumar speaks heavily accented Burmese, nothing in an isolated line of dialogue separates Rajkumar's voice from the representation of a native Burmese speaker. In fact, many of Ghosh's characters in *The Glass Palace* sound remarkably alike. Though readers might easily distinguish his speakers based on the content of what they say, the differences in tone, syntax, grammar, and rhythm are surprisingly slight among dialogues, interior monologues, and free indirect discourse. The major exceptions to this rule are the figures of Dinu and Arjun, who do develop distinctive (and opposing) speech patterns. "'Alison . . . I was just telling you what it's like . . . when I make a picture . . . I didn't mean to put you off,'" Dinu says in a typical moment of his hesitating, elliptical speech (*GP*, 293, ellipses in the original).[21] In contrast, Arjun's language overflows with army jargon and bluff, colloquial "chaps" and "yaars." Apart from these two figures, however, the voices of most characters seem public and even interchangeable. Even Arjun's fondness for slang appears more often in narrative descriptions of his spoken affectations than in his direct speech, his letters, or his inward consciousness.

This commitment to an understated and even old-fashioned form of historical narration has led many readers to downplay the radical ethical potential of Ghosh's style. "Ghosh is a worthy writer, not a scintillating one," Rukmini Bhaya Nair writes in her assessment of *The Glass*

Palace. "*The Glass Palace* is important not because it opens new stylistic or thematic doors, but because it reopens old ones so effectively."[22] The novel often receives more enthusiasm from readers drawn to history and politics than it does from those who seek the defamiliarizing literary tactics associated with fiction. However, although Nair's description provides an understandable response to the conventional realism of Ghosh's novel, I suggest that *The Glass Palace* does actually offer a complicated engagement with the ethics of style. The novel's flattened sense of linguistic difference cannot simply be dismissed as a technical failing. As a stylist, Ghosh has proven in previous books a gift for vocal distinctions, and novels such as *The Shadow Lines* offer much stronger visions of how English might dramatize different forms of spoken alterity. The acerbic and at times demagogic grandmother, the meditative and philosophical Tridib, and the childishly diffident Ila distinguish themselves through their idiosyncratic voices, an effect heightened by the absence of quotation marks or other conventional punctuation that might separate speech from the rest of the story. The narrator's voice in *The Shadow Lines* quietly rebels against what Ghosh has identified as a convention of realist narrative, namely "a rhetoric of description that rigorously segregates direct speech."[23] Although neither the narrator nor the characters speak in dialect or any other pattern indicative of a particular communal identity, the shadow lines between spoken and interior speech subvert the rhetoric of Western realism and its claim to objective documentary narration. Ghosh's foray into science fiction, *The Calcutta Chromosome*, further plays with flamboyant language in the figure of L. Murugan, whose bombastic American colloquialisms complement the emotionless computer speech that shadows the futuristic novel. Compared to these works, the spoken words of *The Glass Palace* appear to reflect a decision not to dramatize the distinctions of vernacular discourse. Its very refusals to engage in particular modes of aestheticized difference, as we will see, work toward a new ethics of surmounting linguistic alterity.

In declining to mimic obvious language differences among its speakers, *The Glass Palace* proffers an alternative to hegemonic patterns of representational violence. Exemplified by Rudyard Kipling's *Kim* (1901), which represents Punjabi as a form of particularly archaic English, a long history of Orientalist writing presents South Asian speech as ridiculous, demotic, pompous, or comically inaccurate. Speaking of her own translation of a Bengali text, Gayatri Spivak notes that in translating "the peculiar Bengali spoken by the tribals . . . it would have been embarrassing to have used some version of the language of D. H. Lawrence's 'common people' or Faulkner's blacks."[24] Ghosh, too, chooses not to take this path. His rejection of dialect resonates with Cairns Craig's more general critique of this form:

> In any novel written in standard or "literary" English, a linguistic hierarchy is established in which, no matter the intent of the author, the dialect-speaking character is always the inhabitant of a linguistically less significant world than that shared by author and reader: the dialect-speaking character is seen as being either in declension from, or in aspiration towards, the moral and intellectual standards—the full humanity—of standard English and its literary traditions.[25]

Given this imbalance in power and knowledge, it should come as no surprise that *The Glass Palace* abjures character-specific dialect as an adequate form of representing linguistic difference. Instead, Ghosh escapes this embarrassment by relying on his plain style to impart a sense of equality to all of the many languages evoked in the novel.

If this choice works against hegemonic forms of representational violence, it also opposes identitarian uses of language. By refusing to create hierarchies among speakers, this plain style works against the idea of a specifically nationalist idiom. Although experimental styles of South Asian writing are often thought to shape new forms of national or regional identity, *The Glass Palace* contests the formation of such nationalist rhetoric. Just as the novel narrates experiences that cannot be mapped onto the birth of nations, it refrains from using language to dramatize national character or assert national distinctions.

The problem of capturing multilingual realities within monolingual prose is one that Ghosh embeds into *The Glass Palace* itself. In doing so, the novel elucidates its aesthetic alternative to the overtly sonic representation of diverse languages. Near the end of the novel, Dinu returns to Burma, where he meets a writer named Ma Thin Thin Aye. Her fiction inspires Dinu to ask the same questions that this chapter inquires of Ghosh:

"You say the people on the street are from many different places . . . from the coasts and the hills . . . Yet in your story they all speak Burmese. How is that possible?"

She was not at all put out.

"Where I live," [Ma Thin Thin Aye] said softly, "every house on the street speaks a different language. I have no choice but to trust my reader to imagine the sound of each house."

(*GP*, 459, ellipses in the original)

If we take Ma Thin Thin Aye's answer as Ghosh's own, *The Glass Palace* invites the reader to collaborate with the novel to create a complete border-crossing fiction. Describing this activity as a mutual effort rather than a singular act of representation, the strategy quietly proposed by Ma Thin Thin Aye places limits on what a writer alone can hope to provide. When Dinu presses Ma Thin Thin Aye to represent the music of each Burmese dialect, she tells him that "a word on the page is like a string on an instrument. My readers sound the music in their heads, and for each it sounds different" (*GP*, 459). Like Ghosh, Ma Thin Thin Aye declines authorial responsibility to make each dialect obviously distinct on the page. A plain style, she suggests, opens up a much wider range for individual readers to hear words differently. *The Glass Palace* invites its readers to exercise that skill by denying clear sonic representations of language while still describing, in vivid detail, the distinctions of different speakers. The crowded style of the novel consists not simply in representing difference on the page but also in encouraging multiple interpretations to be heard in the reader's head. Direct mimicry of dialect and idiosyncratic speech patterns constricts the possible diversity of readerly interpretation. This aesthetic restraint emulates the balance of comprehension and difference toward which an ethics of border crossing strives. As a description of Ghosh's style in *The Glass Palace*, this gentle manifesto suggests how a constraining form of English (or, in Ma Thin Thin Aye's case, Burmese) can offer surprising liberation.

This vision of a crowded style may seem like a paradox: Burmese—and English—become more crowded by refusing to represent other languages directly. Yet it is precisely in this aesthetic sacrifice, when the dominant language confronts its own limitations, that it invites active interpretation on the part of the reader. Out of this confrontation with the style of the novel, the crowded selves of readers may emerge. Ghosh's work implies that novels may require the aesthetic sacrifice of certainty and control in order to forward representations of linguistic difference. As the works of Ghosh and Ma Thin Thin Aye balance the desire to imagine diverse linguistic communities with the desire to avoid constraining them, they insist that readers cannot complacently remain passive consumers of aesthetic works. As these readers become the players of the music they write, they too sacrifice the pleasure of novels in which everything is provided and managed by the work of fiction. By including Dinu's challenge to Ma Thin Thin Aye, the novel teaches its readers to understand the flattened and restrained language of *The Glass Palace* as an aesthetic absence that offers the ethical opportunity to develop a crowded self. What seems like less, in Ghosh's work, is actually more.

In addition to this insistence on readerly participation, Ghosh's work also promotes a second strategy of representing linguistic difference. If the novel dampens the sonic dimension of multiple languages in order to create a coherent but crowded style, *The Glass Palace* also attempts to mimic the nonverbal legibility of the visual arts. In particular, the novel turns to the genre of photography as its model for writing. Although photography is no more transparent than any other art form, it models a different type of accessibility, because audiences can view it no matter what language they speak. A pervasive trope within the novel, photography seeks to link communities across nation and language through its unique aesthetic possibilities. Photographs acquire heightened significance through the figure of Dinu, who finds himself best able to confront the world through the lens of a camera. As his photographs offer a new visual vocabulary for the complex circuits of his life, they help to shape the historical record of Southeast Asia and its diasporas. When Dinu's niece Jaya decides to write her dissertation on the history of photography in India, she finds herself stumbling across Dinu's work as a major force within South Asian photographic art. Her discoveries inspire her to collect the narratives that she passes onto her son, who brings them together to form *The Glass Palace*. As a catalyst and an archival source for transnational narration, photographs provide the best model for the legible but complex representation that the English of the novel seeks to emulate.

Until the 1880s, photography was a pursuit limited to affluent amateur specialists who could afford and comprehend the complicated technical processes of shooting and developing film. When Eastman invented roll film and marketed preloaded cameras in 1888, taking pictures suddenly became available to a much broader audience.[26] Developed in 1900, the Brownie camera offered the most affordable and convenient snapshot device for middle-class consumers. When Dinu receives his first Brownie, he eagerly participates in this new expansion of the art form.[27] Although many users of the Brownie focused their gaze inward on their families, developing new visual idioms for bourgeois leisure, Dinu's own embrace of the technology coincides with an outward focus on new forms of social difference. Given the camera as an incentive to travel with his mother from Burma to Malaya, Dinu links photography to the optic of transition and dispersal.

Photography in South Asia, like the English language, spread beneath a colonial aegis. During the nineteenth and twentieth centuries, it was a common pastime in India for colonial expatriates and Indian elites. The British encouraged the spread of picture taking as a way to document, anthropologize, and master their empire, and the introduction of photography has often been understood as an extension of Western technological modernity that comes to dominate a putatively traditional Indian pictorial culture.[28] Dinu's embrace of the camera, however, is not positioned within the novel as either an extension of empire or a fascination with technological innovation. Instead, like the Indian photographer Raghubir Singh, whose aesthetic forms a model for Dinu's own, Dinu's photography attempts to translate and revise modernist aesthetics to explore the shifting borders between home and world.[29]

Unlike the exotic and primitivist preoccupations of much modernist photography, Dinu's ventures into photography take him farther away from hegemonic or identitarian inscriptions of social difference. Although *The Glass Palace* scrupulously documents and marks the historical effects of racial identity, it attempts to do so without reinforcing a belief in racial essences. As part of this project, Dinu's pictures attempt to find a way of seeing that refuses to fetishize racial markers. This process begins with Dinu's pictures of the shrines, or chandis, on the Malayan mountainside, which first begin as panoramic shots that suggest the power of the camera to contain a foreign landscape. As his early pictures attempt to capture everything—"the frames filled with sweeping vistas" (*GP*, 303)—they resonate with Mary Louise Pratt's influential theory of "the monarch-of-all-I-survey" that affiliates vistas and panoramas with the representational logic of imperialism.[30] Over time, these grandiose shots give way to more intimate and microscopic images: "Soon he could no longer see either the mountain or the forest or the sea" (*GP*, 303). As Dinu's gaze moves away from the markers of geography and into a closer embrace of the chandis, his pictures attempt to evade encapsulating a landscape into a visually manageable vista. This shift away from the grandiose marks the moment when the language of *The Glass Palace* itself becomes less epic, lingering over Dinu's introspective development rather than charting broader social events.

This movement inward achieves fullest elaboration in Dinu's portraits of his beloved Alison, which explore the contours of her body away from the power of a racialized gaze. In Dinu's portraits of Alison as a nude, the novel could easily have chosen to call attention to the aspect of embodied border crossing that sanctions and celebrates multiracial identity. Both Dinu and Alison are multiethnic: Dinu is both Indian and Burmese; Alison is Chinese and Anglo-American by ancestry and Malaysian by upbringing. As Dinu lovingly takes her photograph in the overgrown ruined temple, the novel might have paused to scrutinize the overlapping markers of ethnicity as inscribed on the body. Dinu's camera, however, is not drawn to such marks. Although Ghosh's descriptions of his pictures note in detail the formal patterns of both body and landscape (both of which grow increasingly erotic as Dinu and Alison consummate their romance), the photographs never identify these images in terms of racial rhetoric. Although this moment reaffirms the convention of a woman's body as a natural body of landscape, Dinu refuses to place either the landscape or the body into definable national, racial, or ethnic terms. This refusal to fetishize and hence reaffirm differences of skin is mirrored in Ghosh's prose style, which similarly refuses to articulate its characters in terms of sonic verbal difference.

The flattened language of Ghosh's crowded style thus attempts to approximate the visual register of Dinu's photography, and hence it is no coincidence that both the novel and Dinu's photography salon are called *The Glass Palace*. Late in his life, when Dinu runs the salon from his photography studio in Burma, modernist photographs provide the cover through which Dinu speaks beyond the repressive codes of Burmese military rule. Since speech is not openly possible under the political regime, visual arts provide a solution not only to the question of linguistic difference but also to the problem of repressed linguistic expression. When Jaya finds Dinu in Burma, she watches him present his students with the image of Weston's famous nautilus. Dinu's reproductions of modernist art come to him from the rag pickers, who sort through the trash of foreigners in search of items of value. The image of Weston's nautilus becomes a secret transnational code within the underground Burmese community of photographers, where Dinu uses it to communicate the values of art that cannot be spoken publicly without reprisal. While often modernist aesthetics have been denigrated by postmodern strains in the West, Ghosh seems to suggest that only a position of relative power and luxury can allow one to dispense with the value of modernist rhetoric. If it has been suggested that late twentieth-century Indian writing in English is itself a form of modernism,[31] Ghosh's own choice of a modern rather than postmodern style of narration suggests that the stories he seeks to tell have not yet exhausted their conventions of writing. As each art form attempts to tell border-crossing narratives within a style commensurate with its content, the language of *The Glass Palace* provides an alternative to the flamboyantly vocal rhetoric that characterizes the most prominent mode of South Asian writing in English.

The Glass Palace reveals how Ghosh's own prose might approach such representation. As the novel seeks to speak with many voices, its crowded style of storytelling invites readerly engagement and approaches modernist photography. While the plain style of *The Glass Palace* cannot be considered Ghosh's only solution to the problem of crafting ethically responsive polyphonic narration, it offers one way that border-crossing fictions might navigate between the arrogance of hegemonic knowledge and the silence of identitarian effects. As the novel sacrifices the aesthetic privileges of flamboyance, certainty, and control, it offers new ethical possibilities for storytelling across borders of language.

Nonverbal or Hyperverbal? Amitav Ghosh's The Hungry Tide

In *The Glass Palace*, as Ghosh tests the capacity of the novel to encompass linguistic difference, he ends by locating utopian linguistic diversity in the private experience of the reader and in the visual accessibility of the photograph. With his following novel, *The Hungry Tide*, Ghosh pushes these questions about the significant otherness of language to a deeper and darker place. The back cover of the Harper Collins India paperback edition informs prospective readers that "it is a novel that asks at every turn: what man can take the true measure of another?" Explicitly advertised as an investigation into the central problem of imagining alterity, the novel focuses on the possibilities and limitations of language as a mode of communication and imaginative projection. Expanding the reach of *The Glass Palace*, *The Hungry Tide* is much more radical when it questions the commensurability of language: not simply English but speech and writing in general sustain the scrutiny of the novel.

I will suggest that *The Hungry Tide* sacrifices the privileges of direct and unmediated language, making a place for both silence and translation within the register of English. Within its narration, readers encounter a nonverbal language associated with the natural environment juxtaposed with a hyperverbal language associated with translation. As the novel tests the possibilities of both nonverbal language and hyperverbal translation, it demonstrates the limitations of both approaches to communication. In place of either method, the novel offers a syncretic alternative that incorporates elements of each. This syncretic language presents representational ethics as a form of doubleness, in which the world of the other is perceived simultaneously from within and from without, as an outsider and an insider, and through the nonverbal and the translated. In the ecology of the novel, the moment of grasping one's distance from another provides the paradoxical moment in which those limits may dissolve. The simultaneity of the limits and possibilities of conceptualizing others provides *The Hungry Tide*'s searching contribution to the ethics of imagining across borders.

Set in the muddy Bengali tidelands where fresh and salt water meet, *The Hungry Tide* offers a natural and human ecology where numerous biological and cultural differences find uneasy coexistence. Once the site of a classless and casteless settlement founded by a colonial Scotsman and now reclaimed by twentieth-century Bengali refugees, the tidelands offer spaces of utopian social energy. But the islands and rivers of the jungle also conceal danger and despair. Tigers roam the forests, claiming human lives with relentless regularity, and poverty haunts the fishing communities that commit themselves to life in the Sundarbans. Although novels such as Rushdie's *Midnight's Children*

(1980) envision the Sundarbans as a phantasmagoric space of hallucination, *The Hungry Tide* tethers this dream world to historical problems of class, culture, conservation, and economic development. Defined by the ebb and flood of the silty water that submerges and reveals the land, the tide country provides a rich metaphor for the in-betweenness of life at the turn of the millennium.

Within this landscape, *The Hungry Tide* tells the parallel narratives of two intellectuals who find themselves called to the rural wetlands. When Piya, an Indian American cetologist, boards a train to Canning in search of rare river dolphins, she encounters an urbane and supremely self-confident Indian translator named Kanai. Summoned to the remote island of Lusibari by his aunt, Kanai travels to inherit a series of journals written by his uncle. Though both Piya and Kanai believe themselves to be pursing specific and limited goals on their trip to the tide country, they both find themselves increasingly immersed in the tumultuous worlds of human history and natural calamities that await them there.

Told in alternating third-person chapters, the narratives of Piya and Kanai offer formal and philosophical contrasts that mimic the ebb and flood of the Sundarbans. Most crucially, they offer two radically different approaches toward the problem of linguistic difference. Piya speaks no language but English and spends her days in silence surveying marine mammal life; Kanai, adept in six languages, runs a successful New Delhi company that provides translators for government business and multinational firms. Though he was originally lured to languages by his love of poetry, translation now provides Kanai with his major currency in life. The professional differences between Piya, for whose work "there's not much talk needed," and Kanai, whose survival depends on linguistic interpretation, provide a core set of questions about the best way to overcome linguistic barriers in the novel.[32] Their projects in the Sundarbans reflect and exacerbate these differences: Piya seeks to lose herself in the nonverbal world of rivers and dolphins, whereas Kanai plunges into the Bengali writings of his literary uncle Nirmal, for whom poetry provides a touchstone for all experience. As the novel explores the expressive possibilities of the nonverbal and the hyperverbal, it ultimately demands communicative art that merges the two into an uneasy whole.

In its portrait of complicated contact zones, *The Hungry Tide* explicitly addresses the challenge of imagining social difference. On the river in search of Gangetic and Irrawaddy dolphins, Piya eventually finds herself in the company of a Sundarban fisherman named Fokir. Though both characters share a Bengali heritage and a love of the world of the rivers, their linguistic, social, professional, and educational differences place them far apart in conventional terms of culture and community. This source of social separation compels Piya to muse on Fokir's possible past, and her introspective curiosity offers a moment when the novel reflects openly on the project of engaging significant otherness. While Piya's musings reflect her desire to treat Fokir as more than an instrumental part of her journey, they also provide a glimpse of the difficulties of realizing this desire. As Piya's elaborate musings both succeed and fail, the terms of her success and failure resonate with the ethics of imaginative projection advanced in this book.

> What did he see when he looked back? She pictured a hut like those she had seen on the fringes of Canning, with mud walls and straw thatch and shutters of plaited bamboo. His father was a fisherman like him, with long stringy limbs and a face imprinted by the sun and wind, and his mother was a sturdy but tired woman, worn to the bone by the daily labour of carrying baskets full of fish and crabs to the market. There were many children, many playmates for little Fokir, and although they were poor their lives did not lack for warmth or companionship: it was a family like those she had heard her father talk about—in which want and deprivation made people pull together all the more tightly.
>
> Had he seen his wife's face before the wedding? . . . she would have kept her eyes downcast until it was night and they were lying beside each other in the mud-walled room of their hut. Only then would she allow herself to look at this boy who was her man and thank her fate for giving her a husband who was young, with fine clean limbs and wide, deep eyes, someone who could almost have been the dark god of her prayers and dreams.
>
> (HT, 158)

From the beginning of this passage, the novel calls this meditative fantasy into question. Based on her view from the train into Canning, the portrait of Fokir's home bespeaks a portrait of stability conjured through the optic of transit. Grounded in Piya's brief observations of tidal village life, this theory of Fokir's past is not an unbelievable account of what his life might have been like, but the novel barely allows the reader to believe in Piya's conjectural hypotheses. Only a few pages earlier, Kanai's narrative contradicts Piya's vision of Fokir's wife and wedding night, and a few pages later, Kanai's narrative reveals Fokir's real family history. Where Piya envisions a mud hut, Fokir and his wife Moyna live in hospital barracks; where she conjures a rugged Sundarban fisherman, Fokir's disabled father sold snacks on trains; where she imagines a careworn village wife, Fokir's mother was the luminous and spirited Kusum who haunts the desires of many men in the novel. Enveloped within these conflicting accounts, Piya's imaginative meditation comes to signify the limits of verbal fantasy in apprehending the life of another.

The particular form of Piya's imaginative failure accords with a central element of border crossing: her fantasy can be traced to the unwitting self-projection that colors her vision of Fokir's life. As the novel gently reminds the reader that Piya's attempt does not accurately explain Fokir's life, it suggests that her meditations, in the fashion of the mirror argument, illuminate more about Piya's family than about Fokir's. The warmth of Fokir's imagined family throws into relief the tensions of Piya's upbringing, shadowed by her parents' incessant fighting and her depressive mother's retreat into illness and death. Although nothing in Fokir's reclusive and self-contained manner suggests the gregariousness of his imagined childhood, it speaks to Piya's own loneliness as a daughter without siblings caught within the increasing chill of her parents' estrangement. Even Piya's meditation on Fokir's wedding night suggests residual regrets about her own choice to become a cetologist, a traveling profession that Piya admits makes romantic relationships difficult to sustain. The idealization of Fokir as "the dark god of [his wife's] prayers and dreams" testifies again to the controlled but palpable desire that Piya feels for Fokir. As Piya in her solitary migration continually evades her past, it permeates her life as displaced imaginative projection. If conceptualizing others depends on a robust reconsideration of the self, the failure of Piya's imaginative exercise suggests how insufficient self-consciousness leads to unwitting self-projection.

Although the narrative frame contradicts the accuracy of Piya's thoughts, it nonetheless reveals how her unconscious mirroring can transform itself into a useful representational ethics. The value of representing social difference lies less in its ability to provide positivist portraits than in its attempt to shape responsive and responsible forms of thinking across borders. Such thinking strives for an ethical starting point to engage with others' experiences, and unlike Orientalism, primitivism, or other forms of suffocating rhetorical constraint, it seeks to expand rather than constrict the range of options open to the subject under consideration. The central question is not whether these conjectures are measurably correct but whether they are open to revision. Piya's behavior later in the novel suggests that they are: "She was shamed by her lack of insight," Piya thinks when she learns of Fokir's history (*HT*, 218). A good scientist, Piya does not cling to her preconceptions in the face of new evidence, and her ability to revise her portrait attests to the flexibility of her encounter with significant otherness.

But Piya does not see her failure (or her success) in these terms. Instead, she expresses a far more radical skepticism that challenges her ability to inhabit the interior world of another being. After her vision of Fokir's wedding night, the passage ends with a moment of dark despair about the power of verbal language:

> there was the immeasurable distance that separated her from Fokir. What was he thinking about as he stared at the moonlit river? The forest, the crabs? Whatever it was, she would never know: not just because they had no language in common but because that was how it was with human beings, who came equipped, as a species, with the means of shutting each other out. The two of them, Fokir and herself, they could have been boulders or trees for all they knew of each other: and wasn't it better in a way, more honest, that they could not speak? For if you compared it to the ways in which dolphins' echoes mirrored the world, speech was only a bag of tricks that fooled you into believing that you could see through the eyes of another being.
>
> (*HT*, 159)

As Piya dismisses sympathetic imagination as the illusory ambition of "a bag of tricks," she expresses a desire for a form of communication that exceeds the limitations of human language. Rather than translation, she yearns for nonverbal speech, and as we will see, this nonverbal language tempts her with the possibility of erasing the divide between interior experience and external communication. As *The Hungry Tide* examines the possibility of this form of nonverbal language, it inquires whether speech must be sacrificed to bridge this gap.

Why should the novel contemplate sacrificing speech? In Piya's world, language severs rather than unites. Her desire to escape the ties of language stems back to her childhood, where the sound of Bengali signals her parents' bitter arguments. Carrying messages back and forth between them at the height of their estrangement, Piya understandably flees from the role of the translator or interpreter, for this role marks distance rather than connection in her life. Piya's father encourages her to view language as a constraint and a social barrier, not as a means of expanded communication: "He believes that Indians—Bengalis in particular—don't travel well, because their eyes are always turned backwards, towards home" (*HT*, 250). In fleeing language, Piya seeks to escape the burdens of painful self-reflection.

When Piya critiques the world of human speech, she gestures toward an alternative in the communicative abilities of the dolphins she studies. Throughout the novel, the idea of "dolphin language" offers a utopian vision of nonverbal speech that Piya hopes to replicate in her relations with Fokir. Describing the way the dolphins communicate, Piya "imagined the animals circling drowsily, listening to echoes pinging through the water, painting pictures in three dimensions—images that only they could decode. The thought of experiencing your surroundings in that way never failed to fascinate her: the idea that to 'see' was also to 'speak' to others of your kind, where simply to exist was to communicate" (*HT*, 159). The echolocation of the dolphins erases the divide between verbal and nonverbal, realigning the border between self and other. Given to us through the literal specificity and metaphorical resonance of the marine mammals, this form of communication emerges as a method of perception that Piya idealizes.

As Fokir and Piya navigate the tidal rivers, they develop a mode of communication that evokes this utopian dolphin language more than it resembles human speech. As Piya's guide to the dolphin pods, Fokir calls out when he sees them, and though she cannot comprehend the words, she understands exactly what he means. His words come to Piya like the "pings" of the dolphins, correlating sight with sound in a mimicry of echolocation. This echolocation models the utopian possibility that Piya desires in Fokir. In addition to his expertise, his patience, and his knowledge of the tides, he offers her the hope of a life that mimics those of the dolphins, and his human echolocation seems to offer a nonverbal mapping that cannot be reduced to the deceptive "bag of tricks" of speech. Rather than identifying with another's process of perception, communion takes place outside of their minds in the convergence of their gaze upon a shared object. To valorize this form of communication is to give up on entering another's consciousness and to seek union in the external world of the convergent gaze.

As the story moves further into the watery jungle, it suggests that this voyage away from human habitation is also a voyage into a deeper form of human communion. Fokir's wordless ways help to cut through social differences and arrive at a space beyond conventional categorizations. From Piya's point of view, Fokir is the first individual who treats her neither as the "little East Indian girl" who serves as "a kind of departmental mascot" (HT, 74) for her scientific colleagues nor as the vacant Bengali signifier that provokes obscene responses from men in Canning. When Fokir creates a private space on his boat for Piya to change her wet clothes, the simplicity of the ethical gesture holds tremendous weight for Piya: "It was not just that he had thought to create a space for her; it was as if he had chosen to include her in some simple, practiced family ritual, found a way to let her know that despite the inescapable muteness of their exchanges, she was a person to him and not, as it were, a representative of a species, a faceless, tongueless foreigner" (HT, 71). The novel suggests that it may be *because of*, not despite, their "inescapable muteness" that their encounter eludes common categories that frequently define a constrained first look at social difference. As Piya comes to discover, Fokir's reticence is not merely a practical consequence of their lack of shared language: "in her experience, people almost automatically went through a ritual of naming when they were with a stranger of another language. Fokir was an exception in that he had made no such attempts" (HT, 93).[33] Fokir's gestures and actions provide a nonverbal acknowledgement of Piya's significant otherness that seeks to accommodate difference and strangeness, and the novel suggests that his actions carry significant ethical weight.

The possibilities of Fokir's dolphin language are also generative and erotic. As Piya encounters traces of Fokir's personal life on the boat, her optic lingers over intimate details, such as the salty sweat smell of his gamchaa, that evoke a subtly erotic mood. While this sexual tension sometimes seems awkwardly forced within the emotional world of the novel, *The Hungry Tide* clearly foregrounds the capacity for generative nonverbal connections. In an analysis of literary marshlands, Margaret Doody claims that "the muddy margin is a place to start from— perpetually a point of departure and rebirth. The fertilizing ooze is both unpleasant and pleasurable, the ooze of reality, the undertone of the flesh and the flesh's remaking of itself. . . . Pond and marsh and riverbank offer the muddy site of our desire."[34] Drawing on a long lineage of novelistic imagery that associates marshlands with sexuality, *The Hungry Tide* suggests fertile possibilities within this nonverbal landscape.

Against the utopian fertility of dolphin language, the parallel narrative of Kanai reinforces the novel's emphasis on the inadequacies of human speech. Urbane, sophisticated, but edged with arrogance, Kanai finds many of his own basic principles challenged by the local community on the Sundarban island of Lusibari. Through his aunt Nilima, who runs a local NGO and hospital, he meets Fokir's ambitious and determined wife Moyna. Training to be a nurse at Nilima's hospital, Moyna resents Fokir's commitment to an impoverished fisherman's life and continually struggles with him over the education of their son. When Kanai inquires into the intricacies of Moyna's feelings for her husband, her response suggests not only the gulf between his life and hers but also the inadequacy of linguistic communication:

> She smiled, as if to herself. "You wouldn't understand," she said.
>
> He was nettled by the certainty in her voice. "*I* wouldn't understand?" he said sharply. "I know five languages; I've travelled all over the world. Why wouldn't I understand?"
>
> She let her ãchol drop from her head and gave him a sweet smile. "It doesn't matter how many languages you know," she said. "You're not a woman and you don't know him. You won't understand."
>
> (*HT*, 156)

As with Piya, the erotic connection between Moyna and Fokir is presented as a communion beyond the reach of language. As Moyna refuses the possibility of sympathetic imagination, she disturbs Kanai's complacency about the value of linguistic competence, and she allows the novel to advance the possibilities of the nonverbal.

However, the language of the dolphins is not the only natural language found in *The Hungry Tide*. If the peaceful and communal dolphin pods suggest a form of utopian speech, Ghosh continually reminds us that the tide world is full of other less comradely creatures. Whereas dolphins pull Piya and Fokir together, tigers pry them apart. The tiger, the devastating specter that haunts the Sundarbans, appears throughout the novel as a source of uncontrollable violence. Unlike tigers in other parts of India, as Kanai's aunt Nilima teaches him, the tigers of the tide country regularly attack human settlements without provocation. For many of the local inhabitants, the very word "tiger" cannot be spoken aloud, for to say its name is to summon its presence, and to see a tiger is surely to die. Inverting the generous echolocation of the dolphins, who merge speaking and seeing, the tiger suggests the violence and destruction invested in this form of seamless mapping.

When Piya and Fokir together encounter a tiger trapped in a village settlement, the social barriers between them surge into prominent view. Angry villagers net the tiger within a shed, and with the intensity of a mob, they stab it with sharpened sticks and eventually set it on fire. Appalled by their cruelty, Piya tries to stop the attack, and she turns to Fokir for support. But Fokir is sharpening a stick with the villagers, and he forcibly carries her away from the scene to allow the immolation to occur. In its scrupulously even-handed tone, the novel refrains from taking either side in its portrayal of their first real conflict. The violence toward the trapped animal appears in all its cruelty, but as Kanai tries to explain to Piya, the tiger had already killed several people from the settlement. Despite the appeal of Piya's compassion and conservationist instincts, the novel provides no way for the villagers to set the tiger free without risking their own lives in the process. The scene of the tiger killing marks the divide between the two and shatters Piya's idea of human echolocation. Back on the boat, she says to Kanai, "What you said about there being nothing in common between— . . . You were right. I was just being stupid. I guess it took something like this for me to get it straight" (*HT*, 296–297).

While utopian dolphin language encourages connections through eroticism, the language of the tiger is affiliated with the unities available only in death. Throughout the novel, Fokir emerges as a character deeply marked by a growing desire to die. Well before the monstrous typhoon that takes his life, Fokir alludes to plans to join his mother in death, and he identifies himself with the language of the tiger when he tells Piya, through Kanai, that "when a tiger comes into a human settlement, it's because it wants to die" (*HT*, 295). His own death inverts the tiger's demise: one could argue that Fokir enters the jungle because he too reveals a suicidal impulse. Battered by water rather than fire in a typhoon, Fokir dies from the blows of a natural disaster rather than from the force of human anger, but through this inversion, his fate mirrors that of the tiger.

As the climax of the novel merges eroticism and death, the fullness of nonverbal language achieves perfect communion only in the moment of its extinction. The language of dolphins coincides with the language of tigers in the instant when Fokir dies, strapped with Piya to a tree in the middle of the typhoon. Minutes before his death, they see a tiger, and then the storm begins its assault:

> She could feel the bones of his cheeks as if they had been superimposed upon her own; it was as if the storm had given them what life could not; it had fused them together and made them one. . . .
> She remembered how she had tried to find the words to remind him of how richly he was loved—and once again, as so often before, he had seemed to understand her, even without words.
>
> (HT, 390, 393)

Merging the violent physical syntax of the tiger with the nonverbal communion of the dolphin, this moment fulfills the erotic undertone of the novel only within the moment of erasure. The power of the nonverbal is given as utopian but unsustainable, a force that cannot replace the impulse to understand others through fallible words. If the only moment of perfect nonverbal communication is simultaneously the end of that unity, we are left only with the imperfections of language to chart a path of endurance through the wrecked remains. Reconstruction after the storm, the novel suggests, must embrace—not avoid—the perils of words.

If *The Hungry Tide* tests the possibilities of nonverbal communication only to conclude that such union fulfills itself best in death, what kind of verbal language emerges as a contender for reconstructive representations of social difference? The novel suggests the need for aesthetic sacrifices that emerge when speakers give up the privileges of pure silence and pure speech. Throughout its pages, the novel suggests an aesthetic response through the metaphor of a religious narrative called "The Glory of Bon Bibi." Offering a mythological origin of the tide country, the work—simultaneously narrative, play, poem, and song—provides a vision of crowded style that invites communication across social borders while simultaneously respecting the space beyond human access. Ghosh's prose requires this paradoxical doubleness, which draws upon both the power of the nonverbal and the mediation of translation.

In both its form and its content, "The Glory of Bon Bibi" provides a syncretic melding of different faiths, languages, literary forms, and performance styles that mirrors the complex histories of settlement in the Sundarbans. The story relates how the goddess Bon Bibi rescues a young man from the grasp of the tiger-demon, and Nirmal's journal tells us that *"it was a strange variety of Bangla, deeply interpenetrated by Arabic and Persian."* As Nirmal comes to discover, the story encompasses many contradictory social and literary forms. The narrative passes through an oral lineage, but it also exists in a printed form that Nirmal dates to the nineteenth-century utopian settlement of the Sundarbans. The book is written in Bangla but reads from the right in the Arabic style; it strings its words out in sentence form but uses the meter of Bangla prosody. This *"strange hybrid,"* Nirmal muses, shows how *"the mudbanks of the tide country are shaped not only by rivers of silt, but also by rivers of language: Bengali, English, Arabic, Hindi, Arakanese and who knows what else?"* He compares the merger of languages to the confluence of waters in the regions' mohonas, expansive sites where many different river channels merge together into an open watery landscape: *"a circular roundabout people can use to pass in many directions—from country to country and even between faiths and religions"* (HT, 246–47, italics in original). Piya intuits this linguistic and religious syncretism when she unsuspectingly accompanies Fokir to the shrine of Bon Bibi on a remote island. While his actions remind her of her mother's puja-table, the only word she can understand is "Allah." Idealized within the novel as a perfect language of border crossing, the narrative of Bon Bibi seeks to unite its listeners, readers, and performers within its flexible and surprising forms of transmission, language, and faith.

Although "The Glory of Bon Bibi" is offered as an emblem of crowded style, interpreted by Nirmal's sensitive eye, it also offers a more subtle insight through its confluence of the world of the nonverbal with the world of translation. Piya first encounters the narrative unwittingly when she hears Fokir chanting softly on the boat: "His voice sounded almost hoarse and it seemed to crack and sob as it roamed the notes. There was a suggestion of grief in it that unsettled and disturbed her" (*HT*, 98–99). Unable to decipher the words or their meanings, Piya experiences the song as an entirely nonverbal experience that marks the limits of her knowledge but also invites an emotional identification across borders of language. The next time Fokir sings, his voice becomes a part of the natural landscape that takes shape "against the percussive counterpoint of the dolphins' breathing" (*HT*, 157). Because as readers we perceive his song through Piya's consciousness, we experience the poem as a sensory and nonverbal encounter rather than a linguistic one; it is not until much later in the novel that we realize what Fokir's song must be.

If Fokir suggests the power of nonverbal to Piya, his rival Kanai insists on the importance of translation and language. Falling in love with Piya even though he senses her desire for the elusive (and unavailable) Fokir, Kanai ultimately offers Piya the generous gift of a translation of Fokir's song. In Kanai's preface to the translation, we intuit that Fokir, far from being the silent, nonverbal bearer of natural language, is instead (like Nirmal) deeply shaped by the human artifice of words. "This is my gift to you, this story that is also a song, these words that are a part of Fokir," Kanai writes to Piya (*HT*, 354). Kanai's perspective on Fokir, mediated by Nirmal's journal, suggests that engaging with significant otherness demands engaging with others as subjects of language, not solely as subjects of the natural environment. The doubleness of Piya's perception, which swings from the nonverbal to the translated, suggests that representational ethics require a language that embraces both the "outside" and "inside" of the speaker: it requires Piya to embrace the partiality of her knowledge in order to expand it.

If Piya must accept elements of translation, Kanai must also embrace knowledge beyond human speech. At the syncretic shrine to Bon Bibi, Fokir tells Kanai that on the island of Garjontola "Bon Bibi would show you whatever you wanted to know" (HT, 323). For Kanai, this revelation offers the knowledge that he is not fully the enlightened sophisticate he believes himself to be. In the instant of vulnerable self-realization, when Kanai confronts the residues of class, caste, and geographic prejudice, he becomes best able to move toward a deeper encounter with significant otherness. In this moment of abjection, Kanai suddenly begins to inhabit a new perspective:

> In Kanai's professional life there had been a few instances in which the act of interpretation had given him the momentary sensation of being transported out of his body and into another. In each instance it was as if the instrument of language had metamorphosed—instead of being a barrier, a curtain that divided, it had become a transparent film, a prism that allowed him to look through another set of eyes, to filter the world through a mind other than his own . . . it was exactly this feeling that came upon him as he looked at Fokir: it was as though his own vision were being refracted through those opaque, unreadable eyes, and he were seeing not himself, Kanai, but a great host of people—a double for the outside world, someone standing in for the men who had destroyed Fokir's village, burnt his home and killed his mother; he had become a token for a vision of human beings in which a man such as Fokir counted for nothing, a man whose value was less than that of an animal.
>
> (HT, 326–327)

As he evolves into a crowded self, Kanai combines the project of imagining others with the task of reimagining himself. As the nonverbal and the translated merge into one, the liminal space between water and land offers an opening in the carefully polished social façade that he constructs in his everyday life. When Kanai describes this experience of transmigration, the metaphor of seeing through another's life takes on renewed vigor; it allows him to merge the possibilities of nonverbal physicality with the verbal capacity of translation. As the object of his gaze, Fokir also combines these two qualities: on the one hand, he breaks out of his subaltern silence and speaks directly (his Bengali represented as English), but on the other hand, his steady, challenging gaze prefigures the silent force of the tiger that Kanai will soon see.

As the novel merges the power of the nonverbal with the power of translation, the encounter suggests that representational ethics can require extreme experiences that threaten the safe borders of the self. Kanai's crowded self reverses the asymmetries of power that define his class relation to Fokir, and as he sees his own historical and ethical signification through Fokir's eyes, the novel suggests that Kanai cannot really know another person until he recognizes his own limitations. Confronting the strong social borders between Kanai and Fokir demands encounters with the dangers of the nonverbal physical world and the dangers of verbal speech.

In encouraging us to embrace the simultaneity of the natural and the translated, the novel connects the cognitive process of imagining linguistic alterity with the larger political project that haunts its pages. While the novel, with its exquisite descriptions of the tide country, clearly values environmental conservation, its narration critiques the social institutions that manage environmental protection at the expense of human lives, particularly the lives of the poor and displaced. Fokir's village is burned and his mother killed because their settlement occupied a protected wilderness area, thus rendering the cost of conservation exceedingly expensive in human terms. As Kanai realizes, these policies value refugees less than they do animals. But the reason that they fail is because they refuse to recognize people *as* animals, as a species with needs for habitat and sustenance that parallel those of the tigers and dolphins. It is precisely the division between the world of the natural and the world of the human, or the nonverbal and the linguistic, that underpins these policies. At the end of the novel, when Piya hopes to begin a conservation project through the auspices of Nirmala's pragmatic human-oriented trust, the novel gestures toward a political future for the region that combines the natural with the social and thus the nonverbal with the translated.

This synthesis, often painful but necessary to *The Hungry Tide*'s vision of border crossing, gathers its most eloquent expression in the journal of Nirmal. Writing in Bangla about his time with Fokir and his mother Kusum, Nirmal often chooses to end his entries with poems of

Rainer Maria Rilke (whom he reads in Bangla and English translations). In one of his entries, Nirmal suggests that the nonhuman, nonverbal world is always already caught in the problems of translation. Nirmal's rendering of Rilke's poetic reflection on animals suggests that the natural world may itself be a translated space that precludes the psychological comfort often associated with nonhuman life. In the end, *The Hungry Tide* suggests a demanding representational ethics that integrates silence and speech.

Ghosh's crowded style is all the more striking because, on the surface, his writing does not seem obviously concerned with the workings of language. Works such as Theresa Hak Kyung Cha's *Dictee* (1982) or Gloria Anzaldúa's *Borderlands/La Frontera* (1987) make far greater demands on their audience to read in languages other than English. These works achieve their memorable effects by denying their readers the serviceable illusion of trustworthy translation, enhancing intimacy with similarly bilingual readers while estranging an audience with different linguistic capabilities. Set against such energetic tasks, Ghosh's prose offers a more subtle set of rigors and austerities to confront the durable borders of linguistic alterity.

In representing fictional lives lived through many languages, Ghosh's work frequently nears what Emily Apter calls "the ethical problem that arises when there is, strictly speaking, no 'original' language or text on which the translation is based."[35] Although Ghosh may sometimes think to himself in Bengali and then translate that thought into English, and although the languages of his characters have histories outside his work, we have no Ur-version of *The Glass Palace* or *The Hungry Tide* with parts in English, parts in Burmese, and parts in Bengali. We have no actually existing referent for the thoughts and words of non-English speaking characters represented in his novels. In this situation, it makes less sense to think of his work as translation and more sense to think of it as a form of stylistic imaginative projection. With no specific original against which to evaluate Ghosh's representations, we can only inquire into the linguistic relationships that exist *within* his novels: the inclusions, exclusions, and hierarchies that shape how these many different languages resonate with one another. In both *The Glass Palace* and *The Hungry Tide*, Ghosh's work insists that diverse forms of communication thrive most democratically in a crowded style that, on the surface, seems like uniform and homogenous English prose.

As Ghosh's writing asks how fiction in English might accommodate the multiplicity of multilingual and antilingual experience, it copes with the borders between languages by divesting English of exclusive aesthetic privilege. The flattened language of *The Glass Palace* eschews the hierarchies of dialect, favoring instead the visual techniques of modernist photography, and the crowded selves of *The Hungry Tide* forge a compromise between the utopianism of the unspoken and the fallible speech of translation. These aesthetic renunciations, paradoxically, expand the capacity of English to represent non-English worlds of experience. They testify to possible strategies for lives lived across the borders of language.

6

Sacrificing the Self

How might imagining significant otherness take shape under the most difficult of circumstances? More than any other border-crossing fiction considered in this book, the work of J. M. Coetzee compels exceptionally fraught meditations on the ethics of representation. "Unimaginable perhaps," a character in the novel *Slow Man* (2005) thinks to himself, "but the unimaginable is there to be imagined."[1] This paradox speaks to the heart of Coetzee's singular fiction, where imaginative sympathy under conditions of heightened pressure is simultaneously denied and demanded.

Luring us into violent territory disfigured by extremes of conflict and cruelty, Coetzee's writing stages a series of attempts to imagine the lives of others across historically oppressive social borders. Unafraid to confront diverse legacies of injury in his homeland of South Africa and in other parts of the world, Coetzee's fiction casts the project of sympathizing with others in harsh and unflinching language. His writings layer many different kinds of social divisions, revealing how the problem of crossing race or class is often deeply invested in the question of crossing gender or species. These writings struggle toward an ethics of representation that confronts the many different barriers that divide one self from the rest of its environment. To cross the borders of selfhood without replicating the self-serving distortions of privilege becomes a dangerous undertaking, one that frequently demands individual discomfort, sacrifice, and ultimately disgrace. Coetzee's crowded selves and styles, as we will see, become deeply haunted literary spaces. In taking up the problem of representational ethics at its limit, Coetzee's fiction draws together many of the preoccupations that have emerged in earlier chapters of this book. His work inverts and unsettles my starting point of Ruth Ozeki, returning us to the twinned specters of the rape of women and the predicament of animals while casting the implications of those alignments in a distinctly more disturbing light.

As one of the most prominent postcolonial writers working in English at the turn of the millennium, Coetzee stands out for the exceptional and uncompromising lens that his fiction turns on its world. In the 1970s, Coetzee began his career as a novelist with stylistically innovative and psychologically disturbing portraits of imperial power in a global context. Catapulted into international prominence with *Waiting for the Barbarians* (1980), he gained the reputation for an abiding interest in the problem of liberal complicity with injustice, which led his works to pose formal and ethical challenges to narratives of heroic progress. Stylistically indebted to such European writers as Daniel Defoe, Fyodor Dostoevsky, Franz Kafka, and Samuel Beckett, Coetzee's novels of the 1980s locate themselves within literary and political crises over the reliability of linguistic signifiers.[2] In the 1990s, Coetzee began to craft a more conventionally realist discourse that addresses the haunting consequences of revolutionary terror, the legacy of apartheid in South Africa, and the changing role of postcolonial nations in a globalizing era. Catapulted beyond academic prominence in 2003, when he won the Nobel Prize for Literature, Coetzee's twenty-first-century books struggle with the specter of aging and obsolescence even as his changing career places new demands on him as a public intellectual. *Elizabeth Costello* (2003), *Slow Man* (2005), and *Diary of a Bad Year* (2007) all reflect dizzyingly recursive layerings of realism and metafiction that question the ethical role of the artist in an age of increasingly mediated migration and circulation.

More so than any other novels considered in this book, Coetzee's fiction has come to exemplify the fundamental problem of imagining alterity from the perspective of social privilege. For many of his readers, Coetzee effectively responds to the problem of writing about others by invoking the impossibility of reliable representation. His novels abound with enigmatic ciphers whose silences, gaps, and illegible actions are embedded within the textual fabric of his fiction.[3] A figure such as the tongueless Friday in *Foe* (1986) exemplifies this narrative choice, gesturing toward the impossibility of telling Friday's story adequately within conventional colonial language. To author, and thus to invade, such alterity, the novel suggests, is to position oneself as a "foe" to one's subject in the realm of representable discourse.

Coetzee's novels also invite us to look with suspicion on the very idea of a dominant ethical imperative that would inspire antihegemonic forms of representing others. As these novels distrust the moral privilege of altruistic action, they frequently imply that well-meaning attempts to oppose oppressive states ironically replicate the forms of power that they wish to undo. Suggesting that heroic acts of resistance ultimately resemble the fascist powers they oppose, these writings allow no easy or gentle resolution to problems of discursive domination. Coetzee's twenty-first-century fiction insistently wrestles with the constitutive concept of conviction, offering fictional meditations that undermine the very idea of belief or principle beyond the workings of narrative form.[4] Coetzee frequently lectures at universities by reading stories about an Australian author named Elizabeth Costello, who usually gives her own lecture at an institution unnervingly similar to the venue where Coetzee is reading his story. Because audiences, and later readers, can never quite be sure if Costello's firm opinions are Coetzee's own, these performance pieces invite us to think skeptically about why readers search for ethical impulses in works of art or in the words of their makers. Coetzee is notorious for resisting the conventional give and take of academic interviews, often agreeing to be interviewed only under extremely limited circumstances, offering responses that critique the interviewer's desire for his opinion, and generally sabotaging the form of the interview itself.[5] *Diary of a Bad Year* delves into this question even more keenly, offering three parallel narratives that ask the reader to move between the political opinions of a character who closely resembles Coetzee and a set of diaries that trace this character's involvement within an emerging romantic triangle. Unlike more conventional multivocal texts, which alternate among voices presented in sequence, the graphic layout of *Diary of a Bad Year* divides each page into two and then three discrete sections that feature three simultaneous narratives. The "strong opinions" that constitute the top strand of the novel are thus continually interrupted by the domestic dramas of their maker, and as the diary entries gradually begin to spill over from page to page, they confuse even the linear order that would have us read each page in three parts from top to bottom. This arrangement invites us to appreciate how convictions are formed in contestation with lived experience, destroying any semblance of an ethical imperative that comes from nowhere or that uniformly governs the making of narrative fiction.

However, despite Coetzee's evident respect for the silence of others, his aversion to heroic drama and moral uplift, and his relentless interrogation of ethical beliefs, I contend that Coetzee's novels at the turn of the millennium do not abandon the task of envisioning lives lived outside the reach of easy communion.[6] Honoring the reticence of others can easily conceal apathy or complacency, and it can reaffirm the very borders that contribute to the silencing of others.[7] Although Coetzee has been rebuked for his European literary affiliations and his textual neglect of black South African imaginative traditions,[8] his works anxiously search the archives of European thought for the possibility of imaginative practices that might contest the legacy of discursive domination. As Derek Attridge persuasively argues, any positive ethical gesture we might find in his fiction asserts itself in a space beyond visible moral codes, "not a lesson to be learned or a system to be deployed."[9] Understanding exactly how his work accomplishes this vision, and at what cost, emerges at the center of modern anxieties about what Coetzee means to us as a writer.

As Coetzee's work suggests that the very idea of a lesson is always unsteadily shaped by the potentially disruptive workings of narrative, it invites us to consider the significance of sympathetic imagination. The problem of sympathy speaks to the heart of an ongoing debate about the implications of Coetzee's work, which often divides his readers between those who lament the fictions' constant troubling of political action and those who read this troubling as precisely their contribution to political discourse.[10] Seen more specifically, Coetzee's staging of sympathy suggests to readers a wealth of possible relationships between self and other. The self might *recognize its own limited ability* to know the other, it might *give itself* to the other, it might *come physically close* to the other, and it might *perform* the other.[11] All of these positions seek to describe the competing impulses at work in Coetzee's writing: his fictions appear to refuse liberal or positivist approaches to conceptualizing other lives, while they also appear to refuse to accept significant otherness as absolute, inviolable, or ignorable.

Although scholars in the late 1990s and 2000s have increasingly gravitated toward the rhetoric of sympathy and confirmed its centrality to Coetzee's vision, their work has tended to consider this preoccupation in terms of Coetzee's individual authorial predicament as a writer from South Africa rather than as a symptom of a larger concern with the representational ethics of border crossing in fiction written in English. It is in Coetzee's work, I argue, that this broader preoccupation comes to fullest fruition. Although my readings will stress the importance of South African history, I also approach Coetzee in light of the ethical experiments considered in earlier chapters of this book. Using my keyword of crowding, I propose a new possibility that helps illuminate how Coetzee's work continues and extends a broader millennial concern with the ethics of border crossing: the self might *make room* for the other, diminishing its own claims to literal and metaphoric possession of its place in the world. This act of making room characterizes Coetzee's crowded selves and crowded styles, which grapple with alterity as characters conceptualize each other and as they are imagined in language. These narrative choices resonate with the radical theories of personhood advocated by Derek Parfit, who urges a philosophical understanding of selfhood that diminishes the importance of autonomous personal identity and enhances the importance of experiences (to whomever they occur). Because Parfit's theories of personhood reject the idea of all-or-nothing identity, they emphasize the multiplicity of ways in which one self overlaps with another. While, as Parfit admits, this view of identity destroys many of the traditional privileges of what is considered one's own, embracing the self as a crowd—as Coetzee's characters find—may enable surprising liberation from the endless mirroring of imaginative entrapment that marks discursive domination.

Although these problems arguably shape many of Coetzee's fictions, they emerge most powerfully in two paired works from the turn of the millennium. I begin with his collection of two narratives, *The Lives of Animals* (1999), where Coetzee most explicitly meditates on the ethics of engaging significant otherness. To assess how modern fiction might overcome problems of representation engendered by histories of European imperialism, *The Lives of Animals* confronts the legacy of particular European ideas of sympathy in a postcolonial world. As Coetzee invokes eighteenth- and nineteenth-century theories of sympathetic imagination, his work unsettles many of their guiding assumptions to make room for a new form of sympathy in a globalizing age. This collection, I suggest, offers Coetzee's most explicit defense of imagining alterity, but it also points out its own limitations and contradictions. The crowded selves and styles of the collection, therefore, remain incipient and incomplete. Turning to *Disgrace* (1999), a novel published concurrently with *The Lives of Animals*, I suggest that this novel elaborates, radicalizes, and more fully realizes the ethics of imaginative encounter set forth in its companion volume. *Disgrace* is particularly important, I argue, because it examines the possibility of sympathetic imagination with significant otherness in situations of dramatically unequal social power. In Rita Barnard's description, the novel locates itself within a new South Africa that marks "the site of a painful othering."[12] How best to confront such painful othering, in all its complexity and urgency, forms the central question at the heart of the novel. I begin my discussion of *Disgrace* by examining the novel's interest in crossing social divides of gender. To produce crowded selves across gendered boundaries marked by an optic of sexual privilege, the novel questions the assumptions that bolster Byronic ideas of sympathy and advocates a radical solidarity with loss and dispossession. I follow this exploration with an investigation of how the novel represents race, contending that the novel pursues an ethics of racial-border crossing in a postapartheid landscape through the cipher of the nonhuman. Rejecting liberal principles of imagining alterity, the novel produces crowded selves and crowded styles through a transfiguration rather than a rejection of bestial rhetoric.

Throughout these readings, I argue that to imagine those who are vulnerable, Coetzee's protagonists attempt to embrace their own vulnerability. In developing their crowded selves, they acknowledge the demands of others almost to the point of relinquishing their own claims on individual selfhood. As the novel relies on the figure of animals to demand a new conception of self and community, its characters connect not through modern articulations of human rights but through a larger sense of shared suffering. Drawn together in language as rights losers rather than rights bearers, Coetzee's figures suggest that liberal humanist paradigms cannot surmount intense alterity, and thus his fictions come to embrace a radical antihumanist ethics.

Although these works of fiction are not always optimistic about the ability to conceptualize others, they present this ideal as one worth pursuing even into failure or defeat. These moments of loss and collapse envision an austere ethical practice commensurate to moments when the barriers between selves seem particularly severe. Coetzee's work at the turn of the millennium implies that even figures who strenuously resist representation must nonetheless be confronted, because the cost of failing to engage these figures ultimately demands the higher price. From the most intimate of family relations to the most distant links between strangers, Coetzee's prose suggests both the difficulty and the necessity of imagining across borders. To encounter significant otherness, Coetzee's subjects come to abandon almost all the privileges of what it means to be a person in the modern era: property, bodily integrity, autonomy, and dignity. Coetzee's language performs an analogous sacrifice, opening itself up to make room for troubling rhetorical specters that demand inclusion. The ethics of being and of writing, of crowded selves and crowded styles, ultimately approach the limit where the difference between grace and disgrace is virtually indistinguishable.

The Sympathetic Imagination Abroad: J. M. Coetzee's The Lives of Animals

The question of significant otherness haunts *The Lives of Animals*, two fictionalized academic lectures that also appear in Coetzee's novel-in-lessons *Elizabeth Costello*.[13] In *The Lives of Animals*, an Australian novelist named Elizabeth Costello presents a series of talks at a small college in the United States. In foregrounding the importance of academic institutions, these narratives remind us that the crisis of sympathetic imagination is particularly relevant to the professional readers who interpret Coetzee's career.[14] Although Costello's hosts presumably expect her to lecture on questions of literature, Costello chooses to speak about what she considers a crime of monstrous proportions: the human treatment of animals. As Costello invites her audience to contemplate the ethical implications of how humans behave toward other species, she asks her listeners to consider the lives of beings that seem very much unlike their own. Animals thus come to provide a symbolic way of talking about how broadly and deeply humans can identify themselves with others.[15] Coetzee's work, therefore, not only provides a lecture about the literal lives of animals but also creates a narrative about the difficulty of sympathizing beyond what humans consider their social locations and natural privileges. It provides a fable about how far one can expand the capacity to imagine.

From the beginning, the form of *The Lives of Animals* invites us to recognize how extensively imaginative projection mediates any experience of the world. Setting aside the obvious point that this work is the fiction of Coetzee, who may or may not be expressing his own opinions through the polemical lecture of Elizabeth Costello, we quickly come to realize that Costello is available to us only through the focalizing lens of her son John. Frequently puzzled and frustrated by his mother, who disrupts his workplace and his marriage, yet full of compassion for her as well, John continually attempts to breach the gap that divides Costello from the rest of her world. As his trenchant observations and occasional judgments shape our vision of his mother, they model for us a sensitive running commentary of an active imagination in progress. His role bespeaks the importance of identifying with others (though not necessarily approving of them) as a vital part of everyday embedded life.

If John seems crafted to persuade us of the pervasive presence of imaginative projection, Elizabeth Costello argues for its importance in more grandiose terms. In her speech at Appleton College, Costello expresses a broad optimism that humans can adequately inhabit different cognitive worlds. Invoking the specter of the Holocaust, she reminds her audience that the failure to do so lies at the heart of human atrocity.[16] "The particular horror of the camps," Costello says, "the horror that convinces us that what went on there was a crime against humanity, is not that despite a humanity shared with their victims, the killers treated them like lice. That is too abstract. The horror is that the killers refused to think themselves into the place of their victims, as did everyone else."[17] Locating the atrocity of genocide less in its physical cruelty and more in its imaginative failure, Costello asserts the strongest possible practical importance for an activity associated with the telling of stories. Underlying moral action, she suggests, lies the ability to conceptualize the experience of another in a robust and visceral manner. Costello identifies this ability as sympathy, and she advocates that humans can and should extend the reach of imaginative sympathy across biological borders. "There are no bounds to the sympathetic imagination," she tells her audience with confidence (*LA*, 35). Animals thus come to stand for the outer limits of imaginative capacity, marking the unknown territory that Costello commands her audience to explore.

This affinity between imaginative projection and the treatment of nonhumans places Elizabeth Costello within one vexed legacy of eighteenth- and nineteenth-century European philosophy, when the invention of particular modern ideas of sympathy emerged in concert with the workings of imperial and colonial expansion. As *The Lives of Animals* wrestles with the possibilities and the limitations of this inheritance, it allows us to perceive how Coetzee's work struggles with the adequacy of sympathetic imagination in a postcolonial moment. In advocating for better treatment of animals, Costello echoes the developing concern with animal welfare in eighteenth-century Britain, an era that is often thought to contrast the indifference and cruelty that proliferated during the Restoration.[18] As Costello hints in her reading of Descartes, seventeenth-century scientists often argued that animals had no souls, felt no pain, and existed merely as mechanical objects that could be taken apart to increase scientific knowledge. Public performances of vivisection invited audiences to revel in the spectacle of animal torture as a vital, even pleasurable, aspect of scientific research.[19] Through such grotesque displays, these practices encouraged humans to repress any conceptual identification they might feel for other species.

In contrast, the eighteenth century in England can be seen as inaugurating one form of the modern liberal treatment of animals. During this period, new developments in biological taxonomy, exotic accounts of zoological explorations, and the rise of bourgeois pet keeping suggested potential affinities between humans and other species.[20] These affinities inspired both exuberance and anxiety about what it meant to be human. Not coincidentally, this moment of anxiety about the status of the human emerged in a continent increasingly linked to other parts of the world through exploration and imperialism. Laura Brown argues in her analysis of eighteenth-century culture:

> Animals helped Europeans imagine Africans, Native Americans, and themselves. The many figurative lines of connection between our cohort of nonhuman beings and the non-European human beings who had become vividly present to European experience in the eighteenth century suggest that the fable of the nonhuman being served as a powerful and common resource for structuring the encounter with cultural difference.[21]

By the nineteenth century, this entanglement of European subjects, animals, and human "others" had taken a new turn. "Kindness to animals came to stand high in the index of civilization," Kathleen Kete contends. "It formed part of the project of civilization. The barbarian others—the urban working classes, continental peasants, southern Europeans, Irish Catholics, Russians, Asians, and Turks—were defined in part by their brutality to beasts."[22] When Elizabeth Costello talks about the treatment of animals, then, she implicitly raises the specter of imperialism, its production of particular ideas of the human, and its investment in concepts of cultural difference. Her own identification with beings like Kafka's great ape Red Peter encourages us to think expansively about humans as animals, but it also reminds us of periods when only *some* humans were considered to share essential qualities with beasts, as well as of periods when liberal relationships to animals were thought to constitute defining marks of ethical humanism. This period of uneven sympathy—increased sympathy for certain kinds of animals and diminished sympathy for certain kinds of humans—prefigures Costello's own ambiguous positioning within the genre of the twentieth-century postcolonial animal tale. As we will see, this paradox even characterizes her own promising but ultimately limited approach to significant otherness.

Costello's polemic draws explicitly upon the thought of eighteenth-century British moral philosophers who prefigure her own close connection between sympathy and ethical action.[23] In Adam Smith's *Theory of Moral Sentiments* (1759), the ability to identify with others is central to his explanation of a moral impulse. Sympathy, Smith argues, depends upon imaginative projection rather than upon sensory knowledge. "Though our brother is upon the rack, as long as we ourselves are at our ease, our senses will never inform us of what he suffers," he famously declares. "They never did, and never can, carry us beyond our own person, and it is by the imagination only that we can form any conception of what are his sensations."[24] Such imaginative projection forms the basis for what eighteenth-century thinkers called fellow-feeling, which in turn renders the possibility of action on another's behalf. Although there is no guarantee that conceptualizing the predicaments of others will lead to palpable social change, Costello inherits the guarded optimism of Smith when she suggests that the root cause of injustice and cruelty can be found in the cognitive failure to identify with others.

Despite the title of Smith's work, it is important to note that the idea of sympathy in this sense is not primarily what we might call a sentimental one. Smith does not identify sympathy exclusively with the emphasis on affective bonding through loss with which even his contemporaries associated the word: "Pity and compassion are words appropriated to signify our fellow-feeling with the sorrow of others. Sympathy, though its meaning was, perhaps, originally the same, may now, however, without much impropriety, be made use of to denote our fellow-feeling with any passion whatever," he stresses.[25] Although Elizabeth Costello argues passionately for the extension of sympathy to nonhumans, she is consistently presented as a ruthlessly unsentimental character who belies the typical image of the liberal lover of animals.[26] Unlike the figures of Ozeki's world, who eagerly perform emotionally intense bonding through loss, Costello seems designed as a rejection of this affective conception of sympathy. Her son John considers her "one of those large cats that pause as they eviscerate their victim and, across the torn-open belly, give you a cold yellow stare."[27] As this metaphor proves an apt description for Costello's unflinching style of address, it suggests a distinction between Smith's conception of sympathy and the nineteenth-century Western cult of sentimentality that followed in its wake. Coetzee's work, as we will see, aims to test the ethical possibilities of sympathy without sentiment.

Following Smith, Costello argues that we do not need literal sensory experiences to imagine others sympathetically. She introduces a counterargument through the work of the philosopher Thomas Nagel, whose celebrated essay "What Is It Like to Be a Bat?" suggests the insufficiency of the human mind to grasp alien experiences. In Costello's representation of his work, Nagel suggests that we are trapped inside our own contours of consciousness and cannot fully inhabit the life of a radically different being.[28] Costello quotes from a thought experiment in which Nagel attempts to imagine the experience of a bat: "It will not help to try to imagine that one has webbing on one's arms, which enables one to fly around. . . . Insofar as I can imagine this (which is not very far), it tells me only what it would be like for *me* to behave as a bat behaves. But that is not the question. I want to know what it is like for a *bat* to be a bat" (quoted in *LA*, 31, italics in the original). When Costello challenges Nagel's idea that "we need to be able to experience bat-life through the sense-modalities of a bat" (*LA*, 33), she echoes Smith's argument that the production of sympathetic identification need not rely on the spectator's personal sensory experience. For Costello, the difference between sympathizing with Smith's sufferer and with Nagel's bat signals a difference in degree but not in kind.

In advocating sympathy beyond sensory experience, Costello echoes the arguments of Samuel Johnson, who suggested that it is specifically *language* that enhances our ability to identify with others. Johnson wrote about the importance of imaginative projection in his essays for *The Rambler*, where he argued that the idea of sympathetic imagination helps explain the aesthetic effects of narratives that enable their audience to identify with others. "All joy or sorrow for the happiness or calamities of others is produced by an act of the imagination, that realises the event however fictitious, or approximates it however remote, by placing us, for a time, in the condition of him whose fortune we contemplate," Johnson began an essay on the value of biography.[29] Our ability to feel joy and sorrow while reading testifies to imaginative projection at work; it documents the existence of this invisible capacity. Description offers a link between one life and another, replacing the need for personal sensory experience.

While Coetzee's portrait presents Costello in many ways as a direct descendant of Adam Smith and Samuel Johnson, *The Lives of Animals* offers not only a continuation but also a subversion of their genealogy. Even as both Costello and the narratives at large claim certain affinities with particular strands of eighteenth-century projects, both also subject their discourse to late twentieth-century critiques of values associated with such projects. Most evidently, Costello disavows the faith in rationality with which the period is often associated.[30] In contrast to Smith and Johnson, Costello retains faith in imagination without distinguishing between cognitive projection and the physical body. If Smith and Johnson suggest that thought and language can provide what sensory experience cannot, while the position attributed to Nagel insists that no amount of thought can adequately compensate for the lack of sensory experience, Costello defends a deeply physical sense of what it means to imagine. "To thinking, cogitation, I oppose fullness, embodiedness, the sensation of being," she says, "not a consciousness of yourself as a kind of ghostly reasoning machine thinking thoughts, but on the contrary the sensation—a heavily affective sensation—of being a body with limbs that have extension in space, of being alive to the world" (LA, 33). Her thought experiment on what it might be like to be a corpse produces the feeling of choking, inspiring imaginatively produced physical sensations. This revised vision of sympathy allows Costello to retain elements of Smith's and Johnson's optimism while encompassing one of the strongest late twentieth-century critiques of reason, namely the power of embodied knowledge. In refusing to accept reason as the dominant form of identification between beings, Costello opens up a space for sympathy with nonhumans, and she thus rejects the imperialist logic that excluded non-Europeans from claims upon sympathy. Her emphasis on embodiment, then, helps generate an incipient crowded self that reflects a new ethics of imaginative projection in a postcolonial era—one that is not a positivist claim to another's consciousness but a relational feeling of solidarity through the experience of inhabiting a body.

However, if Costello offers an explicit revision of Smith and Johnson's ideas of sympathy, the rhetoric of *The Lives of Animals* also undermines Costello's own understanding of imaginative projection. Martin Puchner points out that Costello's commitment to the embodied is set against the metafictional moments of the narrative, which perform precisely the disembodied view from nowhere that the content of the narrative denies.[31] In an even more telling fashion, Costello's specific defense of engaging significant otherness raises more questions than it resolves.

There is no limit to the extent to which we can think ourselves into the being of another. There are no bounds to the sympathetic imagination. If you want proof, consider the following. Some years ago I wrote a book called *The House on Eccles Street*. To write that book I had to think my way into the existence of Marion Bloom. Either I succeeded or I did not. If I did not, I cannot imagine why you invited me here today.... If I can think my way into the existence of a being who has never existed, then I can think my way into the existence of a bat or a chimpanzee or an oyster, any being with whom I share the substrate of life.

(*LA*, 35)

Costello's universalist rhetoric seems at odds with many of the details within the narrative, which quietly question the logic of her argument. Because she often defends the value of the literal and the concrete, her invocation of the abstract "substrate of life" seems a contradictory choice. Costello also tries to convince her audience of the breadth of imaginative power through a syllogism that relies on a particular and puzzling comparison between a fictional character and a nonhuman being. Despite the prickly authority of Costello's tone, it is not at all clear why it would be more difficult to imagine the world of a fictional woman than the universe of an oyster or a bat. After all, the Australian Costello at least shares with Marion Bloom the experiences of being a twentieth-century woman with artistic ambitions in an Anglophone nation shaped by colonization. In his response to *The Lives of Animals*, Peter Singer raises this objection when a character in his philosophical dialogue makes the following point: "The fact that a character doesn't exist isn't something that makes it hard to imagine yourself as that character. You can imagine someone very like yourself, or like someone else you know."[32] Costello's analogy between imagining the nonexistent and imagining the alien thus appears distinctly unconvincing as an argument for expansive conceptual projection. In offering us this absurdly weak analogy that contradicts many of Costello's own ideas, Coetzee seems to invite us to question her portrait of how sympathy works.

If, as Costello says, "there are no bounds to the sympathetic imagination," why does Coetzee immediately have Costello say so colloquially that she "cannot imagine" why her hosts would challenge her claims to imaginative success? This seemingly careless turn of phrase plays upon the dissonance between the claims made for expansive imagination and the contrasting constraints of particular language usage. As Marjorie Garber suggests in her response to Coetzee's *The Lives of Animals*, dead metaphors that mirror thematic textual concerns proliferate throughout the story. These colloquial usages, Garber argues, pose philosophical and ethical questions that challenge particular humanist beliefs.[33] In this spirit, the wordplay of the story asks us to question how the phrase "cannot imagine" comments upon the stated philosophy of imagining others that pervades *The Lives of Animals*. The fiction suggests a constitutive problem at work: at the very moment when Elizabeth Costello claims the most robust philosophical power for imaginative projection, her practical use of language ironically contracts and contradicts that power.

Figured as a subtle textual moment in this passage, this contradiction between grand philosophical possibilities and local historical constraints produces the incipient crowded style of *The Lives of Animals*. The narratives in the collection partake of two genres, the academic lecture and the short story, such that the philosophical ideas in the lectures resonate with the realist drama of a family triangle that frames Costello's public discourse. Costello's ideas on the importance of sympathy emerge within a narrative frame that exposes the practical *absence* of sympathy in Costello's personal life. Although Costello has a reasonably strong relationship with her son John, her relationship with her daughter-in-law Norma is scarred by vivid animosity between the two women. Because Norma dislikes her mother-in-law, she views Costello's vegetarianism and philosophical positions on animals as disguised forms of aggression that challenge Norma's own authority. "I would have more respect for her if she didn't try to undermine me behind my back, with her stories to the children about the poor little veal calves and what the bad men do to them," Norma says with anger to John after attending Costello's talks (*LA*, 68). The fictional counterpoint to the nonfictional lecture thus tells a story about the pervasive role of hostility and misunderstanding in Costello's domestic life.

Although most readers tend to take Costello's side against Norma's, suggesting the complicity between "Norma" and her "normal" or "normative" ideas, to deny Norma sympathy is ultimately to replicate the limitations of Costello's position. Although Norma is not sketched in particularly appealing terms, the story gives us convincing reasons for her resentment of her mother-in-law. "Norma holds a Ph.D. in philosophy with a specialism in the philosophy of mind," the narrative reveals. "Having moved with [John] to Appleton, she has been unable to find a teaching position. This is a cause of bitterness to her, and of conflict between the two of them" (*LA*, 17). Norma, not Elizabeth Costello, is the academic expert in philosophy, but while Costello speculates freely to an academic audience on the cognitive capabilities of great apes, Norma works in the shadows on a review essay about language learning in primates. Costello gains a public voice to pontificate on grand ideas that intrigue her; Norma attends academic functions only in her subordinate role as Costello's daughter-in-law. Given Norma's frustrated intellectual career, it is no surprise that she views Costello as a rival for power both in the realm of the family and in the realm of intellectual discourse.

Although Norma's displaced anger makes sense within the story, it is more striking that Elizabeth Costello offers little sympathy for a woman in her position. While Costello speaks with passion of her ability to think herself into the position of any being with whom she shares the substrate of life, she makes no attempt to engage with the perspective of a woman who is, in many ways, much like her—intelligent, unsentimental, and intellectually ambitious. To the contrary, she seems to go out of her way to provoke Norma's anxiety. When Costello asks Norma and John why their children do not join them at the dinner table, the story suggests the insidious impulse concealed within the seemingly innocuous inquiry: "The question is not necessary, because [Elizabeth Costello] knows the answer" (*LA*, 16). The children eat separately because Norma refuses to change their diet to accommodate Costello's vegetarianism, and Costello knows of this practice before she asks. Her question appears to her family as a covert form of manipulation, an attempt to make them feel guilty before her moral stance on the eating of meat. When Norma raises the question of control in public, as part of an academic argument, and in private, as part of the rivalries of a family triangle, she reveals a genuine problem with Costello's position. In Coetzee's work, as we will see more explicitly in *Disgrace*, robust sympathy with others cannot coexist with such disguised exertion of power.

Far from offering sympathy to figures in her life, Costello sympathizes the most with creatures who cannot contradict or resist her claims to imaginative projection—fictional characters and animals. Sympathy thus emerges in *The Lives of Animals* as a deeply inhuman activity that fails to transfigure existing human relationships. In one respect, this troubling omission perhaps should not surprise us, since radical sympathy for the nonhuman can often mask a form of misanthropy. In Swiftian terms, animals frequently figure the ennobled Houyhnhnms against the debased human Yahoos.[34] Yet, while Costello fits within this recognizable paradigm, the narrative makes a point of underscoring the ironies of Costello's investment in grand ideals of compassion that she fails to realize. In fact, no one seems capable of very much human sympathy in the world of the story. "I don't think [Norma] is in a position to sympathize," John tells his mother at the end of her trip. "Perhaps one could say the same for me" (*LA*, 68). Costello only imagines subjects who cannot challenge her imaginative projections, and she denies sympathy to those who can. This paradox returns us to the problem of sympathy as it appears in the writings of Costello's eighteenth-century predecessors. "We are, by our occupations, education, and habits of life, divided almost into different species, which regard one another, for the most part with scorn and malignity," Samuel Johnson despairs in *The Rambler*.[35] For Elizabeth Costello, the barriers that divide humans from one another seem to be much more powerful than the barriers that divide humans from other species. Although she makes claims for the possibility of sympathy with nonhuman subjects, she remains caught within the social divides that Johnson invokes.

Elizabeth Costello, therefore, figures an ambivalent vision of *The Lives of Animals*' search for an ethics of representing alterity. Although she remains committed to the value of expansive imaginative projection, she remains blind to the implications of such sympathy within her most intimate world. Although she advocates the importance of diminishing human privilege with respect to animals, she fails to suggest how this transhuman solidarity might reconfigure relationships between humans. And although she presents her position as the minority view that it is, she refuses to sympathize with subjects who might speak back and challenge her claims to knowledge. As her daughter-in-law intuits, Costello appears to lack the openness to revision that might enable a more persuasive approach to her claims to sympathy. Only in the last few pages of *The Lives of Animals*, when Costello emerges as a figure of vulnerability rather than authority, do we sense a commitment to imagining others that exceeds Costello's desire to avoid painful encounters with other humans or to exert authority over them. This burgeoning vision of sympathy through loss appears in a more fully developed form within *Disgrace*, which seeks to confront Costello's evasions.

Costello's crowded self in Coetzee's narratives, therefore, inhabits the contradiction between the language of expansive imaginative claims and the historically specific colloquialism of "I cannot imagine." Poised on the brink between what she can and cannot conceptualize, like the compelling image of herself alive and dead at the same time, Costello's position suggests both the urgency of imagining others and the limitations of doing so. Indeed, in the one new interview granted to a Swedish publication in the wake of his Nobel Prize, Coetzee expressed beliefs that both concur with and contradict the positions Costello proffers in the narrative. This interview, conducted by *Djurens Rätt* [*Animal Rights*], bespeaks Coetzee's skepticism that the inner lives of animals can ever be known as the lives of humans can be (thus rearticulating Nagel's position), while it nonetheless echoes some of Costello's pronouncements: "my interest is . . . in a change of heart towards animals."[36] This undecidable tension energizes the narrative's crowded style, which merges philosophical claims with dead metaphors and enmeshes the genre of fiction with the ideals of the lecture. Coetzee's work at large often seems to inhabit this contradictory moment, in which the pull between what is possible and what is required reshapes the ethics of engaging significant otherness.

Becoming the Woman: J. M. Coetzee's Disgrace

While *The Lives of Animals* thematizes the possibilities but also dramatizes the limitations of Elizabeth Costello's crowded self, Coetzee's novel *Disgrace* pushes past this impasse to suggest an ethics of representation at the point of loss, suffering, and disgrace.[37] If Costello's vestiges of power prevent her from fully imagining the humans in her life, *Disgrace* suggests that individuals must sacrifice themselves almost to the point of extinction to generate connections with others unlike them. Such crowded selves ultimately allot most of their room to the demands of others.

Disgrace transposes the problems raised in *The Lives of Animals* to the vexed terrain of postapartheid South Africa. Since Coetzee is a writer of Afrikaner and English descent, his work enters the public sphere through the politically volatile history of imperialism and apartheid. Within this social location, his writing is thus always already the focus of stringent ethical demands.[38] Unlike Nadine Gordimer, with whom he is frequently compared, Coetzee has not always embraced the idea that writers within apartheid and postapartheid systems bear political responsibilities to witness the suffering of their nation. However, works such as *Disgrace* contemplate fundamental philosophical questions about sympathy and alterity that underlie these political concerns. In featuring a controversial narrative plot that conjures poisonous histories of sexual and racial relations in South Africa, *Disgrace* represents one of the most difficult stories for a white male writer to tell. Though the implications of the novel unsettle many of its readers, Coetzee's decision to embrace this very difficulty suggests one kind of commitment to the ethics of South African writing.

Since *Disgrace* is a novel that offers no easy vision of imagining others, its readers frequently disagree over how effective its representation of sympathetic imagination can be. Although some claim that Coetzee ultimately offers a successful portrait of sympathy, others are less sure of such an optimistic outcome. In a substantial discussion of sympathy in *Disgrace*, Mike Marais contends that Coetzee enables both points of view. "The meditation on the imagination that one finds in *Disgrace* ultimately argues not for the power of the imagination, but the inspiration that may derive from the sense the imagination imparts of that over which it has no power, of that which its attempts to reveal ultimately destroy," he claims.[39] Like Marais, my readings will emphasize the ethically productive moments of failure that seem to mark Coetzee's portrayal of sympathy. However, while Marais perceives imagination as fundamentally invasive, I suggest that the greatest danger is not to the *object* of imagination but to its *subject*. In the world of *Disgrace*, robust sympathetic imagination may come dangerously close to destroying the sympathizer.

In its stylistic construction, *Disgrace* performs the problem that its characters confront: it immediately makes it difficult for its readers to sympathize with its own narrative voice. Through the free indirect discourse of the novel, we share an uncomfortable stylistic space with a character designed to trouble any easy identification between narrator and reader, even as it holds a troubling mirror to what Coetzee knows will be a substantial academic audience. David Lurie, the white former professor of literature from whose focalizing perspective the story is told, comes to us as a deeply flawed subject whose sensibilities we cannot fundamentally trust. This dissonance speaks to the heart of Coetzee's enterprise, compelling us to acknowledge the claims of a very different perspective without abandoning our own interpretative instincts as readers. As the narrator of Coetzee's *Age of Iron* (1990) famously declares of a fellow character, "Because I cannot trust Vercueil I must trust him."[40] The force of this ethical wager, intensified by the lack of a comma that would separate the sentence into two grammatically comfortable clauses, haunts the stylistic premise of *Disgrace*'s narration. Pushing its readers to inhabit the mind of a character they distrust yet rely upon, this tension helps constitute one element of the novel's crowded style.

Although we often presume that it is more difficult to imagine others across socially enforced borders such as race or nationality, Coetzee (like Jen in chapter 3) reminds us that powerful divisions trouble the most intimate of communities. Focusing upon a troubled bond between a father and a daughter, *Disgrace* explores how the unfolding of their relationship mirrors the divisions of their world at large. Indeed, the novel examines the possibility of sympathy in a world defined precisely by its absence. "Don't expect sympathy from me, David," his former wife declares, "and don't expect sympathy from anyone else either. No sympathy, no mercy, not in this day and age."[41] Shared race, nationality, class, and genes are no guarantee of imaginative sympathy, and like many novelists, Coetzee shows us how hard we must work to understand those closest to us. Situated at the crossroads of the private and the public, Coetzee reveals how the struggle for dialogue between a father and a daughter requires an engagement with broader differences of gender, race, and even species.

Although these forms of significant otherness emerge in many shapes, the novel draws special attention to the cipher of sexuality. "For a man of his age, fifty-two, divorced, he has, to his mind, solved the problem of sex rather well," reads the opening line of *Disgrace* (D, 1). As the novel makes abundantly clear, this beginning ironically commences a book concerned deeply with "the problem of sex" and the social differences entrenched through sexual practices. The novel begins in the multiethnic city of Cape Town, where David initiates a short affair with one of his female students. Called to account for his abuse of professional authority before a university committee, David eventually loses his position and leaves to visit his daughter Lucy on her smallholding in the eastern Cape. During his visit, Lucy's farmhouse is looted by three black men; David is wounded and Lucy is raped. The remainder of the novel attempts to come to terms with this eruption of sexualized violence, describing how David and Lucy seek to reconstruct their lives within varying states of disgrace. David composes an opera and works at a clinic to euthanize abandoned dogs; Lucy, pregnant from the attack, sacrifices her property rights to her black neighbor Petrus in return for her right to endure on the land. As this sketch of the novel suggests, *Disgrace* locates the search for a new ethics of representation within unpromising social geographies that figure both the pathologies of a national past and the problems of material inequality in a globalizing present.[42]

As the relentless preoccupation of the novel implies, the specter of sexualized violence is central to the vexed era of political transition to a postapartheid South African state in the 1990s. While 1994 witnessed the first free elections in South Africa, the nation still found itself haunted by the legacy of European colonialism, the virtual half-century of apartheid governance, the violence of repressive state security and armed struggle, and the pervasive criminalization of politics. Although elite political rhetoric shifted to more compromising accents of racial reconciliation, this era of transitional governance coincided with what many saw as a sharp rise in crime within South African civil society.[43] "The period of political transition," argues Rosalind Morris, "has been marked by a perceived efflorescence of criminality and by a sensation of political crisis."[44] By 2001, South Africa's rates of armed robbery were the highest in the world.[45] This new public sense of danger to person and property was often linked to the specific predations of sexual violence. "Sexual violence is widely thought to lie at the heart of this crisis of crime," Morris contends.[46] In other words, the constitution of South Africa as a new multiracial nation exhibited anxieties about ownership and agency through distinctly gendered divisions. The landscape of *Disgrace* reflects a world where such struggles erupt through public and private sexualized violence.

Within this ironic portrait of a new South Africa, *Disgrace* offers a look at the condition of a man who finds himself trying to inhabit the worlds of others with an urgency hitherto unknown in his life. As a self-perceived aging professor increasingly out of touch with his era, David voices authorial anxieties about representational ethics that bear closely upon the novel's search for a language adequate to the changing social terrain it describes. Though *Disgrace* cannot be said to figure an idyllic, optimistic, or comforting vision of a multiracial South Africa, it ponders the sacrifices that might underlie such a possibility. In asking how David tries to escape the conceptual constraints that mark his life, this chapter charts the fragile emergence of such an ethics of representation during a time of crisis.

This crisis of imaginative sympathy emerges in an era of not only political but also philosophical transition. David's world is the world of the modern university, where what was once a sanctuary for the study of literature has been forced to become a pragmatic site of technology and commerce. Initially appointed as a professor of modern languages, David now serves in what he considers a diminished capacity as an adjunct professor of communications. The handbook of his new department declares that the central goal of language is to communicate human emotions and ideas, prompting David's scorn: "His own opinion, which he does not air, is that the origins of speech lie in song, and the origins of song in the need to fill out with sound the overlarge and rather empty human soul" (*D*, 4). Although David's defense of song invites the reader to share his contempt for the great rationalization of the university, his voice also serves as an unreliable ethical compass within the unfolding events of the novel. While David despises the imperative to teach "Communication Skills" and favors the lessons of his elective on Romantic poetry, the book soon immerses us in narrative conflicts where the need for human communication acquires an undeniable urgency for David himself. Beginning with an intellectual debate over language as a social bond versus language as an artistic and even solipsistic need, the novel explores the bankruptcy of this divide in the landscape of the book. It forces David to reevaluate his own understanding of how communication ironically enables the possibility of song.

As a defender of what he perceives as the prerogatives of the lyrical self, David is unsurprisingly an heir to specific values associated with the British Romantics, in particular to those associated with Byron. Byron is far from the only literary precursor that shadows the pages of *Disgrace*—Sophocles, Wordsworth, Flaubert, Dostoevsky, Hardy, and Kafka, among others, all weave their way through David's allusive consciousness—but Byron takes on a particularly powerful role as the novel unfolds. As a specialist in British Romantic poetry, David introduces Byron's verse to his undergraduates and plans to compose an opera about Byron's life in Italy. As the novel soon makes clear, David also upholds the prerogatives of male heterosexual desire exemplified by Byron's libertine lifestyle. This complicity between lyrical egoism and sexual privilege is no accident, and *Disgrace* illuminates how both Byron's poetry and his practices constrain the workings of David's incipient sympathetic imagination. In offering a stringent critique of Byronic principles, the novel challenges a particular Romantic legacy of sympathy in order to shape new possibilities for a postcolonial moment.

In this first ethical crisis of the book, the limitations of this Byronic performative identity become clear. Sexually adrift after two failed marriages, a long-term arrangement with a prostitute, and a brief incident with his secretary, David finds himself beset by desires that seem to have no appropriate object. On impulse, he invites his student Melanie Isaacs home with him and seduces her over the days that follow. In retrospect, David describes their affair in the heightened language of the Romantics. "Suffice it to say that Eros entered. . . . I became a servant of Eros" (*D*, 52), he claims. "She struck up a fire in me," he says later to Melanie's family (*D*, 166). The novel reveals how such sexual privilege places the lyrical in the service of male-centered power. Though David convinces Melanie that "a woman's beauty does not belong to her alone. . . . She has a duty to share it" (*D*, 16), David perceives no such generous obligation on his own part.

The narcissism of David's desire is further enhanced by the specter of incest (a desire that may be informed by Byron's legendary incestuous affair) that runs throughout much of the novel. David's sexual encounter with Melanie is tinged with confusion between parental and sexual impulses, while his vision of his daughter often speculates explicitly on her sexual life. Indeed, the confusions of incest make themselves felt from the beginnings of *Disgrace*. "Is this your wife?" Melanie asks David, pointing to a photograph. "My mother," he replies (*D*, 15).[47] Taboos and transgressions aside, these hints of incest suggest a form of reproduction that replicates progenitors as closely as possible, and thus it offers another mode of the Byronic egoism that the novel places front and center.

David thus appears not only as a privileged self but as one who privileges the self. After his affair ends ambiguously and Melanie files a sexual-harassment complaint, David leaves his university hearing to tell angry crowds of female students that he was "enriched" by his experience (D, 56). Like the mythologized Byron, David understands his relationship with Melanie only in terms of how she affects his own "overlarge and rather empty human soul," and he evinces little interest in understanding her language for their affair. Refusing even to read her legal charges against him, David manipulates his own disinterest so that the scene of inquiry appears to reflect a Kafkaesque prosecution of unspecified criminality and abstract persecution. He interprets his social censure as the repression of an older man's desire for a young woman, ignoring the fact that he is not called to account for feelings of lust but for abuse of professional authority. It is the absence of communication, not only in pragmatic and legal terms but also in imaginative and compassionate ones, that makes David's so-called enrichment a code for ethical insolvency. As the privilege of pleasure cripples David's capacity for sympathetic imagination, his experience of song continues to render his "overlarge and rather empty" human soul dramatically uncrowded.

David's Byronic defenses for his own actions reappear in significantly more disturbing fashion in the second part of the book, where the metaphors of the city suddenly reappear as literal events in the country. The second plot line of the novel takes David's Byronism to its furthest extreme, suggesting how its values haunt more violent assertions of entitlement. After his daughter Lucy is raped, the description of her suffering suggests that the logical extreme of David's Byronic rhetoric lies not in sublime romance but in agonizing violence. If David claims metaphorical flames for his affair with Melanie, it is injury, not love, that literally sets him alight. Even more excruciatingly, the trope of rape suggests the inexorable end to David's seductive rhetoric that a woman has a duty to share her beauty. Melanie asks, "And what if I already share it?" David replies, "Then you should share it more widely" (D, 16). Lucy, "sharing" her beauty and her body with her three attackers, bespeaks the continuum of sexualized power that runs from courtly seduction to inimical rape. Even David recognizes the ingenuousness of his words: "Smooth words, as old as seduction itself. Yet at this moment he believes in them. She does not own herself" (D, 16). As Lucy shows David what it means not to own oneself, her experience suggests the cruelty of David's romanticized terms. Imagining Lucy's rape, thus, will require abandoning the privileges of Byronic sexuality.

Throughout the novel, the act of rape emerges as an experience so alien that it cannot be represented directly and fully. The elusive moment comes to us through David's agonized consciousness, which imagines the abuse and suffering of his daughter while remaining impotent to stop it. After the attack, Lucy compounds this silence when she refuses to discuss her attack, to press legal charges, or to leave the smallholding. Though the novel never inspires serious doubt that she was in fact raped, Lucy attempts to turn this legacy of intimate violation into an inviolable imaginative experience that no one else can share. "You tell what happened to you, I tell what happened to me," Lucy demands of her father in the immediate aftermath of the attack (D, 99). The novel refuses the reader access to what Lucy tells the police, the doctor, or her closest friend Bev Shaw, intensifying David's position of anxious ignorance. When David challenges her decision to refuse public discussion and legal retribution, Lucy continues to protect her authority over the interpretation of her experience. "What happened to me is a purely private matter," she asserts (D, 112). Unlike Melanie Isaacs, Lucy refuses to allow herself to be represented, whether such representation is understood in legal or literary terms. Often read as a dramatization of Levinas's theories of alterity, Lucy's radical refusals provide the clearest sense of the cost of Levinas's call to face the other.[48] As Emmanuel Levinas would suggest, Lucy attempts to endure hatred, violence, humiliation, and invasion without turning the encounter into an ongoing battle between self and other. Her resolute silence, coupled with her irrevocable decision to remain on the farm, suggest a form of reasoning that cannot find adequate expression in words.[49]

Despite Lucy's attempts to maintain the inviolability of her experience, imagining Lucy's rape is an ethical compulsion that David finds himself unable to abandon. It is not possible for David to simply tell what happened to him, because he is beginning to appreciate, in Derek Parfit's sense, that physical continuity is less important than psychological connectedness, so that experiences have more than one significant relationship to different persons.[50] "Do [Lucy and Bev Shaw] think he has not suffered with his daughter? What more could he have witnessed than he is capable of imagining? Or do they think that, where rape is concerned, no man can be where the woman is? Whatever the answer, he is outraged, outraged at being treated like an outsider" (D, 140–141). Although this question originally emerges from David's paternal concern for Lucy's well-being, the implications of David's question extend beyond the paternalism of his character. His words raise larger anxieties about the possibility and the limits of a crowded self, allowing the novel to examine what it means to think beyond the blind spots of one's sense of the world.

As grappling with the significant otherness of Lucy's rape provides the haunting challenge that David accepts in the book, he soon finds that the process of grasping her experience requires him to examine the source of his exclusion. As David probes the limits of compassion, he comes to embrace the position of "being treated like an outsider" in order to move past its limitations on sympathy and identification. After Lucy finally consents to speak of her experience, David finds himself reflecting on her rape within the context of his own opera on Byron's romance. Though David believes that Byron's own rapes of kitchen maids, and presumably his own seduction of Melanie, do not compare to the humiliating violence of Lucy's attack, his musings suggest the continuities between these three forms of male sexual power and enable him to imagine the rape from the attackers' point of view. "He does understand; he can, if he concentrates, if he loses himself, be there, be the men, inhabit them, fill them with the ghost of himself. The question is, does he have it in him to be the woman?" (D, 160).

This searching skepticism—"does he have it in him to be the woman?"—emerges just after David imagines, in detail, Lucy's experience of rape. "Lucy was frightened, frightened near to death. Her voice choked, she could not breathe, her limbs went numb. *This is not happening*, she said to herself as the men forced her down; *it is just a dream, a nightmare*" (D, 160, italics in original). In recognizing the insufficiency of this fictionalized narration of Lucy's consciousness, David's inner voice suggests the need for an even greater experience of alterity than these sensory narrative details can provide. Laura Tanner describes the possible dangers of such narration, contending that "the dynamics of violence often involve a violator who appropriates the victim's subjectivity as an extension of his own power, turning the force of consciousness against a victim for whom sentience becomes pain, consciousness no more than an agonizing awareness of the inability to escape embodiment."[51] Imagining rape, in these terms, becomes the ultimate form of discursive domination.

Avoiding this kind of domination, therefore, requires radical measures. In a philosophical account of rape, Susan J. Brison speaks of "the disintegration of the self experienced by victims of violence" that challenges central concepts of identity and selfhood.[52] Lucy's experience of such disintegration (she calls herself a dead person) raises historical and political questions about how to imagine subject positions defined by the absence of power or voice. Seeing oneself as the subject of rape means more than reconstructing injurious facts and emotions; instead, it metaphorically demands that one identify with the temporary erasure of selfhood and with the divestment of privilege.[53] When David ultimately rejects an explicit fictionalizing that carries the threat of pornographic (and incestuous) voyeurism, he begins to intuit this new form of ethical sympathy. To develop such a crowded self thus constantly threatens the subject with its own dissolution.

To inhabit this elusive state of self-sacrifice, David attempts to abandon the kind of sexual desire he identifies with the Byronic tradition. For much of the novel, David's approach to women provides an aggressive instance of a classical male gaze. He appreciates the young and beautiful, and he expresses disappointment with women who, like Lucy, do not attempt to make themselves attractive to men. The best exemplar of such a woman appears in Lucy's friend Bev Shaw, whose plainness inspires David to patronizing pity. As David spends more and more time helping Bev euthanize unwanted animals in her primitive country clinic, he finds himself drawn into a brief and surprising affair. In the tradition of Anna Sergeyevna, in *The Master of Petersburg* (1994), and Elizabeth Costello, in "The Humanities in Africa" (2003), who offer themselves sexually to men as acts of spiritual charity, Bev's initiation of their affair comes to exemplify a gift that takes David beyond the realm of sexual pleasure. At first, their awkward trysting on the floor of the clinic signals to David his own diminution in a world where he can no longer command more alluring sexual partners. However, in the final sentence of the chapter that describes their affair, David's interior voice moves away from the condescending tone that laments their distance from Byronic lover and Byronic beloved. "And let him stop calling her poor Bev Shaw," he thinks to himself. "If she is poor, he is bankrupt"

(*D*, 150). This acknowledgment of his own disgrace suggests a palpable distance from the imperatives of masculine desire and sexual confidence. Although this distance is temporary—on a visit to the family of Melanie Isaacs, David kneels before her mother and sister in a Dostoevskian apology to and from suffering while he continues to look lustfully at the young woman before him—it nonetheless marks an important transformation in David's relationship to the literary tradition that shapes him.

If David momentarily forsakes Byronic sexual values in this affair, he makes a more substantial sacrifice through the composition of an opera. In the late section of the novel, David's foray into art provides the most enduring attempt to imagine what it might be like to be a woman. In turning to the genre of the opera, David engages with a form historically associated with the rise of sympathy in secular Western art.[54] His opera explores the relationship between communication and song, or between history and art, as it contributes to the ethics of engaging significant otherness. In everyday life, David's direct communications with Lucy all come to naught; she refuses his spoken and written words of advice and resolutely remains committed to the only path of stoic survival she feels is open to her. As his avenues of dialogue with Lucy collapse, David begins to deflect the problems of their relationship into the composition of his opera. Beginning originally as an exploration of Byron's love affair with a young woman, the opera shifts away from a glorification of masculine heroism and instead meditates upon the mind of Teresa, Byron's adored and eventually discarded mistress. As he begins to compose, David slowly starts to forsake the privilege of male desire and power to imagine a space of female sexuality.[55] This move marks the shift from detached observation to sympathetic imagination: David abandons his initial vision of Teresa, an attractive young woman who resembles Melanie Isaacs, and instead envisions her in a middle age that resonates with the unglamorous Bev Shaw. The novel makes clear that this sympathy corresponds to an absence of conventional sexual desire: "It is not the erotic that is calling to him after all," David realizes (*D*, 184).

In the opera, imagining Teresa is intimately bound to an ethics that links art with compassion. "Can he find it in his heart to love this plain, ordinary woman? Can he love her enough to write a music for her? If he cannot, what is left for him?" (*D*, 182). In asking this question, David makes the crucial connection between imagination and self-reflection that enables his emerging crowded self. In attempting to answer affirmatively to his first question, David turns the opera into a conversation between a lonely Teresa and her long-dead lover Byron. Teresa attempts to pull Byron back from the grave through the power of her voice, compelling him to acknowledge her desire as he refused to in life. Learning to think outside of the boundaries of male heterosexual desire, David finds himself able to produce a Teresa who cannot be reduced to simply a male fantasy of the feminine or a displacement of self. In revising Byronic values within his composition, David might well echo the lines he attributes to Byron in the opera: "*Out of the poets I learned to love . . . but life, I found* (descending chromatically to F), *is another story*" (D, 185, italics in the original). The "other story" that changes the fictional Byron, and by implication David, is the story of Teresa, Bev Shaw, and Lucy.[56] This reevaluation of art proves central to David's inchoate attempts to develop a crowded self—the precise opposite of "the overlarge and rather empty human soul." The opera, limited and fragile as it is, comes to exemplify the workings of a new form of sympathy that unites the imperatives of song with the ethics of communication.

In composing his opera, David seeks to push through what Coetzee once described in *White Writing* (1988) as the dominant metanarrative of unrepresentability in late twentieth-century literature. In this passage, Coetzee lays out a core aspiration of representational ethics:

> Our ears today are finely attuned to modes of silence. . . . Our craft is all in reading *the other*: gaps, inverses, undersides; the veiled; the dark, the buried, the feminine; alterities. . . . It is a mode of reading which, subverting the dominant, is in peril, like all triumphant subversion, of becoming the dominant in turn. Is it a version of utopianism (or pastoralism) to look forward (or backward) to the day when the truth will be (or was) what is said, not what is not said, when we will hear (or heard) music as sound upon silence, not silence between sounds?[57]

Though published more than a decade before *Disgrace*, the rhetoric of this passage resonates with the signature imagery of *Disgrace*, as the novel ponders the ability to move beyond silence to sound. If Lucy seems to insist upon playing "*the other*," whose motives and meanings are mysterious to her father, David's opera attempts to restore the importance of sound through the arias of an abandoned, forsaken Teresa, the simple banjo that plinks out her song, and the young dog whose howling pushes the opera beyond the world of human artifice. As David learns to imagine and to love this middle-aged woman who resembles the women he disdains in his life, the moment of artistic composition becomes the least egoistic and self-centered point of David's experience. Though the book is careful to note that David's epiphanic turn does not always last and is only unevenly integrated into the daily fabric of his life, this moment of possibility holds out the chance for a new beginning and a new language. As a cognitive intimacy replaces a sexual one, this tradeoff between sympathy and desire suggests both the power and the price of the crowded self.

The narrative potential of David's altered imaginative attempt emerges in his final glimpse of Lucy, where he appears to apprehend her as a being who exists beyond his own needs and desires: "now here she is, solid in her existence, more solid than he has ever been. With luck she will last a long time, long beyond him. . . . And from within her will have issued another existence, that with luck will be just as solid, just as long-lasting. So it will go on, a line of existences in which his share, his gift, will grow inexorably less and less, till it may as well be forgotten" (D, 217). As it stresses Lucy's solidity, the free indirect discourse asserts that she now appears to David as something more than an emanation of his desires, something more than what she earlier calls a minor character in the story of his life. In recognizing the emergence of narratives that write him out of their stories, David grasps the need to sacrifice both his biological and his textual control over these future descendants. His approach begins to resemble Parfit's understanding of personhood, which finds comfort in forms of experience that will bear different—not necessarily better or worse, but different—relations to one's present experience. It is thus not a coincidence that the novel is preoccupied not only with sympathy but also with aging and death, implying that a new relationship toward one entails a new relationship toward the other. Releasing himself from the need to preserve his own autonomy allows David a new openness to the lives of others. "Is [this theory of personhood] depressing?" Parfit asks. "Some may find it so. But I find it liberating, and consoling. . . . My death will break the more direct relations between my present experiences and future experiences, but it will not break various other relations. . . . Now that I have seen this, my death seems to me less bad."[58] David, musing on the idea of these "various other relations" with a new equanimity, even arrives at the point where being forgotten is no longer a driving source of anxiety for self-preservation.

As David learns to love Lucy for, not despite, her resistance to his sympathy, this new gaze revitalizes her image in the novel. As long as David perceives Lucy through the debilitating lens of Byronic privilege, she languishes in the novel; here, through this new gaze, "she looks, suddenly, the picture of health" (D, 218). Although this new gaze is not unmediated, as David appreciates Lucy's beauty through Western traditions of landscape painting, his recognition of his own increasing obsolescence pushes against the sexual drive for replication that propels David in earlier moments.[59] This gaze pushes against the subtle specter of David's incestuous desire that haunts his earlier perceptions of his daughter. To abandon this incestuous desire is thus to accept the inability to replicate oneself as closely as possible, diminishing narcissistic impulses to allow for the presence of others. Although many readers of Disgrace have despaired over the possibility of David's ethical growth, and indeed the novel refuses any simple narrative of redemption, this revitalized portrait of Lucy suggests a genuine shift in the effect of David's once corrosive perception. In sacrificing his formerly invasive imagination, David accepts the diminishment of individual privilege within the crowded self that the novel's stringent vision demands.

Racial Discourse and the Nonhuman

If David and Lucy struggle to cross divides of gender, Disgrace also ponders the problem of figuring race. Within the novel, the question of racial discourse is heavily embedded in a rhetoric of the nonhuman, figured through the specter of dogs and monsters. Coetzee thus approaches an ethics of representation by radically reenvisioning relationships between humans and animals. Rather than rejecting the rhetoric of the nonhuman that demeans black subjects in racist discourse, Disgrace transforms this rhetoric by suggesting that the space of the nonhuman offers a potential point of sympathetic connection for white and black figures.[60] In offering us a stark vision of human possibility, the novel abandons the promises of liberal humanism to urge a sterner vision of commonality based upon living creatures' capacity for loss. Not as rights-bearing subjects but as rights-losing subjects do his characters attempt to cross racial boundaries. As the novel demands that its characters and readers extend their sympathetic imagination to dogs and monsters, I will suggest that any hope of engaging significant otherness in the novel must begin in the difficulties of suffering and disgrace.

In telling its provocative story about a white woman raped by three black assailants, *Disgrace* demands that we confront the ethics of representing racial difference on historically explosive terrain. Coetzee's position as a white South African writing in English places him within a long history of debates over the power of representation, in which the ability to represent black South Africans cannot be divorced from the corrosive inequalities of racial oppression. Like Europeans figuring the Orient, white South African literature on black subjects has been seen as saying nothing about black South Africans but much about white anxieties and aspirations. Michael Wade, writing about white representations of black migrant workers, opens his account with the claim that "the [black] migrant has no characteristics other than those allocated to him by the white imagination. . . . Little can be learned about the [black] migrant worker himself from these [white] accounts; but much may be garnered towards an understanding of the group that has dominated the private sector of the South African economy."[61] However, to demand that white South African writers refrain from writing about subjects of color replicates the logic of apartheid and its governing myth of racial separation. Novelists such as Coetzee have embraced the drive to confront multiracial shared histories as a crucial part of their literary ethics.

To intervene in this history of discursive domination, *Disgrace* attempts to rewrite the genre of the *plaasroman*, or farm novel, that traditionally bolstered white authority in colonial South Africa. Oscillating between city and country, the novel locates much of its social critique within an iconic landscape once central to Afrikaner mythologies of self and community. As Coetzee contends in his book *White Writing*, the landscape of South Africa and the laboring world of the farm offered a crucial space in which the emblematic colonial subject attempted to find "a dialogue with Africa, a reciprocity with Africa, that [would] allow him an identity better than that of visitor, stranger, transient" (*WW*, 8). Coetzee claims that this essentialist search for identity often required the erasure of black labor in the imagined African pastoral, focusing on an accommodation with the empty land to avoid thorny questions about the presence of black inhabitants (*WW*, 9). In this context, the movement in *Disgrace* from multiethnic city to farm country attempts to offer an antipastoral vision of the land, even as the novel continues the search for viable dialogue and reciprocity within what is not quite garden nor quite wilderness. In the country, I will suggest, both David and Lucy try to reconstruct lives that broach the boundaries suggested by "visitor, stranger, transient." In doing so, they must first embrace that status. Only by accepting themselves as outsiders, the novel suggests, will they overcome the failure of love that Coetzee has called the heart of white unfreedom in South Africa.[62]

To challenge the historical evasions of the *plaasroman*, the novel foregrounds the contested legacies of its setting in the eastern Cape. As the story shifts from the urban center of Cape Town to the countryside near Grahamstown, *Disgrace* enters a specific social landscape noted for its complex history of racialized violence. In a 1993 review of Noël Mostert's history of the Cape Colony, Coetzee describes Grahamstown as "the cradle of British culture in South Africa" that "lays claim to embodying a link between white English-speaking South Africans and the liberal traditions (real or imagined) of their land of ancestry." In a sentence that anticipates a key theme of *Disgrace*, Coetzee goes on to say that "Mostert shows just how illusory this link is."[63] As Gareth Cornwall suggests, eruptions of nineteenth-century frontier violence in the region prefigure the conflicts that animate the second part of the novel.[64] Drawing as well upon Mostert's characterization of the region, the poet Antjie Krog describes this part of South Africa as "the first frontier between black and white, between the terrestrial endeavor of Africa and the maritime endeavor of Europe." She notes that the eastern Cape was the origin of numerous forms of resistance to apartheid, including the Pan-Africanist Congress and Black Consciousness. It was also a region whose inhabitants suffered disproportionately under apartheid regimes. "From the sixties onward," Krog writes, "the eastern Cape endured an unprecedented escalation of human rights abuses, many of them notorious. . . . Of all those detained without trial in South Africa, one-third came from the eastern Cape." Economically depressed (with

65 percent unemployment), the region was also known as "the dumping ground for those soldiers who got out of hand" during the years of virtual civil war.[65] In era following the end of apartheid, such rural space also served as a central locus for black empowerment initiatives. The African National Congress, in alliance with nongovernmental associations, put forward a Reconstruction and Development Programme that sought to address the underdevelopment of black communities as part of the fundamental injustice of apartheid. In 1996, to promote land redistribution, the Land Reform (Labour Tenants) Act sought to assure laborers tenure on the land they cultivated. Yet, as the sociologists Sam Kariuki and Lucien Van der Walt argue, "the land reform programme implemented by the ANC massively fell short of achieving its stated goal of redistributing 30 percent of South African land by the 1999 national elections."[66] David's desire for pastoral refuge in the countryside, therefore, ironically draws him into a terrain that exemplifies the complex social, political, and material inequities in both old and new South Africa.[67]

Within this fraught landscape, *Disgrace* exploits the visible proximity between humans and animals to reevaluate race relations in postapartheid territory. Rather than avoiding the language of bestiality that insinuatingly dehumanizes black subjects, the novel makes the disturbing narrative choice to embrace the rhetoric of the nonhuman in its portrait of life in the eastern Cape. Almost all of the black characters within the novel are described as dogs, jackals, or other nonhuman figures, suggesting distinctly unelevated visions of their character. The animals in *Disgrace* conjure emotions of disgust, fear, disdain, and possibly pity; none of them evoke images of the sublime or the beautiful. Petrus, the laborer turned landlord who jointly owns Lucy's farm, enters the story as "the dog-man" (D, 64) who initially helps care for Lucy's boarding kennels. As Petrus's rise in power mirrors Lucy and David's fall, Petrus gains adjacent land and renounces his role as the keeper of dogs. At a party to celebrate Petrus's land transfer, an emblem of national land reform from white to black ownership, Petrus chooses this moment to remind Lucy and David of the significance of this shift in status. "He does not play the eager host, does not offer them a drink, but does say, 'No more dogs. I am not any more the dog-man,' which Lucy chooses to accept as a joke" (D, 129). Although Lucy has tried to develop progressive relations with local farmers like Petrus, the bitter edge of Petrus's remark suggest the tensions that still beset a relationship Lucy has tried her best to liberalize.

In more sinister terms, David and Lucy both conceive of their attackers as dogs, interpreting the drive to mark Lucy as the territorial instincts of men who roam and prey in packs. Lucy is the closest figure we have to a fully ethical subject in the novel, and when she uses the language of animality, she indicates how central it appears to Coetzee's design. "They spur each other on," Lucy says in a rare commentary on her rape. "That's probably why they do it together. Like dogs in a pack" (D, 159). When the men first arrive with unclear intentions on the farm, they approach her kennels in a threatening manner, and Lucy's repressed anxieties burst forth when she addresses them as one would a dog. "Get away from the dogs!" she shouts. "*Hamba!*" (D, 92). Using a command commonly used to shoo an animal, Lucy unwittingly suggests the racial identity of her attackers well before other narrative clues imply the men are black.[68]

As part of their violation of Lucy's life, the attackers shoot her watchdogs in defiance of traditional signs of white authority.[69] Lucy hints at this legacy of fortification when she tries to persuade David that "dogs still mean something. The more dogs, the more deterrence" (D, 60). The irony of this belief resounds with full force during the attack. David imagines how the assailants might have boasted of their slaughter to Lucy: "*Call your dogs! they said to her. Go on, call your dogs! No dogs? Then let us show you dogs!*" (D, 160, italics in original). Evoking the specter of violent sexual assertion, canine rhetoric frequently bespeaks libidinal desire in the minds of Coetzee's characters.[70] This language reinforces not only the attackers' racial identity but also their sexualized demands for power.

In choosing to use such a proliferation of animal metaphors to describe black characters, Coetzee's work abandons liberal strategies of writing about others. The novel could easily have refrained from such comparisons, or it could have opposed them with black characters less complicit with the violence of the attack. (Only a figure such as Manas Mathabane, a sympathetic professor who presides over David's sexual-harassment case, seems to offset these representations, but he plays only a very small part in the novel.)[71] Although the third-person narration reflects David's imperfect consciousness and cannot be taken as Coetzee's implicit narrative optic, the lack of substantial alternative visions creates a resounding silence throughout the novel. In choosing to embrace rather than avoid such racially charged rhetoric, *Disgrace* suggests that racial borders cannot adequately be crossed through liberal strategies of writing. Instead, its narrative choices produce a crowded style through this incorporation of literally disgraceful language.[72]

As part of this austere and difficult vision, the novel casts doubt on the power of revivifying comedy to transgress social boundaries. This skepticism emerges in David's description of a play called *Sunset at the Globe Salon*, which dramatizes a more flamboyant approach toward representing racial difference. David visits a rehearsal to watch Melanie's performance in this "comedy of the new South Africa," where a gay hairdresser in Johannesburg banters with his black and white clients (*D*, 23). "Patter passes among the three of them: jokes, insults. Catharsis seems to be the presiding principle: all the coarse old prejudices brought into the light of day and washed away in gales of laughter" (*D*, 23). Like *Disgrace*, *Sunset at the Globe Salon* embeds itself within a history of charged racial rhetoric, but the play's tactics of choice—bracing, purgative humor and slapstick physical comedy—conspicuously elude the emotional spectrum of the novel. (Indeed, Coetzee's oeuvre stands out for its general lack of humor.) Unlike Johnson and Jen, who productively turn to the resources of the comic, Coetzee suggests the insufficiency of such choices in a world of entrenched social violence. When David surreptitiously returns to Cape Town to watch Melanie in a public performance, his critique could well be *Disgrace*'s own rebuttal of the dramatic tactics of the comedy: "he finds the play, with its crude humour and nakedly political intent, as hard to endure as before" (*D*, 191). Though David later comes to embrace a different view of comic potential in his opera, his rejection of cathartic comedic laughter signals the commitment of the novel to a darker view of an inescapable past.

Coetzee's rejection of liberal and comic strategies can be seen as an enormously risky move that threatens to repeat the demeaning rhetoric of apartheid, and *Disgrace* has been read in some quarters as a deeply offensive narrative. In an Afrikaans essay called "Is *This* the Right Image of Our Nation?" (2002), the scholar and political figure Jakes Gerwel laments "the almost barbaric post-colonial claims of black Africans" and the portrayal of mixed-race figures as "whores, seducers, complainers, conceited accusers" to indict the implied author of the novel.[73] The book warranted a mention in an African National Congress submission to the Human Rights Commission's Inquiry Into Racism in the Media, in which the authors suggested that the world within the novel resonated with racist portraits of primitive Africans.[74] Many readers have seen the work as one that easily plays into the hands of white paranoia, arguing that its colonial myths of black sexuality and savagery might fuel or vindicate racist fears of rising black power in a postapartheid order.[75] Others have suggested that the novel's preoccupation with animality displaces the need to confront racialized thinking, understanding them as discourses that compete for ethical transformation in the novel.[76]

The reason why Coetzee cannot be read as simply a white writer whose novel disparages black Africans, and the reason why his risky gamble requires attention, is because the portrayal of race in the novel demands a radical redefinition of what it means to be human. The use of animal imagery for black Africans exceeds its demeaning legacy of racist metaphor, although such connotations comprise parts of the history that the novel provocatively commands us to confront, because this dehumanizing rhetoric ultimately generates crowded selves and crowded styles. As Lucy argues, "there is no higher life. This the only life there is. Which we share with animals" (D, 74). The novel suggests that the only place where subjects can converge across gender, race, and species is not within the promises of liberal humanism but within the site of literal and literary disgrace that animals come to figure. Through this interest in challenging humanist limits on sympathy, *Disgrace* demands an expansion of ethics to its fullest capacity.

Such an expansion occurs as the rhetoric of dogs gradually characterizes not only black characters but also white figures as well. As David and Lucy begin to understand themselves in the language of dogs, the hierarchy "human/dog" no longer maps onto the hierarchy "white/ black" in an uncomplicated manner. Working in the country clinic to euthanize strays and incinerate their corpses with honor, David explicitly places himself in continuity with the lives of animals: "A dog-man, Petrus once called himself. Well, now he has become a dog-man: a dog undertaker; a dog psychopomp; a *harijan*" (D, 146). When David comes to think of himself as "the dog-man," he places himself not only into an antihumanist place of possible redemption but also into the metaphorical condition of South Africans of color. His choice of Gandhian rhetoric alludes to South Africa's multiracial population as well as to political marginality across the globe. Killing the dogs and burning their bodies invites David to surrender the privileges of skin color, masculinity, and humanity, suggesting that such sacrifice is necessary to imagine across lines of race. David's irony, his last defense against vulnerability, grows markedly weaker in his attitude toward animals. Though his acceptance of being a dog-man does not lead to interracial reconciliation in a liberal or literal sense (David remains angry, skeptical, and ironic toward Petrus and the attackers), the novel suggests that he must learn to identify with the loss of authority that dogs embody.

Lucy, as well, throughout the novel develops an increasingly radical relationship with animals, which challenges the division between people and other species. The novel gives us to understand that initially her affinity for rural life bespeaks her commitment to liberal idealism (she comes to the farm with a commune of basket weavers). However, Lucy's persona becomes terrifyingly resolute over the course of the novel. In contrast to a critique that stresses a patronizing continuity between liberal attitudes toward Africans and animals,[77] Lucy embodies and articulates what Elizabeth Costello calls "*kind-ness*"—appreciation of shared kind, rather than conventional kindness—without sentimentality (*LA*, 61, italics in original). Although sentiment may offer ethical possibility within worlds of only moderate social division, as we see in the work of Ruth Ozeki, it proves powerless in the face of extreme violence and conflict. As Lucy abandons sentimental impulses, she begins to embody a more radically crowded self.

When Lucy treats the aftermath of her rape as a chance to divest herself of human privilege and begin anew, she identifies her sense of honor as a rights-losing subject rather than as a rights-asserting one. "Perhaps that is what I must learn to accept," Lucy tells her father. "To start at ground level. With nothing. Not with nothing but. With nothing. No cards, no weapons, no property, no rights, no dignity . . . like a dog" (*D*, 205). This deliberate abandonment of particular kinds of power represents the only power Lucy feels is still available to her, and it suggests that the project of reconstructing her life changes the metaphoric meaning of dogs from protectors of privilege to emblems of loss.[78] In rejecting the importance of property and status, Lucy works against what Coetzee, paraphrasing Noël Mostert's history, describes as the particularly British investment in "the ideology of social self-advancement" embedded in the social capital of their "furnishings, books, heirlooms," which led the British to understand attacks on property as attacks on selfhood.[79] As Lucy rejects the logic of the British settlers who preceded her in the eastern Cape, her more radical identification with the propertyless nonhuman suggests new terms of contact between the two. Humans and animals converge not by affording rights to animals and thus elevating them to human status but by diminishing human rights and acknowledging kinship and kind-ness at a place without property, at "ground level."[80]

It is only by beginning at this point that Lucy develops an expanded sense of self within multiracial kinship networks. As she accepts Petrus's protection as his third wife, she demands a place for her unborn child within Petrus's extended family. (In this sense, it may be significant that Lucy is half Dutch, since Mostert argues that the Boers, unlike the British, did not understand the loss of possession as the loss of social identity.)[81] Offering increasing amounts of room to the needs of others, she diminishes the amount she claims as her own within her crowded self. This novel visualizes this process through the metaphors of house and land: Lucy agrees to sign over her property to Petrus and retains only her house as a private sanctuary. This sacrificial gift stands in sharp contrast to her earlier willingness to partake in the neoliberal reform practice of *selling* Petrus land, again suggesting the inadequacy of liberal strategies for managing relations between neighbors.[82] As Lucy's pregnant body literally suggests the crowding of her character, the novel makes clear that this ethical achievement comes at great cost to the comforts and privileges of her life.

If the metaphoric space of dogs seems to promise the possibility of multiracial communion in *Disgrace*, the Byronic strand of the novel furthers this ethical possibility of engaging significant otherness at the site of the nonhuman. Byron's poetry divides the world into a tripartite realm of angels, humans, and monstrous things, and as David interprets his poem, Byron places the world of things outside the possibility of sympathetic imagination. As with the Byronic sexual privileges that David unlearns in order to imagine across gender, the novel demands that David reject this hierarchy in order to imagine across race. As Byron haunts the world of *Disgrace*, his presence serves in many different ways to constrain the workings of sympathy. When David teaches the poetry of Byron in his undergraduate elective, his chosen passage raises the question of sympathetic imagination that the novel implicitly pursues. Expounding on Byron's Lucifer to his students, David argues:

> Note that we are not asked to condemn this being with the mad heart, this being with whom there is something constitutionally wrong. On the contrary, we are invited to understand and sympathize. But there is a limit to sympathy. For though he lives among us, he is not one of us. He is exactly what he calls himself: a *thing*, that is, a monster. Finally, Byron will suggest, it will not be possible to love him, not in the deeper, more human sense of the word. He will be condemned to solitude.
>
> (*D*, 33–34, italics in original)

Because the world of the poem is divided into the tripartite formation of divine beings, humans, and things, this description of the fallen angel suggests that humans cannot fully extend themselves beyond the borders that inscribe such social, religious, and metaphysical distinctions. In offering us a Lucifer whom "it will not be possible to love," Byron's poetry articulates the stopping point of sympathy. As a "thing" or "a monster" who ultimately exceeds human comprehension, Lucifer occupies a space very similar to the position of animals in the lectures of Elizabeth Costello. Much as Byronic sexual privilege constrains David from sympathizing across lines of gender, this tripartite world of angels, men, and monsters similarly attempts to contract his imaginative horizon.

However, it is this space of monstrous things that David and Pollux, one of Lucy's rapists, ironically inhabit together. David appears as a Byronic Lucifer from the early pages of the novel: "He doesn't act on principle but on impulse, and the source of his impulses is dark to him" (*D*, 33), David says of Lucifer in language that suggests his own impulsive erotic seduction of Melanie. The waywardness of David's actions can be read as a variant on such satanic perversity, and when Melanie files charges against him at the university, David resists providing a public confession for motives that seem as prideful as Lucifer's own. The "mad heart" (*D*, 33) that Byron ascribes to Lucifer recurs when David's daughter smilingly refers to him as "mad, bad, and dangerous to know" (*D*, 77). Even the names of the characters offer a suggestive play on words: as Lucy's father who brings her into the world, David can be read as the "Lucy-bearer" (Lucifer, or light-bearer) within the world of the novel. If David comes to us as a Luciferian figure, the description of the youngest rapist, Pollux, echoes David's interpretation of Byron's Lucifer in more sinister form. Haunting Lucy's farm under the protection of his relative Petrus, Pollux lurks on the fringes of Lucy's life much as Lucifer furtively explores the new world of earth. In a guise more extreme than David, Pollux is also a creature with a "mad heart" who appears as an incompletely rational subject: "I suspect there is something wrong with him," Lucy tells David (*D*, 200). When David finds Pollux peering in the window to spy on Lucy, he confirms her judgment: "Lucy is right. Something is wrong with him, wrong in his head" (*D*, 207). This mysterious quality of Pollux offers a living version of Byron's Lucifer, who dwells outside the human world as a figure once an angel, now "a *thing*." Although David's purchase on violence is distinctively different from that of Pollux, the stylistic imagery of the novel crowds them together within its Luciferian metaphor.

The incommensurability between the two, the irreconcilability of their differences, is precisely what pushes this project of representational ethics to its limit. David and Pollux are offered in many respects as antitheses: the first possesses an extraordinary sense of control over the operations of his own mind; the second lacks even the rudiments of self-consciousness (even, as Lucy and David suggest above, to the point of cognitive disability). Echoing patterns found in Coetzee's previous novels, they pair hyperconscious and subconscious states of mind in ways that, as Ato Quayson suggests, enact "a coincidence between inarticulacy, racialization, and disability."[83] Recognizing Pollux as a part of David's Luciferian crowded self will not mean learning to like him or even expressing patronizing pity for his condition; indeed, David resents the feeling of being crowded together with Pollux, raging at "the thought that like a weed he has been allowed to tangle his roots with Lucy and Lucy's existence" (*D*, 209). Instead, the novel suggests that as long as David remains within the grip of "the thought," he will be unable to experience the significant otherness of Pollux's existence. Toward the end of the novel, David ultimately comes to realize that his deeply prized mental mastery over his consciousness constitutes the last barrier that separates himself from the lives of others. If developing a crowded self entails reimagining one's own position, David's predicament takes us to the furthest paradoxical point where such reconception demands abandoning control over the self.

This transformation occurs in displaced form through David's growing attachment to an unwanted dog, young like Pollux, whose nonintellectual overtures compel David to abandon the protective armor of self-consciousness in an acknowledgement of alterity. Though David dislikes the feel and smell of animals, he succumbs to the power of a nonrational sympathy with another being. In a passage that echoes a moment from *The Master of Petersburg*, the novel that perhaps best prefigures the concerns of *Disgrace*, Coetzee writes: "The dog wags its crippled rear, sniffs his face, licks his cheeks, his lips, his ears. He does nothing to stop it" (*D*, 220). Presented as one of the more redemptive experiences in the novel, this instant both attests to David's changed relationship to sexual desire (the lick of the dog replaces the kiss of a woman) and bespeaks his willingness to abandon the ironic distancing that constitutes him discursively as a focalizing perspective in the novel. As he works with Bev Shaw to euthanize the animal with honor, he finds himself "giving it what he no longer has difficulty in calling by its proper name: love" (*D*, 219). To love this animal at the moment of its death helps David surmount traditional Byronic limits on sympathizing with the Luciferian, thus offering him a possible point of connection with Pollux.[84] With its "crippled rear," the dog evokes descriptions of Byron himself, who was said to have a withered leg; through this figure of disability, the novel locates itself within the residual discourse of Byron but radically undermines its sexual privilege and its limits on sympathy.[85] Love, after all, is what David hopes to offer to the child growing in Lucy's womb, who offers inescapable evidence of what binds David and Pollux together.[86] Though—or perhaps because—this mystifying relation to dogs does not permit sympathy in a politically utilitarian sense, it does suggest continuity between human kinship and the kind-ness of living beings.

If the novel demands a necessary compression of the human with the nonhuman, lowering humans to places of loss rather than elevating animals to places of privilege, it suggests that this crowded space of disgrace is nonetheless visible to the sight of divinity. This shift furthers the novel's critique of the tripartite division of angels, men, and beasts that David inherits from Byron's poetry. In an early section of the novel,

David (in contrast to Lucy) describes the difference between the human and the nonhuman as a matter of the soul. " 'The Church Fathers had a long debate about [animals], and decided they don't have proper souls,' he observes. 'Their souls are tied to their bodies and die with them' " (D, 78). Against Lucy's skepticism about the existence of the immaterial, David asserts that being human necessitates a soul: "You are a soul. We are all souls. We are all souls before we are born" (D, 79). Though David does not identify himself as a religious believer, he accepts the division that makes humans visible to divine sight while nonhumans partake only temporarily in such spirituality. Later in the novel, David tells a different story: "The business of dog-killing is over for the day, the black bags are piled at the door, each with a body and a soul inside" (D, 161). The dead bodies of the dogs, iconic emblems of the disgrace that pervades the novel, suggest that there exists no hierarchical division between god, human, and animal. Drawing strength from the palindromic intimacy between dogs and gods, the haunting presence of dogs in *Disgrace* echoes the simultaneously subhuman and divine role that characterizes their earlier appearances in Coetzee's fiction. Imagined as a possible guardian angel in *Age of Iron* and as a son returned in *The Master of Petersburg*, the dog collapses the distinctions between least and most. The space where living creatures are visible to the divine is not in the comfortable space of human privilege, as David earlier implies, but in the monstrous space of the rights-losing subject.

This space, enabled by the language *of* the novel but beyond the language of the characters *in* the novel, bespeaks *Disgrace*'s own anxiety about the power of rhetoric to forge engagements with significant otherness. As we see in the middle of the novel, when David is attacked on the farm, European languages enter the text as contaminants of a discursive domination that surges up, both ironically and unwittingly, in David's consciousness: "He speaks Italian, he speaks French, but Italian and French will not save him here in darkest Africa. He is helpless, an Aunt Sally, a figure from a cartoon, a missionary in cassock and topi waiting with clasped hands and upcast eyes while the savages jaw away in their own lingo preparatory to plunging him into their boiling cauldron" (D, 95). Throughout this passage, David's capacity for representational violence appears through his European linguistic affiliations. Although David acknowledges that a fuller sense of comprehension will need to elude these linguistic constraints, expressing the desire to hear

Petrus's story in a language other than English, the novel nonetheless suggests that liberal acts of learning isiXhosa will not fully address the matter of alterity at stake. (Lucy does make efforts to speak isiXhosa, but, as with her other liberal instincts, this gesture does not protect her from the onslaught of violence or offer her a clear path toward a reconstructed life.) Although European languages, including English, may be contaminated, the novel suggests that they cannot simply be replaced with indigenous African languages. Instead, the rhetoric of the novel creates a crowded style by working through its own disgraceful racial contamination with the language of animality, just as David ultimately elects to move into a world beyond human language through his strange kinship with actual dogs.[87] In both cases, the rhetoric and the plot of *Disgrace* resist liberal solutions to language politics by gesturing toward deeply antihumanist modes of encounter with others.

As these nonhuman images help produce extreme and troubling visions of crowded selves and crowded styles, they do so in a way that compels us to consider their importance as animals, not simply as displaced signifiers for human activities. In other words, the dogs of *Disgrace* are not only dogs in a fable, where they gesture toward recognizably human ideas or characters, but also dogs whose irreducible embodiment enables the most basic connection between living beings.[88] "A dog sitting in a patch of sun licking itself," says a character in *Elizabeth Costello*, "is at one moment a dog and at the next a vessel of revelation" (*EC*, 229). This doubled presence expands David's world to its fullest capacity, so that in the moments when David connects with a dog most fully (before or after its death), the novel offers an elaborated sense of the many different and strange lives that populate the experience of a single individual. If sympathetic engagement with alterity, as at times Coetzee has suggested,[89] is limited to humans and not returned by animals, it nonetheless refuses its own claim as a marker of human particularity by collapsing distinctions among animal, human, and divine. Any possible grace must come from this point of disgraceful sympathy, the space of the impossibly crowded self and style.

For much of his career, Coetzee has been read as a masterful novelist of deconstruction whose fictions and metafictions ponder the crises of literary signification, textual authority, and linguistic rupture that drive many questions of poststructuralist theory. However, *The Lives of*

Animals and *Disgrace* are also very much fictions of the search for reconstruction. In posing the question of sympathetic imagination within fraught historical moments, Coetzee's writing asks how it might be possible to move past silence toward a visible way of representing others. As his stories wrestle with what it means for individuals to reconstruct themselves in the aftermath of violence and disgrace, they ask what new form of imaginative projection might arise from the wreckage of an agonizing past. With Elizabeth Costello in *The Lives of Animals*, Coetzee most explicitly raises the problem of sympathetic imagination and meditates on its genealogy, its modern reformation, and its possibilities and limitations. As Elizabeth Costello's character performs constitutive contradictions in her search for a crowded self, the novel both defends and critiques her model for representational ethics. With *Disgrace*, Coetzee's emergent vision of postcolonial sympathy comes to fullest fruition. The ethical decisions of Coetzee's characters and the narrative choices of his fiction all turn to radical renunciation and self-conscious vulnerability to transgress social borders. This emphasis on the ethical possibility of the rights losing may help to explain why so few of Coetzee's black and colored figures, newly enfranchised in the world of postapartheid South Africa, serve as emblems for sympathetic engagement. The crowded selves of David and Lucy abandon many of their claims to liberal rights, and the crowded style of *Disgrace* inhabits the terrain of racist discourse to reconfigure it into an antihumanist mode of representational ethics.

In offering us this austere vision of perpetual sacrifice, Coetzee models sympathetic perception when pushed to its limit. As the last line of *Disgrace* reminds us, engagements with significant otherness are progressive rather than perfective.[90] "Yes, I am giving him up," David says as he sends a stray dog to its death (*D*, 220). In relinquishing the dog, David, now "the dog-man," metaphorically gives up more and more of his own claims to the privileges of personhood, in what Louis Tremaine calls "growing small."[91] This diminishment, however, makes room for the lives of others within evolving crowded selves and styles, enacting the paradoxical logic of grace and disgrace.

Although I suggest that this paradoxical maneuver may be the only ethical response commensurate to the extreme barriers represented in *Disgrace*, it is possible to read Coetzee's emphasis on unending sacrifice in a distinctly more disturbing light. Many will surely share Zoë Wicomb's sense that a mystifying and ethically fraught relationship with dogs cannot adequately substitute for renewed political bonds.[92] With its emphasis on euthanasia, *Disgrace* could be seen as a novel of depopulation that challenges the very existence of a crowded self. Most crucially, the unlimited imperative to imagine alterity pushes the ethics of this gesture so far that it threatens to turn sympathy into an identification with evil. The implications of this gesture emerge most vividly in Coetzee's *The Master of Petersburg*, when Coetzee's Dostoevsky speaks of a short story in which a young revolutionary murders a member of the older landowning generation, a plot that alludes to the historical *The Brothers Karamazov* (1880). This narrative provokes a mediation on novelistic and readerly sympathetic imagination:

> "When you read about Karamzin or Karamzov or whatever his name is, when Karamzin's skull is cracked open like an egg, what is the truth: do you suffer with him, or do you secretly exult behind the arm that swings the axe? You don't answer? Let me tell you then: reading is being the arm and being the axe *and* being the skull; reading is giving yourself up, not holding yourself at a distance and jeering."[93]

As the imperative to enter into the lives of others admits no limit on identification, the crowded self of the reader and writer—at once murderer, weapon, and murdered—is threatened with its own destruction. Coetzee suggests that there is a point at which the impulse to project oneself into the life of another can only occur through an act of violence—perhaps, like the murderer, literally opening up the mind of his hated enemy, or perhaps, like Dostoevsky himself at the end of the novel, penning sadistic scenes that will destroy the fragile innocence of the child who will find them. Indeed, one might read the rhetoric of rape in *Disgrace* as just such an intrusion into the life of another. Even David's opera, which opens itself up to the voices of women and dogs, does so because, as David thinks, "in a work that will never be performed, all things are permitted" (*D*, 215)—a phrase that echoes Ivan's famous claim in *The Brothers Karamazov* that, in a world without God, all things are permitted. The specter of amorality and immorality thus haunts the workings of imaginative projection.

In such terrifying moments, when sympathy has lost almost all of its comforting associations, one might recall Elizabeth Costello's injunction against representations of depravity in "The Problem of Evil" (2003). "She is no longer sure that people are always improved by what they read," Coetzee writes. "Furthermore, she is not sure that writers who venture into the darker territories of the soul always return unscathed" (EC, 160). Yet, in the paradoxical style that characterizes the Costello lectures, even its own rhetoric cannot retreat into a decorous silence; it too compels us to encounter stories of atrocity even as its protagonist rails against them. Costello herself, in "At the Gate" (2003), defends her surrender to the deeply unethical lives of others. "I am open to all voices, not just the voices of the murdered and violated," she says. "If it is their murderers and violators who choose to summon me instead, to use me and speak through me, I will not close my ears to them, I will not judge them" (EC, 204). This paradoxical space, where inhabiting the perspectives of others becomes both the most *and* the least ethical of endeavors, pushes the act of border crossing to yet another limit.[94]

When Coetzee's Dostoevsky declares that "reading is giving yourself up, not holding yourself at a distance and jeering," he might well serve as a prophet for the not yet invented David Lurie. The end of *Disgrace* performs these words in a new ritual of sacrifice, abandoning David's characteristic irony as he relinquishes the dog that serves as both self and other. The novel suggests that this surrender to all kinds of voices is the necessary condition for an ethics of representation, despite the dangers that such surrender may entail. Against this specter of dissolution, the Christian language of the ending, which describes the dog as "like a lamb" (D, 220), reinforces the redemptive possibility latent within the dog's imminent death. The novel's emphasis on the progressive tense of David's unending sacrifice thus enables a surprising form of hope. Even as the privileges of David's selfhood recede almost to the point of extinction, they never actually reach the point of their own annihilation. Slender as it is, the novel's final commitment to the progressive tense keeps David, and an ethics of imagining others, alive: just enough to sympathize with more and more subjects through increasingly crowded selves and styles. Giving up, or enacting endless sacrifice, circles into giving oneself up, or sympathizing with the lives of others.

As the postscript to *Elizabeth Costello* suggests, this vision of imaginative absorption, in which the presence of other lives crowds around one ever more intensely, offers both ecstasy and agony. For Lady Chandos's husband, captivated by the process of reading the world, "each creature is key to all other creatures" (*EC*, 229). But for Lady Chandos, this enmeshment is frightening indeed. "And perhaps he speaks the truth," she writes, "perhaps in the mind of our Creator (*our Creator*, I say) where we whirl about as in a millrace we interpenetrate and are interpenetrated by fellow creatures by the thousand. But how I ask you can I live with rats and dogs and beetles crawling through me day and night, drowning and gasping, scratching at me, tugging me, urging me deeper and deeper into revelation—how?" (*EC*, 229, italics in original). How to go on living as such a crowded self: this question takes us, quite literally, past the end of Coetzee's narrative into an as yet unimagined future.

POSTSCRIPT

As powerful forms of seduction, novels may play a role in how their readers perceive the world around them. Although this effect is not readily measurable or consistent from reader to reader, fiction nonetheless lends weight to ideas—dominant, oppositional, or both—that circulate across different times and places. Although modern adult reading is usually individual and private, it occurs within larger interpretative fields that encourage readers to connect the worlds on the page with the worlds of their historical experience. While few readers aspire to the extremes of a Don Quixote or a Catherine Morland, who map the course of their lives through chivalric romances and Gothic tales, works of fiction often inspire complicity from both witting and unwitting audiences in shaping specific ideas about human capacity. When we consider how an education in European literature affected colonial subjects or how portraits of women shaped ideas about femininity, we often conclude that literature contributed subtly (and sometimes obviously) to the making of readers' beliefs about their world. Even if readers resist the values embedded within a work of fiction and champion the marginal voice over the central chorus, their very desire to read against the grain suggests the potential for novels to spark reflection on social norms and ethical values.

As a central part of this legacy, one strong tradition of late twentieth-century reading exposes the persuasive power of novels as negative and reprehensible, stressing the subtle and not-so-subtle ways that works of fiction reinforce repressive ideas about human capacity. Even among scholars who refrain from explicit evaluative judgment, their interpretations often unveil how particular novels bolster ideas and practices that twenty-first-century readers would hope to resist. This widespread critical metanarrative encourages a trajectory from innocence to experience, compelling readers to recognize how deeply appealing pieces of fiction can contribute to discursive domination. Through what Eve Kosofsky Sedgwick calls the "tracing-and-exposure project," many scholars have understood novelistic attempts to cross social borders as mere projections of individual, cultural, or national fantasy.[1] Border-crossing fiction, seen in this light, illuminates only the world of the novel, narrowly construed, rather than anything beyond its local origins. Although authors who write from positions of comparative marginality about positions of power are seen to effectively represent social difference, because they shed light on the workings of power and knowledge that the privileged cannot always perceive, novelists who complicate this paradigm are often viewed with suspicion. Informed by such governing assumptions, many scholars locate the real worth of imaginative border crossing in silences, omissions, and exclusions. In such readings, the lives of others appear most ethically as those who cannot be represented.

This book has proposed theoretical and empirical alternatives to these scholarly metanarratives of displacement and silence. If novels have the power to promote and perpetuate ideologies of inferiority, they may logically have the capacity to help us begin to question them. As these border-crossing fictions attend to problems of unequal privilege that define many social landscapes of globalization, they work to contest the hierarchical optic that seeks to control whatever enters its gaze. These novels help their readers contemplate what it would mean to imagine across borders without imperial eyes, and though we may not always agree with their narrative choices, we can approach these novels as shared seekers in a mutual search for effective ways of considering the lives of others.

The ethics of representing social difference I have defended springs from the tension between the desire to challenge constraining representations and the desire to engage with significant otherness. Although imagining alterity is often vexed, *not* writing about others ultimately exacts its own ethical price. Unlike conventional defenses of artistic freedom of expression, which stress the right to create new representations without regard to differentials in power, the practices I defend invite us to understand writing about others as a responsibility that attends to the nuances of historical, intellectual, and material privilege. The purpose of such fiction is not to claim the objective accuracy of positivist portraits but to open paths for dialogue, debate, and meditation across socially defined borders. Such imaginative projection struggles toward the utopian form of communication that the artist Guillermo Gómez-Peña describes in his reflection on social-border crossing. "Dialogue is a two-way, ongoing communication between peoples and communities that enjoy equal negotiating powers," Gómez-Peña asserts. "In order to dialogue, we must learn each other's language, history, art, literature, and political ideas. We must travel south and east, with frequency and humility, not as cultural tourists but as civilian ambassadors."[2] While "equal negotiating powers" may frequently prove elusive in a world marked by intensifying inequality, the crowded selves and styles considered in this study nonetheless work toward the practice that Gómez-Peña asks of his readership.

As novels at the turn of the millennium invent new forms of writing across borders, their narrative choices ask readers to move beyond visions of otherness that only mirror the self or vanish beyond the power of representation. The novels considered in this study thus merge concerns of formal representation with those of ethical desire. Though it is not possible to know anyone, including the self, with a claim to absolute and objective truth, some forms of representation are more desirable— less dominating and diminishing—than others. We need not believe in perfect objectivity to make distinctions between representations anchored in cruelty, indifference, or alterity and those inspired by a desire for democratic, compassionate, or just ways of writing. Although many border-crossing fictions cannot completely meet the standards they assign themselves, they still compel us to ask difficult questions about what ideal forms of representation might actually look like in fallible prose. If dominant critical metanarratives encourage us, in David

Parker's words, to believe that "the judgments we make merely tell us about ourselves and not about the world,"[3] these diverse works of fiction suggest the possibility of different kinds of judgments formed through the creation of crowded selves and styles. Derek Attridge gestures toward this middle space when he argues that "when I experience alterity, I experience not the other as such (how could I?) but the remolding of the self that brings the other into being as, necessarily, no longer entirely other."[4] The significance of border-crossing representational practices lies in what it suggests about this remolding.

In offering a spectrum of responses to this question, the novels considered in this book respond specifically to entrenched practices of representational violence that vary across time, place, and circumstance. As these novels confront increasingly intransigent social borders, their narrative choices move from reformist impulses to radical sacrifices. The visions considered in the first half of this book resonate with the philosophical stance of Kwame Anthony Appiah, who argues that not all ethical actions at a distance require asceticism.[5] In insisting that it is possible to practice border-crossing ethics and experience pleasure at the same time, Appiah offers a defense of the kind of world that Ozeki, Johnson, and Jen describe. By the time we reach the realm of Ghosh and especially Coetzee, an ethics of representation requires such severe renunciation that most individuals would not voluntarily create such uncomfortably crowded selves. A theorist like Peter Singer places Coetzee-like pressures on us when he refuses to specify when the demands of the other must stop and the comforts of the self can begin.[6] I argue that both approaches are necessary in our modern world: we need visions that work within the chronic comedies of getting and spending in daily first-world existence, and we need visions that sustain us in darker, implacable, and disgraceful circumstances. Making space for both kinds of literary perspective, these novels produce crowded selves and crowded styles in both moderate and extreme guises.

As the novels in this study lead from the most pleasurable visions to the most demanding, they elucidate possible roles for many different novelistic subgenres. Ozeki, Johnson, and Jen, while not avoiding painful representations, testify to the power of sentimentality and comedy in forging new representational ethics. Sentiment produces affective bonding between willing subjects, while comic incongruity undermines conventional assumptions about identity and difference. Eugenides and

Bajwa turn to the conventions of tragicomic styles of narration, and in doing so, they shape new images of engagement through the middle grounds between different claims to knowledge and different claims to class privilege. Ghosh and Coetzee offer works of fiction that favor the elegant, high styles of historical epic and tragic drama, and although they both ultimately offer a form of hope, they force their readers to confront dramatic personal and aesthetic sacrifices along the way.

As these novels seek to contest invasive imagination, they gesture toward a burgeoning future for planetary idealism. Drawing upon Benedict Anderson's classic thesis of the nation as an imagined community, Peter Singer applies Anderson's logic toward the possibility of larger global sentiment. "If Anderson is right, and the modern idea of the nation rests on a community we imagine ourselves to be part of, rather than one that we really are part of, then it is also possible for us to imagine ourselves to be part of a different community," he argues.[7] In seeking to represent the lives of others across social borders, the novels I explore envision such expansive forms of public cultures. Although novels cannot bring about new and enduring solidarity by themselves, they may still work to enlarge their readers' horizons of possibility. They struggle to create, in Paul Gilroy's terms, "a more generous and creative view of how human beings might communicate or act in concert across racial, ethnic, or civilizational lines."[8]

While we need constitutions, laws, media, religions, schools, and many other factors to make a broader imagined community, novels and other forms of art are particularly well-suited to expanding conceptions of responsibilities to others. Many philosophers, including Singer, argue with undeniable logic that when we limit concern for others to those who share our nation, race, tribe, gender, class, or other social group, we rely on what Martha Nussbaum calls morally irrelevant attributes to make these important decisions about whom we value and why. Rationally speaking, we would find it hard to defend why we should care about a fellow national and not someone suffering in an unfamiliar part of the world. Critics of Nussbaum and Singer's position, however, argue that it is precisely our irrational attachments that drive commitments to those other than ourselves. To remove passionate feelings and loyalties, they claim, is to remove the most enduring of ethical impulses.[9] Leo Tolstoy famously articulates this perspective in *Anna Karenina* (1877), where both Anna Karenina and Constantine Levin find themselves called to explain their distrust of grand social schemes and egalitarian compassion. In both cases, Anna and Levin confess that no matter what they might wish, their ethical impulses follow personal loyalties rather than abstract commandments. In pleading that "no activity can endure if it is not based on personal interest," Levin anticipates late twentieth-century defenses of the waywardness of the human heart.[10]

In light of this persistent debate about the proper scope for ethical concern, an art form like the novel offers a powerful accommodation between the rational imperative to imagine the lives of others and the emotional need to consider them within intimate communities of passionate commitment. When novels ask readers to expand their attention, they typically do so through the power of specific stories rather than through remote abstractions. Indeed, as Nussbaum would argue, novels suggest the rational work that emotions can perform in helping individuals understand what they value and how they value it. In modeling for their readers how to imagine others across social borders, these novels gesture toward a larger world of concern through immersion in the specificity, contradiction, and eccentricity of individual lives.

Though invasive imagination continues to abound in the millennial world, we need to celebrate moments in which imaginative projection surmounts the temptation to replicate familiar forms of discursive domination. As the writers throughout this study show, although no representation is above critique, it is possible to dramatize the process of conceptualizing others without inevitably trapping them within the prisons of one's needs and desires. Understanding these efforts helps illuminate a new scholarly metanarrative for cultural study. "For the professors in the academy," reflects a character in Ian McEwan's *Saturday* (2005), "for the humanities generally, misery is more amenable to analysis: happiness is a harder nut to crack."[11] While we still require rich and robust understandings of how fiction gets things wrong, we also need momentary celebrations of crowded selves and crowded styles.

APPENDIX

CREATIVE WRITING MANUALS

Aronie, Nancy Slonim. *Writing from the Heart: Tapping the Power of Your Inner Voice*. New York: Hyperion, 1998.

Bauer, Douglas. *The Stuff of Fiction: Advice on Craft*. Ann Arbor: University of Michigan Press, 2000.

Bell, Julia, and Paul Magrs, eds. *The Creative Writing Coursebook: Forty Writers Share Advice and Exercises for Poetry and Prose*. London: Macmillan, 2001.

Bernays, Annie, and Pamela Painter. *What If? Writing Exercises for Fiction Writers*. New York: Harper Collins, 1990.

Bly, Carol. *Beyond the Writers' Workshop: New Ways to Write Creative Nonfiction*. New York: Anchor Books, 2001.

Boran, Pat. *The Portable Creative Writing Workshop*. Cliffs of Mohur: Salmon Publishing, 1999.

Cooper, Donna. *Writing Great Screenplays for Film and TV*. New York: Macmillan, 1994.

Dawson, Jonathan. *Screenwriting: A Manual*. Oxford: Oxford University Press, 2000.

Goldberg, Bonnie. *Room to Write: Daily Invitations to a Writer's Life*. New York: Jeremy P. Tarcher/Putnam, 1996.

Goldberg, Natalie. *Writing Down the Bones: Freeing the Writer Within*. Boston: Shambhala, 1986.

Hemley, Robin. *Turning Life Into Fiction*. Cincinnati, Oh.: Story Press, 1994.

Keyes, Ralph. *The Courage to Write: How Writers Transcend Fear*. New York: Henry Holt, 1995.

Kitson, Norma. *Creative Writing: A Handbook with Exercises and Examples*. Harare: Baobab Books, 1997.

Mills, Paul. *Writing in Action*. London: Routledge, 1996.

Minot, Stephen. *Three Genres: The Writing of Poetry, Fiction, and Drama*. 3rd ed. Englewood Cliffs, N.J.: Prentice-Hall, Inc., 1982.

O'Conner, Patricia T. *Words Fail Me: What Everyone Who Writes Should Know About Writing*. New York: Harcourt Brace and Co., 1999.

Rico, Gabriele Lusser. *Writing the Natural Way: Using Right-Brain Techniques to Release Your Expressive Powers*. Los Angeles: J. P. Tarcher, Inc., 1983.

Rubie, Peter. *The Elements of Storytelling: How to Write Compelling Fiction*. New York: John Wiley and Sons, 1996.

Safire, William, and Leonard Safir, eds. *Good Advice on Writing: Writers Past and Present on How to Write Well*. New York: Simon and Schuster, 1992.

Singleton, John, and Mary Luckhurst, eds. *The Creative Writing Handbook: Techniques for New Writers*. 2nd ed. London: Macmillan, 2000.

Stafford, Kim. *The Muses Among Us: Eloquent Listening and Other Pleasures of the Writer's Craft*. Athens: The University of Georgia Press, 2003.

Winokur, Jon, ed. *Advice to Writers: A Compendium of Quotes, Anecdotes, and Writerly Wisdom from a Dazzling Array of Literary Lights*. New York: Pantheon Books, 1999.

Wolf, Robert. *Jump Start: How to Write from Everyday Life*. Oxford: Oxford University Press, 2001.

NOTES

INTRODUCTION: TOWARD AN ETHICS OF
BORDER-CROSSING FICTION

1. Coetzee, *Disgrace*, 140–141. Subsequent citations will be abbreviated *D* and cited parenthetically in the text.

2. My definition here draws upon Tzvetan Todorov's taxonomy, emphasizing in particular the mode of alterity that Todorov describes as "a specific social group to which *we* do not belong." In his formulation, "This group in turn can be interior to society: women for men, the rich for the poor, the mad for the 'normal'; or it can be exterior to society, i.e. another society which will be near or far away, depending on the case: beings whom everything links to me on the cultural, moral, historical plane; or else unknown quantities, outsiders whose language and customs I do not understand, so foreign that in extreme instances I am reluctant to admit they belong to the same species as my own." Todorov, *The Conquest of America*, 3. Subsequent references will be abbreviated *CA* in the text. My use of the adjective "social" also resembles Arjun Appadurai's description of the adjective "cultural," which he deploys to denote "a contrastive rather than a substantive property of certain things." Because I am interested in many different articulations of difference,

some of which (such as gender) are at best awkwardly understood as "cultural," I use the broader word "social." See Appadurai, *Modernity at Large*, 12.

3. I suggest that nonhuman animal otherness could fall under this definition to the extent that other species animate questions pertaining to human social life: for example, debates over whether or not to kill, eat, live in proximity with, or afford animals cognizable rights all posit nonhumans within a shared social world.

4. I will discuss the conceptual underpinnings of these works in chapter 1, so I will simply mention here three of the most influential arguments in this field: the scholarship of Edward Said, whose foundational *Orientalism* (1978) contends that Western representations (and inventions) of the Orient suggest complicity with imperialism; the work of Mary Louise Pratt, which reveals the operations of "imperial eyes" in Western travel writings; and the writing of Marianna Torgovnick, whose study of Western representations of Africa and South America applies Said's logic to Western modernists' fascination with premodern societies. See Pratt, *Imperial Eyes*; Said, *Orientalism*; Torgovnick, *Gone Primitive*.

5. Mohanty, *Literary Theory and the Claims of History*, 122.

6. Rey Chow makes this point when she argues that "attempts to salvage the other often turn into attempts to uphold the other as the non-duped—the site of authenticity and true knowledge. Critics who do this also imply that, having absorbed the primal wisdoms, they are the non-duped themselves." For Chow, "our fascination with the native, the oppressed, the savage, and all such figures is therefore a desire to hold on to an unchanging certainty somewhere outside our own 'fake' experience. It is a desire for being 'non-duped,' which is a not-too-innocent desire to seize control." Chow, *Writing Diaspora*, 52–53.

7. One of the earliest promulgators of such a turn to ethics is Wayne Booth, whose work advocates a model of book as friend. Booth encourages a shift away from ethics as morality to ethics as a form of character building, arguing that works of literature affect their readers by inviting them to exercise forms of judgment through the act of shared reading. I take from Booth the sense that books do have the capacity to speak intimately to their audiences, although (as my subsequent chapters will show) I do not see all novels as encouraging a friendly relationship with their readers. My account is also indebted to the work of Richard Rorty and Martha Nussbaum, whose writings on the representation of otherness approach literature for new ways of reasoning, ways formal philosophical argumentation cannot always provide. While I believe that Rorty and Nussbaum pose crucial questions about imagining alterity, however, I will be setting forth a set of novels that frequently challenge the liberalism upon which their readings (Nussbaum's in particular) depend. See Booth, *The Company We Keep*; Nussbaum, *Love's Knowl-*

edge; Nussbaum, *Cultivating Humanity*; Nussbaum, *Poetic Justice*; Rorty, *Contingency, Irony, and Solidarity*.

8. In using the language of responsibility, my definition builds upon Katherine Stanton's description of ethics, which is designed to include "my responsibility to and for the other—a particular response owed to a particular other." Stanton, *Cosmopolitan Fictions*, 3. The qualification I add—a responsibility opposed to representational violence—is certainly not the only form of responsibility that might count as ethical. However, it best describes the specific impulse with which this book is concerned.

9. My understanding of ethics thus draws upon, but also distinguishes itself from, an extremely open definition that radically rejects the affiliation of ethics with virtue and morality. Such an open account characterizes Adam Zachary Newton's work, in which ethics comes to mean "an armature of intersubjective relation accomplished through story" and "recursive, contingent, and interactive dramas of encounter and recognition." Newton's definition underwrites John Su's work on late twentieth-century Anglophone fiction, who declares that "my notion of ethics does not signify normative codes of behavior or depictions of virtue." Instead, Su understands ethics "as a communal process of negotiating needs," bound in his account to nostalgia, in which individuals reconstruct images of place to express their needs through social interactions. See Newton, *Narrative Ethics*, 7, 12; Su, *Ethics and Nostalgia in the Contemporary Novel*, 12, 52. To the extent that these accounts seek to distance themselves from rigid codes and to insist on the primacy of particular encounters, my account draws upon theirs. However, I believe that defining ethics in an overly broad way is to sacrifice precisely that which ethics was designed to indicate, namely the workings of value and judgment. My conception of ethics thus calls attention to the explicit ideals at stake in my analysis. In similar fashion, my understanding of ethics builds upon but also departs from the (differently) open account of John Guillory, who argues against ethics as a choice between right and wrong and in favor of ethics as a choice between goods. Drawing upon Foucault's concept of self-care, Guillory rewrites ethical practice into a form of self-cultivation. I find myself drawn to much in Guillory's account, especially as he describes what might be considered ethical about reading. The interpretative lens I propose in this book should help reformulate the (explicitly or implicitly) moralizing language of difference criticism, presenting instead the representation of otherness as an act that is a crucial part of what we might call fiction's equivalent of seeking the good life. However, I do not think that Guillory's division between ethics as moralizing and ethics as self-care can always be sustained. Choosing among goods, if it is to deserve the language of ethics rather than of consumption,

implies judgments about what is more or less valuable, and these judgments remain crucial to the novels I explore and to the reading practices I propose. See Guillory, "The Ethical Practice of Modernity," 29–46.

10. Haraway, *The Companion Species Manifesto*, 7.

11. My approach draws upon current work like Sedgwick's, which seeks to explore alternatives to givens of critical reading. As a complementary alternative to these "paranoid methodologies," Sedgwick proposes a "recuperative" position, based on the work of Melanie Klein, that she associates with "ethical possibility" and with Foucault's "care of the self." This practice, however, is vulnerable to Michael Warner's critique that "Sedgwick's reparative reading seems to be defined less by any project of its own than by its recoil from a manically programmatic intensification of the critical. It is not so much a method as (principled?) avoidance of method." The interpretative practice I propose in this book might be understood as one form of recuperative reading, but, as I will describe in chapter 1, it also seeks to offer the more systematized and focused lens that Warner calls for. See Sedgwick, "Paranoid Reading and Reparative Reading," 4, 7, 15, 21; Warner, "Uncritical Reading," 18.

12. Appadurai, *Modernity at Large*, 33.

13. Barber, *Jihad vs. McWorld*.

14. To take only one example of a literary precursor, nineteenth-century British romantic poets such as Shelley and Wordsworth energetically defended the value of imaginative perspective taking. In "A Defence of Poetry" (1821), Shelley boldly declared: "The great secret of morals is Love; or a going out of our own nature, and identification of ourselves with the beautiful which exists in thought, action, or person, not our own. A man, to be greatly good, must imagine intensely and comprehensively; he must put himself in the place of another and of many others; the pains and pleasures of his species must become his own. The great instrument of moral good is the imagination; and poetry administers to the effect by acting upon the cause." While many late twentieth- and early twenty-first-century writers do inherit Shelley's confidence in the possibility and value of this undertaking, many others are warier of being accused of insensitive universalism. Shelley, "A Defence of Poetry," 785.

15. I am grateful to Adrian Lurssen for this phrase.

16. The novel, Michael McKeon argues, should not be conflated indiscriminately with fiction, which "rules out factuality," or with narrative, which "rules out discourse that isn't told, or whose telling doesn't take the form of a story." McKeon, ed., *Theory of the Novel*, xiii. While I respect McKeon's decision to assert the distinctiveness of the genre, my argument does not hinge upon a strong distinction between

the novel and other forms of prose fiction. Throughout this book, I use "fiction" and "novel" interchangeably to indicate my focus of study: "fiction," because not all of my examples are novels (I occasionally consider short stories and works that have been published both as independent short pieces and as parts of novels), and "novel," because the great majority of my examples do indeed fall into this category. When I use "fiction," I mean the narrow sense of "prose fiction"; when I use "novel," I do so with the caveat that my observations could also apply to short stories. The argument I wish to make depends more on the resources available to prose fiction than on the distinctions between different kinds of prose fiction; in other words, I seek to conflate these terms *discriminately*. (In contrast, I do not wish to merge prose fiction with poetry, plays, or other forms of expressive writing, which bring very different formal resources to bear, or with nonfiction narrative, which entails a different conception of ethical obligation to its referent.) I use "narrative," as in "narrative choices," to point to the particular ways in which novels and short stories choose to relate their engagements with significant otherness. These choices sometimes lie in what particular stories are told, but they also appear in how these stories are told.

17. Said, *Culture and Imperialism*, xiii.

18. In particular, novels have been credited with helping invent Western conceptions of human rights. Lynn Hunt argues that reading eighteenth-century novels promoted new kinds of psychological identification with a wide range of figures, and she claims that this new imaginative sympathy enabled the formulation of expanded views of human rights. Joseph Slaughter understands the relationship between the novel (in particular, the *Bildungsroman*) and human rights as mutually constitutive, claiming that "human rights and the *Bildungsroman* are mutually enabling fictions: each projects an image of the human personality that ratifies the other's vision of the ideal relations between individual and society." See Hunt, *Inventing Human Rights*, 35–69; Slaughter, "Enabling Fictions and Novel Subjects," 1407. Whether or not novels actually affected all their readers in such ways is debatable. Suzanne Keen, for instance, argues that broad claims for the social effects of novel reading are not firmly supported by psychological and empirical studies of reading. However, whether or not novels lead to prosocial behavior, the *perception* that they can influence ideas and actions remains a strong one. See Keen, *Empathy and the Novel*, 35.

19. I will call attention here to only a few of the most obvious differences between prose fiction and other expressive literary forms. Poetry may be most able to evade mimetic representations of border crossing, but, as Jahan Ramazani suggests in his reading of Derek Walcott, it can call most powerfully upon nonlinear language

connections (such as those enabled by metaphor) to surmount the impasses of representing alterity. See Ramazani, *The Hybrid Muse*, 49–71. The specific resources of theater and performance offer rich strategies for representing alterity that are fundamentally different from the techniques of the novel, including (though not limited to) the interplay between the marked body of the actor, the social identity of the role, and the social context of the performance. Katrin Sieg, in her study of ethnic drag in twentieth-century German theatrical practices, points to the ways in which white performances of ethnic others (such as Jews or Native Americans) reflect a complex triangulated relationship between actor, role, and referent. Sieg's findings analyze the productive use of ethnic drag but also emphasize the limits of impersonating practices, when adopted by relatively privileged groups, to counter ideologies of inferiority. Sieg, *Ethnic Drag*, 21–22. "Vernacularizing" a play written in one language into another set of linguistic and theatrical practices also affords another specifically performative way of engaging alterity, as the work of Rustom Bharucha explores. His analysis of his work as a director inquires into the possibility of theatrical "spaces left within community that are open to non-sectarian interaction and dialogue." Bharucha, *The Politics of Cultural Practice*, 66. While nonfiction narrative may be closest to the novel or story in terms of structure and style, I believe that it belongs in a different category because it implies an ethical responsibility to an actually existing referent, whereas fiction implies such a responsibility to a *category* of actually existing referent.

20. Ghosh, "Interview with the Author"; Johnson, *Turning the Wheel*, 104.

21. Perhaps the most robust of these three enabling categories is that of the nation. In challenging the self-evidence of this category, my work shares an interest in the growing trend that questions the link between national territory and literary history. Wai Chee Dimock, for example, critiques the "reproductive logic" that "assumes that there is a seamless correspondence between the temporal and spatial boundaries of the nation and the boundaries of all other expressive domains." Dimock, *Through Other Continents*, 3. Other recent exemplars of this shift include Dimock and Buell, eds., *Shades of the Planet*; Doyle and Winkiel, eds., *Geomodernisms*.

22. My comparative practice, of course, is not unlimited: all of the works considered here share a language (English), a genre (prose fiction), and a quarter century (1980–2005). I hope that the work of scholars with different disciplinary training will allow us to push beyond this archive.

23. Attridge, *J. M. Coetzee and the Ethics of Reading*, 98–99. Italics in original.

1. Rushdie, *Shalimar the Clown*, 37.

2. Shuman, *Other People's Stories*, 3.

3. Updike, "Questions of Character," 238–239.

4. One might also ask why Updike describes this representational right as specifically American, as if voting rights correlated directly with representational rights.

5. See the appendix for a list of manuals consulted.

6. See Shuman, *Other People's Stories*, 121.

7. Lamott, *Bird by Bird*, 4.

8. Goldberg, *Writing Down the Bones*, 19.

9. Though Said is perhaps the first and certainly the most influential to make this argument in a systematic fashion, insights about power inequities and representation existed well before the publication of *Orientalism*. Writing in 1969, Joseph R. Levenson argued that "there is all the difference in the world between thinking about China as exotic—an old way of annexing China to the domain of western consciousness—and thinking about exoticism in China, which is a universal subject." See Levenson, *Revolution and Cosmopolitanism*, 2. This interest in how different parts of the world are annexed to the domain of Western consciousness has inspired a wide range of interdisciplinary investigation. Rana Kabbani, for instance, discusses how European representations of the Middle East were colored by what European writers believed would interest their target audience. Evaluating the intellectual debates over the underpinnings of Orientalism, Richard King suggests that "the general tenor of the arguments furnished by Foucault, Said, and Gadamer, despite their many differences, does seem to imply that the very act of interpretation by Western Orientalists when approaching the Orient inevitably involves an appropriation and 'colonialization' of the material under consideration." Christina Klein, approaching Orientalism as an historian, both revises and confirms Said's thesis in her account of postwar American representations of Asia. Klein does not understand these American images as monolithically constraining, but she does present them as acts that work to legitimate U.S. expansion in Asia. See Kabbani, *Imperial Fictions*; King, *Orientalism and Religion*, 95; Klein, *Cold War Orientalism*, 13.

10. Torgovnick, *Gone Primitive*, 246.

11. Defending Hispanic Orientalism, Julia Kushigian argues that this phenomenon allows for the blending of opposing visions and allows the self to know itself better through its engagement with the other. This perspective is thus quite different

from the approach I will set forth, which seeks to move away from a self-directed model of representation. See Kushigian, *Orientalism in the Hispanic Literary Tradition.*

12. JanMohamed, "The Economy of Manichean Allegory," 85.

13. Austen, *Persuasion*, 209.

14. In their introduction, the editors "offer a literary history of Chinese American and Japanese American writing concerning the real and the fake. We describe the real, from its sources in the Asian fairy tales and the Confucian heroic tradition, to make the work of these Asian American writers understandable in its own terms. We describe the fake—from its sources in Christian dogma and in Western philosophy, history, and literature." Chan et al., "The Big Aiiieeeee!" xv.

15. Hobson, "The Rise of the White Shaman as a New Version of Cultural Imperialism," 414, 416.

16. Kabbani, *Imperial Fictions*, x.

17. For instance, the editors of *The Big Aiiieeeee!* identify numerous Asian American writers as "fake," while Sheng-mei Ma shows how "Orientalist *mis*representations conceivably become *self*-representations." Chan et al., "The Big Aiiieeeee!" xv; Ma, *The Deathly Embrace*, xiii. Italics in original.

18. This shift toward a more circumscribed authority for speaking to and about others finds emblematic articulation in Rich, "Notes Toward a Politics of Location [1984]," 210–231.

19. Neil Lazarus's influential Marxist account of culture in an age of globalization, for instance, offers hope for a form of critical materialist transcultural dialogue but also appears to relinquish the possibility of something more than self-knowledge. As he concludes his study with a meditation on the international reception of Afropop, Lazarus argues that "the implicit proposal is not that we (in the West) listen to world music for what it can tell us about life 'over there,' but that we listen to it for what it can suggest to us about radically different ways of living 'over here,' ways of living that are unimaginable under prevailing social conditions." Lazarus, *Nationalism and Cultural Practice in the Postcolonial World*, 224–225.

20. Kabbani, *Imperial Fictions*, 3. While Kabbani's book primarily concerns European representations, she begins by identifying this pattern in medieval Arab travel narratives.

21. Richards, *Masks of Difference*, 289, 290.

22. Lowe, *Critical Terrains*, 7, 32.

23. For example, see Richards, *Masks of Difference*; Said, *Culture and Imperialism*.

24. Sieg, *Ethnic Drag*, 259.

25. Moya, *Learning from Experience*, 38.

26. Richards, *Masks of Difference*, 290.

27. Spivak, "Can the Subaltern Speak?" 90. Some scholars, such as B. Venkat Mani, perceive more openings for ethical representations of others in Spivak's work. However, these possibilities appear to me much weaker than her more forceful articulations of silencing. See Mani, *Cosmopolitical Claims*, 60.

28. For an example of the affirmative position, see Coronil, "Listening to the Subaltern," 37–55.

29. Bhabha, *The Location of Culture*, 34. Italics in the original.

30. Bhabha, *The Location of Culture*, 37.

31. David Richards, for example, adopts this approach. While Richards frequently uses the mirror argument to help him explain Western representations of worlds considered savage or primitive, he also turns to Bhabha to explore alternatives to an anthropological style of representation. "Bhabha inserts the misrepresented, forgotten or omitted historical presence. . . . Paradoxically, this is done by denying the possibility of representation and of history. . . . What is gained [in Bhabha's approach] is an awareness of those who lie outside representation; what is lost is the perception of the anthropological 'persona': an identity of social roles, obligations, connections, contexts and histories." Richards, *Masks of Difference*, 240.

32. We might also understand Rey Chow's meditations on representations of the "native" in a similar light. Chow argues against both defilements and sanctifications of the image of the native, arguing instead for a theoretical position that critiques the desire to know the other in a nondeceived manner. "The native is not the defiled image and not not the defiled image," she concludes. "And she stares indifferently, mocking our imprisonment within imagistic resemblance and our self-deception as the non-duped." Any ethical possibility we might read into this indifferent stare is certainly a deeply minimalist one. Chow, *Writing Diaspora*, 54.

33. Judith Butler makes this argument in the case of gender, arguing that "power seemed to be more than an exchange between subjects or a relation of constant inversion between a subject and an Other; indeed, power appeared to operate in the production of that very binary frame." From this position, the very fact that critics speak of oppositions such as self and other represents an effect of regulatory social power rather than an innocent description of social reality. Butler, vii–viii.

34. Haraway, *Primate Visions*, 11.

35. Graham Huggan identifies the pressures of this assumption when he argues that "ethnic autobiography, like ethnicity itself, flourishes under the watchful eye of the dominant culture; both are caught in the dual processes of commodification and surveillance. . . . This might help explain why the work of writers who come from, or are perceived as coming from, ethnic minority backgrounds continues to

be marketed so resolutely for a mainstream reading public as 'autobiographical.'" Huggan, *The Postcolonial Exotic*, 155.

36. Lundeen, "Who Has the Right to Feel?" 92.

37. Sedgwick understands this form of reading as problematic not in itself but in its tight monopoly over critical practice. "The trouble with a narrow gene pool, of course, is its diminished ability to respond to environmental (for instance, political) change," she contends. Similarly, I believe that readings based on the metanarrative of the mirror argument or the unrepresentability argument are often necessary, but I do not feel they should offer the only practices of reading in an era when many writers are just as conscious of the pitfalls of representing others as are literary critics. Sedgwick, "Paranoid Reading and Reparative Reading," 21.

38. We find one such attempt in Stuart Hall's cultural-studies textbook *Representations*, which evaluates the value of stereotype reversal, positive imagery, and what the text calls "the eye of representation." However, Hall remains skeptical of the efficacy of such techniques, and he argues that even the more sophisticated techniques of "the eye of representation" can enable fetishization and othering. Hall, "The Spectacle of the Other," 274. A more optimistic attempt appears in the work of Timothy Weiss, who argues for an understanding of Orientalist representation that escapes the determinative correlation between knowledge and power. Drawing upon Buddhist theories of a middle space between subject and object, Weiss advances a heuristic that provides an alternative to Said's framework. "Viewing cultures as interdependent and therefore groundless as autonomous entities, and as capable of being understood only through a recursive loop of ongoing interpretations, offers a way out of the *cul-de-sac* of the archaeological-genealogical methods of Foucault and Said," Weiss contends. This model, however, is oriented toward the broader operations of cultural translation rather than toward an ethics of representing social difference. See Weiss, *Translating Orients*, 11.

39. Said, "Criticism, Culture, and Performance," 115.

40. "Throughout this study," Torgovnick writes, "I have given hints of more positive forms of Western primitivism lurking behind the forms I have criticized. . . . Each of these possibilities exists within certain forms of primitivism I have examined, though they are, in each case, variously turned aside or undeveloped, often under the pressure of our culture's dominant ideas of selfhood or masculinity." Torgovnick, *Gone Primitive*, 246–247. For an overview of scholarship that seeks to give such hints in other fields, see MacKenzie, *Orientalism*, 1–42.

41. Even a work as committed to a Manichean reading of self-other representations as Abdul JanMohamed's essay on colonialist writing, which speculates that "every desire is at base a desire to impose oneself on another," does seek to identify alter-

native practices. However, the locus of his greatest optimism appears in Jan-Mohamed's curiously flat reading of Isak Dinesen's work, which offers only the broadest generalities about how Dinesen's emancipatory strategy emerges. The gestures found in Torgovnick and JanMohamed's work thus suggest how magnetically drawn their critical optics are to the failures of (in their examples) racialized representations and how weak these alternative practices appear in contrast. See JanMohamed, "The Economy of Manichean Allegory," 85, 102.

42. Mani offers some of the most explicit, useful, and imaginative work on this question, turning to German representations of Turkish subjects to explore novelistic techniques that combat discursive domination. His work on Sten Nadolny points to specific practices, such as narrative aphasia, strategic use of stereotypes, and reversals of guest-host relationships, that enable Nadolny's work to surmount Orientalist and multicultural assumptions. My account builds upon these claims, and many of the emancipatory practices Mani identifies provide important support for the vision set forth in this book. See Mani, *Cosmopolitical Claims*, 44–86, 191. In broader theoretical terms, Sara Ahmed also proposes a useful vision of an ethics of encounter. "In my notion of ethical encounters, hearing does not take place in my ear, or in yours, but in between our mouths and our ears, in the very proximity and multiplicity of this encounter," she argues. My account, with its emphasis on crowded selves and crowded styles, draws upon this generative idea of a shared space between subjects. Ahmed, however, is inclined to understand such encounters as rare and rarified. Her work on the concept of strangers makes strong use of the mirror argument and tends to read border crossing in light of paradigms of mastery and consumer fetishizations. Ahmed, *Strange Encounters*, 158. Marianna Torgovnick further identifies the promise of "the ethics of identification," which enables her to explore the possibilities of connection in the modern literature of what she calls "the war complex." In the work of W. G. Sebald, who exemplifies this impulse, Torgovnick perceives "identifications based not on what one might call a biographical imperative but on an ethical relationship to the world's dead . . . [a set of relationships] in which Otherness (alterity) does not preclude a sense of connection, but demands it." Though similar in spirit to my own investigation, Torgovnick's objects and methods of inquiry are quite different. Her literary analysis prefers to allow the ethics of identification to remain elusive; in the chapter on Sebald, for instance, the closest readers can come to understanding Sebald's connective impulse is to appreciate the palpable effect that his work has had on Torgovnick. Torgovnick, *The War Complex*, 125–126.

43. Greer, "Reality Bites."

44. Hassan, "Queries for Postcolonial Studies," 335.

45. Mohanty, *Literary Theory and the Claims of History*, 116.

46. Todorov, "'Race,' Writing, and Culture," 374.

47. Todorov limits his optimism in two crucial ways. First, most of his work articulates the workings of hegemonic vision in Spanish representations of Indians, even and especially in the writings of the early Las Casas. Second, Todorov is cautious not to extol the practice of understanding the other as inherently positive. His account reveals the "understanding-that-kills" (CA, 127), showing how detailed ethnographic description enables the colonizer to take control of native subjects. More radically, he suggests that claiming the ability to identify with the other often constitutes a superiority claim in itself (CA, 248). Nonetheless, Todorov's work still remains one of the most important sustained models for a new metanarrative of reading encounters with others.

48. For the argument that attention to neoliberal constructs of cultural difference can conceal callousness toward material inequality, see Abdul JanMohamed and David Lloyd's claim that "the semblance of pluralism disguises the perpetuation of exclusion insofar as it is enjoyed only by those who have already assimilated the values of the dominant culture. . . . It refuses to acknowledge the class basis of discrimination and the systematic economic exploitation of minorities that underlie postmodern culture." JanMohamed and Lloyd, "Introduction," 8. A more recent revision of this idea appears in Michaels, *The Trouble with Diversity*.

49. Ghosh, *In an Antique Land*, 210.

50. Keen, *Empathy and the Novel*.

51. See Jèmeljan Hakemulder's evaluation of psychological research on how reading affects norms and values, moral development, empathy, outgroup attitudes, sex-role concepts, self-esteem, critical thinking, and anxiety reduction. After assessing the reliability of fifty-four experiments, Hakemulder argues that we find positive results that link reading to moral development, self-esteem, anxiety, and especially sex-role concepts. More mixed results characterize the studies of norms and values, empathy, and outgroup attitudes, while studies linking reading to critical thinking provide only low results. Hakemulder, *The Moral Laboratory*, 32–37. Psychological studies of multicultural book programs also show ambiguous effects in changing readers' attitudes about ethnic identity and social diversity. Jennifer Serena Lee's study of how multicultural book programs affect the development of ethnic identity provides mixed results on the effectiveness of reading. Lee measured Asian American and European American students' feelings about ethnic identity, self-esteem, and attitudes toward Chinese Americans before and after they participated in a multicultural book program that featured Chinese American narratives. While European American children's self-esteem increased

after the program, Asian American children's self-esteem actually decreased, although their self-esteem nonetheless remained higher than that of European Americans. This statistically significant drop leads Lee to suggest that reading may need to be combined with other activities to combat possible feelings of stigmatization. Despite these limitations, Lee did find that students in the multicultural book program increased "their knowledge about Chinese Americans (KNOW) and their positive attitudes toward diversity and Chinese Americans." See Lee, "Ethnic Identity Development and the Influence of Multicultural Children's Literature," 123–126. For a summary of the ways in which media and educational interventions may or may not help alleviate stereotype-based prejudice, see Schneider, *The Psychology of Stereotyping*, 415–418.

52. Scarry, "The Difficulty of Imagining Other Persons," 40–62.

53. In this respect, these novels offer something more than a complexity traditionally valued for its own sake, a complexity whose value is questioned in Knapp, *Literary Interest*, 88–105.

54. Appadurai, *Modernity at Large*, 5.

55. This theory is popularized in Gilbert, *Stumbling on Happiness*.

56. This emphasis on theory-mediated experience allows Mohanty to describe an expanded sense of identity in Toni Morrison's *Beloved*, where he claims that "the community sought in *Beloved* involves as its essence a moral and imaginative expansion of oneself, in particular one's capacity to experience." Such a process is precisely what I will defend in my readings of border-crossing fiction. Mohanty's particular choice of example, however, raises questions about the possible limits attached to his understanding of this expansion. While Paul D learns to conceptualize slave motherhood in a new way and thus comes to sympathize with Sethe's agonizing choice, this expanded sense of ancestry is defined in important ways by experiences of slavery and by blackness. Might it be possible for a figure who is not the biological descendant of slave mothers to develop a sense of community that acknowledges their history? In other words, is Paul D's particular expansion dependent on his blackness? Mohanty's reading of *Beloved* leaves this question unanswered. Mohanty, *Literary Theory*, 206, 208, 217.

57. Anderson, *Imagined Communities*.

58. Too strong an emphasis on external perception also threatens to strip individuals of important kinds of agency. Multiethnic individuals, for example, are often assimilated to existing racial categories in the eyes of their beholders in ways that often flatten their own sense of group affiliation.

59. Michaels, *Our America*, 15.

60. Michaels, *The Shape of the Signifier*, 139.

61. Another path toward this troubling of identitarian logic appears in Gayatri Spivak's discussion of the art of Jamelie Hassan. "To feel one is from an origin is not a pathology," Spivak contends. "It belongs to that group of grounding mistakes that enable us to make sense of our lives." Yet precisely because it constitutes a grounding mistake, a sense of origin needs to destabilized. Describing Hassan's use of an Indian signifier (Salman Rushdie's *Midnight's Children*) to describe images of Egyptian children, Spivak records the unbalancing effect of watching a marker of her origin migrate in unexpected directions. "I stood in front of the installation stripped, precisely, of my 'identity.' This is the kind of stripping that must be undertaken together if ethnic identities in the so-called First World are to become culturally and politically productive." Spivak, "Acting Bits/Identity Talk," 781, 785. Chapter 3 will examine the effects of such productive stripping.

62. One might object to this softening of borders between "Indian" and "non-Indian" by pointing to material and legal factors: Indian passports, for example, are not handed out on the basis of how many works of Indian literature a person has read. Of course, there are formal limits imposed upon different kinds of identity by governments and institutions, not to mention informal limits imposed by, for example, discriminatory or oppressive practices, and these limits help shape the identity that an individual considers his or her own. However, it seems to me deeply problematic to take such imposed limits as imaginative ones.

63. Delany, *Atlantis*, 114–115.

64. Ghosh, "The Indian Story," 39.

65. Evelyn Ch'ien offers an account of this reshaping in twentieth-century literature by explaining how postcolonial and ethnic-minority authors turn vernacular speech patterns into new forms of written English. Dohra Ahmad offers an anthology of such vernacular literature, noting its rise in the late twentieth century and celebrating "the stunningly unanticipated ways in which English has changed as it grew into a global language." In the context of twentieth-century American education, which devalues language learning, Werner Sollors excavates older American multilingual traditions of writing. See Ahmad, *Rotten English*, 16; Ch'ien, *Weird English*; Sollors, ed., *Multilingual America*.

66. Perhaps the most extreme evocation of this hypothesis can be found in the work of Thomas Nagel, to whom I return in chapter 6 in my discussion of J. M. Coetzee. In his famous thought experiment, "What Is It Like to Be a Bat?" Nagel defends the impossibility of identifying with an alien point of view. "Our own experience provides the basic material for our imagination, whose range is therefore limited," Nagel claims. His own imagination "tells me only what it would be like for *me* to behave as a bat behaves. But that is not the question. I want to know what it is like

for a *bat* to be a bat." Simply projecting one's consciousness into an alien body does not actually provide an empathetic act of perspective taking, in Nagel's view, because the selfhood of the imagining subject remains unchanged. While Nagel did not argue for the impossibility of perspective taking in all situations, his position offers a way of describing the problem of inevitably narcissistic subjectivity. Nagel, "What Is It Like to Be a Bat?" 439. Italics in original.

67. Johnson, *Oxherding Tale*, 53. Johnson reiterates a similar image of endless mirroring as discursive domination, this time explicitly linked to imperialism, in his portrait of Captain Falcon in *Middle Passage* (1990). "Only I'm real to me," Falcon confides. Such imagery linking solipsism to imperialism can be traced back to much earlier works; for example, it characterizes Kurtz in Joseph Conrad's *Heart of Darkness* (1899). Johnson, *Middle Passage*, 95.

68. Hungerford, *The Holocaust of Texts*, 97–121.

69. Passing is most commonly discussed as a racial phenomenon, but it can also apply to gender or even class.

70. Randall Kennedy, in his discussion of black American passing, specifically excludes "a person who is mistaken about his background" and "a person whose appearance leads observers to think of him as white in the absence of any purposeful conduct on his part that reinforces this (mis)perception," though he admits that, in the latter case, "the line between innocent silence and fraudulent silence can be thin." Kennedy, *Sellout*, 144–145, 145n.

71. Gayle Wald makes this argument about Griffin's *Black Like Me*, claiming that "based upon a false opposition between the white researcher's theoretical apprehension and the black subject's non-thetic 'experience' or non-consciousness, Griffin's ethnojournalistic experiment is unequipped to imagine black people elaborating their own ontology of blackness or voicing their own opposition to segregation." Wald identifies several troubling elements in Griffin's work, including its very status as "experiment" rather than life commitment, its refusal to include black voices, and its ultimate appropriation by others as a source of authority on black experience (an appropriation that Griffin himself came to disavow). Wald, "A Most Disagreeable Mirror," 154.

72. Through her discussion of Gail Ching-Liang Low's work, Ahmed links passing to a hegemonic white masculinity that presumes it can be anywhere at any moment. Ahmed, *Strange Encounters*, 131.

73. I make two important distinctions here: Charles Johnson's *Oxherding Tale*, discussed at more length in chapter 3, is in fact a novel of passing that ends with its multiracial former slave Andrew living as a white man. However, the aspect of *Oxherding Tale* that concerns me is Johnson's use of Asian spiritual tropes, which do

not invoke the identity effects of passing. Jeffrey Eugenides' *Middlesex*, treated in chapter 4, also involves a hermaphroditic narrator who appears to many in his world as a heterosexual man. The novel, though, emphasizes the ultimate disclosure of his identity.

74. Wispé, *The Psychology of Sympathy*, 59.

75. This preoccupation with interconnection has also become a dominant thread in early twenty-first-century cultural production at large, inspiring such films as *Crash* and *Babel*.

76. Johnson, *Dr. King's Refrigerator and Other Bedtime Stories*, 29.

77. Parfit, *Reasons and Persons*, 275. Subsequent references will be abbreviated *RP* and cited parenthetically in the text.

78. Robbins, "The Sweatshop Sublime," 84–85.

79. Rorty, *Contingency, Irony, and Solidarity*, xvi.

80. My account of self-concern is thus distinct from John Guillory's account, which emphasizes ethics as a care of the self. Despite the appeal of its emphasis on pleasure and cultivation rather than on duty and obligation, ethics as only self-care seems to me vulnerable to narcissism and to treating others instrumentally. See Guillory, "The Ethical Practice of Modernity, 34–38.

81. My argument here coincides with the work of Rajini Srikanth, whose study of South Asian American writing discusses the question of representing ethnic groups other than one's own. "How do we avoid essentializing those whom we wish to know?" she asks. Srikanth ultimately suggests that the most important factor may be "whether the text gives evidence of the writer's having struggled with the difficulties of crossing boundaries." Though I concur with this insight, her approach is one that resists (to a great degree, I believe, deliberately) a clear and rigorous analytical perspective. As a result, while Srikanth's book explores many promising directions, it also produces a series of readings that tend to favor an untheorized language of appraisal. Representations, thus, are praised for nuance or critiqued for thinness, so that it is sometimes difficult to differentiate her method of analysis from the conventional critiques of effective writing that a book review might provide. Though I am sympathetic to Srikanth's desire to avoid prescriptive criticism (and I admire her decision to understand representing others as part of ethnic-minority literature), my account seeks to show how the principle of self-aware struggle fits into a larger analytic paradigm that provides a clear interpretative lens. See Srikanth, *The World Next Door*, 158, 200.

82. Posnock, *Color and Culture*, 20.

83. Hanssen, "Ethics of the Other," 166.

84. Kingston, "The Novel's Next Step," 39.

85. Naipaul, *Guerillas*, epigraph.

86. Pratt, *Imperial Eyes*, 201.

87. Ahmed, *Strange Encounters*, 157.

88. Lugones, "Playfulness, 'World'-Traveling, and Loving Perception," 17. Playfulness, Venkat Mani suggests, is necessary to help theories that emphasize personal experience (such as those of Satya Mohanty) avoid relying on the idea of authentic or inauthentic representation. Lugones's "openness to being a fool" also resonates with Mani's desire to eliminate "the fear of losing epistemic privilege, which informs and fuels orthodox multiculturalism." Mani, *Cosmopolitical Claims*, 65, 85.

89. Keen, *Empathy and the Novel*, 29–35. Keen tests this hypothesis in an experiment where she offers her students three kinds of writing. The first is an unsolicited e-mail proposing a business opportunity in Africa, the second is a handwritten letter from a child in Uganda asking for help, and the third is a novel that features an African wheelchair-bound orphan. Keen reports that her students responded most positively to the novel, which places no demand on them for financial support. I should note that Keen does not find strong evidence for empathy in her students' readings of the novel, but she does note a range of other responses (such as perspective taking and recognition) that fall within my understanding of engaging significant otherness.

90. Moya, *Learning from Experience*, 14–15.

91. Cheah, "Given Culture."

92. I should, however, make some crucial distinctions between my approach and the postpositivist realism articulated by Moya and Mohanty. In their arguments, the idea of objective knowledge plays a larger role than it does in my account. I do not believe that fiction is necessarily required to produce objective knowledge; instead, I understand fiction as helping create conditions that combat discursive domination. These conditions, as Mani argues, can include ironic or playful representations as well as realistic ones. What I do take from their accounts, however, is their sense that representations are not inevitably specular displacements. As Mohanty argues, "To have a cognitivist view of experience is to claim that its truth content can be evaluated, and thus potentially shared with others." Mani, *Cosmopolitical Claims*, 65; Mohanty, *Literary Theory*, 122, 232.

93. Moya's chapter "Learning How to Learn from Others" discusses this question in light of multicultural education. Her proposals for postpositivist pedagogical practices defend multicultural education in universalist terms, claiming that studying different cultures allows individuals to select practices from those cultures that might be beneficial in their lives. "When we realize that our identities and life chances are not wholly determined by our cultures of origins or the social

context within which we grew up, we enliven the possibility that we can learn about and adopt ways of living in the world that are more conducive to human flourishing than those we may have grown up with," she argues. I suggest that this process of evaluation and adoption means that individuals must be free to imagine and resignify these new ways of living. Moya, *Learning from Experience*, 159.

94. My description offers an alternative to accounts of imagining across borders that stress such self-completion, such as Wendy Lesser's theories of male representations of femininity. See Lesser, *His Other Half*.

95. Mary Esteve points to the dangers of the crowd when she distinguishes between "the illiberal crowd mind" and "the liberal public square," while Timothy Brennan notes the pleasures of alternative mass culture that emerge from socialist collectivity. See Brennan, *At Home in the World*, 285–305; Esteve, *The Aesthetics and Politics of the Crowd in American Literature*, 21. For a wide range of meditations on the significance of crowds in modern cultural history, see Schnapp and Tiews, eds., *Crowds*.

96. Canetti, *Crowds and Power*, 17.

97. Schnapp and Tiews, "Introduction: A Book of Crowds," x.

98. See Canetti, *Crowds and Power*, 15–16.

99. Schnapp and Tiews, "Introduction: A Book of Crowds," xi.

100. JanMohamed and Lloyd, "Toward a Theory of Minority Discourse," 8. Their claim of Americans "tolerating" salsa may seem somewhat dated in 2009, as salsa is the most widely used condiment in the nation, but their fundamental critique remains very relevant.

101. See, for example, Nussbaum, *Cultivating Humanity*, 85–112; Nussbaum, *Poetic Justice*. One particular moment where I perceive this tension in Nussbaum's approach lies in her desire to read Richard Wright's *Native Son* as part of a program of civic education. "For literature to play its civic function it must be permitted, and indeed invited, to disturb us," Nussbaum claims. "The challenge of Wright's *Native Son* was and is to look into the life of a violent criminal who kills his lover Bessie more casually than he kills a rat." While I agree with Nussbaum's emphasis on the power of fiction to disturb, her actual reference to Wright fails to acknowledge that *Native Son* critiques precisely the rationalist liberal desire "to look into the life" of Bigger Thomas. Bigger's other victim, of course, is the white liberal Mary Dalton, who exemplifies such an inquisitive gaze. While I do not believe that this resistance to representation constitutes the novel's final word on the subject, I suggest that imagining Bigger requires more extreme measures than Nussbaum implies. Nussbaum, *Cultivating Humanity*, 98.

102. Rushdie has returned to this image in his later work, as we see in this passage from *The Enchantress of Florence* (2008): "He, Akbar, had never referred to himself as 'I,' not even in private, not even in anger or dreams. He was—what else could he be?— 'we.' He was the definition, the incarnation of the We. . . . This 'we' was what it meant to be a king—but commoners, he now allowed himself to consider, in the interest of fairness, and for the purposes of debate, no doubt occasionally thought of themselves as plural, too. . . . Perhaps this idea of self-as-community was what it meant to be a being in the world, any being; such a being being, after all, inevitably a being among other beings, a part of the beingness of all things." Rushdie, *The Enchantress of Florence*, 31.

103. In the passage cited above, Parfit compares a person to a nation. He also compares a person to a political party or a club, suggesting that the importance of the central metaphor lies in its evocation of general collectivity.

104. Rushdie, *Midnight's Children*, 200. Subsequent references will be abbreviated *MC* and cited parenthetically within the text.

105. I confine my discussion of crowded style to its appearance in fiction, but it might be possible to consider other written discourses in this light as well. Todorov, for example, describes his own style of historical narrative in terms that resonate with the conceptual underpinnings of crowded style. See Todorov, *The Conquest of America*, 253–254.

106. Walkowitz, *Cosmopolitan Style*, 4.

107. Esty, *A Shrinking Island*, 30.

108. "As many scholars have shown," Walkowitz argues, "Conrad is critical of norms in some cases and reproduces nature in others: his novels present racism as an arbitrary science and an instrument of exploitation, but they also invoke racist stereotypes. . . . Conrad does not imagine more inclusive or more flexible paradigms of belonging, but neither does he allow the old paradigm to function as it did, invisibly and timelessly." While the argument of her book is primarily concerned with presenting continuity between early and late twentieth-century writers, it also illuminates some of their key distinctions. Walkowitz, *Cosmopolitan Style*, 37.

109. Johnson, "An Interview with Charles Johnson," 228–229.

110. See Hardt and Negri, *Empire*, 142. While hybridity is frequently treated as an emancipatory discourse, one might note that Homi Bhabha's formulation links it intimately to the practice of domination. "In the very practice of domination," Bhabha claims of a colonial text, "the language of the master becomes hybrid— neither the one thing nor the other." Bhabha, *The Location of Culture*, 33.

111. Desai, *Diamond Dust*, 88.

112. Ghosh, *The Shadow Lines*, 24.

113. Ghosh, *The Shadow Lines*, 29.

114. Scarry, *Dreaming by the Book*, 15.

115. Alcoff, "The Problem of Speaking for Others," 5.

116. Alcoff, "The Problem of Speaking for Others," 27.

117. Maracle, "Moving Over," 9.

118. Maracle, "Conversations at the Book Fair," 31.

119. Maracle, "Nobody Home," 110.

120. Cameron, *Dzelarhons*, 19. Subsequent references will be abbreviated *DZ* and cited parenthetically in the text.

121. Robbins, *Feeling Global: Internationalism in Distress*, 16, 174.

122. Benhabib, *Situating the Self*, 3.

123. Sommer reads such marks of resistance in the work of writers like Rigoberta Menchu, whose "techniques include maintaining the secrets that keep readers from knowing her too well." Sommer, *Proceed with Caution, When Engaged by Minority Writing in the Americas*, 8–9, 116.

124. Gilroy, *Postcolonial Melancholia*, xv.

2. EVERYDAY SENTIMENT

1. Robbins, *Feeling Global*, 23.

2. Chow does not regard these new images as particularly emancipatory, referring to them as "a newly fetishistic practice in an exponentially expanding and accelerating virtual field of global visibility." In contrast, I will defend what I see as productive about such alternative images. Although Chow here describes visual media in opposition to prose fiction, her claim speaks to the role of visual media as represented within the world of *My Year of Meats*. Her argument that the new political battleground is the terrain of late capitalist simulacra seems appropriate to Ozeki's representation of transnational filmmaking. Chow, *Sentimental Fabulations, Contemporary Chinese Films*, 11.

3. Ozeki, *My Year of Meats*, 15. Subsequent references will be abbreviated *YM* and cited parenthetically within the text.

4. For a brief examination of how Ozeki's work speaks to narratives about food and identity, see Ecker, "Eating Identities—From Migration to Lifestyle," 171–183.

5. Julie Sze locates *My Year of Meats* within the larger history of DES, arguing that the particular representation of hybridity in the novel allows Ozeki to contest ideas

of racial purity while still critiquing the technological pollution of the body. See Sze, "Boundaries and Border Wars," 791–814.

6. In particular, Hunt argues that eighteenth-century novels invited their readers to feel deeply with the lives of their characters. This practice implied that while all humans were not equal in terms of social position or skill, all humans could claim equally rich interior lives. See Hunt, *Inventing Human Rights*, 35–69.

7. Dobson, "Reclaiming Sentimental Literature," 266.

8. Nussbaum, *Upheavals of Thought*, 320.

9. For critiques of the commercialism of Akiko's desire, see Chiu, "Postnational Globalization and (En)Gendered Meat Production in Ruth L. Ozeki's *My Year of Meats*"; Palumbo-Liu, "Rational and Irrational Choices: Form, Affect, and Ethics," 55.

10. Images of border crossing through commodity purchases are subject to a wide range of critiques, such as fetishization and commodification. However, I suggest that the desire for encounters untainted by practices of late capital may be unrealistic expectations at the turn of the millennium. I do not understand such practices as ineffective or necessarily inauthentic, although I do perceive them as ethically limited.

11. Akiko's fax thus draws upon what June Howard has identified as a formative paradox of sentimentality: "sentimentality at the same time locates us in our embodied and particular selves and takes us out of them." Howard, "What Is Sentimentality?" 77. I suggest that it is precisely this doubled direction that makes sentimentality useful for engaging significant otherness.

12. As a form of sentiment that follows and critiques the global flows of images that enable it, Akiko's fax provides an important alternative to sentimental bondings associated with the legitimation of U.S. economic expansion. Writing about programs that encouraged Americans to bond with citizens of other nations in the cold war of the 1950s, Christina Klein argues that "one has the sense that Eisenhower believed that if he could stimulate the flow of feelings across national borders, he would also smooth the international flows of capital, manufactured goods, and raw materials." This description articulates exactly the impulse at work in the capitalist imperative of *My American Wife!*, but *My Year of Meats* complicates this pattern by showing how flows of feeling can also challenge the hierarchies and interests that structure those global flows. Klein, *Cold War Orientalism*, 53.

13. Cohen, "Sentimental Communities," 107. Emphasis in the original.

14. Cohen examines how different national spaces influenced the role of sentimental literature; Lynn Festa shows how this differentiation also takes place within international consumer culture. Cohen, "Sentimental Communities," 108; Festa, "Sentimental Bonds and Revolutionary Characters," 75.

15. Cohen, "Sentimental Communities," 112.

16. Alliston, "Transnational Sympathies, Imaginary Communities," 134. Italics in the original.

17. Ch'ien, *Weird English*, 5.

18. Ch'ien's reflections on Chinese American English may also be helpful in this context, even though Akiko's nonstandard form of writing reflects the English she learned as a second language in Japan rather than a language produced through immigration in America. "Why should standard English be preferred as the literary language conveying the bicultural experience of Chinese Americans? The psychoanalytic repercussions of immigration convey that Chinglish most accurately represents the formation of Chinese American identity," Ch'ien argues. Akiko's sense of self is altered and expanded not by immigration (at this point in the novel) but by the incursions of American television spectacles into her home in Japan. Ch'ien, *Weird English*, 116.

19. Palumbo-Liu, "Rational and Irrational Choices."

20. For accounts of the debates over the significance of compassion for suffering, see Berlant, "Poor Eliza"; Berlant, ed., *Compassion*; Spelman, *Fruits of Sorrow*.

21. Joanne Dobson, for instance, begins her analysis of sentimental literature by noting that such writing has never been subject to the kind of formal evaluation of quality that other subgenres, such as romanticism and realism, have demanded. Instead, from nineteenth-century attacks on female writing to midcentury New Criticism to late twentieth-century cultural critique, sentimental literature has been explicitly defined as a genre lacking the marks of elite formal craft. This association continues to persist at the turn of the millennium; as we will see, J. M. Coetzee is also compelled by many of the questions of sympathy that preoccupy Ozeki but goes to great lengths to remove any trace of sentimentality from the tone of his fiction. See Dobson, "Reclaiming Sentimental Literature," 263.

22. Warhol, *Having a Good Cry*, 29–30.

23. For an analysis of masochism that challenges both celebratory and critical accounts of sentimentality, see Noble, *The Masochistic Pleasures of Sentimental Literature*.

24. Rorty, "Human Rights, Rationality, and Sentimentality," 129.

25. Palumbo-Liu, "Rational and Irrational Choices," 66.

26. Ahmed, *The Cultural Politics of Emotion*, 171.

27. Sontag, *Regarding the Pain of Others*, 101.

28. Woolf, *Three Guineas*, 109.

29. Rupp, *Worlds of Women*, 201.

30. Morgan, "Introduction," 23.

31. "'Women,' we are told, 'really have nothing in common with one another, given class, race, caste, and comparable barriers.' (The speaker of such Portentous Truth almost invariably is a man.)" Morgan, "Introduction," 19.

32. Pollock et al., "Cosmopolitanisms," 583–584.

33. For a sample of analyses that challenge Morgan's assumptions about the intersections of women, imperialism, and nationalism, see Grewal and Kaplan, eds., *Scattered Hegemonies*; Anne McClintock et al., eds., *Dangerous Liaisons*; Yang, ed., *Spaces of Their Own*.

34. Mohanty, "Under Western Eyes," 68.

35. Freedman, *No Turning Back*, 115.

36. For evidence of this dismantling, see Basu, "Introduction," 3–4; Kaplan, "The Politics of Location as Transnational Feminist Critical Practice," 137–152; Weisser and Fleischner, eds., *Feminist Nightmares*. In Robin Morgan's most recent anthology, she moves away from international feminism to focus on the U.S. women's movement. See Morgan, "Introduction," xv–xix.

37. Coomaraswamy, "Are Women's Rights Universal?" 1–18; Mohanty, *Feminism Without Borders*.

38. Ahmed, *Strange Encounters*, 166.

39. See, for instance, Denise deCaires Narain's work, which seeks to further Ahmed's project and move toward feminist dialogue. Narain, "What Happened to Global Sisterhood?" 240–251.

40. Keck and Sikkink, *Activists Beyond Borders*, 168. Subsequent references will be abbreviated *AB* and cited parenthetically within the text.

41. Violence against women also emerged as the area of greatest consensus within American multicultural feminism in the mid-1990s. According to a survey of eight thousand American women activists, "the majority of survey respondents defined violence against women as the top priority issue for the women's movement in the future." Wolfe and Tucker, "Feminism Lives," 457.

42. Scarry, *The Body in Pain*, 4.

43. In an early precursor to this chapter, I argue that *My Year of Meats* politicizes female reproduction in a transnational context to allow for the articulation of a new global feminist community. See Black, "Fertile Cosmofeminism," 226–256.

44. Basu, "Globalization of the Local/Localization of the Global," 71, 74.

45. Bunch, "Women's Human Rights," 138.

46. Eiser, "Violence and Transcultural Values," 164; Keck and Sikkink, *Activists Beyond Borders*, 198.

47. See Robbins, *Feeling Global*, 141.

48. Schuler, "Violence Against Women," 11.

49. Gelles and Strauss, quoted in Schuler, "Violence Against Women," 10. Violence connected to health issues, a crucial theme of *My Year of Meats*, is only defined in terms of very short and direct causal chains, such as deprivation of food. See Schuler, "Violence Against Women," 14.

50. In their discussion of women's health, Julie H. Levinson and Sandra P. Levinson consider domestic violence, rape, reproductive rights, and healthy work environments among their catalogue of concerns, but they omit any mention of drugs, pesticides, or other indirect forms of harm against women's bodies. See Levinson and Levinson, "Women's Health and Human Rights," 125–151. One exception to this narrow usage can be found in Natalie Dandekar's analysis of international development, which adopts a nonphysical definition of violence. See Dandekar, "International Development Paradigms and Violence Against Women," 179–180.

51. Basu, "Globalization of the Local/Localization of the Global," 75.

52. One might note the structural similarities between Ozeki's novel and entertainment-education television programs that similarly combine melodramatic narratives with explicit issue advocacy. Entertainment-education programs frequently end with an epilogue in which an actor stresses the message of the program, asking rhetorical questions of the viewer and analyzing the behavior of the characters. While it remains unclear whether or not these extranarrative messages make a difference in influencing viewer behavior, Ozeki's turn to "documentary interludes" suggests a similar logic at work. See Slater, "Entertainment Education and the Persuasive Impact of Narratives," 162–163.

53. Mackie, "Feminist Critiques of Modern Japanese Politics," 189.

54. Sontag, *Regarding the Pain of Others*, 102–103.

55. Ozeki, "A Conversation with Ruth Ozeki," 13.

56. Ozeki, "A Conversation with Ruth Ozeki," 13.

57. In this sense, Ozeki's position resonates with some of the critiques of an automatic valorization of complexity articulated in Brennan, *At Home in the World*, 71–88.

58. *My Year of Meats* locates itself in the space that Lisa Lowe and David Lloyd have described as "sites of contradiction that are effects of [transnational capitalism's] always uneven expansion but that cannot be subsumed by the logic of commodification itself." See Lowe and Lloyd, "Introduction," 1.

59. Cornyetz, "The Meat Manifesto," 208.

60. http://www.ruthozeki.com/weblog. September 9, 2006.

61. Ahmed, *The Cultural Politics of Emotion*, 170–171.

62. See, for example, Pinsky, "Eros Against Esperanto," 85–90.

63. Rorty, "Human Rights, Rationality, and Sentimentality," 119.

64. Robbins, *Feeling Global*, 23.

3. ETHNIC REVERSALS

1. Johnson, *Turning the Wheel*, 98. Subsequent citations will be abbreviated *TW* and cited parenthetically in the text.

2. Bhabha, *The Location of Culture*, 66. Ellipses in the original.

3. Michaels, *Our America*, 139.

4. Chow's account differs from mine in its impatience with the idea of escaping representational violence, which Chow considers a naïve and utopian goal. Instead, through her reading of Derrida's stereotype of Chinese as an ideographic language and Hong Kong cartoons that deploy stereotypical graphics, she offers two related but distinct defenses of the stereotype's productive power. In the case of Derrida, Chow figures the stereotype as an engagement with surfaces (what she calls "*the-other-as-face*") that offers the precondition for representation and critical thought but that remains an encounter of exteriors that leaves the object of encounter "in the intermediate state of the living dead." In this kind of encounter, Chow implies that "one can only dart back into the interiority of one's own speech": in short, it seems to evoke the return of the mirror argument. Her reading of the Hong Kong comic strips of Larry Feign, in contrast, offers a vision of stereotypes that more closely resembles my understanding of Johnson's and Jen's comic postures. Although I share her sense that stereotypes serve a generative role, I suggest that the kind of explosive inhabitation we find in Johnson and Jen (and that Chow herself identifies in the comic strips of the Hong Kong artist Larry Feign) deforms the stereotype into a viable ethics of representing social difference. Chow, *The Protestant Ethic and the Spirit of Capitalism*, 64–65, 67, 84, 89. Italics in original.

5. Schlote, "The Sketch's the Thing Wherein We'll Catch the Conscience of the Audience," 187.

6. Erichsen, "Smiling in the Face of Adversity," 28–29. See also Gayatri Spivak's reading of Mahasweta Devi's "Draupadi," which suggests to Spivak that the laugh of the subaltern thwarts Western attempts to understand it. Spivak, *In Other Worlds*, 179–180.

7. Such a function of laughter might be considered in light of Doris Sommer's interest in resistance to reading, in which she argues that minority texts often produce a "rhetoric of selective, socially differentiated understanding. . . . The question, finally, is not what 'insiders' can know as opposed to 'outsiders'; it is how those positions are being constructed as incommensurate or conflictive." Sommer, *Proceed with Caution, when Engaged by Minority Writing in the Americas*, 8–9.

8. Theories of comic incongruity are often traced to the work of the eighteenth-century philosopher Francis Hutcheson, as seen in Stott, *Comedy*, 135–136. See also Erichsen, "Smiling in the Face of Adversity," 29.

9. This chapter focuses on comedy as tone and stance. Although neither Johnson nor Jen maintain a consistently comic tone in their novels, their comic articulations comprise a dominant part of their novels' ethos.

10. Ling, "Cultural Cross-Dressing in *Mona in the Promised Land*," 232.

11. Radhakrishnan, "Toward an Eccentric Cosmopolitanism," 821.

12. wa Wamwere, *Negative Ethnicity*.

13. Gilroy, *Postcolonial Melancholia*, 63.

14. Posnock, *Color and Culture*, 5. The back cover of Posnock's book includes a testimonial by Johnson, who calls the book "the work on black literature that I have been waiting to read for three decades, one that both liberates and enlarges our discussions on racial identity and a century of black intellectual commerce from Du Bois to Samuel Delany."

15. Posnock, *Color and Culture*, 28.

16. Johnson, *Dr. King's Refrigerator and Other Bedtime Stories*, 27.

17. Byrd, *Charles Johnson's Novels*; Conner and Nash, eds., *Charles Johnson*; Nash, *Charles Johnson's Fiction*; Storhoff, *Understanding Charles Johnson*. The first single-author study of Johnson's work appeared in 1997; see Little, *Charles Johnson's Spiritual Imagination*.

18. Johnson, "I Call Myself an Artist," 7.

19. Little, *Charles Johnson's Spiritual Imagination*, 48–49.

20. On the troubled link between black and Asian communities, see Prashad, *The Karma of Brown Folk*.

21. Johnson, *Turning the Wheel*, xvi.

22. Johnson, *Oxherding Tale*, xi. Subsequent citations will be abbreviated *OT* and cited parenthetically in the text.

23. For example, Henry Louis Gates Jr. bases his theory of an indigenous black criticism on West African trickster gods. Gates, *The Signifying Monkey*. Similarly, Houston A. Baker's interest in "spirit work" focuses on voodoo, conjure, and forms of spiritual life that suggest links back to Africa. Baker, Alexander, and Redmond, *Workings of the Spirit*, 80–81. In addition to Afrocentric spiritual discourse, black Christianity is also seen as a strong sign of an African American spiritual community forged in the crucible of slavery. As Johnson himself acknowledges, "no other institution's influence compares with that of the black church, and I believe it will continue to be the dominant spiritual orientation of black Americans." Johnson, "A Sangha by Another Name," 45.

24. Most of the writing on Johnson's turn to Asia has focused on source studies, such as Johnson's use of the Ten Oxherding Pictures or Hesse's *Siddhartha*. Although these works offer careful readings of the way these sources structure Johnson's novels and provide key ideas for his philosophical fiction, they refrain from probing the ethics of representing social difference. See, for example, Byrd, *Charles Johnson's Novels*, 61–101; Byrd, "*Oxherding Tale* and *Siddhartha*," 549–558; Gleason, "The Liberation of Perception," 705–728; Little, *Charles Johnson's Spiritual Imagination*, 80–108. More skeptical readings of Johnson's portrayal of Asian discourses frequently critique them for apolitical quietism, suggesting that the real representational danger is not to the Asian discourses (as with Orientalism) but to their interpretations of African American experience. On this note, see Nash, *Charles Johnson's Fiction*, 110–111. Approaching the texts more critically, Bill Brown's study of "China" provides a materialist critique of Johnson's cultural signifiers. See Brown, "Global Bodies/Postnationalities," 24–48.

25. Kamakshi P. Murti writes, "As the Orient of Europe, Germany would speak for the Orient most effectively, a gesture that has continued into the late twentieth century." Murti, *India*, 12.

26. Said, *Orientalism*, 40.

27. On Du Bois's interest in Asian discourses, see Edwards, *The Practice of Diaspora*, 233–238; Gilroy, *The Black Atlantic*, 140–145; Mullen, "Du Bois, *Dark Princess,* and the Afro-Asian International," 217–239; Posnock, *Color and Culture*, 170–177; Rampersad, "Du Bois's Passage to India."

28. See Deutsch, "The Asiatic Black Man," 193–208.

29. In placing Johnson within a specific genealogy of black-Asian engagements, I hope to suggest that Johnson's interest in Asian discourses helps make the nature of his investment in border crossing less of an investment exclusively in whiteness. Because Johnson rejects cultural-nationalist defenses of black identity and experience, his work has been read (as in Richard Hardack's thoughtful essay) as a work that ultimately subscribes to a universalism that is, in the end, a cipher for whiteness. Hardack makes this argument by treating the Asian discourses in *Oxherding Tale* as essentially emanations of Emersonian philosophy, a move that makes Johnson's novel seem more invested in whiteness than I believe it is. See Hardack, "Black Skin, White Tissues," 1028–1053.

30. Johnson's reworking of this parable is part of a long tradition dating back to the eleventh century. For explorations of how Johnson uses the Ten Oxherding Pictures, see Byrd, "*Oxherding Tale* and *Siddhartha*"; Gleason, "The Liberation of Perception."

31. A handful of Asian characters do appear in his work, such as the martial-arts instructor in the short story "China" or the head monk in *Dreamer*. However, these

characters are minor figures who do not stretch Johnson's considerable powers of invention.

32. Parfit, *Reasons and Persons*, 273.

33. On the tradition of interracial representation, see Sollors, *Neither Black nor White yet Both*.

34. Rushdy understands *Oxherding Tale* in light of Johnson's critique of 1960s cultural nationalist ideologies, such as those found in the Black Arts movement. Rushdy, *Neo-Slave Narratives*, 170.

35. Chakrabarty, *Provincializing Europe*, 5–6.

36. Thanks to Hongfan Lu for confirming my suspicions that most of the characters are not recognizable units of language.

37. Johnson includes six ideographs that resemble Chinese characters. One, *tu*, is recognizable as the character for "soil" or "earth." The other five resemble the characters *li* ("stand" or "set up"), *ming* ("life" or "command"), *guo* ("nation"), *guo* ("fruit"), and *hui* ("can," "will," or "know"), but all are missing particular strokes.

38. Although it is possible that the "mistakes" in this passage are Johnson's rather than Andrew's, I am treating these transfigured characters as purposeful on Johnson's part. I do so because these changes reflect mistakes that even a beginner probably would not make: they deform radicals, or basic units of character composition, and they violate elementary techniques of stroke composition. For example, the character that is almost *hui* should separate its middle box from its lower box. Boxes are almost always composed in a particular stroke order: one begins at the top left and draws a vertical line, then one returns to the top left and draws the top and right side of the box as one stroke, and eventually one completes the box by drawing its bottom side from left to right. Johnson's character omits the top part of the box, which means that drawing it feels distinctly unnatural for even an elementary student of written Chinese.

39. Walkowitz, *Cosmopolitan Style*, 131.

40. Rey Chow describes a similar joke played with characters in one of Larry Feign's cartoons, in which getting the joke requires one to know enough Chinese to know what is *not* Chinese. It is this element which allows Chow to defend Feign against critics who dismiss his work as racist and insulting to Hong Kong. See Chow, *The Protestant Ethnic and the Spirit of Capitalism*, 91.

41. Frye, "Anatomy of Criticism," 10.

42. Erichsen, "Smiling in the Face of Adversity," 28; Stott, *Comedy*, 133.

43. Hanis, "Heredity Crisis."

44. Dunant, "Introduction," xi–xii.

45. Littlewood and Pickering, "Heard the One About the White Middle-Class Heterosexual Father-in-Law?" 307.

46. Bakhtin, *Rabelais and His World*, 11–12.

47. Jen, *Mona in the Promised Land*, 3. Subsequent citations will be abbreviated *M* and cited parenthetically in the text.

48. Bloom, "Introduction," xv; Freedman, "Who's Jewish?" 232–233; Furman, "Immigrant Dreams and Civic Promises," 213.

49. Hanis, "Heredity Crisis."

50. Sollors, *Beyond Ethnicity*, 6.

51. One might also understand Seth's performative border crossing in light of Satya Mohanty and Paula Moya's defense of learning from other ways of life. Mohanty and Moya argue that acknowledging difference is important because cultures provide experimental laboratories for new and better forms of living. See Mohanty, *Literary Theory and the Claims of History*, 240–241; Moya, *Learning from Experience*, 159.

52. Erika Lin also identifies the liberating comedy that occurs when stereotypes experience their "surprise reversal" in Jen's prose. See Lin, "Mona on the Phone," 50.

53. Syal, "PC: GLC," 125.

54. Walkowitz, *Cosmopolitan Style*, 133.

4. MIDDLE GROUNDS

1. Eugenides, *Middlesex*, 3. Subsequent citations will be abbreviated *M* and cited parenthetically in the text.

2. On how the novel negotiates middle grounds through its plot of immigration and migrancy, see Collado-Rodriguez, "Of Self and Country," 71–83.

3. Fetterly, "Introduction," 564. Subsequent references will be abbreviated *PL* and cited parenthetically in the text. This skepticism about the politics of representation characterizes many of the seminal 1970s essays anthologized in *Feminisms*. One might point to Shoshana Felman's discomfort with "speaking in the name of," Sandra Gilbert and Susan Gubar's critique of male stereotypes (such as "passive angel" or "active monster"), or Laura Mulvey's psychoanalytic theory of the male gaze. See Felman, "Women and Madness", 9; Gilbert and Gubar, "Infection in the Sentence," 29; Mulvey, "Visual Pleasure and Narrative Cinema," 438–448.

4. Lesser, *His Other Half*, 9.

5. What third-person pronoun should we use for an intersex character? Because the story is narrated by Cal from a point when he identifies as a man, I generally use the pronoun "he." However, when I refer to the narrator's childhood as Callie, I use "she."

6. Eugenides, interviewed in Weich, "Jeffrey Eugenides Has It Both Ways."

7. Eugenides, in Weich, "Jeffrey Eugenides Has It Both Ways."

8. Woolf, *A Room of One's Own*, 97.

9. Appiah, "Cosmopolitan Patriots," 106.

10. Hungerford, *The Holocaust of Texts: Genocide, Literature, and Personification*, 148.

11. On *Middlesex*'s relationship to queer theories of the body, see Sifuentes, "Strange Anatomy, Strange Sexuality," 145–157.

12. Warhol, *Gendered Interventions*.

13. Tannen, *You Just Don't Understand*.

14. Cixous, "The Laugh of the Medusa," 347–362.

15. Warhol, "Physiology, Gender, and Feeling," 229fn.

16. A different approach to this middle ground emerges in Kenneth Womack and Amy Mallory-Kani's reading, which understands *Middlesex* as what they call an "adaptationist" novel. This critical approach tries to account for what they see as the strong biological and genetic impulse working in the fiction, rejecting the poststructuralist elements that I continue to regard as important to Eugenides' vision. See Womack and Mallory-Kani, "Why Don't You Just Leave It up to Nature?" 157–173.

17. Eugenides, in Weich, "Jeffrey Eugenides Has It Both Ways."

18. As the cultural map of *Feminisms* reveals, critiques abound over the way women's cultural production can repress working-class women, lesbians, ethnic minorities, or subaltern subjects. Cora Kaplan discusses the vexed relationship between liberal feminism and socialist feminism, Barbara Smith documents the repression of lesbian representations, Gayatri Spivak contends that liberal feminism reproduces the axes of imperialism, and Susan Willis argues that white consumer culture fails to offer creative representations of blacks. See Kaplan, "Pandora's Box"; Smith, "The Truth That Never Hurts"; Spivak, "Three Women's Texts and a Critique of Imperialism"; Willis, "I Shop Therefore I Am."

19. Felski, *Doing Time*, 36.

20. Felski, *Doing Time*, 47.

21. Bajwa, *The Sari Shop*, 25. Italics in the original. Subsequent references will be cited parenthetically as *SS* in the text.

22. Nussbaum, *The Fragility of Goodness*, 384.

1. Ghosh's interest in border crossing forms a central thread of criticism on his work. John Hawley, for instance, describes Ghosh's work in terms of "subaltern cosmopolitanism," and many scholars have elaborated on Ghosh's interest in reclaiming idealized international formations of history. See Black, "Cosmopolitanism at Home," 45–65; Dixon, "Travelling in the West," 3–24; Grewal, *Transnational America*, 48–58; Hawley, *Amitav Ghosh*, 89; Kaul, "Separation Anxiety," 125–145; Viswanathan, "Beyond Orientalism," 19–34. These readings illuminate Ghosh's often idealized images of syncretism in premodern and postcolonial formations, but they do not focus on the role of language politics or multilingualism in his work.

2. For a brief version of Ghosh's defense of indigenous sources for modern critique, see Ghosh and Chakrabarty, "A Correspondence on *Provincializing Europe*," 156–157.

3. On the novel's engagement with postcolonial nationalism, see Moral, "In the Time of the Breaking of Nations," 139–154.

4. For evidence of Ghosh's concern with the history and historiography of Asia, see Ghosh and Chakrabarty, "A Correspondence on *Provincializing Europe*." Many of Ghosh's historical arguments resonate, as he acknowledges, with passages from *The Glass Palace*. For a brief analysis of the novel's engagement with colonial historiography, see Gupta, "That Which a Man Takes for Himself No One Can Deny Him."

5. Ghosh, "Interview by Neluka Silva and Alex Tickell," 173.

6. Ghosh, "Letter to Sandra Vince."

7. Khair, "Open Letter."

8. For a useful sample of such linguistic anxiety in Indian writing, see Bailey, "Attitudes Toward English," 40–45. Bailey cites the work of Yasmine Gooneratne, Zulfikar Ghose, Rajagopal Parthasarathy, Lakdasa Wikkramasinha, and Abdul Ghani Hazari.

9. Ghosh, *When Borne Across*, 49.

10. For a discussion of the problems of Indian writing, language choice, and their relationship to emblematic cosmopolitanism, see Mukherjee, "The Anxiety of Indianness," 166–186. For an analysis of the patterns and problems of literary circulation that affect writers such as Ghosh, see Ghosh, *When Borne Across*, 47–79.

11. Appiah, *In My Father's House*, 57.

12. Ghosh, "The Indian Story," 39.

13. Ghosh, *The Glass Palace*, 470. Subsequent references will be abbreviated *GP* and cited parenthetically in the text.

14. For a brief discussion of how different characters use or refuse English for political ends, see Glasgow and Fletcher, "Palimpsest and Seduction," 79–80.

15. Ghosh, "Interview with the Author."

16. Rushdie, *The Satanic Verses*, 44.

17. Ghosh, "Interview with the Author."

18. See the discussion of language politics in Khair, *Babu Fictions*, 105.

19. See the discussion of English vernaculars in Ghosh, *When Borne Across*, 80–120.

20. Ghosh, "Interview with the Author."

21. The way I hear Dinu's speech is at odds with descriptions of his dialogue in the novel. Although the heavy use of ellipses suggests to me slowness and hesitation, Bela describes Dinu's language as "explosive little bursts, as though his thoughts were spurting out of him in jets." Ghosh, *The Glass Palace*, 237.

22. Nair, "The Road from Mandalay," 174.

23. Ghosh, "The Indian Story," 43.

24. Spivak, *In Other Worlds*, 186. Spivak has since changed her mind about translating dialect, as her translation of Devi's *Chotti Munda and His Arrow* attests. See Spivak, "Translator's Foreword," vii.

25. Craig, *The Modern Scottish Novel*, 78.

26. Slater, "Consuming Kodak," 50, 52.

27. Rosenblum, *A World History of Photography*, 625.

28. Rosenblum, *A World History of Photography*, 73, 122.

29. On the relationship between Singh and Dinu, see Freedman, "On the Ganges Side of Modernism," 114–129.

30. Pratt, *Imperial Eyes*, 201.

31. *The Glass Palace* is presented as a specifically modernist novel in Freedman, "On the Ganges Side of Modernism," 122–126. More generally, in her study of Indian writing in English, Priya Joshi claims that such literature from the 1980s is best understood as an alternative modernism, and Rebecca Walkowitz describes late twentieth-century postcolonial writing as "modernist cosmopolitanism." See Joshi, *In Another Country*, 230–234; Walkowitz, *Cosmopolitan Style*.

32. Ghosh, *The Hungry Tide*, 11. Subsequent citations will be abbreviated *HT* and cited parenthetically in the text.

33. This passage is a little odd, because Fokir does actually go through this naming ritual with Piya (*HT*, 63). However, its inclusion perhaps testifies how strongly the novel wants to emphasize how Piya views Fokir as a subject beyond human language.

34. Doody, *The True Story of the Novel*, 335.

35. Apter, "Translation with No Original," 160.

6. SACRIFICING THE SELF

1. Coetzee, *Slow Man*, 44.

2. The earliest influential studies of Coetzee's work explore this crisis of signification. See Dovey, *The Novels of J. M. Coetzee*. Although Dovey's readings emphasize the textual and psychoanalytic play of the novels, a competing thread of scholarship contends that Coetzee's stylistic experimentation speaks directly to historical and often specifically South African predicaments. For exemplars of such historically oriented readings, see Attwell, *J. M. Coetzee*; Gallagher, *A Story of South Africa*.

3. "It has been suggested that in these occlusions and absences Coetzee manages to evade the problematic inscription of Otherness, the appropriation of voice: the absences speak of an unviolated presence outside the realm of representation." Meffan and Worthington, "Ethics Before Politics," 137. See also Attwell, *J. M. Coetzee*, 5.

4. On how the question of authorial belief affects Coetzee's persona and his novels, see Brouillette, *Postcolonial Writers in the Global Literary Marketplace*, 112–143.

5. For an example of Coetzee's elusiveness within, and even hostility toward, the interview format, see "J. M. Coetzee in Conversation with Jane Poyner," 21–24.

6. One might also argue that earlier works support this idea as well. *Waiting for the Barbarians*, for instance, can be read as the story of how the Magistrate *produces* the idea of the barbarian girl's alterity rather than as the narrative of her actual unknowability.

7. For the argument that Coetzee's own strategies silence others under the guise of respecting their alterity, see Parry, "Speech and Silence in the Fictions of J. M. Coetzee," 149–165.

8. As David Attwell describes Coetzee's position, "his relationship with the European canon entails an accusation of complicity in a history of domination." Attwell, *J. M. Coetzee*, 4.

9. Attridge, *J. M. Coetzee and the Ethics of Reading*, 190–191.

10. For an overview of this split with respect to the question of sympathy, see Baker, "The Limits of Sympathy," 27–49. Baker argues for a middle road between these readings that centers on the private possibilities and limitations of interpersonal sympathy.

11. On recognizing the limits of knowing the other, see Meffan and Worthington, "Ethics Before Politics," 145. On giving the self to the other, see Marais, "The Possibility of Ethical Action," 62. On seeking bodily proximity with the other, see Durrant, "J. M. Coetzee, Elizabeth Costello, and the Limits of the Sympathetic

Imagination," 130. On performing the other, see Wright, *Writing "Out of All the Camps,"* 13.

12. Barnard, *Apartheid and Beyond*, 40.

13. As the generic status of *The Lives of Animals* is purposefully indeterminate (its components can be read as short stories, framed lectures, and chapters of a larger novel), I refer to those pieces as narratives, fictions, and stories.

14. The title of Jane Poyner's 2006 edited collection, *J. M. Coetzee and the Idea of the Public Intellectual*, testifies to this growing interest. As a special section on Coetzee's work in the journal *American Anthropologist* suggests, his narratives speak not only to the problems of literary criticism but also to the practice of modern anthropology. See *American Anthropologist* 108, no. 1 (March 2006). An early book-length study of Coetzee's writing by Dick Penner anticipates this interest, drawing heavily upon Coetzee's role as an intellectual specifically positioned in American and South African institutional spaces. See Penner, *Countries of the Mind*.

15. For broader meditations on how conceptions of animals affect conceptions of the human in literature and critical theory, see Norris, *Beasts of the Modern Imagination*; Simons, *Animal Rights and the Politics of Literary Representation*; Wolfe, *Animal Rites*.

16. Costello forwards a much-discussed analogy between the genocide of the Jews and the modern treatment of animals, arguing that the Nazis learned how to process human bodies from the stockyards of Chicago, and thus she implies that capacious imaginative practices toward humans and animals are conjoined—to lack the second is ultimately to lack the first. She does not mention that the Nazis also created some of the most stringent animal-protection laws of modern Europe, based on a system that placed certain kinds of beings (Aryans and predatory species) above others (Jews and vermin). The Nazis also associated cruelty to animals with Jewish practices (such as kosher butchering), so that compassion for animals became a justification for cruelty to Jews. To what extent these ironies are intentional in Coetzee's work is open to debate. See Kete, "Animals and Ideology," 29–30.

17. Coetzee, *The Lives of Animals*, 34. Subsequent references will be denoted *LA* and cited parenthetically in the text.

18. Harwood, "Love for Animals and How It Developed in Great Britain," 126.

19. "After the Restoration, the continental mania for dissection and vivisection developed in England, so that anatomizing and experimenting became very much *a la mode*. The great and near-great entertained their friends with vivisection parties and a dish of tea, or trotted across town to see what the virtuosi of the Royal Society were about." Harwood, "Love for Animals," 103.

20. Brown, *Fables of Modernity*, 224–233.

21. Brown, *Fables of Modernity*, 262.

22. Kete, "Animals and Ideology," 26.

23. Although Adam Smith remains the best-known eighteenth-century philosopher of sympathy, many other seventeenth- and eighteenth-century British moral philosophers wrestled with new ideas about the existence and importance of sympathetic imagination. As we see from the entries of the word in the *Oxford English Dictionary*, the idea of sympathy surged in English around the turn of the seventeenth century. The *OED* defines the relevant meaning of sympathy as "the quality or state of being affected by the condition of another with a feeling similar or corresponding to that of the other; the fact or capacity of entering into or sharing the feelings of another or others; fellow-feeling." The definition also notes a more specialized meaning that focuses on the particular power of pain and prefigures contemporary associations between sympathy and suffering: "the quality or state of being thus affected by the suffering or sorrow of another; a feeling of compassion or commiseration." As quotations from Robert Burton's *The Anatomy of Melancholy* (1621) suggest, the verb "sympathize" was originally used as a medical term that described the correspondence between various bodily parts. English writers in the mid-seventeenth century began to use sympathy as a psychological rather than a physiological word, and the eighteenth century broadened its scope to include political as well as personal emotions. Eighteenth-century philosophers such as Adam Smith, David Hume, Samuel Johnson, Francis Hutcheson, Dugald Stewart, and other members of the Scottish Common-Sense School all employed the rhetoric of sympathetic imagination to further their theories of psychology, aesthetics, and morality. In his work on eighteenth-century conceptions of sympathetic imagination, Walter Jackson Bate argues that Hume and especially Smith locate moral sense in the ability to sympathize. Bate, "The Sympathetic Imagination in Eighteenth-Century English Criticism," 146–147.

24. Smith, *The Theory of Moral Sentiments*, 11. Many scholars have been intrigued by the dual dimension of Smith's work as a theorist of modern capitalism and a theorist of sympathy, and the possibility of connections between these two aspects of his thought provokes what is known as "the Adam Smith problem." I am grateful to Roy Tsao for introducing me to this debate. Although my analysis does not focus on *Disgrace*'s representation of global capital, it is possible to read the novel as an inquiry into the possibility of sympathy in an era of capitalist circulation. Katherine Stanton analyzes the role of global capital in *Disgrace*, showing how it maintains structural inequalities that render humans (and women in particular) as interchangeable goods rather than as candidates for sympathetic engagement. See

Stanton, *Cosmopolitan Fictions*, 73, 76. The tension Stanton evokes between sympathy and global capital emerges even more keenly in *Diary of a Bad Year*, which associates the embrace of capitalist principles with a form of particularly invasive imagination represented by computer spyware.

25. Smith, *The Theory of Moral Sentiments*, 13.

26. Her son John hints at this distance when he wonders querulously, "if she wants to open her heart to animals, why can't she stay home and open it to her cats?" Coetzee, *The Lives of Animals*, 38. As Barbara Smuts points out in her response to the narratives, Costello consistently refrains from making use of her own experience with animals. Smuts, in Coetzee, *The Lives of Animals*, 107–108.

27. Coetzee, *Elizabeth Costello*, 5. Subsequent references will be abbreviated *EC* and cited parenthetically in the text.

28. For the argument that Costello misreads Nagel's position, see Bell, "What Is It Like to Be a Nonracist?" 177.

29. *Rambler* 60, in Johnson, *The Rambler*, 105.

30. At least, this is how Costello herself describes the period despite the suggestion that she oversimplifies it. At a luncheon, she encounters a scholar of eighteenth-century studies: " 'My husband is in the eighteenth century,' says Mrs. Godwin. 'Ah yes,' [says Costello]. 'A good place to be. The Age of Reason.' 'I do not believe we see the period in quite so uncomplicated a way nowadays,' says Professor Godwin." Coetzee, *Elizabeth Costello*, 126.

31. Puchner, "Performing the Open," 26.

32. Singer, in Coetzee, *The Lives of Animals*, 90–91.

33. Garber, in Coetzee, *The Lives of Animals*, 81.

34. The logical extent of such misanthropy can be found in the history of modern ecoterrorism.

35. *Rambler* 160, in Johnson, *The Rambler*, 276.

36. "Animals, Humans, Cruelty, and Literature: A Rare Interview with J. M. Coetzee."

37. Interestingly, my comparison between the two novels leads toward the opposite of the conclusion that Laura Wright draws. For Wright, *The Lives of Animals* offers the more successful portrait of sympathy, as it emphasizes the productive power of impersonation and performance. See Wright, *Writing "Out of All the Camps."*

38. Coetzee has rejected the label of "South African writer" and has emigrated to Australia, but *Disgrace* makes his positioning in relation to South African identity unavoidable.

39. Marais, "J. M. Coetzee's *Disgrace* and the Task of the Imagination," 89.

40. Coetzee, *Age of Iron*, 130.

41. Coetzee, *Disgrace*, 44. Subsequent references will be abbreviated *D* and cited parenthetically in the text.

42. In her reading of *Disgrace*, Katherine Stanton argues that the novel explores the ethical relationship between the national and the global by showing how practices of global capital come to endanger national projects of economic justice. These forms of violence thus intensify the social barriers confronted in the novel. See Stanton, *Cosmopolitan Fictions*, 71–77.

43. Some analysts claim that the South African crime rate began to rise in the mid-1980s rather than in the early or mid-1990s. See Shaw and Gastrow, "Stealing the Show," 238–239.

44. Morris, "The Mute and the Unspeakable," 57.

45. Shaw and Gastrow, "Stealing the Show," 246.

46. Morris, "The Mute and the Unspeakable," 57.

47. The confusions of incest make themselves felt within many parts of the novel. Lucy's habit of calling David by his first name pushes against conventional naming practices of parenthood, while David's first glimpse of Lucy leads him to speculate that "her hips and breasts are now (he searches for the best word) ample" (*D*, 59). As David contemplates Lucy's sexual life, he admits that "as a father grows older he turns more and more—it cannot be helped—toward his daughter. She becomes his second salvation, the bride of his youth reborn" (*D*, 86).

48. Lucy, and *Disgrace* in general, is often read with reference to the theories of Levinas. Michael Marais argues that the possibility of ethics in Coetzee depends not on sympathy but on, paraphrasing Levinas, "the *substitution* of self with the other. Instead of affirming itself by foreclosing on the other, the self *gives* itself to the other and this gift takes the form of a sacrifice." Marais, "The Possibility of Ethical Action," 62. See also Marais, "Little Enough, Less Than Little: Nothing," 159–182. Italics in original.

49. For the argument that Lucy's choices lead to a problematic gendering of suffering, see Boehmer, "Not Saying Sorry, Not Speaking Pain," 29–46. It is very possible to claim that Lucy simply makes a virtue of necessity or that the novel unnecessarily (and disturbingly) rationalizes this gendered suffering. I am in agreement with many scholars that Lucy's refusal to pursue her rights offers a troubling vision, but I am less sure that this refusal is specifically gendered by the novel. Instead, I read it as part of a larger vision that critiques the idea of human rights more broadly.

50. On this point, see Parfit, *Reasons and Persons*, 282–287.

51. Tanner, *Intimate Violence*, 3.

52. Brison, "Surviving Sexual Violence," 13.

53. Sam Durrant also identifies the importance of such a "radical loss of subjectivity," although he describes this choice as an alternative to sympathy rather than one of its constitutive forms. See Durrant, *Postcolonial Narrative and the Work of Mourning*, 27.

54. HaCohen, "The Music of Sympathy in the Arts of the Baroque," 611.

55. In their reading of ethics in *Disgrace*, James Meffan and Kim L. Worthington argue, as I do, that imagining Lucy's rape represents David's ethical response to the social divide between himself and his daughter. Reading his attempt to "be the woman" through the philosophy of Levinas, Meffan and Worthington suggest that it is his attempt, not his success or failure, that counts as an ethical gesture. "Lurie, a man, cannot 'be the woman,' unless by imagining her in his gendered terms. But it is precisely this failure, the necessary failure of the imaginative attempt, that may be ethically productive, for it issues in self-critique a recognition of the limitations of his own perceptions." Meffan and Worthington, "Ethics Before Politics," 145. Although I concur that David often fails in his imaginative attempts, I suggest that his changing perception of Teresa allows him to escape "his gendered terms" for a vital moment.

56. Laura Wright suggests that because the opera will never be performed, it loses its ability to figure a robust enactment of sympathy. I venture to suggest that, in *Disgrace*, the idea of performance is intimately linked to the idea of *sexual* performance. David's attempts to relinquish masculinized desire thus may necessitate this sacrifice of artistic performance, allowing us to read ethical possibility within this closet opera. See Wright, *Writing "Out of All the Camps,"* 105.

57. Coetzee, *White Writing*, 81. Italics in original. Subsequent references will be abbreviated *WW* in the text.

58. Parfit, *Reasons and Persons*, 281.

59. In a reading of this scene in relation to the tradition of the pastoral, Rita Barnard suggests that its emphasis on bodily experiences "hints at a newness that still eludes the descriptive language of its observer, who continues to rely on outmoded, foreign phrases." I understand this "newness" as central to David's changing ability to represent Lucy. Barnard, *Apartheid and Beyond*, 38.

60. As Jopi Nyman suggests through a reading of David's dream of Thoth, dogs are not the only link between race and animality in the novel, but they offer particularly prominent figurations of this affinity. See Nyman, *Postcolonial Animal Tale from Kipling to Coetzee*, 140–141.

61. Wade, *White on Black in South Africa*, 1.

62. "At the heart of the unfreedom of the hereditary masters of South Africa is a failure of love." Coetzee, "Jerusalem Prize Acceptance Speech (1987)," 97.

63. See "Noël Mostert and the Eastern Cape Frontier," in Coetzee, *Stranger Shores*, 276.

64. See Cornwell, "*Disgrace*land," esp. 43–55.

65. Krog, *Country of My Skull*, 46–47.

66. Kariuki and Van der Walt, "Land Reform in South Africa," 19.

67. For an exploration of the competing trends of dwelling and exile within the landscape of *Disgrace*, see Strode, *The Ethics of Exile*, 218–228.

68. I would like to thank Jonathan Fork for suggesting that Lucy's "*Hamba!*" is directed not to the dogs but to the men.

69. Lucy Graham argues that "in South Africa, guard dogs have been synonymous with the protection of the propertied classes, and thus dogs have generally acted in the interests of white power." Graham, "Yes, I Am Giving Him Up," 8.

70. David uses the image of dogs to talk about his own relationship to sexual desire (*D*, 90). Costello's son John and his wife "do not mind a puppy but foresee a grown dog, with a grown dog's sexual needs, as nothing but trouble." Coetzee, *The Lives of Animals*, 17.

71. For a defense of Coetzee's portrait of black characters, see Attwell, "Race in *Disgrace*," 335–336. Attwell argues that race is the least important feature of these narrative portraits.

72. My account of Coetzee's crowded style as constituted through inclusion of its disgraceful other, racist language, elaborates on what Sanders calls the "motivated privation" of language in *Disgrace*. See *Ambiguities of Witnessing*, 178.

73. Jakes Gerwel, quoted in McDonald, "Disgrace Effects," 325. Italics in original.

74. In his reading of the ANC's submission, David Attwell argues that "the more interesting tension in the ANC document, I would suggest, is between the attempt to avoid the philistinism of accusing Coetzee of racism and wanting to use him nevertheless as a celebrity witness to its prevalence." Attwell, "Race in *Disgrace*," 334.

75. McDonald, "Disgrace Effects," 326.

76. Barney, "Between Swift and Kafka," 22–23. Barney's reading implies that the mediation of race through animality is a less than ideal indirection: a surprising perspective, given his essay's defense of Coetzee's indirection.

77. Graham, "Yes, I Am Giving Him Up," 8.

78. Josephine Donovan suggests the exceptionality of such gestures in her reading of the novel: "Although many modern writers . . . succeed in granting subjectivity to the animals who figure in their work, few—if any—of their human characters exhibit the intense empathetic identification with animal suffering and loss of dignity as do Coetzee's." See Donovan, "Miracles of Creation," 85–86.

79. Coetzee, *Stranger Shores*, 276.

80. Coetzee has suggested that the right to life will never be afforded to animals; perhaps the novel's suspicion of rights emerges from this fundamental exclusion. See "Animals, Humans, Cruelty, and Literature: A Rare Interview with J. M. Coetzee."

81. See Coetzee, *Stranger Shores*, 276.

82. Kariuki and Van der Walt argue that South African land-reform plans stalled because they drew too heavily on neoliberal "willing-buyer–willing-seller" models inherited from the World Bank. See Kariuki and Van der Walt, "Land Reform in South Africa," 19.

83. Quayson, *Aesthetic Nervousness*, 149.

84. For a very different understanding of dog love, see Haraway, *The Companion Species Manifesto*. In Coetzee's fiction, dogs are not governed by the mode of "companion species" that attracts Haraway's attention. Indeed, Coetzee has expressed the greatest sense of connection with animals, such as frogs and birds, that are precisely not companion species in a conventional sense. See "Animals, Humans, Cruelty, and Literature: A Rare Interview with J. M. Coetzee."

85. I thank Alexis Fitts for calling to my attention the link between Byron's leg and the legs of the dog.

86. On the importance of proximity as a counter to the limits of imaginative projection, see Durrant, "J. M. Coetzee, Elizabeth Costello, and the Limits of the Sympathetic Imagination," 130.

87. Although Travis Mason offers the intriguing speculation that the dogs in *Disgrace* may actually speak to each other, this reading is not particularly plausible in light of the tone of the novel, which bears no trace of the fabulist tradition of speaking animals. See Mason, "Dog Gambit," 137–138.

88. For the argument that dogs in *Disgrace* are precisely *not* signs, see Tremaine, "The Embodied Soul," 587–612.

89. In his interview with a Swedish animal-rights publication, Coetzee claims that "I have what I consider to be personal relations to the birds and frogs that visit or live upon the land I 'own,' but I do not for a minute believe they have personal relations with me." "Animals, Humans, Cruelty, and Literature: A Rare Interview with J. M. Coetzee."

90. For more on the role of the progressive and perfective tenses in the novel, see Sanders, "*Disgrace*," 363–373; Wicomb, "Translations in the Yard of Africa," 209–223.

91. Tremaine, "The Embodied Soul," 607.

92. Even for those who take the matter of animals seriously, the novel is often read as enacting a tradeoff between human and nonhuman priorities. Onno Oerlemans, for instance, argues that even as sympathy for animals intensifies, the "novel con-

cludes by displacing human tragedies with those of actual animals." See Oerlemans, "A Defense of Anthropomorphism," 189.

93. Coetzee, *The Master of Petersburg*, 47. Italics in original.

94. Karin Andriolo suggests that Coetzee's portrait of sympathetic imagination reflects a "bipolar inclination" that can both mitigate and exacerbate human suffering. See Andriolo, "The Twice-Killed," 111.

POSTSCRIPT

1. Sedgwick, "Paranoid Reading and Reparative Reading," 4.

2. Gómez-Peña, "The Multicultural Paradigm," 48.

3. Parker, *Ethics, Theory, and the Novel*, 11.

4. Attridge, "Innovation, Literature, Ethics," 21.

5. Appiah, *Cosmopolitanism*, 155–174.

6. Singer specifies minimal demands but refuses to identify optimal ones in Singer,
One World, 185–195.

7. Singer, *One World*, 171.

8. Gilroy, *Postcolonial Melancholia*, 63.

9. For example, see McConnell, "Don't Neglect the Little Platoons"; Pinsky, "Eros
Against Esperanto"; Walzer, "Spheres of Affection."

10. Tolstoy, *Anna Karenina*, 291.

11. McEwan, *Saturday*, 77–78.

BIBLIOGRAPHY

Ahmad, Dohra. *Rotten English: A Literary Anthology*. New York: Norton, 2007.

Ahmed, Sara. *The Cultural Politics of Emotion*. Edinburgh: Edinburgh University Press, 2004.

——. *Strange Encounters: Embodied Others in Post-Coloniality*. London: Routledge, 2000.

Alcoff, Linda. "The Problem of Speaking for Others." *Cultural Critique* (1991–1992): 5–32.

Alliston, April. "Transnational Sympathies, Imaginary Communities." In *The Literary Channel: The Inter-National Invention of the Novel*, ed. Margaret Cohen and Carolyn Dever, 133–148. Princeton, N.J.: Princeton University Press, 2002.

Anderson, Benedict R. *Imagined Communities: Reflections on the Origin and Spread of Nationalism*. London: Verso, 1991.

Andriolo, Karin. "The Twice-Killed: Imagining Protest Suicide." *American Anthropologist* 108, no. 1 (2006): 100–113.

"Animals, Humans, Cruelty, and Literature: A Rare Interview with J. M. Coetzee." *Satya* (2004).

Appadurai, Arjun. *Modernity at Large: Cultural Dimensions of Globalization*. Minneapolis: University of Minnesota Press, 1996.

Appiah, Kwame Anthony. "Cosmopolitan Patriots." In *Cosmopolitics: Thinking and Feeling Beyond the Nation*, ed. Pheng Cheah and Bruce Robbins, 91–114. Minneapolis: University of Minnesota Press, 1998.

———. *Cosmopolitanism: Ethics in a World of Strangers.* New York: Norton, 2006.

———. *In My Father's House: Africa in the Philosophy of Culture.* New York: Oxford University Press, 1992.

Apter, Emily. "Translation with No Original: Scandals of Textual Reproduction." In *Nation, Language, and the Ethics of Translation,* ed. Sandra Bermann and Michael Wood, 159–174. Princeton, N.J.: Princeton University Press, 2005.

Attridge, Derek. "Innovation, Literature, Ethics: Relating to the Other." *PMLA* 114, no. 1 (1999): 20–31.

———. *J. M. Coetzee and the Ethics of Reading: Literature in the Event.* Chicago: University of Chicago Press, 2004.

Attwell, David. *J. M. Coetzee: South Africa and the Politics of Writing.* Berkeley: University of California Press, 1993.

———. "Race in *Disgrace.*" *Interventions* 4, no. 3 (2002): 331–341.

Austen, Jane. *Persuasion.* New York: Bantam Books, 1984.

Bailey, Richard W. "Attitudes Toward English: The Future of English in South Asia." In *South Asian English: Structure, Use, and Users,* ed. Robert J. Baumgardner, 40–52. Urbana: University of Illinois Press, 1996.

Bajwa, Rupa. *The Sari Shop.* New York: Norton, 2004.

Baker, Geoffrey. "The Limits of Sympathy: J. M. Coetzee's Evolving Ethics of Engagement." *ARIEL: A Review of International English Literature* 36, no. 1–2 (2005): 27–49.

Baker, Houston A., Jr., Elizabeth Alexander, and Patricia Redmond. *Workings of the Spirit: The Poetics of Afro-American Women's Writing.* Chicago: University of Chicago Press, 1991.

Bakhtin, Mikhail. *Rabelais and His World.* Translated by Helene Iswolsky. Cambridge, Mass.: The MIT Press, 1968.

Barber, Benjamin R. *Jihad vs. McWorld: How the Planet Is Both Falling Apart and Coming Together—And What This Means for Democracy.* New York: Times Books, 1995.

Barnard, Rita. *Apartheid and Beyond: South African Writers and the Politics of Place.* Oxford: Oxford University Press, 2007.

Barney, Richard A. "Between Swift and Kafka: Animals and the Politics of Coetzee's Elusive Fiction." *World Literature Today* 78, no. 1 (2004): 17–23.

Basu, Amrita. "Globalization of the Local/Localization of the Global: Mapping Transnational Women's Movements." *Meridians: feminism, race, transnationalism* 1, no. 1 (2000): 68–84.

———. "Introduction." In *The Challenge of Local Feminisms: Women's Movements in Global Perspective,* ed. Amrita Basu with C. Elizabeth McGrory, 1–21. Boulder, Colo.: Westview Press, 1995.

Bate, Walter Jackson. "The Sympathetic Imagination in Eighteenth-Century English Criticism." *ELH: A Journal of English Literary History* 12, no. 2 (1945): 144–164.

Bell, Michael. "What Is It Like to Be a Nonracist? Costello and Coetzee on the Lives of Animals and Men." In *J. M. Coetzee and the Idea of the Public Intellectual*, ed. Jane Poyner, 172–192. Athens: Ohio University Press, 2006.

Benhabib, Seyla. *Situating the Self: Gender, Community, and Postmodernism in Contemporary Ethics*. New York: Routledge, 1992.

Berlant, Lauren. "Poor Eliza." *American Literature* 70, no. 3 (1998): 635–668.

——, ed. *Compassion: The Culture and Politics of an Emotion*. New York: Routledge, 2004.

Bhabha, Homi K. *The Location of Culture*. London: Routledge, 1994.

Bharucha, Rustom. *The Politics of Cultural Practice: Thinking Through Theatre in an Age of Globalization*. Hanover, N.H.: Wesleyan University Press, 2000.

Black, Shameem. "Cosmopolitanism at Home: Amitav Ghosh's *The Shadow Lines*." *The Journal of Commonwealth Literature* 41, no. 3 (2006): 45–65.

——. "Fertile Cosmofeminism: Ruth Ozeki and Transnational Reproduction." *Meridians: feminism, race, transnationalism* 5, no. 1 (2004): 226–256.

Bloom, Harold. "Introduction." In *Asian American Women Writers*, ed. Harold Bloom, xv–xvii. Philadelphia: Chelsea House Publishers, 1997.

Boehmer, Elleke. "Not Saying Sorry, Not Speaking Pain: Gender Implications in *Disgrace*." In *Resistance and Reconciliation: Writing in the Commonwealth*, ed. Bruce Bennett et al., 29–46. Canberra: Association for Commonwealth Literature and Language Studies, 2003.

Booth, Wayne C. *The Company We Keep: An Ethics of Fiction*. Berkeley: University of California Press, 1988.

Brennan, Timothy. *At Home in the World: Cosmopolitanism Now*. Cambridge, Mass.: Harvard University Press, 1997.

Brison, Susan J. "Surviving Sexual Violence: A Philosophical Perspective." In *Violence Against Women: Philosophical Perspectives*, ed. Stanley G. French, Wanda Teays, and Laura M. Purdy, 11–26. Ithaca, N.Y.: Cornell University Press, 1998.

Brouillette, Sarah. *Postcolonial Writers in the Global Literary Marketplace*. Basingstoke: Palgrave Macmillan, 2007.

Brown, Bill. "Global Bodies/Postnationalities: Charles Johnson's Consumer Culture." *Representations* 58 (1997): 24–48.

Brown, Laura. *Fables of Modernity: Literature and Culture in the English Eighteenth Century*. Ithaca, N.Y.: Cornell University Press, 2001.

Bunch, Charlotte. "Women's Human Rights: The Challenges of Global Feminism and Diversity." In *Feminist Locations: Global and Local, Theory and Practice*, ed. Marianne DeKoven, 129–146. New Brunswick, N.J.: Rutgers University Press, 2001.

Butler, Judith. *Gender Trouble: Feminism and the Subversion of Identity*. New York: Routledge, 1990.

Byrd, Rudolph P. *Charles Johnson's Novels: Writing the American Palimpsest*. Bloomington: Indiana University Press, 2005.

——. "*Oxherding Tale* and *Siddhartha*: Philosophy, Fiction, and the Emergence of a Hidden Tradition." *African American Review* 30, no. 4 (1996): 549–558.

Cameron, Anne. *Dzelarhons: Myths of the Northwest Coast*. Madeira Park, B.C.: Harbour, 1986.

Canetti, Elias. *Crowds and Power*. Translated by Carol Stewart. New York: Viking Press, 1963.

Chakrabarty, Dipesh. *Provincializing Europe: Postcolonial Thought and Historical Difference*. Princeton, N.J.: Princeton University Press, 2000.

Chan, Jeffrey Paul, et al. "Introduction." In *The Big Aiiieeeee! An Anthology of Chinese American and Japanese American Literature*, ed. Jeffrey Paul Chan et al., xi–xvi. New York: Meridian, 1991.

Cheah, Pheng. "Given Culture: Rethinking Cosmopolitical Freedom in Transnationalism." In *Cosmopolitics: Thinking and Feeling Beyond the Nation*, ed. Pheng Cheah and Bruce Robbins, 290–328. Minneapolis: University of Minnesota Press, 1998.

Ch'ien, Evelyn Nien-Ming. *Weird English*. Cambridge, Mass.: Harvard University Press, 2004.

Chiu, Monica. "Postnational Globalization and (En)Gendered Meat Production in Ruth L. Ozeki's *My Year of Meats*." *LIT* 12, no. 1 (2001): 99–128.

Chow, Rey. *The Protestant Ethnic and the Spirit of Capitalism*. New York: Columbia University Press, 2002.

——. *Sentimental Fabulations, Contemporary Chinese Films: Attachment in the Age of Global Visibility*. New York: Columbia University Press, 2007.

——. *Writing Diaspora: Tactics of Intervention in Contemporary Cultural Studies*. Bloomington: Indiana University Press, 1993.

Cixous, Helene. "The Laugh of the Medusa." In *Feminisms: An Anthology of Literary Theory and Criticism*, ed. Robyn R. Warhol and Diane Price Herndl, 347–362. New Brunswick, N.J.: Rutgers University Press, 1997.

Coetzee, J. M. *Age of Iron*. Penguin: New York, 1990.

——. *Disgrace*. London: Secker & Warburg, 1999.

——. *Elizabeth Costello: Eight Lessons*. London: Secker & Warburg, 2003.

——. "Jerusalem Prize Acceptance Speech (1987)." In *Doubling the Point: Essays and Interviews*, ed. David Attwell, 96–99. Cambridge, Mass.: Harvard University Press, 1992.

——. *The Lives of Animals*. Princeton, N.J.: Princeton University Press, 1999.

——. *The Master of Petersburg*. New York: Penguin, 1995.

——. *Slow Man*. New York: Penguin, 2006.

——. *Stranger Shores: Literary Essays 1986–1999*. New York: Viking, 2001.

———. *White Writing: On the Culture of Letters in South Africa.* New Haven, Conn.: Yale University Press, 1988.

Cohen, Margaret. "Sentimental Communities." In *The Literary Channel: The International Invention of the Novel*, ed. Margaret Cohen and Carolyn Dever, 106–132. Princeton, N.J.: Princeton University Press, 2002.

Collado-Rodriguez, Francisco. "Of Self and Country: U.S. Politics, Cultural Hybridity, and Ambivalent Identity in Jeffrey Eugenides' Middlesex." *International Fiction Review* 33, no. 1–2 (2006): 71–83.

Conner, Marc C., and William R. Nash, eds. *Charles Johnson: The Novelist as Philosopher.* Jackson: University Press of Mississippi, 2007.

Coomaraswamy, Radhika. "Are Women's Rights Universal? Re-Engaging the Local." *Meridians: feminism, race, transnationalism* 3, no. 1 (2002): 1–18.

Cornwell, Gareth. "*Disgrace*land: History and the Humanities in Frontier Country." *English in Africa* 30, no. 2 (2003): 43–68.

Cornyetz, Nina. "The Meat Manifesto: Ruth Ozeki's Performative Poetics." *Women and Performance: A Journal of Feminist Theory* 12, no. 1 (2001): 207–224.

Coronil, Fernando. "Listening to the Subaltern: Postcolonial Studies and the Poetics of Neocolonial States." In *Postcolonial Theory and Criticism*, ed. Laura Chrisman and Benita Parry, 37–55. Cambridge: D. S. Brewer, 2000.

Craig, Cairns. *The Modern Scottish Novel: Narrative and the National Imagination.* Edinburgh: Edinburgh University Press, 1999.

Dandekar, Natalie. "International Development Paradigms and Violence Against Women." In *Violence Against Women: Philosophical Perspectives*, ed. Stanley G. French, Wanda Teays, and Laura M. Purdy, 168–181. Ithaca, N.Y.: Cornell University Press, 1998.

Desai, Anita. *Diamond Dust: Stories.* Boston: Houghton Mifflin, 2000.

Deutsch, Nathaniel. "'The Asiatic Black Man': An African American Orientalism?" *Journal of Asian American Studies* 4, no. 3 (2001): 193–208.

Dimock, Wai Chee. *Through Other Continents: American Literature Across Deep Time.* Princeton, N.J.: Princeton University Press, 2006.

Dimock, Wai Chee, and Lawrence Buell, eds. *Shades of the Planet: American Literature as World Literature.* Princeton, N.J.: Princeton University Press, 2007.

Dixon, Robert. "'Travelling in the West': The Writing of Amitav Ghosh." *Journal of Commonwealth Literature* 31, no. 1 (1996): 3–24.

Dobson, Joanne. "Reclaiming Sentimental Literature." *American Literature* 69, no. 2 (1997): 263–288.

Donovan, Josephine. "'Miracles of Creation': Animals in J. M. Coetzee's Work." *Michigan Quarterly Review* 43, no. 1 (2004): 78–93.

Doody, Margaret Anne. *The True Story of the Novel*. New Brunswick, N.J.: Rutgers University Press, 1996.

Dovey, Teresa. *The Novels of J. M. Coetzee: Lacanian Allegories*. Craighall: A. D. Donker, 1988.

Doyle, Laura, and Laura Winkiel, eds. *Geomodernisms: Race, Modernism, Modernity*. Bloomington: Indiana University Press, 2005.

Dunant, Sarah. "Introduction: What's In a Word?" In *The War of the Words: The Political Correctness Debate*, ed. Sarah Dunant, vii–xv. London: Virago Press, 1994.

Durrant, Sam. "J. M. Coetzee, Elizabeth Costello, and the Limits of the Sympathetic Imagination." In *J. M. Coetzee and the Idea of the Public Intellectual*, ed. Jane Poyner, 118–134. Athens: Ohio University Press, 2006.

——. *Postcolonial Narrative and the Work of Mourning: J. M. Coetzee, Wilson Harris, and Toni Morrison*. Albany: State University of New York Press, 2004.

Ecker, Gisela. "Eating Identities—From Migration to Lifestyle: Mary Antin, Ntozake Shange, Ruth Ozeki." In *Wandering Selves: Essays on Migration and Multiculturalism*, ed. M. Porsche and C. Berkemeier, 171–183. Essen: Verlag Die Blaue Eule, 2001.

Edwards, Brent Hayes. *The Practice of Diaspora: Literature, Translation, and the Rise of Black Internationalism*. Cambridge, Mass.: Harvard University Press, 2003.

Eiser, Arnold R. "Violence and Transcultural Values." In *Violence Against Women: Philosophical Perspectives*, ed. Stanley G. French, Wanda Teays, and Laura M. Purdy, 161–167. Ithaca, N.Y.: Cornell University Press, 1998.

Erichsen, Ulrike. "Smiling in the Face of Adversity: How to Use Humour to Defuse Cultural Conflict." In *Cheeky Fictions: Laughter and the Postcolonial*, ed. Susanne Reichl and Mark Stein, 27–41. Amsterdam: Rodopi, 2005.

Esteve, Mary. *The Aesthetics and Politics of the Crowd in American Literature*. Cambridge: Cambridge University Press, 2003.

Esty, Jed. *A Shrinking Island: Modernism and National Culture in England*. Princeton, N.J.: Princeton University Press, 2004.

Eugenides, Jeffrey. *Middlesex*. New York: Farrar, Straus and Giroux, 2002.

Felman, Shoshana. "Women and Madness: The Critical Phallacy." In *Feminisms: An Anthology of Literary Theory and Criticism*, ed. Robyn R. Warhol and Diane Price Herndl, 7–20. New Brunswick, N.J.: Rutgers University Press, 1997.

Felski, Rita. *Doing Time: Feminist Theory and Postmodern Culture*. New York: New York University Press, 2000.

Festa, Lynn. "Sentimental Bonds and Revolutionary Characters: Richardson's *Pamela* in England and France." In *The Literary Channel: The Inter-National Invention of the Novel*, ed. M. Cohen and C. Dever. Princeton, N.J.: Princeton University Press, 2002.

Fetterly, Judith. "Introduction: On the Politics of Literature." In *Feminisms: An Anthology of Literary Theory and Criticism*, ed. Robyn R. Warhol and Diane Price Herndl, 564–573. New Brunswick, N.J.: Rutgers University Press, 1997.

Freedman, Ariela. "On the Ganges Side of Modernism: Raghubir Singh, Amitav Ghosh, and the Postcolonial Modern." In *Geomodernisms: Race, Modernism, Modernity*, ed. Laura Doyle and Laura Winkiel, 114–129. Bloomington: Indiana University Press, 2005.

Freedman, Estelle B. *No Turning Back: The History of Feminism and the Future of Women*. New York: Ballantine, 2002.

Freedman, Jonathan. "'Who's Jewish?' Some Asian American Writers and the Jewish American Literary Canon." *Michigan Quarterly Review* 42, no. 1 (2003): 230–254.

Frye, Northrop. "Anatomy of Criticism: Four Essays." In *Theory of the Novel: A Historical Approach*, ed. Michael McKeon, 5–13. Baltimore, Md.: The Johns Hopkins University Press, 2000.

Furman, Andrew. "Immigrant Dreams and Civic Promises: (Con-)testing Identity in Early Jewish American Literature and Gish Jen's *Mona in the Promised Land*." *MELUS* 25, no. 1 (2000): 210–226.

Gallagher, Susan VanZanten. *A Story of South Africa: J. M. Coetzee's Fiction in Context*. Cambridge, Mass.: Harvard University Press, 1991.

Gates, Henry Louis. *The Signifying Monkey: A Theory of Afro-American Literary Criticism*. New York: Oxford University Press, 1988.

Ghosh, Amitav. *The Glass Palace*. London: HarperCollins, 2000.

——. *The Hungry Tide*. New Delhi: HarperCollins Publishers India, 2004.

——. *In an Antique Land: History in the Guise of a Traveler's Tale*. New York: Vintage, 1994.

——. "The Indian Story: Notes on Some Preliminaries." *Civil Lines* 1 (1994): 35–49.

——. "Interview by Neluka Silva and Alex Tickell." *Kunapipi* 19, no. 3 (1997): 171–177.

——. "Interview with the author." Barker Center, Harvard University, May 3, 2004.

——. "Letter to Sandra Vince." March 18, 2001. Available online at http:/www.amitav ghosh.com/cwprize.html.

——. *The Shadow Lines*. Delhi: Ravi Dayal, 1988.

Ghosh, Amitav, and Dipesh Chakrabarty. "A Correspondence on *Provincializing Europe*." *Radical History Review* 83 (2002): 146–172.

Ghosh, Bishnupriya. *When Borne Across: Literary Cosmopolitics in the Contemporary Indian Novel*. New Brunswick, N.J.: Rutgers University Press, 2004.

Gilbert, Daniel. *Stumbling on Happiness*. New York: Vintage Books, 2007.

Gilbert, Sandra M., and Susan Gubar. "Infection in the Sentence: The Woman Writer and the Anxiety of Authorship." In *Feminisms: An Anthology of Literary Theory and*

Criticism, ed. Robyn R. Warhol and Diane Price Herndl, 21–32. New Brunswick, N.J.: Rutgers University Press, 1997.

Gilroy, Paul. *The Black Atlantic: Modernity and Double Consciousness.* Cambridge, Mass.: Harvard University Press, 1993.

——. *Postcolonial Melancholia.* New York: Columbia University Press, 2005.

Glasgow, Melita, and Don Fletcher. "Palimpsest and Seduction: The Glass Palace and White Teeth." *Kunapipi: Journal of Postcolonial Writing* 27, no. 1 (2005): 75–87.

Gleason, William. "The Liberation of Perception: Charles Johnson's *Oxherding Tale.*" *Black American Literature Forum* 25, no. 4 (1991): 705–728.

Gómez-Peña, Guillermo. "The Multicultural Paradigm: An Open Letter to the National Arts Community (1989)." In *Warrior for Gringostroika: Essays, Performance Texts, and Poetry*, 45–54. Saint Paul, Minn.: Graywolf Press, 1993.

Graham, Lucy. "'Yes, I am giving him up': Sacrificial Responsibility and Likeness with Dogs in J. M. Coetzee's Recent Fiction." *Scrutiny 2* 7, no. 1 (2000): 4–15.

Greer, Germaine. "Reality Bites." *The Guardian* (July 24, 2006).

Grewal, Inderpal. *Transnational America: Feminisms, Diasporas, Neoliberalisms.* Durham, N.C.: Duke University Press, 2005.

Grewal, Inderpal, and Caren Kaplan, eds. *Scattered Hegemonies: Postmodernity and Transnational Feminist Practices.* Minneapolis: University of Minnesota Press, 1994.

Guillory, John. "The Ethical Practice of Modernity: The Example of Reading." In *The Turn to Ethics*, ed. Marjorie Garber, Beatrice Hanssen, and Rebecca L. Walkowitz, 29–46. New York: Routledge, 2000.

Gupta, R. K. "'That which a man takes for himself no one can deny him': Amitav Ghosh's *The Glass Palace* and the Colonial Experience." *International Fiction Review* 33, no. 1–2 (2006): 18–26.

HaCohen, Ruth. "The Music of Sympathy in the Arts of the Baroque; or, the Use of Difference to Overcome Indifference." *Poetics Today* 22, no. 3 (2001).

Hakemulder, Jèmeljan. *The Moral Laboratory: Experiments Examining the Effects of Reading Literature on Social Perception and Moral Self-Concept.* Amsterdam: John Benjamins, 2000.

Hall, Stuart. "The Spectacle of the Other." In *Representation: Cultural Representations and Signifying Practices*, ed. Stuart Hall, 223–290. London: Sage, 1997.

Hanis, Andrea. "Heredity Crisis: Mona Takes Witty Look at Ethnicity." *Chicago Sun-Times* (June 23, 1996).

Hanssen, Beatrice. "Ethics of the Other." In *The Turn to Ethics*, ed. Marjorie Garber, Beatrice Hanssen, and Rebecca L. Walkowitz, 127–179. New York: Routledge, 2000.

Haraway, Donna. *The Companion Species Manifesto: Dogs, People, and Significant Otherness.* Chicago: Prickly Paradigm Press, 2003.

——. *Primate Visions: Gender, Race, and Nature in the World of Modern Science*. New York: Routledge, 1989.

Hardack, Richard. "Black Skin, White Tissues: Local Color and Universal Solvents in the Novels of Charles Johnson." *Callaloo* 22, no. 4 (1999): 1028–1053.

Hardt, Michael, and Antonio Negri. *Empire*. Cambridge, Mass.: Harvard University Press, 2000.

Harwood, Dix. "Love for Animals and How It Developed in Great Britain." Ph.D. Dissertation, Columbia University, 1928.

Hassan, Ihab. "Queries for Postcolonial Studies." *Philosophy and Literature* 22, no. 2 (1998): 328–342.

Hawley, John C. *Amitav Ghosh: An Introduction*. New Delhi: Foundation Books, 2005.

Hobson, Geary. "The Rise of the White Shaman as a New Version of Cultural Imperialism." In *From Totems to Hip-Hop: A Multicultural Anthology of Poetry Across the Americas, 1900–2002*, ed. Ishmael Reed, 410–423. New York: Thunder's Mouth Press, 2003.

Howard, June. "What Is Sentimentality?" *American Literary History* 11, no. 1 (1999): 63–81.

Huggan, Graham. *The Postcolonial Exotic: Marketing the Margins*. London: Routledge, 2001.

Hungerford, Amy. *The Holocaust of Texts: Genocide, Literature, and Personification*. Chicago: University of Chicago Press, 2003.

Hunt, Lynn. *Inventing Human Rights: A History*. New York: Norton, 2007.

"J. M. Coetzee in Conversation with Jane Poyner." In *J. M. Coetzee and the Idea of the Public Intellectual*, ed. Jane Poyner, 21–24. Athens: Ohio University Press, 2006.

JanMohamed, Abdul R. "The Economy of Manichean Allegory: The Function of Racial Difference in Colonialist Literature." In *"Race," Writing, and Difference*, ed. Henry Louis Gates, 78–106. Chicago: University of Chicago Press, 1986.

JanMohamed, Abdul R., and David Lloyd. "Introduction: Toward a Theory of Minority Discourse: What Is to Be Done?" In *The Nature and Context of Minority Discourse*, ed. A. R. JanMohamed and D. Lloyd, 1–16. New York: Oxford University Press, 1990.

Jen, Gish. *Mona in the Promised Land*. New York: Knopf, 1996.

Johnson, Charles. *Dr. King's Refrigerator and Other Bedtime Stories*. New York: Scribner, 2005.

——. "I Call Myself an Artist." In *I Call Myself an Artist: Writings by and About Charles Johnson*, ed. Rudolph P. Byrd, 3–30. Bloomington: Indiana University Press, 1999.

——. "An Interview with Charles Johnson: Interview by Jonathan Little." In *I Call Myself an Artist: Writings by and About Charles Johnson*, ed. Rudolph P. Byrd, 225–243. Bloomington: Indiana University Press, 1999.

——. *Middle Passage*. New York: Plume, 1991.

——. *Oxherding Tale*. Bloomington: Indiana University Press, 1982.

——. "A Sangha by Another Name." *Tricycle* 9, no. 2 (1999): 43ff.

——. *Turning the Wheel: Essays on Buddhism and Writing*. New York: Scribner, 2003.

Johnson, Samuel. *The Rambler*. London: Jones and Company, 1825.

Joshi, Priya. *In Another Country: Colonialism, Culture, and the English Novel in India*. New York: Columbia University Press, 2002.

Kabbani, Rana. *Imperial Fictions: Europe's Myths of Orient*. London: Pandora, 1988.

Kaplan, Caren. "The Politics of Location as Transnational Feminist Critical Practice." In *Scattered Hegemonies: Postmodernity and Transnational Feminist Practices*, ed. Inderpal Grewal and Caren Kaplan, 137–152. Minneapolis: University of Minnesota, 1994.

Kaplan, Cora. "Pandora's Box: Subjectivity, Class, and Sexuality in Socialist Feminist Criticism." In *Feminisms: An Anthology of Literary Theory and Criticism*, ed. Robyn R. Warhol and Diane Price Herndl, 956–975. New Brunswick, N.J.: Rutgers University Press, 1997.

Kariuki, Sam, and Lucien Van der Walt. "Land Reform in South Africa: Still Waiting." *Southern Africa Report* 15, no. 3 (2000): 19.

Kaul, Suvir. "Separation Anxiety: Growing Up Inter/National in Amitav Ghosh's *The Shadow Lines*." *Oxford Literary Review* 16, no. 1–2 (1994): 125–145.

Keck, Margaret E., and Kathryn Sikkink. *Activists Beyond Borders: Advocacy Networks in International Politics*. Ithaca, N.Y.: Cornell University Press, 1998.

Keen, Suzanne. *Empathy and the Novel*. New York: Oxford University Press, 2007.

Kennedy, Randall. *Sellout: The Politics of Racial Betrayal*. New York: Pantheon Books, 2008.

Kete, Kathleen. "Animals and Ideology: The Politics of Animal Protection in Europe." In *Representing Animals*, ed. Nigel Rothfels, 19–34. Bloomington: Indiana University Press, 2002.

Khair, Tabish. *Babu Fictions: Alienation in Contemporary Indian English Novels*. Delhi: Oxford University Press, 2001.

——. "Open Letter." March 19, 2001. Available online at http:/www.amitavghosh.com/cwprize.html.

King, Richard. *Orientalism and Religion: Postcolonial Theory, India, and "The Mystic East."* London: Routledge, 1999.

Kingston, Maxine Hong. "The Novel's Next Step." *Mother Jones* 14, no. 10 (1989): 37–41.

Klein, Christina. *Cold War Orientalism: Asia in the Middlebrow Imagination, 1945–1961*. Berkeley: University of California Press, 2003.

Knapp, Steven. *Literary Interest: The Limits of Antiformalism*. Cambridge, Mass.: Harvard University Press, 1993.

Krog, Antjie. *Country of My Skull: Guilt, Sorrow, and the Limits of Forgiveness in the New South Africa.* New York: Three Rivers Press, 1998.

Kushigian, Julia A. *Orientalism in the Hispanic Literary Tradition: In Dialogue with Borges, Paz, and Sarduy.* Albuquerque: University of New Mexico Press, 1991.

Lamott, Anne. *Bird by Bird: Some Instructions on Writing and Life.* New York: Anchor Books, 1995.

Lazarus, Neil. *Nationalism and Cultural Practice in the Postcolonial World.* Cambridge: Cambridge University Press, 1999.

Lee, Jennifer Serena. "Ethnic Identity Development and the Influence of Multicultural Children's Literature." Dissertation, University of California, Davis, 2000.

Lesser, Wendy. *His Other Half: Men Looking at Women Through Art.* Cambridge, Mass.: Harvard University Press, 1991.

Levenson, Joseph Richmond. *Revolution and Cosmopolitanism: The Western Stage and the Chinese Stages.* Berkeley: University of California Press, 1971.

Levinson, Julie H., and Sandra P. Levinson. "Women's Health and Human Rights." In *Women, Gender, and Human Rights,* ed. Marjorie Agosin, 124–151. New Brunswick, N.J.: Rutgers University Press, 2001.

Lin, Erika T. "Mona on the Phone: The Performative Body and Racial Identity in *Mona in the Promised Land.*" *MELUS* 28, no. 2 (2003): 47–57.

Ling, Amy. "Cultural Cross-Dressing in *Mona in the Promised Land.*" In *Asian American Literature in the International Context: Readings on Fiction, Poetry, and Performance,* ed. Rocio G. Davis and Sami Ludwig, 227–236. Hamburg: LIT, 2002.

Little, Jonathan. *Charles Johnson's Spiritual Imagination.* Columbia: University of Missouri Press, 1997.

Littlewood, Jane, and Michael Pickering. "Heard the One About the White Middle-Class Heterosexual Father-in-Law? Gender, Ethnicity, and Political Correctness in Comedy." In *Because I Tell a Joke or Two: Comedy, Politics, and Social Difference,* ed. Stephen Wagg, 291–312. London: Routledge, 1998.

Lowe, Lisa. *Critical Terrains: French and British Orientalisms.* Ithaca, N.Y.: Cornell University Press, 1992.

Lowe, Lisa, and David Lloyd. "Introduction." In *The Politics of Culture in the Shadow of Capital,* ed. L. Lowe and D. Lloyd, 1–32. Durham, N.C.: Duke University Press, 1997.

Lugones, Maria. "Playfulness, 'World'-Travelling, and Loving Perception." *Hypatia* 2, no. 2 (1987): 3–19.

Lundeen, Kathleen. "Who Has the Right to Feel? The Ethics of Literary Empathy." In *Mapping the Ethical Turn: A Reader in Ethics, Culture, and Literary Theory,* ed. Todd F. Davis and Kenneth Womack, 83–92. Charlottesville: University Press of Virginia, 2001.

Ma, Sheng-mei. *The Deathly Embrace: Orientalism and Asian American Identity*. Minneapolis: University of Minnesota Press, 2000.

MacKenzie, John M. *Orientalism: History, Theory, and the Arts*. Manchester: Manchester University Press, 1995.

Mackie, Vera. "Feminist Critiques of Modern Japanese Politics." In *Global Feminisms Since 1945*, ed. Bonnie G. Smith, 180–201. London: Routledge, 2000.

Mani, B. Venkat. *Cosmopolitical Claims: Turkish-German Literatures from Nadolny to Pamuk*. Iowa City: University of Iowa Press, 2007.

Maracle, Lee. "Conversations at the Book Fair: Interview by Susanne de Lotbinière." *Trivia* 14 (1989): 24–36.

——. "Moving Over." *Trivia* 14 (1989): 9–12.

——. "Nobody Home." *Trivia* 16/17 (1990): 108–118.

Marais, Michael. "'Little enough, less than little: nothing': Ethics, Engagement, and Change in the Fiction of J. M. Coetzee." *MFS: Modern Fiction Studies* 46, no. 1 (2000): 159–182.

Marais, Mike. "J. M. Coetzee's *Disgrace* and the Task of the Imagination." *Journal of Modern Literature* 29, no. 2 (2006): 75–93.

——. "The Possibility of Ethical Action: J. M. Coetzee's *Disgrace*." *Scrutiny* 2 5, no. 1 (2000): 57–63.

Mason, Travis V. "Dog Gambit: Shifting the Species Boundary in J. M. Coetzee's Recent Fiction." *Mosaic* 39, no. 4 (2006): 129–144.

McClintock, Anne, Aamir Mufti, Ella Shohat, and Social Text Collective, eds. *Dangerous Liaisons: Gender, Nations, and Postcolonial Perspectives*. Minneapolis: University of Minnesota Press, 1997.

McConnell, Michael W. "Don't Neglect the Little Platoons." In *For Love of Country: Debating the Limits of Patriotism*, ed. Joshua Cohen, 78–84. Boston: Beacon Press, 1996.

McDonald, Peter D. "Disgrace Effects." *Interventions* 4, no. 3 (2002): 321–330.

McEwan, Ian. *Saturday*. New York: Random House, 2005.

McKeon, Michael, ed. *Theory of the Novel: A Historical Approach*. Baltimore, Md.: The John Hopkins University Press, 2000.

Meffan, James, and Kim L. Worthington. "Ethics Before Politics: J. M. Coetzee's *Disgrace*." In *Mapping the Ethical Turn: A Reader in Ethics, Culture, and Literary Theory*, ed. T. F. Davis and K. Womack, 131–150. Charlottesville: University Press of Virginia, 2001.

Michaels, Walter Benn. *Our America: Nativism, Modernism, and Pluralism*. Durham, N.C.: Duke University Press, 1995.

——. *The Shape of the Signifier: 1967 to the End of History*. Princeton, N.J.: Princeton University Press, 2004.

———. *The Trouble with Diversity: How We Learned to Love Identity and Ignore Inequality.* New York: Metropolitan Books, 2006.

Mohanty, Chandra Talpade. *Feminism Without Borders: Decolonizing Theory, Practicing Solidarity.* Durham, N.C.: Duke University Press, 2003.

———. "Under Western Eyes: Feminist Scholarship and Colonial Discourses." In *Third World Women and the Politics of Feminism*, ed. C. T. Mohanty, A. Russo, and L. Torres, 51–80. Bloomington: Indiana University Press, 1991.

Mohanty, Satya P. *Literary Theory and the Claims of History: Postmodernism, Objectivity, Multicultural Politics.* Ithaca, N.Y.: Cornell University Press, 1997.

Moral, Rakhee. "'In the Time of the Breaking of Nations': *The Glass Palace* as Postcolonial Narrative." In *Amitav Ghosh: Critical Perspectives*, ed. Brinda Bose, 139–154. Delhi: Pencraft International, 2003.

Morgan, Robin. "Introduction: New World Women." In *Sisterhood is Forever: The Women's Anthology for a New Millennium*, ed. Robin Morgan, xv–lv. New York: Washington Square Press, 2003.

———. "Introduction: Planetary Feminism: The Politics of the Twenty-First Century." In *Sisterhood Is Global: The International Women's Movement Anthology*, ed. Robin Morgan, 1–37. Garden City, N.Y.: Anchor Press, 1984.

Morris, Rosalind C. "The Mute and the Unspeakable: Political Subjectivity, Violent Crime, and the 'Sexual Thing' in a South African Mining Community." In *Law and Disorder in the Postcolony*, ed. J. Comaroff and J. L. Comaroff, 57–101. Chicago: University of Chicago Press, 2006.

Moya, Paula M. L. *Learning from Experience: Minority Identities, Multicultural Struggles.* Berkeley: University of California Press, 2002.

Mukherjee, Meenakshi. "The Anxiety of Indianness." In *The Perishable Empire: Essays on Indian Writing in English*, 166–186. New Delhi: Oxford University Press, 2000.

Mullen, Bill V. "Du Bois, *Dark Princess*, and the Afro-Asian International." *positions: east asia cultures critique* 11, no. 1 (2003): 217–239.

Mulvey, Laura. "Visual Pleasure and Narrative Cinema." In *Feminisms: An Anthology of Literary Theory and Criticism*, ed. Robyn R. Warhol and Diane Price Herndl, 438–448. New Brunswick, N.J.: Rutgers University Press, 1997.

Murti, Kamakshi P. *India: The Seductive and Seduced "Other" of German Orientalism.* Westport, Conn.: Greenwood, 2001.

Nagel, Thomas. "What Is It Like to Be a Bat?" *The Philosophical Review* 83, no. 4 (1974).

Naipaul, V. S. *Guerillas.* New York: Vintage International, 1990.

Nair, Rukmini Bhaya. "The Road from Mandalay: Reflections on Amitav Ghosh's *The Glass Palace*." In *Amitav Ghosh: A Critical Companion*, ed. Tabish Khair, 162–174. Delhi: Permanent Black, 2003.

Narain, Denise deCaires. "What Happened to Global Sisterhood? Writing and Reading 'the' Postcolonial Woman." In *Third Wave Feminism: A Critical Exploration*, ed. G. Howie, S. Gillis, and R. Munford, 240–251. Basingstoke: Palgrave Macmillan, 2004.

Nash, William R. *Charles Johnson's Fiction*. Urbana: University of Illinois Press, 2003.

Newton, Adam Zachary. *Narrative Ethics*. Cambridge, Mass.: Harvard University Press, 1995.

Noble, Marianne. *The Masochistic Pleasures of Sentimental Literature*. Princeton, N.J.: Princeton University Press, 2000.

Norris, Margot. *Beasts of the Modern Imagination: Darwin, Nietzsche, Kafka, Ernst, and Lawrence*. Baltimore, Md.: The Johns Hopkins University Press, 1985.

Nussbaum, Martha C. *Cultivating Humanity: A Classical Defense of Reform in Liberal Education*. Cambridge, Mass.: Harvard University Press, 1997.

——. *The Fragility of Goodness: Luck and Ethics in Greek Tragedy and Philosophy*. Cambridge: Cambridge University Press, 1986.

——. *Love's Knowledge: Essays on Philosophy and Literature*. New York: Oxford University Press, 1990.

——. *Poetic Justice: The Literary Imagination and Public Life*. Boston: Beacon Press, 1995.

——. *Upheavals of Thought: The Intelligence of Emotions*. Cambridge: Cambridge University Press, 2001.

Nyman, Jopi. *Postcolonial Animal Tale from Kipling to Coetzee*. New Delhi: Atlantic, 2003.

Oerlemans, Onno. "A Defense of Anthropomorphism: Comparing Coetzee and Gowdy." *Mosaic* 40, no. 1 (2007): 181–196.

Ozeki, Ruth L. "A Conversation with Ruth Ozeki." In *My Year of Meats*, 6–14. New York: Penguin, 1998.

——. "fall." Available online at http://www.ruthozeki.com/weblog.

——. *My Year of Meats*. New York: Penguin, 1998.

Palumbo-Liu, David. "Rational and Irrational Choices: Form, Affect, and Ethics." In *Minor Transnationalism*, ed. Francoise Lionnet and Shu-mei Shih, 41–72. Durham, N.C.: Duke University Press, 2005.

Parfit, Derek. *Reasons and Persons*. Oxford: Clarendon Press, 1984.

Parker, David. *Ethics, Theory, and the Novel*. Cambridge: Cambridge University Press, 1994.

Parry, Benita. "Speech and Silence in the Fictions of J. M. Coetzee." In *Writing South Africa: Literature, Apartheid, and Democracy, 1970–1995*, ed. Derek Attridge and Rosemary Jolly, 149–165. Cambridge: Cambridge University Press, 1998.

Penner, Dick. *Countries of the Mind: The Fiction of J. M. Coetzee*. New York: Greenwood, 1989.

Pinsky, Robert. "Eros Against Esperanto." In *For Love of Country: Debating the Limits of Patriotism*, ed. Joshua Cohen, 85–90. Boston: Beacon Press, 1996.

Pollock, Sheldon, Homi K. Bhabha, Carol A. Breckenridge, and Dipesh Chakrabarty. "Cosmopolitanisms." *Public Culture* 12, no. 3 (2000): 577–589.

Posnock, Ross. *Color and Culture: Black Writers and the Making of the Modern Intellectual.* Cambridge, Mass.: Harvard University Press, 1998.

Prashad, Vijay. *The Karma of Brown Folk.* Minneapolis: University of Minnesota Press, 2000.

Pratt, Mary Louise. *Imperial Eyes: Travel Writing and Transculturation.* London: Routledge, 1992.

Puchner, Martin. "Performing the Open: Actors, Animals, Philosophers." *TDR: The Drama Review* 51, no. 1 (2007): 21–32.

Quayson, Ato. *Aesthetic Nervousness: Disability and the Crisis of Representation.* New York: Columbia University Press, 2007.

Radhakrishnan, R. "Toward an Eccentric Cosmopolitanism." *positions: east asia cultures critique* 3, no. 3 (1995): 814–821.

Ramazani, Jahan. *The Hybrid Muse: Postcolonial Poetry in English.* Chicago: University of Chicago Press, 2001.

Rampersad, Arnold. "Du Bois's Passage to India: *Dark Princess*." In *W. E. B. Du Bois on Race and Culture: Philosophy, Politics, and Poetics*, ed. Bernard W. Bell, Emily Grosholz, and James B. Stewart, 161–176. New York: Routledge, 1996.

Rich, Adrienne. "Notes Toward a Politics of Location (1984)." In *Blood, Bread, and Poetry: Selected Prose 1979–1985*, 210–231. New York: Norton, 1986.

Richards, David. *Masks of Difference: Cultural Representations in Literature, Anthropology, and Art.* Cambridge: Cambridge University Press, 1994.

Robbins, Bruce. *Feeling Global: Internationalism in Distress.* New York: New York University Press, 1999.

——. "The Sweatshop Sublime." *PMLA* 117, no. 1 (2002): 84–97.

Rorty, Richard. *Contingency, Irony, and Solidarity.* Cambridge: Cambridge University Press, 1989.

——. "Human Rights, Rationality, and Sentimentality." In *On Human Rights: The Oxford Amnesty Lectures 1993*, ed. S. Shute and S. Hurley, 111–134. New York: Basic Books, 1993.

Rosenblum, Naomi. *A World History of Photography.* 3rd ed. New York: Abbeville Press, 1997.

Rupp, Leila J. *Worlds of Women: The Making of an International Women's Movement.* Princeton, N.J.: Princeton University Press, 1997.

Rushdie, Salman. *The Enchantress of Florence*. New York: Random House, 2008.

——. *Midnight's Children*. London: Avon Books, 1982.

——. *The Satanic Verses*. New York: Henry Holt, 1988.

——. *Shalimar the Clown*. New York: Random House, 2005.

Rushdy, Ashraf H. A. *Neo-Slave Narratives: Studies in the Social Logic of a Literary Form*. New York: Oxford University Press, 1999.

Said, Edward W. "Criticism, Culture, and Performance." In *Power, Politics, and Culture: Interviews with Edward W. Said*, ed. Gauri Viswanathan, 94–117. New York: Pantheon, 2001.

——. *Culture and Imperialism*. New York: Vintage Books, 1994.

——. *Orientalism*. New York: Vintage, 1979.

Sanders, Mark. *Ambiguities of Witnessing: Law and Literature in the Time of a Truth Commission*. Stanford, Calif.: Stanford University Press, 2007.

——. "Disgrace." *Interventions* 4, no. 3 (2002): 363–373.

Scarry, Elaine. *The Body in Pain: The Making and Unmaking of the World*. New York: Oxford University Press, 1985.

——. "The Difficulty of Imagining Other Persons." In *The Handbook of Interethnic Coexistence*, ed. Eugene Weiner, 40–62. New York: Continuum, 1998.

——. *Dreaming By the Book*. New York: Farrar, Straus and Giroux, 1999.

Schlote, Christiane. "'The Sketch's the Thing Wherein We'll Catch the Conscience of the Audience': Strategies and Pitfalls of Ethnic TV Comedies in Britain, the United States, and Germany." In *Cheeky Fictions: Laughter and the Postcolonial*, ed. Susanne Reichl and Mark Stein, 177–190. Amsterdam: Rodopi, 2005.

Schnapp, Jeffrey T., and Matthew Tiews, eds. *Crowds*. Stanford, Calif.: Stanford University Press, 2006.

Schneider, David J. *The Psychology of Stereotyping*. New York: Guilford Press, 2004.

Schuler, Margaret. "Violence Against Women: An International Perspective." In *Freedom from Violence: Women's Strategies from Around the World*, ed. Margaret Schuler, 1–45. New York: UNIFEM, 1992.

Sedgwick, Eve Kosofsky. "Paranoid Reading and Reparative Reading; or, You're So Paranoid, You Probably Think This Introduction Is About You." In *Novel-Gazing: Queer Readings in Fiction*, ed. E. K. Sedgwick, 1–37. Durham, N.C.: Duke University Press, 1997.

Shaw, Mark, and Peter Gastrow. "Stealing the Show: Crime and Its Impact in Postapartheid South Africa." *Daedalus: Journal of the American Academy of Arts and Sciences* 130, no. 1 (2001): 235–258.

Shelley, Percy Bysshe. "A Defence of Poetry." In *The Norton Anthology of English Literature*, ed. M. H. Abrams. New York: Norton, 1983.

Shuman, Amy. *Other People's Stories: Entitlement Claims and the Critique of Empathy.* Urbana: University of Illinois Press, 2005.

Sieg, Katrin. *Ethnic Drag: Performing Race, Nation, Sexuality in West Germany.* Ann Arbor: The University of Michigan Press, 2002.

Sifuentes, Zachary. "Strange Anatomy, Strange Sexuality: The Queer Body in Jeffrey Eugenides' *Middlesex*." In *Straight Writ Queer: Non-Normative Expressions of Heterosexuality in Literature*, ed. Richard Fantina, 145–157. Jefferson, N.C.: McFarland, 2006.

Simons, John. *Animal Rights and the Politics of Literary Representation.* Houndmills: Palgrave, 2002.

Singer, Peter. *One World: The Ethics of Globalization.* New Haven, Conn.: Yale University Press, 2002.

Slater, Don. "Consuming Kodak." In *Family Snaps: The Meanings of Domestic Photography*, ed. Jo Spence and Patricia Holland, 49–59. London: Virago, 1991.

Slater, Michael D. "Entertainment Education and the Persuasive Impact of Narratives." In *Narrative Impact: Social and Cognitive Foundations*, ed. M. C. Green, J. J. Strange, and T. C. Brock, 157–181. Mahwah, N.J.: Lawrence Erlbaum Associates, 2002.

Slaughter, Joseph R. "Enabling Fictions and Novel Subjects: The *Bildungsroman* and International Human Rights Law." *PMLA* 121, no. 5 (2006): 1405–1423.

Smith, Adam. *The Theory of Moral Sentiments*, ed. Knud Haakonssen. Cambridge: Cambridge University Press, 2002.

Smith, Barbara. "The Truth That Never Hurts: Black Lesbians in Fiction in the 1980s." In *Feminisms: An Anthology of Literary Theory and Criticism*, ed. Robyn R. Warhol and Diane Price Herndl, 784–806. New Brunswick, N.J.: Rutgers University Press, 1997.

Sollors, Werner. *Beyond Ethnicity: Consent and Descent in American Culture.* New York: Oxford University Press, 1986.

——. *Neither Black nor White yet Both: Thematic Explorations of Interracial Literature.* New York: Oxford University Press, 1997.

Sollors, Werner, ed. *Multilingual America: Transnationalism, Ethnicity, and the Languages of American Literature.* New York: New York University Press, 1998.

Sommer, Doris. *Proceed with Caution, When Engaged by Minority Writing in the Americas.* Cambridge, Mass.: Harvard University Press, 1999.

Sontag, Susan. *Regarding the Pain of Others.* New York: Farrar, Straus and Giroux, 2003.

Spelman, Elizabeth V. *Fruits of Sorrow: Framing Our Attention to Suffering.* Boston: Beacon Press, 1997.

Spivak, Gayatri Chakravorty. "Acting Bits/Identity Talk." *Critical Inquiry* 18, no. 4 (1992): 770–803.

——. "Can the Subaltern Speak?" In *Colonial Discourse and Post-Colonial Theory: A Reader*, ed. Patrick Williams and Laura Chrisman, 66–111. New York: Harvester Wheatsheaf, 1993.

——. *In Other Worlds: Essays in Cultural Politics.* New York: Routledge, 1988.

——. "Three Women's Texts and a Critique of Imperialism." In *Feminisms: An Anthology of Literary Theory and Criticism*, ed. Robyn R. Warhol and Diane Price Herndl, 896–912. New Brunswick, N.J.: Rutgers University Press, 1997.

——. "Translator's Foreword." In *Chotti Munda and His Arrow*, vii–viii. Malden: Blackwell Publishing, 2002.

Srikanth, Rajini. *The World Next Door: South Asian American Literature and the Idea of America.* Philadelphia: Temple University Press, 2004.

Stanton, Katherine. *Cosmopolitan Fictions: Ethics, Politics, and Global Change in the Works of Kazuo Ishiguro, Michael Ondaatje, Jamaica Kincaid, and J. M. Coetzee.* New York: Routledge, 2006.

Storhoff, Gary. *Understanding Charles Johnson.* Columbia: University of South Carolina Press, 2004.

Stott, Andrew. *Comedy.* New York: Routledge, 2005.

Strode, Timothy Francis. *The Ethics of Exile: Colonialism in the Fictions of Charles Brockden Brown and J. M. Coetzee.* New York: Routledge, 2005.

Su, John J. *Ethics and Nostalgia in the Contemporary Novel.* Cambridge: Cambridge University Press, 2005.

Syal, Meera. "PC: GLC." In *The War of the Words: The Political Correctness Debate*, ed. Sarah Dunant, 116–132. London: Virago Press, 1994.

Sze, Julie. "Boundaries and Border Wars: DES, Technology, and Environmental Justice." *American Quarterly* 58, no. 3 (2006): 791–814.

Tannen, Deborah. *You Just Don't Understand: Women and Men in Conversation.* New York: Morrow, 1990.

Tanner, Laura E. *Intimate Violence: Reading Rape and Torture in Twentieth-Century Fiction.* Bloomington: Indiana University Press, 1994.

Todorov, Tzvetan. *The Conquest of America: The Question of the Other.* Translated by Richard Howard. New York: Harper and Row, 1984.

——. "'Race,' Writing, and Culture." In *"Race," Writing, and Difference*, ed. Henry Louis Gates, 370–380. Chicago: The University of Chicago Press, 1986.

Tolstoy, Leo. *Anna Karenina.* Translated by Louise and Alymer Maude. New York: Knopf, 1992.

Torgovnick, Marianna. *Gone Primitive: Savage Intellects, Modern Lives.* Chicago: University of Chicago Press, 1990.

——. *The War Complex: World War II in Our Time.* Chicago: University of Chicago Press, 2005.

Tremaine, Louis. "The Embodied Soul: Animal Being in the Work of J. M. Coetzee." *Contemporary Literature* 44, no. 4 (2003): 587–612.

Updike, John. "Questions of Character: There's No Ego as Wounded as a Wounded Alter Ego." In *Writers on Writing: Collected Essays from* The New York Times, 236–240. New York: Times Books, 2001.

Viswanathan, Gauri. "Beyond Orientalism: Syncretism and the Politics of Knowledge." *Stanford Humanities Review* 5, no. 1 (1995): 19–34.

wa Wamwere, Koigi. *Negative Ethnicity: From Bias to Genocide*. New York: Seven Stories Press, 2003.

Wade, Michael. *White on Black in South Africa: A Study of English-Language Inscriptions of Skin Colour*. London: Macmillan, 1993.

Wald, Gayle. "'A Most Disagreeable Mirror': Reflections on White Identity in *Black Like Me*." In *Passing and the Fictions of Identity*, ed. Elaine K. Ginsberg, 151–177. Durham, N.C.: Duke University Press, 1996.

Walkowitz, Rebecca L. *Cosmopolitan Style: Modernism Beyond the Nation*. New York: Columbia University Press, 2006.

Walzer, Michael. "Spheres of Affection." In *For Love of Country: Debating the Limits of Patriotism*, ed. Joshua Cohen, 125–127. Boston: Beacon Press, 1996.

Warhol, Robyn R. *Gendered Interventions: Narrative Discourse in the Victorian Novel*. New Brunswick, N.J.: Rutgers University Press, 1989.

——. *Having a Good Cry: Effeminate Feelings and Pop-Culture Forms*. Columbus: The Ohio State University Press, 2003.

——. "Physiology, Gender, and Feeling: On Cheering Up." *Narrative* 12, no. 2 (2004): 226–229.

Warner, Michael. "Uncritical Reading." In *Polemic: Critical or Uncritical*, ed. Jane Gallop, 13–38. New York: Routledge, 2004.

Weich, Dave. "Jeffrey Eugenides Has It Both Ways." Available online at http://www .powells.com/authors.eugenides.html.

Weiss, Timothy. *Translating Orients: Between Ideology and Utopia*. Toronto: University of Toronto Press, 2004.

Weisser, Susan Ostrov, and Jennifer Fleischner, eds. *Feminist Nightmares: Women at Odds: Feminism and the Problem of Sisterhood*. New York: New York University Press, 1994.

Wicomb, Zoë. "Translations in the Yard of Africa." *Journal of Literary Studies/Tydskrif vir Literatuurwetenskap* 18, no. 3–4 (2002): 209–223.

Willis, Susan. "I Shop Therefore I Am: Is There a Place for Afro-American Culture in Commodity Culture?" In *Feminisms: An Anthology of Literary Theory and Criticism*, ed. Robyn R. Warhol and Diane Price Herndl, 992–1008. New Brunswick, N.J.: Rutgers University Press, 1997.

Wispé, Lauren. *The Psychology of Sympathy*. New York: Plenum Press, 1991.

Wolfe, Cary. *Animal Rites: American Culture, the Discourse of Species, and Posthumanist Theory*. Chicago: University of Chicago Press, 2003.

Wolfe, Leslie R., and Jennifer Tucker. "Feminism Lives: Building a Multicultural Women's Movement in the United States." In *The Challenge of Local Feminisms: Women's Movements in Global Perspective*, ed. Amrita Basu and C. Elizabeth McGrory, 435–462. Boulder, Colo.: Westview Press, 1995.

Womack, Kenneth, and Amy Mallory-Kani. "'Why don't you just leave it up to nature?' An Adaptationist Reading of the Novels of Jeffrey Eugenides." *Mosaic* 40, no. 3 (2007): 157–173.

Woolf, Virginia. *A Room of One's Own*. San Diego, Calif.: Harcourt Brace Jovanovich, 1989.

——. *Three Guineas*. San Diego, Calif.: Harcourt Brace, 1938.

Wright, Laura. *Writing "Out of All the Camps": J. M. Coetzee's Narratives of Displacement*. New York: Routledge, 2006.

Yang, Mayfair Mei-hui, ed. *Spaces of Their Own: Women's Public Sphere in Transnational China*. Minneapolis: University of Minnesota Press, 1999.

INDEX

Bakhtin, 9, 121, 173

Barber, Benjamin, 6

Barnard, Rita, 205, 294*n*59

Basu, Amrita, 89–90

Benhabib, Seyla, 63

Bhabha, Homi: hybridity and, 275*n*110;
   stereotype and, 101; Third Space and,
   28, 265*n*31

Bhaskar, Sanjeev, 102

Bon Bibi metaphor, 194–96

Bone People, The (Hulme), 167

book, as friend, 258*n*7

Booth, Wayne, 258*n*7

border-crossing fiction: antecedents of, 7,
   260*n*14; author goals regarding, 4–5;
   author's comparative methodology
   and, 11–12; common attributes of, 9–10;
   criteria of, 3–4; critical metanarrative
   concerning, 250; diversity of, 9, 10,
   12; ethics of representation and, 3–4,
   250–52; ethnic / comic reversal and, 15;
   globalization regarding, 6–7; history
   regarding, 7–8; imagining process in,
   4; language and, 16–17; middlebrow,
   12–13; middle ground and, 16; minority
   literary traditions and, 11; narrative
   choices in, 12–14; novel and, 8–9;
   novel subgenres and, 252–53; Ozeki
   vs. Coetzee regarding, 5–6; planetary
   idealism and, 253–54; publication /
   translation and, 8; range of, 252;
   self-sacrifice and, 17; sentimental
   fiction / feminist politics and, 14–15;
   sentiment in, 69; social change and,
   33–34, 268*n*51; tracing-and-exposure
   project and, 5

Brennan, Timothy, 274*n*95

Brison, Susan J., 226

Bronte, Charlotte, 145–46

Brown, Laura, 209

Butler, Judith, 265*n*33

Byron, Lord (George Gordon), 221–24,
   226–28, 238–39, 241

Cal (book character). *See Middlesex*

Calcutta Chromosome, The (Ghosh), 168, 177

Cameron, Anne: literary authority and,
   61–63; Maracle and, 60–61

Canetti, Elias, 48

"Can the Subaltern Speak?" (Spivak), 27–28

capital, 90–91, 95, 277*n*12, 280*n*58, 291*n*24

Chakrabarty, Dipesh, 113

Ch'ien, Evelyn: language and, 270*n*65; on
   weird English, 80, 278*n*18

Chow, Rey: images and, 68, 276*n*2; native
   representation and, 265*n*32; other and,
   258*n*6; stereotypes and, 101–2, 281*n*4

Circle of Reason, A (Ghosh), 167–68

Cixous, Hélène, 145

Cleage, Pearl, 110

Clifton, Lucille, 109–10

Coetzee, J. M., 1–2; on animals, 296*n*80,
   296*n*84, 296*n*89; background / works
   of, 201–3, 289*nn*2–5; bipolar
   inclination and, 297*n*94; crowding
   regarding, 204–6; ethics of
   representation and, 228; ethnic
   writers and, 29; narrative choice
   regarding, 5–6; problem of sympathy
   and, 200–201, 203–4, 205, 289*nn*10–11;
   professional readers and, 202, 206–7,
   290*n*14; search for reconstruction
   and, 244; sentimentality and, 210,
   278*n*21; silence of others and, 203,
   289*nn*6–7; South Africa regarding,
   217–18, 292*n*38; style overview of, 17;

white unfreedom and, 232, 294n62. *See also Disgrace; Lives of Animals, The*

Cohen, Margaret, 79, 277n14

comedy: British fiction and, 100–101; comic reversal and, 15; *Disgrace* regarding, 235; incongruity regarding, 102–3, 282n8; laughter regarding, 102, 121, 281nn6–7; satire, 119–20; of slavery, 133; as tone/stance, 102, 282n9

Commonwealth Prize, 169–70

Conquest of America, The (Todorov): representing alterity and, 32–33; social difference and, 257n2

Cornwall, Gareth, 232

Cornyetz, Nina, 95

Costello, Elizabeth (book character). *See Lives of Animals, The*

Crossing the River (Phillips), 136

cross voicing, 151, 286n18

crowded self: Coetzee and, 204–6; definition of, 47; *Disgrace* illustrating, 217, 226, 228–30, 236–40, 243; expansion limits of, 51; *The Hungry Tide* and, 196–97, 199; hybridity and, 55–56; imaginative absorption and, 246–47; intersubjectivity and, 54; Jen and, 102, 104, 123–32, 124, 133–34; Charles Johnson and, 102, 104, 133–34; language of crowds and, 48–50; literary authority and, 60–63; *The Lives of Animals* illustrating, 212, 217; Maracle/Cameron story regarding, 60–63; *Middlesex* illustrating, 142–44, 163–64; *Mona in the Promised Land* and, 124–25, 127, 129, 130; multicultural tolerance and, 49; *My Year of Meats* and, 76–83; Ozeki and, 69, 70; Parfit and, 41–42, 50, 204, 275n103; readerly participation creating, 179–80;

Rushdie's work regarding, 50, 275n102; *The Sari Shop* and, 154–58, 163–64; self-completion regarding, 47, 274n94; *The Shadow Lines* illustrating, 57–60; as subjectivity metaphor, 47–49; sympathy and, 40, 90; "The Man Who Saw Himself Drown" illustrating, 56–57; theory of, 34–66

crowded style: Coetzee and, 204–6; definition of, 51–54; of *Disgrace*, 218–19, 234–35, 236, 243, 295n72; Ghosh and, 53, 166, 179–83, 194–99; of *The Glass Palace*, 53, 171–72, 174–75, 179–80, 183; of *The Hungry Tide*, 194–95; hybridity and, 55–56; intersubjectivity and, 54; Jen and, 104, 119–20, 133–34; Charles Johnson, and, 53–54, 104, 111, 114–18, 133–34; literary authority and, 61–63; literary/historical/intellectual contexts and, 52–53, 275n108; of *The Lives of Animals*, 214, 217; "The Man Who Saw Himself Drown" illustrating, 57; Maracle/Cameron story regarding, 60–63; of *Middlesex*, 144–46, 149–50, 163; of *My Year of Meats*, 75–76, 85–86, 92–93; of *Oxherding Tale*, 53–54, 114–15, 117–18; range of, 51–52, 275n105; of *The Sari Shop*, 162–63; theory of, 34–66; Todorov regarding, 275n105

crowds, 48–49, 274n95

Crowds and Power (Canetti), 48

culture: adjective and, 257n2; cultural anachronism and, 113; cultural cross-dressing and, 103; dialogue and, 264n19; global flows and, 6; secrecy regarding, 72–73; Sieg on, 27; Todorov on, 32; tolerance and, 49, 274n101

Culture and Imperialism (Said), 8

Dandekar, Natalie, 280n50

Dangor, Achmat, 167

Delany, Samuel, 37

Diamond Dust (Desai), 56–57

Diary of a Bad Year (Coetzee), 202–3

Dimock, Wai Chee, 262n21

discursive domination: definition of, 3; English and, 167; history regarding, 7–8; in imagining others, 29–30; Satya Mohanty and, 3; representation theories and, 2–3, 258n4, 258n6; Said and, 109, 258n4

Disgrace (Coetzee), 217–46; affair in, 222; altered imagination in, 229–30, 294n59; anger / resistance and, 64–65; animal rights and, 237–38, 296n80; black characters regarding, 234–35, 295n71; Byron concerning, 221–24, 226–28, 238–39, 241; comedy regarding, 235; communication and, 221; crisis of representation and, 1–2; crowded self and, 217, 226, 228–30, 236–40, 243; crowded style of, 218–19, 234–35, 236, 243, 295n72; depravity representation and, 245–46; dog rhetoric and, 233–34, 236–38, 241, 242, 243, 244–45, 246, 247, 295nn68–70, 296nn84–85, 296n87, 296n88, 296n92; eastern Cape regarding, 232–33; ethics issues in, 219–20, 226, 293n42, 293n48, 294n53, 294n55; farm novel and, 231–32; grasping another's experience and, 224–26; house / land and, 238, 296n82; hyperconscious / subconscious and, 240–41; incest and, 222, 230, 293n47; "kind-ness" in, 237; language and, 242–43; loss concerning, 237, 295n78; Lucifer metaphor in, 239–40,

241; monstrous things and, 238–41; nonhuman representation and, 230–31, 294n60; as offensive narrative, 235–36, 295n74, 295n76; opera in, 227–29, 294n56; overview of, 205–6; privileged self and, 223; progressive / perfective and, 244, 296n90; race and, 230–43; refused representation in, 224, 293n49; search for reconstruction and, 244; self-erasure and, 226–27, 229–30, 294n53; sexualized violence regarding, 220; silence / sound regarding, 228–29; soul regarding, 242; South Africa regarding, 217–18, 220, 292n38, 293n43; surrender and, 246; sympathy and, 218, 219, 221–30, 236–41, 245; white writers and, 231

Distant Shore, A (Phillips), 136

Dobson, Joanne, 76

Doody, Margaret, 191

"Dr. King's Refrigerator" (Johnson), 40–41

Dreamer (Johnson), 106

Du Bois, W. E. B., 109

Dunant, Sarah, 121

Durrant, Sam, 294n53

Dzelarhons: Myths of the Northwest Coast (Cameron), 61–63

Elizabeth Costello (Coetzee), 246–47

entertainment-education fiction, 14–15, 68

entitlement position, 21–23, 25, 28

Esteve, Mary, 274n95

Esty, Jed, 52

ethics: definitions, 3, 258n7, 259nn8–9, 260n11; *Disgrace* and, 219–20, 226, 293n42, 293n48, 294n53, 294n55

ethics of border crossing. *See* ethics of representation

ethics of representation: anger / resistance and, 64–65; border-crossing fiction and, 3–4, 250–52; characteristics of, 40–45; Coetzee and, 228; ethics definitions and, 2–3, 258*n*7, 259*nn*8–9; feminism and, 85; globalization regarding, 7; interpretive lens and, 31–32; Charles Johnson, Gish Jen, and, 132–34; *My Year of Meats* and, 96–98; negative vs. positive, 19–20; novel and, 8–9; novel subgenres and, 252–53; overview of, 14; Ozeki vs. Coetzee regarding, 5–6; postpositivist realism and, 45–46; principles for, 20; sacrifice of, 28; self-awareness and, 42–43, 272*n*80; selfhood and, 35–37; self / style expansion and, 40–42; surrender and, 246; universalism and, 63–64; vulnerability and, 44–45

ethnic borders, 138

ethnicity, multi-, 30, 71–72, 100, 122, 182, 269n58

ethnic power differentials, 109–10, 283*n*29

ethnic reversals: British comic fiction regarding, 100–101; comic incongruity and, 102–3, 282*n*8; laughter regarding, 102, 281*n*7; nondominant groups and, 104; overview of, 15; romantic Orientalism and, 103–4, 108–18; stereotype and, 101–2, 281*n*4; *Uncle Tom's Cabin* regarding, 99–100; via social identity, 103, 127–31

ethnic writers, 29, 265*n*35

Eugenides, Jeffrey: background on, 140; Bajwa compared with, 150; Bronte and, 145–46; individual identity and, 142–43; language of hermaphrodism and, 141–42; middle ground regarding,

136–37, 149–50; multiple literary expression and, 149; shared gender and, 141; social borders and, 138, 140; social categories and, 143; style overview of, 16. *See also Middlesex*

European philosophy, 208–10, 212, 290*n*19, 291*nn*23–24

Ezekiel (book character). *See Oxherding Tale*

false teeth metaphor, 171–72

farm novel (*plaasroman*), 231–32

Feign, Larry, 284*n*40

Felski, Rita, 151

feminism: Austen and, 24; cross voicing and, 151, 286*n*18; gender issues and, 138–39; imagining others and, 24, 84–93, 138–40, 151, 286*n*18; politics and, 14–15

feminism across borders: challenges faced by, 84–85, 279*n*33, 279*n*36; concrete action and, 82–83; ethical task of, 85; *My Year of Meats* and, 85–86; shared gender and, 83, 279*n*31; transnational feminist community and, 83–85; violence against women influencing, 86–92, 279*n*41, 280*nn*49–50

Festa, Lynn, 277*n*14

Fetterly, Judith, 139, 285*n*3

fiction: British, 100–101; critical metanarrative concerning, 250; definitions surrounding, 8–9, 260n16, 261*n*18; entertainment-education, 14–15, 68; prose, 8–9, 260n16, 261*nn*18–19; readers of, 249. *See also* border-crossing fiction; novel

Flanders, Laura, 89

Frye, Northrop, 119

Garber, Marjorie, 214

Gates, Henry Louis, Jr., 282*n*23

gender: ethnic / national borders and, 138;
feminism regarding, 138–39; Fetterly
and, 139, 285*n*3; individual identity
and, 142–43; middle space and,
136–37, 163–64; norms, 143–44, 286*n*11;
novelist predicament concerning, 141;
postmodernist / essentialist views of,
146–48; rhetorical styles regarding,
144–46; shared, 83, 84, 141, 279*n*31;
as social border, 138–40; social
constructionism and, 146–47; social
vs. biological, 150. *See also Disgrace;
Middlesex; Sari Shop, The*

genocide, 207–8, 290*n*16

Gerwel, Jakes, 235

Ghosh, Amitav: background on, 167;
Commonwealth Prize rejection
by, 169–70; criticism on, 287*n*1;
crowded style regarding, 53, 166,
179–83, 194–99; English / South Asian
literature and, 170–71, 287*n*10;
historical scholarship of, 169, 287*n*4;
on Indian languages / literature, 171;
introductory comments on, 165–67;
on language, 11, 37; language equality
and, 174–75; modernist aesthetics and,
183, 288*n*31; on multiple language use,
173; narration language of, 53; plain
style of, 175–76; social distinctions
and, 33; style overview of, 16–17; works
by, 167–68. *See also Glass Palace, The;
Hungry Tide, The; Shadow Lines, The*

Gilroy, Paul, 66, 104, 253

Glass Palace, The (Ghosh), 167–83;
character voices regarding, 176–78,
288*n*21; Commonwealth Prize
rejection and, 169–70; crowded style
in, 53, 171–72, 174–75, 179–80, 183; epic
sweep of, 168–69; false teeth metaphor
in, 171–72; historical storytelling and,
169, 176; introductory comments on,
166–67; language and, 169–80, 182–83,
288*n*14, 288*n*21; modernist aesthetics
and, 183, 288*n*31; multilingualism in,
172–73; nonverbal communication
in, 180; nude portraits and, 182;
photography concerning, 180–83;
plain style of, 175–76, 178; postcolonial
nationalism regarding, 287*n*3; readerly
participation with, 178–80

globalization: border-crossing fiction
and, 6–7; "Dr. King's Refrigerator"
regarding, 40–41; English / South Asian
publishing and, 171, 287*n*10; *The Glass
Palace* and, 168–69; interconnection
and, 40, 272*n*75

God of Small Things, The (Roy), 136

Goldberg, Natalie, 23

Gómez-Peña, Guillermo, 251

Graham, Lucy, 295*n*69

Greer, Germaine, 30–31

Griffin, John Howard, 40, 271*n*71

Guerillas (Naipaul), 43

Guillory, John: ethics and, 259*n*9;
self-awareness and, 272*n*80

Hakemulder, Jèmeljan, 268*n*51

Hall, Stuart, 266*n*38

Hanssen, Beatrice, 43

happy endings, 94–95, 280*n*57

Haraway, Donna, 3, 29, 296*n*84

Hardt, Michael, 55, 275*n*110

Hassan, Ihab, 31

hermaphrodism, language of, 141–42

Hilton, James, 108

Hispanic Orientalism, 263*n*11

Hobson, Geary, 25

hooks, bell, 109

Howard, June, 277*n*11

How Late It Was, How Late (Kelman), 167

Huggan, Graham, 265*n*35

Hughes, Langston, 109

Hulme, Keri, 167

human rights, 88, 261*n*18

Hungerford, Amy, 39, 143

Hungry Tide, The (Ghosh), 183–98; Bon
   Bibi metaphor in, 194–96; Bon Bibi
   shrine in, 196; crowded self in,
   196–97, 199; crowded style of, 194–95;
   dolphin language and, 189–90; human
   communion in, 190–91; introductory
   comments on, 166–67; language and,
   183–85, 188–98; language limitations
   and, 183–84, 191–92; Nirmal's journal
   in, 194–95, 197–98; nonverbal speech
   in, 189–91, 193, 195; nonverbal /
   translation melding regarding,
   194–98; parallel narratives of, 185;
   Piya's self-projection in, 186–87; Piya's
   skepticism in, 188; politics regarding,
   197; social difference and, 185–88;
   tidelands as metaphor in, 184–85; tiger
   language and, 192–93

Hunt, Lynn: human rights and, 261*n*18;
   sentimental discourse and, 76, 277*n*6

hybridity, 55–56, 275*n*110

identity: border softening regarding, 35–38,
   270*nn*61–62; confusion, 140–41, 286*n*5;

external construction of, 36, 269*n*58;
impersonation and, 39; individual, 143;
intimate relationship regarding, 37,
270*n*61; *Mona in the Promised Land* and,
123–26; Parfit and, 41–42; passing and,
39–40; pluralist conception of, 36–37;
selfhood and, 35–37; social, 35, 103;
theorization of experience and, 35–36,
269*n*56; unchanged, 38, 270*n*66

imaginative projection: globalization and,
40–41; Parfit regarding, 41–42; passing
and, 39–40, 271*nn*69–73; postpositivist
realism and, 45–46; relational practice
of, 46; self-awareness and, 42–43,
272*n*80; self / style expansion and,
40–42; sympathy and, 40; unchanged
identity and, 38, 270*n*66; unconscious
mirroring and, 42, 272*n*81; vulnerability
and, 44–45

imagining others: allegory / entitlement
and, 21–23; ambivalent approach to,
135, 136; Coetzee paradox of, 200–201;
criticism of, 30–31; discursive
domination in, 29–30; ethics
interpretive lens for, 31–32; ethnic
writer and, 29, 265*n*35; feminism and,
24, 84–93, 138–40, 151, 286*n*18; grasping
another's experience and, 224–26;
intimate relationship regarding,
37, 270*n*61; issues surrounding, 21;
language regarding, 21, 25, 264*n*19;
minority / postcolonial writings and,
24–25, 264*n*14; mirror argument and,
26–27, 29; Orientalism and, 23–24;
positive approaches to, 29–30, 266*n*38,
266*nn*40–41, 267*n*42; power / privilege
and, 135–36; power relations in, 28–29,
265*n*33; primitivism and, 24; principles

imagining others (*continued*)

    for, 20; self-representation and, 25, 264*n*17; social change and, 33–34; subaltern regarding, 27–28; uneasiness from, 19; unrepresentability and, 28, 265*nn*31–32

impersonation, 39

In an Antique Land (Ghosh), 168

intersubjectivity, 54

It's Lonely at the Top (Johnson), 106

Jane (book character). *See My Year of Meats*

JanMohamed, Abdul: material exploitation and, 268*n*48; multicultural tolerance and, 49; positive representation and, 266*n*41

Jen, Gish: background on, 118; border rigidity and, 121–22; crowded self and, 102, 104, 123–32, 133–34; crowded style regarding, 104, 119–20, 133–34; ethics of border crossing and, 132–34; introductory comments on, 100, 101, 103–4; Judaism and, 123; political correctness regarding, 120–21; satire and, 119–20; style overview of, 15; works by, 118–19. *See also Mona in the Promised Land*

Johnson, Charles: Asian characters and, 111, 283*n*31; Asian influences on, 105–8; background on, 105; comedy of slavery and, 133; comic techniques and, 100, 102–4, 111–15, 118, 132–34; crowded self and, 102, 104, 133–34; crowded style regarding, 53–54, 104, 111, 114–18, 133–34; ethnic power differentials and, 109–10, 283*n*29; on intersubjectivity, 54; introductory comments on, 100, 101, 103–4; mirroring and, 38, 271*n*67;

Orientalist stereotypes regarding, 108–9, 283*n*25; Posnock and, 105, 282*n*14; on racial Other, 11, 100; spirituality / ancestry and, 107, 282*n*23; style overview of, 15; on *Uncle Tom's Cabin*, 99–100; works by, 106; writings on, 108, 283*n*24. *See also Oxherding Tale*

Johnson, Samuel, 211

Judaism, 123

Kabbani, Rana: mirror argument and, 26; on self-representation, 25

Kafka's Curse (Dangor), 167

Kaplan, Cora, 286*n*18

Kariuki, Sam, 233

Keck, Margaret, 86–87

Keen, Suzanne: empathy and, 45, 273*n*89; social effects of novel and, 34, 261*n*18

Kelman, James, 167

Kennedy, Randall, 271*n*70

Kete, Kathleen, 209, 290*n*16

Kincaid, Jamaica, 136

King, Martin Luther, Jr., 109

Kingston, Maxine Hong, 43

Klein, Christina, 43, 263*n*9, 277*n*12

Krog, Antjie, 232–33

Kunzru, Hari, 100–101

Kushigian, Julia, 263*n*11

Lamott, Anne, 23

language: Akiko's English and, 80; border-crossing fiction and, 16–17; Commonwealth Prize rejection regarding, 169–70; of crowds, 48–49; dialect and, 177–79; discursive domination and, 165, 177–78; *Disgrace* and, 230–31, 233–35, 242–43; dolphin, 189–90, 193; equality, 174–75; Ghosh and, 11, 37, 53, 171, 173, 174–75; *The Glass Palace* and, 169–80, 182–83, 288*n*14, 288*n*21; of hermaphrodism, 141–42; *The Hungry Tide* and, 183–85, 188–98; imagining others regarding, 21, 25, 264*n*19; Indian, 171; politics of, 173–74; *The Sari Shop* and, 162–63; as socially shaped, 37–38, 270*n*65; Sollors and, 127, 270*n*65; South Asian literature and, 170–71, 287*n*8, 287*n*10; tiger, 192–93; use of multiple, 173; weird English and, 80, 278*n*18

Lazarus, Neil, 264*n*19

Learning from Experience (Moya), 46, 273*n*93

Lee, Jennifer Serena, 268*n*51

Lesser, Wendy, 139, 274*n*94

Levinas, Emmanuel, 44, 224, 293*n*49

Levinson, Julie H., 280*n*50

Levinson, Sandra P., 280*n*50

Levy, Andrea, 136

Ling, Amy, 103

literary criticism, 2–3

literary guidebooks, 22–23

Lives of Animals, The (Coetzee), 206–17; Costello as unsentimental in, 210, 292*n*26; crowded self and, 212, 217; crowded style of, 214, 217; embodied knowledge / reason and, 212, 292*n*30; European philosophy / sympathy and, 208–10, 212, 290*n*19, 291*nn*23–24; genocide and, 207–08, 290*n*16; imaginative sympathy and, 207–17; limits of imagining and, 207, 290*n*15; misanthropy and, 215–16, 292*n*34; overview of, 205–7; power exertion in, 214–15; rhetoric contradiction in, 212–14; search for reconstruction and,

244; sensory experience and, 210–11; uneven sympathy regarding, 209

Lloyd, David, 49, 268*n*48, 280*n*58

Londonstani (Malkani), 167

Love Wife, The (Jen), 119

Lowe, Lisa, 26

Luce (book character). *See Middlesex*

Lucifer metaphor, 239–40, 241

Lucy (Kincaid), 136

Lugones, María, 45

Lundeen, Kathleen, 29

Mackie, Vera, 92

Malkani, Gautam, 167

Mallory-Kani, Amy, 286*n*16

Mani, B. Venkat: playfulness and, 273*n*88; positive representation and, 30, 267*n*42

"Man Who Saw Himself Drown, The" (Desai), 56–57

Maracle, Lee, 60–61

Marais, Michael, 218, 293*n*48

Mason, Travis, 296*n*87

Master of Petersburg, The (Coetzee), 245

Maugham, Somerset, 108

McEwan, Ian, 254

McKeon, Michael, 260*n*16

metaphor: Bon Bibi, 194–96; false teeth, 171–72; Lucifer, 239–40, 241; subjectivity, 47–49; taxi, 141; theft, 75; tidelands, 184–85

Michaels, Walter Benn: pluralist identity conception of, 36–37; pluralist logic and, 101

middle ground: gender and, 136–37, 163–64; *Middlesex and*, 136–37, 149–50, 163–64; overview of, 16; power / privilege and, 135–36; resistance to alterity and, 135;

middle ground (*continued*)

   The Sari Shop and, 137, 163–64; social /
   material and, 137; tragicomic form and,
   136. *See also Middlesex; Sari Shop, The*

Middle Passage (Johnson), 106

Middlesex (Eugenides), 137–50; as
   adaptationist novel, 286n16; Bronte
   and, 145–46; Cal's "I" in, 142–43;
   conclusions about, 163–64; crowded
   self in, 142–44, 149–50, 163–64;
   crowded style of, 144–46, 149–50, 163;
   embodiment / biology and, 148–49;
   gender norms and, 143–44, 286n11;
   identity confusion and, 140–41,
   286n5; immigration / migration plot
   regarding, 138, 285n2; language of
   hermaphrodism and, 141–42; Luce as
   postmodernist / essentialist in, 146–48;
   Luce's report in, 147; middle ground
   regarding, 136–37, 149–50, 163–64;
   multiple literary expression in, 149;
   overview of, 140; pornographic video
   in, 147–48; queer body theories and,
   144n11; rhetorical styles regarding,
   144–46; shared gender and, 141;
   social categories and, 143; social
   constructionism and, 146–47; social vs.
   biological gender and, 150

Midnight's Children (Rushdie), 50

minority literary traditions, 11, 24–25,
   264n14

mirror argument: imagining others and,
   26–27, 29; Charles Johnson and, 38,
   271n67; unconscious mirroring and,
   42, 272n81

misanthropy, 215–16, 292n34

modernist aesthetics, 183, 288n31

Mohanty, Chandra Talpade, 85

Mohanty, Satya, 3, 32, 35, 269n56, 273n88,
   273n92, 285n51

Mona (book character). *See Mona in the
   Promised Land*

Mona in the Promised Land (Jen), 118–32;
   community collision concerning,
   122–23; crowded self in, 124–25, 127,
   129, 130; identity issues in, 123–26; love
   pairings in, 129–31; mother / daughter
   reconnection in, 131–32; overview of,
   122; Sherman / Mona relationship in,
   125; Sherman / Seth transformation
   in, 125–26; stereotype and, 127–29,
   285n52; switching / flipping in, 126–28;
   telephone calls regarding, 125–26,
   127–28

Montagu, Mary Wortley, 26

Moor's Last Sigh, The (Rushdie), 55

Morgan, Robin, 84–85, 279n33, 279n36

Mostert, Noël, 232, 237–38

Moya, Paula, 285n51; epistemic privilege
   and, 27; learning from others and, 46,
   273n93; postpositivist realism of, 46,
   273n92

multiethnicity, 30, 71–72, 100, 122, 182,
   269n58

My Year of Meats (Ozeki), 71–98; action at
   a distance and, 67–68; Akiko's English
   and, 80; Akiko's fax in, 78–81,
   277nn11–12; capital and, 90–91, 95,
   280n58, 291n24; class action influenced
   by, 96; commodity purchases and,
   77–78, 277n10; crowded self in, 76–83;
   crowded style of, 75–76, 85–86, 92–93;
   cultural secrecy in, 72–73; difficulties
   surrounding, 70; "Documentary
   Interlude" in, 90–91, 280n52; educated
   feelings and, 92–93; emotion and, 83;

as entertainment-education fiction, 14–15, 68; feminism across borders and, 85–86; happy endings and, 93–95; imagery production / consumption and, 73–74; introductory comments about, 67–71; Jane / Akiko as connected in, 74–75; Jane's sentimentality in, 80–81; marketing activism in, 95; multiethnicity and, 71–72; narrative construction of, 73; representational ethics of, 96–98; sentimental literature regarding, 79, 81–82; sentimental realignment in, 76, 77; shortcomings of, 97–98; theft metaphor in, 75; violence against women and, 87–88, 90–93, 279n43, 280n49

Nadolny, Sten, 267n42
Nagel, Thomas, 211, 217, 270n66
Naipaul, V. S., 43
Nair, Mira, 106
Nair, Rukmini Bhaya, 176–77
Narain, Denise deCaires, 279n39
narrative choices: in border-crossing fiction, 12–14; Coetzee / Ozeki and, 5–6; meaning of, 260n16
nationality, shared, 11, 262n21
Negri, Antonio, 55, 275n110
Newton, Adam Zachary, 259n9
Nirmal (book character). *See Hungry Tide, The*
nonfiction narrative, 9, 261n19
novel: critical metanarrative concerning, 250; crossing borders via, 8–9, 250–52; definitions surrounding, 8–9, 260n16, 261n18; farm, 231–32; human rights and, 261n18; vs. other literary forms, 9, 261n19; politics of language

and, 173–74; readers regarding, 249; rhetorical advantages of, 9; in *The Sari Shop*, 160–62; social difference and, 8–9, 261n18; social effects and, 33, 261n18; subgenres of, 252–53
Nussbaum, Martha, 253, 254; multicultural tolerance and, 49, 274n101; otherness and, 77, 258n7; spectatorship and, 152–53
Nyman, Jopi, 294n60

Oerlemans, Onno, 296n92
Orientalism: Hispanic, 263n11; Charles Johnson and, 108–9, 283n25; Lowe and, 26; romantic, 103–4, 108–18; Said and, 23–24; simian, 29
Orientalism (Said): discursive domination and, 258n4; imperialist assumptions and, 23–24
Oxherding Tale (Johnson), 105–18; Chinese characters and, 114, 284nn37–38, 284n40; crowded style regarding, 53–54, 114–15, 117–18; cultural anachronism in, 113; Ezekiel's teaching in, 112–13; mirroring in, 38; narrator in, 111–12; passing and, 271n73; polyphony used in, 114–18; Trishanku tale in, 115–16; uncarved block parable in, 116–17; Zen parable regarding, 110, 283n30
Ozeki, Ruth: background of, 71; class action and, 96; crowded self and, 69, 70; entertainment-education fiction of, 14–15, 68; food regarding, 73, 276n4; on happy endings, 94–95, 280n57; multiethnicity and, 71–72; narrative choice regarding, 5–6; style overview of, 14–15. *See also My Year of Meats*

Palumbo-Liu, David, 81, 82, 277*n9*

Parfit, Derek: Buddhist ideas and, 111; crowded self and, 41–42, 50, 204, 275*n103*; on death, 229–30; expanded self and, 41–42, 224

Parker, David, 251–52

passing, discourse of, 39–40, 271*nn69–73*

performance, 9, 261*n19*, 294*n56*

Persuasion (Austen), 24

Phillips, Caryl, 136

Piya (book character). *See Hungry Tide, The*

plaasroman (farm novel), 231–32

playfulness, 45, 273*n88*

pluralist logic, 36–37, 101

poetry, 9, 261*n19*

politics: feminist, 14–15; *The Hungry Tide* and, 197; of language, 173–74; political correctness and, 120–21; transnational, 88–89

positive representation, 29–30, 266*n38*, 266*n40*, 267*nn41–42*

Posnock, Ross: Charles Johnson and, 105, 282*n14*; unconscious mirroring and, 42

postpositivist realism, 46, 273*n92*

Pratt, Mary Louise: authority and, 44, 181; discursive domination and, 258*n4*

primitivism, 24

"Problem of Speaking for Others, The" (Alcoff), 60

prose fiction: definitions surrounding, 8–9, 260*n16*, 261*n18*; vs. other literary forms, 9, 261*n19*

Puchner, Martin, 212

Radhakrishnan, R., 104, 120

Ramchand (book character). *See Sari Shop, The*

readerly participation, 178–80

Reasons and Persons (Parfit), 41–42

recuperative reading, 260*n11*

representation theories, 2–3, 258*n4*, 258*n6*

responsibility, 2, 44, 259*n8*

Richards, David: Bhabha and, 265*n31*; euphemisation of power and, 26, 27

Rina (book character). *See Sari Shop, The*

Robbins, Bruce, 89, 98; distant action and, 67–68; feelings / knowledge and, 63

Room of One's Own, A (Woolf), 141

Rorty, Richard: otherness and, 258*n7*; self-awareness and, 42; sentimental education and, 82, 97

Roy, Arundhati, 136

Rushdie, Salman, 53, 166, 173, 176, 184–85, 270*n61*; crowded self and, 50, 275*n102*; England and, 174; hybridity and, 55; unsettlement and, 19

Rushdy, Ashraf, 112, 284*n34*

Said, Edward, 28, 266*n38*; discursive domination and, 109, 110, 258*n4*, 263*n9*; Orientalism and, 23–24, 26, 27, 29; positive representation and, 29; on power to narrate, 8

Sanders, Mark, 295*n72*, 296*n90*

Sari Shop, The (Bajwa), 150–63; class-oriented middle ground in, 151–53; conclusions about, 163–64; cross-voicing regarding, 151, 286*n18*; crowded self in, 154–55, 163–64; crowded style of, 162–63; darkness rhetoric in, 157; end of, 163; expansion of self in, 154–55; imaginative gender crossing and,

Sontag, Susan, 83, 92, 96

spectatorship, 152–53

Spivak, Gayatri Chakravorty, 286n18; imaginative relationship and, 37, 270n61; subaltern and, 27–28, 265n27, 281n6; translation and, 178, 288n24

Srikanth, Rajini, 272n81

Stanton, Katherine, 259n8, 291n24, 293n42

stereotype: ethnic reversals and, 101–2, 281n4; *Mona in the Promised Land* and, 127–29, 285n52; Orientalist, 108–9, 283n25

Stowe, Harriet Beecher, 99–100

Su, John, 259n9

subaltern, 27–28, 281n6

subjectivity metaphor, 47–49

Syal, Meera, 100, 102, 132

sympathy: Alliston on, 79; crowded self from, 90; *Disgrace* regarding, 218, 219, 221–30, 236–41, 245; European philosophy and, 208–10, 212, 290n19, 291nn23–24; genocide and, 207–8, 290n16; imaginative, 207–17; imaginative projection and, 40; problem of, 200–201, 203–4, 205, 289nn10–11; *The Sari Shop* and, 154–55, 156, 158–59; sensory experience and, 210–11; Sontag on, 83, 92; uneven, 209, 215–16

Sze, Julie, 276n5

Tannen, Deborah, 145

Tanner, Laura, 225–26

taxi metaphor, 141

theft metaphor, 75

Third Space, 28, 265n31

tidelands metaphor, 184–85

Tiews, Matthew, 48–49, 274n95

Todorov, Tzvetan: crowded style regarding, 275n105; on culture, 32; optimistic perspective of, 32–33, 268n47; others and, 12; social difference and, 257n2

Tolstoy, Leo, 253–54

Toomer, Jean, 109

Torgovnick, Marianna: discursive domination and, 258n4; positive representation and, 29–30, 266n40, 267n42; primitivism and, 24

tracing-and-exposure project, 5, 250

Trainspotting (Welsh), 167

Trishanku tale, 115–16

Typical American (Jen), 118

uncarved block parable, 116–17

Uncle Tom's Cabin (Stowe), 99–100

universalism, 63–64

Updike, John, 22

Van der Walt, Lucien, 233

violence against women: capital and, 90–91; definitions surrounding, 89–90, 280nn49–50; feminism across borders and, 86–92, 279n41, 280nn49–50; Keck / Sikkink and, 86–87; Mackie on, 92; *My Year of Meats* and, 87–88, 90–93, 279n43, 280n49; sexualized, 220; transnational politics vs., 88–89; by women, 91–92

vulnerability, 44–45, 59–60, 157–58

Wade, Michael, 231

Walkowitz, Rebecca, 52–53, 114, 133, 275n108

Warhol, Robyn, 145

Warner, Michael, 260n11

wa Wamwere, Koigi, 104

weird English, 80, 278*n*18

Weiss, Timothy, 266*n*38

Welsh, Irvine, 167

White Writing (Coetzee), 228, 231–32

Who's Irish (Jen), 118–19

Wicomb, Zoë, 245, 296*n*90

Willis, Susan, 286*n*18

Wispé, Lauren, 40

Womack, Kenneth, 286*n*16

women. *See* feminism; feminism across borders; gender; violence against women

Woolf, Virginia, 84, 141

Wright, Laura, 290*n*11, 292*n*37, 294*n*56

Wright, Richard, 109, 274*n*101

Zen parable, 110, 283*n*30